(Re)imagining Translanguaging Pedagogies through Teacher–Researcher Collaboration

MW01633816

TRANSLANGUAGING IN THEORY AND PRACTICE

Series Editors: **Li Wei**, *University College London*, **Angel Lin**, *Simon Fraser University*, **Yuen Yi Lo**, *The University of Hong Kong* and **Saskia Van Viegen**, *York University.*

Translanguaging in Theory and Practice aims to publish work that highlights the dynamic use of an individual's linguistic repertoire and challenges the socially and politically defined boundaries of languages and their hierarchy. We invite research from across disciplines by both established and emergent researchers in multifarious settings, including everyday use, educational, digital and workplace contexts. We also actively welcome and solicit studies on translanguaging in contexts where English is not the mainstream language and where other modalities and semiotic resources take prominence over speech and writing. The series is transdisciplinary and encourages scholars to publish empirical research on translanguaging, especially that which aims to disrupt power relations, to create new identities and communities, to engage in the discussion of translanguaging theories and pedagogies, and/or to help the field of translanguaging consolidate its scholarship.

Topics to be covered by the series include:

- Theoretical underpinnings of Translanguaging.
- Translanguaging Pedagogies.
- Translanguaging in Assessment.
- Translanguaging and Language Policy.
- Translanguaging in Everyday Social Practices in Different Contexts and Communities, including Digital/ Social/ Media.

All books in this series are externally peer-reviewed.

Full details of all the books in this series and of all our other publications can be found on http://www.multilingual-matters.com, or by writing to Multilingual Matters, St Nicholas House, 31–34 High Street, Bristol, BS1 2AW, UK.

TRANSLANGUAGING IN THEORY AND PRACTICE: 5

(Re)imagining Translanguaging Pedagogies through Teacher–Researcher Collaboration

Edited by

Leah Shepard-Carey and Zhongfeng Tian

MULTILINGUAL MATTERS
Bristol • Jackson

DOI https://doi.org/10.21832/SHEPAR3177
Library of Congress Cataloging in Publication Data
A catalog record for this book is available from the Library of Congress.
Names: Shepard-Carey, Leah, editor. | Tian, Zhongfeng, editor.
Title: (Re)imagining Translanguaging Pedagogies through Teacher–Researcher Collaboration/Edited by Leah Shepard-Carey and Zhongfeng Tian.
Description: Bristol, UK; Jackson, TN: Multilingual Matters, 2023. | Series: Translanguaging in Theory and Practice: 5 | Includes bibliographical references and index. | Summary: "By promoting and highlighting teacher-researcher partnerships as one avenue for improvement and transparency, the chapters in this book demonstrate the potential of translanguaging pedagogies in classrooms and further resist the linguistic hierarchies that exist in educational institutions today"— Provided by publisher.
Identifiers: LCCN 2023005586 (print) | LCCN 2023005587 (ebook) | ISBN 9781800413160 (paperback) | ISBN 9781800413177 (hardback) | ISBN 9781800413184 (pdf) | ISBN 9781800413191 (epub)
Subjects: LCSH: Language and education. | Multilingual education. | Translanguaging (Linguistics) | Teachers—Professional relationships. | Education—Research. Classification: LCC P40.8 .R44 2023 (print) | LCC P40.8 (ebook) | DDC 418.0071—dc23/eng/20230314
LC record available at https://lccn.loc.gov/2023005586
LC ebook record available at https://lccn.loc.gov/2023005587

British Library Cataloguing in Publication Data
A catalogue entry for this book is available from the British Library.

ISBN-13: 978-1-80041-317-7 (hbk)
ISBN-13: 978-1-80041-316-0 (pbk)

Multilingual Matters
UK: St Nicholas House, 31–34 High Street, Bristol, BS1 2AW, UK.
USA: Ingram, Jackson, TN, USA.

Website: www.multilingual-matters.com
Twitter: Multi_Ling_Mat
Facebook: https://www.facebook.com/multilingualmatters
Blog: www.channelviewpublications.wordpress.com

Copyright © 2023 Leah Shepard-Carey and Zhongfeng Tian and the authors of individual chapters.

All rights reserved. No part of this work may be reproduced in any form or by any means without permission in writing from the publisher.

The policy of Multilingual Matters/Channel View Publications is to use papers that are natural, renewable and recyclable products, made from wood grown in sustainable forests. In the manufacturing process of our books, and to further support our policy, preference is given to printers that have FSC and PEFC Chain of Custody certification. The FSC and/or PEFC logos will appear on those books where full certification has been granted to the printer concerned.

Typeset by Nova Techset Private Limited, Bengaluru and Chennai, India.

Contents

Contributors

Laura Ascenzi-Moreno is currently a professor and the bilingual program coordinator in the Childhood, Bilingual and Special Education Department at Brooklyn College. Dr Ascenzi-Moreno's research is focused on the literacy development of emergent bilinguals, the literacy assessment of emergent bilinguals, the development of teacher knowledge, and how these intersect with equity. She co-authored the book, along with Dr Cecilia Espinosa, *Rooted in Strength: Using Translanguaging to Grow Multilingual Readers and Writers* (Scholastic, 2021). Her articles can be found in *Language Arts*, *The Reading Teacher*, the *Journal of Literacy Research*, *Literacy Research and Instruction*, *Voices from the Middle*, among others.

Maria José Botelho is Full Professor of Language, Literacy & Culture at the University of Massachusetts Amherst. Her three-pronged research agenda includes: critical multicultural analysis of children's literature; how critical literacies, multiliteracies, and Waldorf language arts pedagogies converge and diverge; and, ethnography and critical literacies as pre-service/inservice professional learning. She is the lead author of *Critical Multicultural Analysis of Children's Literature: Mirrors, Windows, and Doors* (2009) and the faculty director of the Five College Doors to the World Project (https://doors2world.umass.edu). Presently, she is working on *Reimagining Literacy Teaching with Critical Literacies and Ethnography: Teaching as Text* (Routledge).

Derek Braun is a doctoral student in the Department of Teaching and Learning at The Ohio State University. He teaches English Learner science classes at World Language Middle School located in Columbus, Ohio. His research focuses on adolescent Multilingual Learners in content classes. His current work is based on reviewing outcomes of problem-based learning in multilingual environments.

Sally Brown is a Professor of Literacy Education at Georgia Southern University where she teaches pre-service and in-service teachers. Her research focuses on supporting emergent bilingual children as they navigate learning English in classrooms while maintaining the first language. Sally is interested in the ways that digital tools can support a multimodal approach to literacy learning where emergent bilinguals draw from their vast resources in order to construct meaning. She is the co-editor of *Multimodal Literacies in Young Emergent Bilinguals: Beyond Print-Centric Practices* (2022).

Lena Cataldo-Schwarzl currently works at the University College of Teacher Education in Vienna/Krems (Austria) at the Department of Initial Teacher Education in Vienna. She holds a teaching degree in Italian, Psychology and Philosophy and a doctoral degree in Applied Linguistics. Her research interests and teaching are in the fields of multilingualism, self-efficacy and self-concept, teacher education and teacher professionalization.

Toni Dobinson is an Associate Professor and Discipline Lead in Applied Linguistics, TESOL and Languages in the School of Education at Curtin University, Australia. She coordinates and teaches the Post Graduate Programmes at the Bentley Campus and at a provider institution in Vietnam (SEAMEO RETRAC). She is the winner of multiple teaching awards at faculty, university and national level (Australian Awards for University Teaching (AAUT)) for her culturally inclusive approach to teaching. She researches in the areas of language teacher education, language and identity, language and social justice, translingual practices and language in migrant communities.

Stephanie Dryden is a PhD candidate at the School of Education, Curtin University, with a background of teaching English as an additional language in Australia, Colombia, and Vietnam. Her research interests include critical applied linguistics, the sociolinguistic experiences of migrants in an Australian context, and translingual practices. She has published multiple applied linguistics peer-reviewed research articles, on the topics of sociolinguistics, translingualism, semiotics, linguistic discrimination, and foreign language anxiety.

Elizabeth J. Erling, PhD, is Professor of ELT Research and Methodology at the University of Education Upper Austria and Elise-Richter Senior Postdoctoral Fellow at the University of Vienna. She is particularly interested in using multilingualism as a resource and supporting equity in (English) language education.

Caitlin G. McC. Fine is an Assistant Professor of Elementary Education at Metropolitan State University of Denver. Her research explores how teachers customize science instructional materials and assessments to expand multilingual students' sensemaking opportunities. She is particularly interested in how science teachers integrate translanguaging in their pedagogical practices and classroom culture. She taught at a Spanish/English dual-language elementary school for eight years as a science teacher and as an ESOL teacher. Her scholarship has been published in *Journal of Language, Identity, and Education, Science Education, The Science Teacher* and *Science and Children.*

Ofelia García is Professor Emerita in the PhD programs in Urban Education and Latin American, Iberian and Latino Cultures at The Graduate Center of the City University of New York. García has published widely in the areas of bilingualism/multilingualism and bilingual education, language education, language policy, and sociology of language. The American Educational Research Association has awarded her two Lifetime Research Achievement Awards–Distinguished Contributions to Social Contexts in Education (2019) and Bilingual Education (2017), as well as Second Language Acquisition Leadership through Research Award (2019). She is a member of the US National Academy of Education. For more, visit www.ofeliagarcia.org.

Paul Gardner is a Senior Lecturer in Primary English in the School of Education at Curtin University, Australia. Paul is a leading researcher in the Centre for Excellence in the Explicit Teaching of Literacy, funded by the Western Australian Government. He is a member of the Board of the Primary English Teachers Association of Australia (PETAA); the United Kingdom Literacy Association's (UKLA) Ambassador to Australia and he is vice-president of the Western Australian Institute for Educational Research (WAIER). He writes in the field of writer identity and compositional processes and is a regular contributor to Arena.

Maren Getz has been a public school educator in Aurora Public Schools for 22 years. She taught at the elementary level for 18 years and is now a middle school science teacher. Maren received her undergraduate degree from the University of Northern Colorado, her Masters degree from the University of Colorado and her CLDE endorsement from Regis University.

Kao Chia-Ling Gupta is a PhD candidate in the Faculty of Education at the University of Hong Kong with an MSc in Applied Linguistics and SLA from the University of Oxford and a BA in Applied Foreign Languages from National Taiwan University of Science and Technology. She is researching Content and Language Integrated Learning (CLIL), specifically with a critical approach.

Laura Hamman-Ortiz is Assistant Professor of TESOL and Bilingual Education in the School of Education at the University of Rhode Island. Her research explores how classroom language practices, policies and ideologies shape learning experiences for emergent bilingual students. She is particularly interested in the role of translanguaging pedagogies in destabilizing monoglossic ideologies, nurturing students' bilingual identities, and cultivating critical consciousness. Her scholarship has been published in *TESOL Quarterly*, *Language and Education*, the *Journal of Second Language Writing*, the *Journal of Literacy Research* and the *International Journal of Bilingual Education and Bilingualism*.

Chris Hoadley (he/him) is a professor and director of the learning sciences initiative at the University at Buffalo of the State University of New York (SUNY), jointly appointed in the departments of Learning and Instruction, Information Sciences, and Computer Science. His research focuses on collaborative technologies, computer support for cooperative learning (CSCL), and design-based research methods. Hoadley is a fellow of the International Society for the Learning Sciences (ISLS), and previously taught at NYU, Penn State, Mills College, and Stanford University.

Susana Ibarra Johnson is an assistant professor in bilingual/TESOL education in the department of Curriculum and Instruction at New Mexico State University. Dr Ibarra Johnson is one of the co-authors of *The Translanguaging Classroom: Leveraging Student Bilingualism for Learning*. Her commitment to improving the education of bilingual students is grounded in her experience as a bilingual learner and teacher. She has been a professional development specialist and researcher for WIDA, director of bilingual multicultural education programs at Bernalillo Public Schools, and most recently a district biliteracy specialist for Albuquerque Public Schools. Her research focuses on translanguaging pedagogy in bilingual education and English language development contexts.

Mishelle Jurado is a veteran bilingual teacher from New Mexico. A Biliteracy Coach, Mishelle and her colleagues have developed a portfolio process for the Biliteracy Seal offered by Albuquerque Public Schools. Mishelle received a BA in Spanish and Sociology, a MA in Language, Literacy, and Sociocultural studies with an emphasis in Bilingual Education, and is in her 7th year of her doctoral program – all completed at the University of New Mexico. Mishelle and her husband have two bilingual children. For the Jurado family bilingualism is celebrated; it is not just something out of a book or a theory paradigm – it is their way of life.

Somin Kim is a language educator and researcher. She has worked at pre K-12 schools and universities in different countries. Her research is focused on language and literacy practices of school-aged multilingual students, particularly those of adolescent newcomers in English-medium content area classrooms.

Sunny Man Chu Lau, Full Professor at Bishop's University in Quebec, Canada, is Canada Research Chair (Tier 2) in Integrated Plurilingual Teaching and Learning. Her research focuses on teachers' cross-language and cross-curricular collaborations to mobilize students' entire semiotic repertoire for language and content learning for critical engagements. As co-researcher in two recent SSHRC-funded projects, she explores multilingual approaches to assessment in education and the promotion of critical/media literacies in plurilingual and pluricultural teacher education. She co-edited the book *Plurilingual Pedagogies: Critical and Creative Undertakings for Equitable Language in Education* (Lau & Van Viegen, 2020) and serves as co-editor of *Critical Inquiry in Language Studies.*

Marsha Jing-Ji Liaw is curriculum director at a K-12 Chinese immersion school in the US. Her research and educational leadership work centers around critical biliteracies; that is, how children develop criticality in two language systems, and how knowing two (or more!) languages can contribute to children being critical. Other interests include literacy education, second language writing, multiliteracies, and ethnographic methodology. She earned her PhD in Language, Literacy and Culture from the University of Massachusetts Amherst. She was a teacher, curriculum specialist, and administrator in a leading K-12 bilingual school in Taiwan.

Angel M.Y. Lin received her doctoral degree from the Ontario Institute for Studies in Education (OISE), University of Toronto, in 1996. Her research and teaching have focused on classroom discourse analysis, bilingual plurilingual education, academic literacies, language across the curriculum, Content and Language Integrated Learning (CLIL), and translanguaging and trans-semiotizing. She has published six research books and over 100 research articles and book chapters. In 2018 Angel Lin moved from the University of Hong Kong to Simon Fraser University to take up the position of Tier 1 Canada Research Chair in Plurilingual and Intercultural Education.

Haeyoung Littich has been a public school educator in Aurora Public Schools for 7 years. She taught at the middle school level for 5 years as a science teacher and STEM teacher. Haeyoung is currently teaching Biology in Project Based Learning high school. Haeyoung received her BS in Biology and MA in Curriculum Design and Instruction from the University of Connecticut.

Paul Mercieca is a Senior Adjunct Research Fellow in the School of Education, at Curtin University. He has coordinated and taught in the areas of Applied Linguistics/TESOL both overseas in Egypt, the UK and Oman and on Curtin's transnational provider campus in Ho Chi Min City. His research interests are in the areas of language teacher education, critical transcultural literacy and translanguaging and he has published widely in these areas including his monograph, *To the Ends of the Earth: Northern Soul and Southern Nights in Western Australia* (2013) which explores theories about migrant identity and literacy.

Soy **María Elena Orozco.** Nací en Albuquerque, Nuevo México en 1976 en Los Padillas. Tengo una familia cariñosa, grande, y hablantes de español de la herencia. Así que Nuevo México es mi corazón. Comencé a enseñar en Head Start. Me gradué de la Universidad de Nuevo México en la educación bilingüe y saqué mi máster en la secundaria. He enseñado en las Escuelas Públicas por 20 años. Ahora enseño en Valley High School. Recibí mi certificación de National Boards en inglés como segundo idioma. Estoy estudiando para un máster en lengua y cultura española de la Universidad de Granada.

Ashlyn Pierson is an assistant professor of STEM education at the Ohio State University. She earned her PhD at Vanderbilt University's Peabody College of Education, specializing in Math & Science Education and Learning Sciences & Learning Environment Design. Her research merges theory and practice by using design studies to explore the interplay between disciplinary STEM practices (such as scientific modeling and computer programming) and students' everyday practices and diverse linguistic resources.

Margarita Pomare-McDonald is a teacher in the Savannah-Chatham County Public School System where she teaches first grade. Her family background supports her role in the classroom when working with bilingual students. Margarita is interested in helping students to make connections in and out of the classroom. By fostering a love for reading and expressing who they are, bilingual students are able to bloom and engage in the classroom more confidently.

Shakina Rajendram is an Assistant Professor, Teaching Stream and the Coordinator of the Language Teaching Field at the Ontario Institute for Studies in Education (OISE), University of Toronto, Canada. Shakina has taught at the K-12 and post-secondary levels in Malaysia and Canada for over 12 years. Her current teaching and research focus on second language teaching methodologies, pre-service and in-service teacher education, and supporting multilingual learners and international students through translanguaging and multiliteracies pedagogies.

Brian Seilstad received his PhD from the Ohio State University's department of Education/Teaching and Learning with a focus on Multicultural and Equity Studies. Currently he is the Director of Internationalization and Partnerships at Al Akhawayn University in Ifrane, Morocco. Prior to this position, he received his MA in Classical Languages from Bryn Mawr College, taught high school Greek and Latin, served in Peace Corps/ Morocco, was the Deputy Director of Youth Service California, and held teaching and leadership positions at Al Akhawayn University and American Academy/College Casablanca. He focuses on linguistic diversity and equity in educational spaces.

Kate Seltzer is an Assistant Professor of Bilingual and ESL Education at Rowan University. A former high school English Language Arts teacher in New York City, she currently teaches pre- and in-service teachers of bilingual students. Her current research involves working with English teachers to cultivate a critical stance and approach to teaching emergent bilinguals. She is co-author of the book, *The Translanguaging Classroom: Leveraging Student Bilingualism for Learning* as well as several book chapters and articles in journals such as *English Education, Language, Identity and Education, Research in the Teaching of English* and *TESOL Quarterly.*

Leah Shepard-Carey is an Assistant Professor of Graduate Studies in the School of Education at Drake University (Iowa, United States). She teaches courses for programs in ESL education, Literacy education, and Culturally Responsive Leadership. Her research explores multilingual pedagogies in English-medium settings, supporting critical language awareness and culturally-sustaining pedagogies in teacher education, and collaborative and design-based approaches to educational research. Her research has been featured in *TESOL Quarterly*, *TESOL Journal*, *Linguistics and Education*, *Language Awareness*, *Classroom Discourse*, and *The Journal of Early Childhood Literacy.*

Zhongfeng Tian is Assistant Professor of Bilingual Education at Rutgers University–Newark, USA. His research centers on working with pre- and in-service teachers to provide bi/multilingual students with equitable and inclusive learning environments in ESL and dual language immersion contexts. Dr Tian has published extensively in the field of ESL/bilingual education and teacher education, including four books (with Multilingual Matters, Springer and De Gruyter Mouton), five special issues and numerous articles which can be found in *International Journal of Bilingual Education and Bilingualism*, *Journal of Multilingual and Multicultural Development*, *Journal of Language, Identity & Education*, *TESOL Quarterly*, to name a few. Most recently, based on his scholarly contributions in Chinese-English bilingual education, Dr Tian has received an Early Career Award from ACTFL (American Council on the Teaching of Foreign Languages) Research SIG.

Michele Trujillo has worked as an early childhood educator in Albuquerque, New Mexico for 20 years. She holds three degrees from the University of New Mexico, including a MA in Language, Literacy, and Sociocultural Studies with an emphasis in Bilingual Education. She loves guiding young children through their first years of school and is honored to be a part of their bilingual journey. Michele also cherishes her community of bilingual educators and has established an online space for colleagues to network and collaborate; *Maestr@s Bilingües NM* celebrates its fifth year of online comunidad.

Ralph Vacca is an assistant professor in the Department of Communication and Media Studies and affiliated faculty in the New Media and Digital Design Program at Fordham University. He studies how information, design, and technology are used by youth, with a focus on how co-design can promote innovation, and address issues of marginalization in education and mental health.

Sara Vogel is a born-and-raised Brooklynite and an education researcher whose work focuses on the intersection of bilingual, social justice, and computing education. A former bilingual public school teacher and out-of-school digital media educator, she has worked at institutions such as Hunter College and Bank Street Graduate School of Education guiding pre- and in-service educators to invite and build on the dynamic languaging practices of bilingual learners. She currently leads research efforts for the Computing Integrated Teacher Education initiative at the City University of New York.

Gerard Winkler is a Primary School Teacher currently focusing on Early Childhood Education. His research interests include explicit teaching, high impact teaching models and students with languages other than English. He has contributed to the School Curriculum and Standards Authority (SCSA) in curriculum development and has developed local school networks for early childhood teachers. This is his first research project.

Preface

We entered upon this collaboration to expand understanding about teacher-researcher partnerships within the context of translanguaging pedagogies research. As we note in the introduction, while much translanguaging scholarship employs collaborative approaches, few talk about collaboration explicitly and the unique opportunities and tensions that emerge from these collaborations. The contributions in this volume detail the affordances, constraints, tensions and context-driven nature of working in partnerships in complex school environments. All of the contributions embrace translanguaging as an integral and worthwhile pedagogical approach to create more just schooling environments for multilingual students. Additionally, all contributions underscore the situated and immense expertise of the educators involved in these studies, further aiming to resist bifurcated conceptualizations of 'teacher' and 'researcher.' The multidimensional processes and perspectives detailed by the contributions all reflect the complexity of multilingual approaches across a variety of primary and secondary classroom contexts and educational systems, noting the structural, historical, and social obstacles.

We wrote this book for teachers, teacher educators, and classroom-research oriented scholars in the fields of TESOL and bilingual education. However, as we are all teachers of language and content, teacher educators in a variety of content areas who seek to support translanguaging pedagogies may find this book helpful as well. Additionally, this book is intended for graduate students in a variety of language education fields and applied linguistics who are interested in equitable and critical approaches of working with educators within and beyond translanguaging research.

This book is a continuation of the work of Ofelia García, Susana Ibarra Johnson and Kate Seltzer, (and many from the CUNY-NYSIEB team) and their conceptualization of the *stance, design, shifts* framework for translanguaging pedagogies, and more broadly, translanguaging pedagogies as an approach to leverage and embrace the identities and dynamic language practices of multilingual students. This volume was made possible by the translanguaging scholarship that has preceded ours. We would also like to thank Ofelia García and Kate Seltzer for their thoughtful commentary on this volume. Additionally, we would like to thank TESOL International Association for their Research Mini-Grants, which supported our work as doctoral students and introduced us (Zhongfeng and Leah) to each other's work. We also have a very special thank you to all of the contributors and to the external reviewers whose hard work and thoughtful reflection made this volume possible. In addition, without the careful copyediting eye, graphic support, and diligent work ethic of Jessica McConnell, we could not have brought this volume to the finish line. Thank you to Martha Samaniego Calderón for her talent in creating our cover art. Thank you to Multilingual Matters, Anna Roderick, Florence McClelland, and our Translanguaging in Theory and Practice Series Editors: Li Wei, Angel Lin, Yuen Yi Lo and Saskia Van Viegen for their generous guidance through this project. Finally, we are grateful to the many teachers, teacher educators who willingly and generously shared their collaborative journeys in co-designing and implementing translanguaging pedagogies.

Leah Shepard-Carey
Des Moines, IA, USA

Zhongfeng Tian
Newark, NJ, USA

Foreword: Doing Translanguaging Research/ Teaching/Learning Juntos

Ofelia García

In this book Shepard-Carey and Tian advance the notion of juntos/together that was used to describe a translanguaging stance in García *et al.* (2017) and that was taken up in the portrayal of the work we did juntos in The City University of New York-New York State Initiative on Emergent Bilinguals (CUNY-NYSIEB, 2021). We defined the juntos stance as the teacher's mindset of joint collaboration among themselves and their students, and their families and communities, as well as the joint elaboration of students' language and cultural practices. Here Shepard-Carey and Tian take the juntos stance one step further, focusing on how teachers and researchers collaborate to jointly develop translanguaging pedagogies by acting on their co-stance, a co-design and co-shifts (Tian & Shepard-Carey, 2020). As a theory, translanguaging effaces boundaries – between named languages and their speakers, between school and communities, between so-called 'speech communities.' The work that this book describes and attests effaces another boundary – that between university researchers and teachers.

Teacher–Researcher Collaboration Juntos

Teachers are often constrained by school policies and curricula. For example, policy in immersion programs requires that only the 'target language' be used, whereas in dual language bilingual programs in the US the two languages are strictly separated. However, in all classrooms, bilingual students do language with a unitary repertoire which usually does not fit the strict monolingual/monoglossic language policies and practices of schools. Teachers often do not know how to negotiate the tension between school policy and children's languaging. On the other hand, researchers are often disconnected from school practices and children's and communities' lives. They are well versed in the scholarly literature but may be clueless about the everyday life of classrooms, which teachers know well.

By putting researchers and teachers to work through the tensions juntos, the authors in these chapters advance our understandings of translanguaging pedagogical practices. The chapters weave a fabric that tells the story of translanguaging in classrooms, while noticing the gaps that allow us to see power differentials and the contextual specificities of participating communities. Translanguaging pedagogies emerge in classrooms of different types – English-medium classrooms, both English as a second language (ESL) and English as a foreign language (EFL); bilingual education classrooms that are said to be immersion or dual language; classrooms that follow the approach known as Content and Language Integrated Learning (CLIL); as well as in science, arts, technology and other content classrooms where there are multilingual learners. Teachers and researchers support each other in understanding how translanguaging operates and designing lessons that leverage the students' translanguaging in ways that respond to different national and community wishes.

In taking up the translanguaging juntos stance, everyone becomes a learner, creating a cycle of discovery and learning that extends beyond the student to the educator and to the researcher. The direction is not simply top-down from university researchers to educators on the ground who must be instructed. Instead, the juntos relationship is fully bi-directional, as everyone becomes a co-learner.

Translanguaging: Transforming Research and Pedagogical Practices Juntos

This volume not only extends relationships, but transforms the mere idea of what research is, as well as the purpose of research. Some scholars have proposed that translanguaging is a research methodology, a way of looking and analyzing language data without the prior categorical imposition of named languages. Translanguaging theory also requires a different way of capturing language data. Li Wei (2011) has proposed moment analysis as one way of generating the data. And in a 2022 issue of *Research Methods in Applied Linguistics*, Won Lee, Li Wei, Phyak and Vogel (2022) have proposed that a translanguaging lens leads to a more grounded research methodology. Finex Nhdlovu (2022) has described how translanguaging is best captured without the strictures of an apriori method, spontaneously, as it occurs in real life. Here Shepard-Carey and Tian advance the idea that translanguaging research in classrooms must be about working juntos, with researchers taking up a parallel position to teachers and becoming co-learners/co-educators as they take up a co-stance, a co-design and co-shifts. In many ways, traditional educational research is hereby disrupted. Instead of legitimizing an external perspective, that is, understandings that stem from the top down, from outside of classrooms, from the academy, from expert accounts, this collaborative research juntos honors the internal perspective of classroom practice, legitimizing teacher knowledge as important expertise. As researchers work collaboratively with teachers, they start owning their own vulnerabilities. For example, the chapter by Hamman-Ortiz shows how vulnerable the researcher felt when the teacher observed her, teaching what she was preaching.

Not only does this collaborative juntos translanguaging perspective transform educational research, but also does so regarding teaching methodology. Translanguaging pedagogy is a way of teaching emergent bilinguals without the prior categorical imposition of named languages, instead following the students' translanguaging corriente. The pedagogy is again not externally created by experts but is co-designed by teachers according to the local context, the students, the community, and their practices and desires. The ways in which Shepard-Carey and Tian have conceptualized translanguaging in this volume responds to what Kumaravadivelu (2001) has called post-method because of three characteristics: (1) a context-sensitive language education; (2) the rupture of relationship between theorists and practitioners; and (3) the tapping into educators' and learners' sociopolitical consciousness.

In the opening chapter, Johnson *et al.* call translanguaging pedagogical practices 'pedagogía a lo natural.' This 'a lo natural' does not mean the same as natural in the 'natural communicative approach.' In the second sense, the word 'natural' responds to the ways that monolingual so-called 'native' speakers use language. In the Johnson *et al.* sense, 'a lo natural' means the ways in which teachers respond and adjust to the natural ways of doing language of racialized bilingual communities whose language practices are not legitimized in classrooms and that disrupt the boundaries of normed named languages. This pedagogía a lo natural involves a constant 'regar the rows del jardín,' to water the language flowers, to grow the students' language practices (Johnson *et al.*), and an acompañamiento of the children (as Vacca *et al.* call it in their chapter). The growth only happens with a stance of patience, of aguante, that 'the children will eventually get it' (Lau *et al.*), and that 'from little things big things grow.' (Dobinson *et al.*). A translanguaging pedagogía a lo natural requires translinguistas, transladoras and translanguerreras, as Johnson *et al.* describe the work of teachers/researchers. These warriors are capable of building the stamina, el aguante, so as to open up spaces in the traditional language policies and curricula which teachers face. Teachers not only need stamina to face these obstacles, they also must understand that teaching bilingual children in institutions that are not necessarily open to differences must also build their children's aguante. This aguante consists of the stamina to continue to language in ways that are their own, and to try out and develop new features to add to their unitary repertoire. That is, the students must develop a stamina to be sociocognitively aware of when they must suppress certain features of their repertoire, and when they must select some features to interact with different interlocutors.

Through the work with university researchers, teachers become aware of when they can leverage the students' translanguaging a lo natural, and yet, when they must guide them to become socially aware of which features and practices they must select, and which to suppress from their unitary repertoire. In turn, university researchers become socially aware of the limitations that language policies and curricula impose on teachers as they attempt to transform their pedagogical practices to follow the students' translanguaging corriente.

Bilingual children do not require stamina to engage in translanguaging – that is why it is so important to leverage it in educating them. Bilingual children find it natural to engage in translanguaging and it is a most important resource to learn. But stamina is required to use only certain features of their repertoire, especially those associated with a minoritized language. Teachers then must learn to mediate the vulnerability that bilingual children feel when they are asked to perform linguistically as monolinguals, whether in a dominant global language like English or in a minoritized language like Spanish. In turn, researchers and educators must mediate for each other the vulnerabilities that they face as they work in each other's space.

Mediating Vulnerabilities of Researchers and Teachers

This volume also makes visible the tensions that translanguaging work brings to schools. A monolingual/monoglossic ideology has always permeated education, with the purpose of schooling often being the teaching of a named language norm, and the eradication of other language differences. Thus, teachers often interpret translanguaging as language mixing, as code-switching and, as the teachers report in Rajendram's contribution, as the ways of languaging of incompetent bilinguals. Teachers also must disrupt their own learning experiences, often in immersion classrooms where only the target language is said to be used. We learn through these contributions that it is not only the children, but also the teachers, who 'will eventually get it,' if we all work juntos.

But it is not only misunderstandings that cause teachers' hesitancy. Many teachers report that they are reprimanded by the administration for violating the strict monolingual/monoglossic language policies that have been established. There are also teachers who report fear of losing control of the classroom if they allow the children to use language practices that they simply do not understand (Cataldo-Schwarzl & Erling). It turns out that for teachers it is not simply a case of 'not getting it.' Courage is needed, a 'sin miedo,' a without fear, that echoes the call that Sánchez and García made in their 2022 book. Furthermore, the collaborative work also makes researchers name and acknowledge their own privilege, with teachers often reporting that they have little time to reflect on their practices. In fact, the collaborative work between researchers and teachers is difficult to carry out because of the little time that teachers have for planning and discussion.

Researchers learn that they must adjust to the realities of classroom policies and practices. For example, although teachers slowly change their stance towards translanguaging through the collaboration, researchers adapt to how teachers negotiate the school's language policies and curricula in designing translanguaging instruction. For example, the teachers in Lau *et al.*'s chapter report that they decided to model only the use of the target language, as they created bridges between the two languages. However, they were able to open up translanguaging spaces for students' practices. Lau *et al.* report that the researchers 'came to appreciate this more structured yet flexible approach in coordinating teacher and student-directed translanguaging practices.' It is also researchers who 'will eventually get it.' Researchers' own idealized translanguaging stances shift in response to institutional realities and the pedagogical needs of the students.

Translanguaging Futures

In the last 10 years, language educators and researchers have begun opening spaces for translanguaging in classrooms, disrupting the monolingual/monoglossic ideology that has dominated the field. As we see in these chapters, researchers and teachers are collaboratively designing translanguaging pedagogical practices that disrupt much traditional language education policy, curricula and practices. Opening up translanguaging spaces to educate racialized bilinguals will always be difficult if we continue to only view language and language communities with western/modern hegemonic lenses. These lenses enable us to perceive histories and experiences only from the side of the colonial line (Santos, 2007) where 'white listening subjects' are positioned, that is, those with institutional power who are mostly white monolingual heterosexual males (Flores & Rosa, 2015). Raciolinguistic ideologies often do not enable us to see the full human potential of racialized and colonized people who language differently, who language outside of the boundaries established by dominant institutions such as schools.

To enact translanguaging pedagogical practices requires researchers and teachers to work together as a political act (García *et al.*, 2021), to listen to and perceive those who have been made invisible by the colonial logic that protects the privilege of those with power. If we were to listen to racialized bilinguals as speakers with languaging human capacity, we would recognize their full potential, and we would recognize their use of complex dynamic bilingualism as ways of being academic, critical and creative. We would understand that being bilingual does not simply mean having or maintaining a first language as a static entity to which a second language can be added whole. Instead, we would understand that racialized bilinguals do language by assembling a repertoire of language and semiotic features and practices from all the different communities and individuals with whom they interact.

If we truly appreciated the bilinguals' translanguaging, we would then want to jointly study them and teach them in ways that extend their repertoire, that adds features, practices, discourses and experiences that they can then make their own. It is not about adding a second language. It is not about eradicating features (or even named languages) that are considered impure, ill-sounding, improper. It is not even about maintaining what are seen as 'mother tongues.' It is about recognizing bilingual practices as important to potentialize how language enables us to think, create, be critical, make meaning for ourselves as people who live 'entre mundos,' in borderlands (Anzaldua, 1987). Only by leveraging the children's own features and practices and then extending them, as one adds pearls to a single string, will learners be able to use THEIR language to learn, exist, live and make meaning. As Anishinaabe cultural theorist Gerald Vizenor (1999) says, translanguaging is a way of 'survivance,' languaging for survival as people, while building the aguante to resist the dominance of others. This requires a strong teacher–researcher collaboration.

To me, translanguaging entails understanding that a named language has an important social reality that is the result of nation-building and colonialism. This is not, however, what people draw on to language and make meaning because ways of languaging always go beyond the boundaries that schools have drawn around the concept of academic or school language to protect the privilege of some. The bilingual's unitary linguistic/semiotic competence must be leveraged in education. Of course, this also means that bilinguals must be made socially aware of their interlocutors, and of which features to use with whom. But the selection or suppression of certain linguistic/semiotic features relies on a sociocognitive awareness that named languages have a very important external social reality with which bilinguals must learn to cope. This, however, has little to do with the cognitive capacity of bilinguals who language with their own resources. For this complex understanding to emerge, the collaboration of researchers–teachers is most important.

Only by recognizing the plurilingualism of individual speakers, especially of those who have been racialized and colonized, and understanding how speakers orchestrate their many linguistic and semiotic resources in encounters, both with monolingual and other plurilingual individuals, will teachers and researchers develop the courage to name translanguaging as it is – a unitary repertoire that requires political consciousness to recognize it as such because it carves out space for different and equitable languaging practices. Translanguaging requires assessment that taps into a unitary competence that has little to do with the concept of language proficiency in one named language or two that continues to permeate educational discourse.

One more collaborative step will be required beyond effacing the boundary between teacher and researcher that this book highlights. We will also need to work juntos with educational policymakers and school authorities. There is a contradiction between national, state and local authorities' sense of language standards as *universal* and applicable to all populations and the *pluriversal* notion that translanguaging requires. The pluriverse, according to Latin American decolonial theorist Arturo Escobar (2020), is a world that fits many worlds with their own ontological and epistemic grounding. A pluriverse politics is required to design different possible futures that can transform the linguistic hierarchies with which schools operate. In other words, pluriverse politics in education requires that the concept of social justice and equity go beyond simple sameness in standards that then produce hierarchies of ability and power. Pluriverse politics in language education would require that we ground our teaching on the ontologies and epistemes of all speakers, and their language practices, as different as these might be from the ones that have been posited as the norm. For this to occur, researcher–teachers collaborations of the types described in this book are urgently needed.

References

Anzaldúa, G. (1987) *Borderlands/La frontera. The new mestiza.* Aunt Lute Books.

CUNY-NYSIEB (City University of New York-New York State Initiative on Emergent Bilinguals) (eds) (2021) *Translanguaging and Transformative Teaching for Emergent Bilingual Students. Lessons from the CUNY-NYSIEB Project.* New York: Routledge.

Escobar, A. (2020) *Pluriversal Politics. The Real and the Possible.* Durham, NC: Duke University Press.

Flores, N. and Rosa, J. (2015) Undoing appropriateness: Raciolinguistic ideologies and language diversity in education. *Harvard Educational Review* 85 (2), 149–171.

García, O., Flores, N., Seltzer, K., Li, W., Otheguy, R. and Rosa, J. (2021) Rejecting abyssal thinking in the language and education of racialized bilinguals: A manifesto. *Critical Inquiry in Language Studies* 18 (3), 203–228. https://doi.org/10.1080/15427587.2021.1935957

Kumaravadivelu, B. (2001) Toward a postmethod pedagogy. *TESOL Quarterly* 35 (4), 537–560.

Lee, J.W. (2022) Translanguaging research methodologies. *Research Methods in Applied Linguistics* 1 (1). https://doi.org/10.1016/j.rmal.2022.100004.

Li, W. (2011) Moment analysis and translanguaging space: discursive construction of identities by multilingual Chinese youth in Britain. *Journal of Pragmatics* 43 (5), 1222–1235. https://doi.org/10.1016/j.pragma.2010.07.035.

Li, W. (2022) Translanguaging as method. *Research Methods in Applied Linguistics* 1 (1) https://www.sciencedirect.com/science/article/pii/S2772766122000234?via%3Dihub

Phyak, P. (2022) Decolonizing translanguaging research methodologies: A commentary and self-reflection. *Research Methods in Applied Linguistics* 1 (1). https://doi.org/10.1016/j.rmal.2022.100032

Sánchez, M.T. and García, O. (eds) (2022) *Transformative Translanguaging Espacios: Latinx Students and Teachers Rompiendo Fronteras sin Miedo.* Bristol: Multilingual Matters.

Santos, B. de S. (2007) Beyond abyssal thinking: From global lines to ecologies of knowledges. *Review (Fernand Braudel Center)* 30 (1), 45–89.

Tian, Z. and Shepard-Carey, L. (2020) (Re)imagining the future of translanguaging pedagogies in TESOL through teacher-researcher collaboration. *TESOL Quarterly* 54 (4), 1131–1143.

Vizenor, G. (1999) *Manifest Manners: Narratives on PostIndian Survivance.* Lincoln: Bison Books.

Vogel, S. (2022) Attending to and transforming power dynamics in translanguaged research relationships and methodology. *Research Methods in Applied Linguistics* 1 (1). https://www.sciencedirect.com/science/article/pii/S2772766122000234?via%3Dihub

Introduction: Teacher–Researcher Collaboration as a Pathway for Sustaining Translanguaging Pedagogies

Leah Shepard-Carey and Zhongfeng Tian

Research surrounding translanguaging pedagogies and multilingual pedagogies more broadly has increased over the last 10 years across a variety of educational contexts (e.g. Cenoz & Gorter, 2017; David *et al.*, 2022; Gort & Sembiante, 2015; Machado & Hartman, 2019; Paulsrud *et al.*, 2021; Rajendram, 2021; Tian & Link, 2019; Tian *et al.*, 2020). This increase in scholarship exemplifies growing engagement with culturally and linguistically sustaining approaches (Paris & Alim, 2014) in education that integrate the lived experiences of multilingual students. Theoretically, translanguaging frameworks assume that multilinguals have a holistic linguistic repertoire from which they strategically choose features to adapt to the communicative context (García & Li, 2014). In practice, translanguaging pedagogies represent an epistemic and pedagogical commitment to multilingual learners by legitimizing and intentionally incorporating their multilingualism and multilingual identities in the classroom (García & Li, 2014; García *et al.*, 2017). Translanguaging pedagogies have demonstrated numerous benefits to multilingual students, such as building cross-linguistic awareness, reading comprehension, conceptual knowledge and sense of belonging (e.g. Daniel *et al.*, 2019; García-Mateus & Palmer, 2017; Leonet *et al.*, 2020; Rajendram, 2021; Sayer, 2013). We position translanguaging pedagogies as critical avenues to dismantle monoglossic and elite bilingualism discourse and policies that pervade many educational settings (Flores & Rosa, 2015), and as an integral part of building schooling systems that 'sustain and support bi- and multilingualism and bi- and multiculturalism' (Paris, 2012: 95). While the theoretical and psycholinguistic conceptualizations of translanguaging have been contested (e.g. MacSwan, 2017, 2022; Otheguy *et al.*, 2015, 2019), our emphasis for this volume is the improvement of pedagogical practice and building partnerships with teachers and researchers, and consequently, the creation of more equitable schooling experiences for multilingual learners. As such, while we contend that translanguaging pedagogies have demonstrated much promise to serve multilingual students, we have yet to encounter translanguaging pedagogies as consistent and intentional practices across K-12 educational settings.

The editors of this volume suggest one pathway towards advancement of translanguaging pedagogies: teacher–researcher partnerships. Although literature alludes to the value of teacher–researcher relationships in translanguaging pedagogies inquiry (e.g. David *et al.*, 2022; García & Kleyn, 2016; Zapata & Laman, 2016), we see a dearth of research that explicitly describes the processes of designing and implementing translanguaging pedagogies in primary and secondary school settings (K-12) across various international contexts. By promoting and highlighting teacher–researcher partnerships as one possible avenue for improvement and transparency, we believe that we can build upon the potential of translanguaging pedagogies in classrooms and further resist linguistic hierarchies that exist in educational institutions today. Translanguaging pedagogies are not an easy endeavor, as many of the authors in this volume illustrate; they often co-occur within and against problematic institutional policies, strict curriculum and language ideologies, along with the everyday problems of practice in the classroom. However, collaborative approaches between researchers and educators may help further the aims of translanguaging pedagogies through mutual support in addressing everyday issues, sharing information on best practice and the expertise of educators and their knowledge of their context. García *et al.* (2021) also highlight the power of collaboration in their own partnerships:

> In our collaborations with teachers, we have found that as they explore new theories and take them up in their pedagogical practices, they also make them their own, shaping them in ways that align with their teaching. It is this reshaping of theory through practice – and through continuing collaborations with researchers and teacher-educators – that pushes the theory forward *and* creates more dynamic, sustaining, and equitable learning environments for racialized bilingual students. (2021: 221, original emphasis)

Drawing on García *et al.*'s (2021) work, we also believe that teacher–researcher collaboration may advance theory and practice and build classroom environments that sustain translanguaging pedagogies as everyday practice and embrace the linguistic realities of multilingual students.

The editors of this volume expand García *et al.*'s (2017) stance, design and shifts framework to recognize the power of equitable teacher–researcher partnerships. We ground this volume in our framework of co-stance, co-design and co-shifts (Tian & Shepard-Carey, 2020), which is a heuristic for designing and examining collaborative approaches to translanguaging pedagogies and further recognizes the dynamic nature of collaboration. In the paragraphs that follow, we each narrate one of our own collaborative partnerships and rationale for the volume, provide an overview of the literature and theoretical framework guiding this book and then provide descriptions of the chapters.

This framework and volume came into fruition when we, Leah Shepard-Carey and Zhongfeng Tian (editors), met at a conference panel in 2019 sharing our research, and subsequently discussed many of our observations in our teacher–researcher collaborations focused on translanguaging pedagogies. We have both worked as educators and teacher-educators in various capacities, and have wrestled with the sustainability of translanguaging pedagogies in our current educational climate. We wondered how other educators and researchers were adapting to and/or resisting institutional constraints, negotiating raciolinguistic and monoglossic ideologies and circumventing everyday problems of practice. We believe that translanguaging pedagogies require a transformative stance that cultivates multilingual and multicultural spaces and further questions and resists monolingual and monocultural bias (Flores, 2020; Flores & Rosa, 2015; García & Kleyn, 2016). In agreement with García and Otheguy, 'in conceptualizing translanguaging, we have focused on *its consequences* for minoritized bilinguals, and how it has shaped the dominance of monolinguals' (2021: 4, original emphasis) in schooling, and hence we strive, as current researchers and teacher-educators, to better collaborate with our colleagues in K-12 education to make translanguaging pedagogies a norm in the school experiences of multilinguals.

As a former elementary English-as-an-additional language educator, Leah's research has focused on working with young multilinguals and with less-common languages (Shepard-Carey, 2020a, 2021). Her dissertation research (Shepard-Carey, 2020b, 2022) involved a three-year participatory design research project (Bang & Vossoughi, 2016) in an English-medium classroom with her former second-grade colleague Ms Hassan (pseudonym). In this project, they redesigned Ms Hassan's reading instruction to incorporate translanguaging pedagogies to better meet the needs of students from a less-common language background, Somali. During this collaboration, Ms Hassan and Leah encountered several challenges and successes, including materials design for less-common languages, student internalization of language ideologies and incorporating a multilingual morning meeting routine. Close collaboration in design and teaching of lessons involved constant negotiation of ideologies and flexible approaches to design work, which we believe, allowed us to more deeply understand the challenges and implications of doing translanguaging pedagogies.

To leverage bilingual learners' full linguistic repertoires as resources and move beyond strict language separation in dual language immersion (DLI) programs, Zhongfeng's (2020) dissertation study explored how

Sánchez *et al.*'s (2018) translanguaging allocation policy could be strategically and purposefully designed in a US Mandarin-English DLI classroom where the majority of the students were English-dominant speakers. Also taking the form of participatory design research, Zhongfeng worked alongside a grade 3 Mandarin teacher, Ms Li, to co-design *translanguaging documentation*, *translanguaging rings* and *translanguaging transformation* spaces across different content areas – Chinese Language Arts, Science and Social Studies. Findings revealed that translanguaging pedagogies took many shapes based on contextual factors, such as the different pedagogical purposes and curricular demands across content areas. Students were able to develop deeper content understandings, build cross-linguistic connections and develop their bi/multilingual identities and critical consciousness in those flexible bilingual spaces (Tian, 2022a, 2022b). Findings also demonstrated that the ideological (re)negotiation between the researcher and the teacher was a bumpy and discursive journey, replete with tensions, confusions and difficult conversations. Overall, it was a balancing act to create translanguaging spaces while maintaining the language-minoritized (Mandarin) space and privileging students' use of Mandarin.

As in other areas of literature, we found that our participatory and collaborative partnerships not only led to many successes and long-term change in ideologies and curriculum (Gutiérrez & Vossoughi, 2010), but allowed us to permeate the teacher–researcher binary and trouble the on-the-ground and systemic issues that come with implementing translanguaging pedagogies (McKinley, 2019). Hence, our inquiry and purpose for this book is truly grounded in work in schools, and seeks to illuminate both *processes* and *products* that result from collaborative design and implementation of translanguaging pedagogies in primary and secondary school contexts, in order to better understand how such pedagogies can be developed across a range of contexts. Specifically, with an expanded focus on collaborative processes in translanguaging pedagogies, we seek to reveal the benefits and challenges of engaging in this work with reference to everyday design processes, broader ideological discourses and systemic structures.

Teacher–Researcher Collaboration and Translanguaging Pedagogies

In this volume, the editors and authors aim to emphasize the invaluable expertise and experience of K-12 educators as co-designers, as part of efforts across educational contexts to resist the dichotomous positioning of research and practice, and further make transparent the 'messiness' of classroom research (McKinley, 2019). As Rose (2019) notes, classroom research needs to be recognized for its 'ecological validity' as it can assist in strengthening the knowledge-base of translanguaging. Additionally, with the vast theoretical shifts in multilingualism, we need teacher perspectives and input on how these new 'perspectives can improve their language teaching practices' (Rose, 2019: 4) and in general, improve approaches that serve multilingual learners. We define teacher–researcher collaboration broadly as joint work and/or negotiation in design and implementation of programs and/or educational practices between K-12 teachers, teacher-leaders, administrators and university-level teacher educators/researchers. In educational research more broadly, teacher–researcher collaboration functions along a continuum, with varying levels of involvement and direction from practitioners and researchers (Wagner, 1997). There are many frameworks from which to approach this work, including design-based research, community-based research, social design experiments, Indigenous methodologies, participatory design research and research–practice partnerships (e.g. Bang *et al.*, 2010; Bang & Vossoughi, 2016; Coburn *et al.*, 2013; Gutiérrez, 2008; Gutiérrez & Vossoughi, 2010; McKenney & Reeves, 2018; Sylvester *et al.*, 2020). In alignment with critical and participatory approaches to research and with the social justice aims of translanguaging pedagogies, equitable and bidirectional partnerships may induce more transformative change by attending to the nuanced needs and desires of the participating communities (Gutiérrez & Vossoughi, 2010).

Translanguaging research has highlighted teacher–researcher partnerships in various forms, often as a key part of the mobilization of these translanguaging pedagogies in schools. Generally, there are two strands of teacher–researcher collaboration with regard to translanguaging pedagogies, professional development and direct collaboration in classrooms, and many studies take up one or both (e.g. Daniel *et al.*, 2019; David *et al.*, 2022; Galante, 2020; Liu *et al.*, 2020; Machado & Hartman, 2019; Ollerhead, 2019). Arguably, one of the most notable and often cited teacher–researcher collaborations in translanguaging pedagogies is the CUNY-NYSIEB project which was a partnership between principal investigators Drs Ofelia García, Ricardo Otheguy and Kate Menken (including many colleagues and doctoral students) at the City University of New York and public schools in New York City lasting several years, involving many schools, educators and researchers. The schools and teachers involved made commitments to engage with students' bilingualism as a resource and to cultivate multilingual school ecologies (see CUNY-NYSIEB, 2021; García & Kleyn, 2016). With a multilevel approach, the researchers worked with principals and teachers to provide professional development and classroom support as teachers gained pedagogical knowledge in translanguaging pedagogies. Professional development seems to be a productive avenue for teacher–researcher collaboration in translanguaging pedagogies, as numerous studies have reported changes in teacher practices and beliefs (e.g. David *et al.*, 2022; Gorter & Arocena, 2020; Liu *et al.*, 2020). David *et al.* (2022) worked with secondary content teachers in a culturally and linguistically diverse school setting to provide professional development on translanguaging pedagogies. While translanguaging pedagogies were seemingly new to many of the teachers, they found 'entry point' strategies such as word-walls and same-language groups to be beneficial. Additionally, many of the educators reported that this professional development caused them to think more deeply about students' multilingualism. Similarly, Liu *et al.* (2020) found that teacher–researcher collaboration in the form of professional development helped English language teachers in China trouble monolingual language ideologies. Direct partnerships between a researcher (or multiple) and a classroom teacher have also been reported consistently in the literature (e.g. Allard, 2017; Allard *et al.*, 2019; García & Kleyn, 2016; Machado & Hartman, 2019; Tian, 2022a; Zapata & Laman, 2016). While few of these studies actually comment on the collaborative processes themselves, we see evidence of the benefits of this collaboration for both students and teachers in these settings, as the authors often report a change in pedagogical practice, ideologies and/or student engagement with translanguaging. However, without explicit description about many of these partnerships, we are left to infer about, what we imagine to be, the time-intensive processes of negotiating stances, designs and shifts (García *et al.*, 2017) as teachers and researchers carry out translanguaging pedagogies. Hence, the editors created a framework to better help us and other partnerships explore the complex web of translanguaging ideologies, products and practices that occur in collaborative classroom endeavors.

Co-Stance, Co-Design, Co-Shifts

In this volume, we center teacher–researcher collaboration through our conceptual framework, 'co-stance, co-design, and co-shifts' (Tian & Shepard-Carey, 2020) which is adapted from García *et al.*'s (2017) stance, design and shifts framework. Our framework emphasizes equitable collaboration as one way to unleash the potential of translanguaging pedagogies in K-12 settings, though we recognize it is certainly not the only way. Yet, we believe in the power of collective and collaborative engagement, whether it be between researchers and teachers, teachers and administrators, colleagues, etc., because it allows for multiple points of entry and problem-solving in design work. Additionally, while not all partnerships are equitable or even balanced, this is a central goal of our framework. In their framework, García *et al.* (2017) explained that teachers need to have language ideologies (stance) that see students' multilingualism as valuable and as a resource. Educators also need to intentionally incorporate students' multilingualism into lesson designs and assessments (design), and shift as needed to respond to students' needs in the moment. Our framework situates theory, practice and research as interrelated and denotes porous roles between teachers and researchers, subverting dichotomous

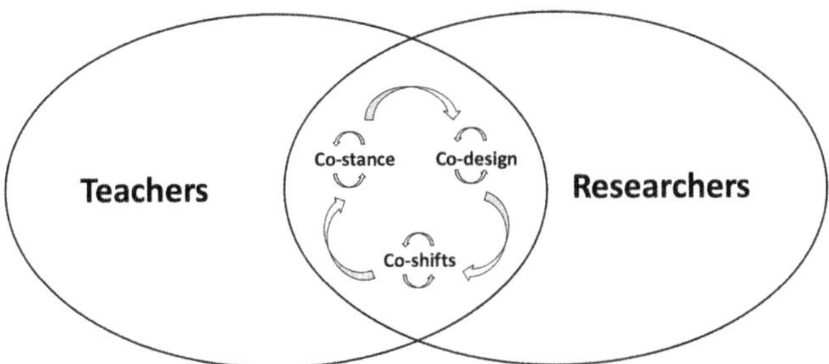

Figure 0.1 Translanguaging co-stance, co-design and co-shifts framework

conceptualizations of 'researcher' and 'teacher.' We position collaboration as a dynamic process, during which researchers and teachers must negotiate co-stances, develop co-designs and make co-shifts to address the needs of the students (see Figure 0.1[1]). Like many action and design-based research approaches, we conceptualize our co-stance, co-design and co-shifts processes as iterative and interconnected. Each element functions in concert with the other, influencing the flow of collaborative processes, and is situated within the nexus of teacher–researcher collaboration.

We expand our 2020 framework to suggest collaboration as a worthwhile endeavor for researchers and teachers across all educational contexts (with and beyond language teaching and TESOL). With modification of our 2020 framework (p. 1130–1134), the interrelated strands are described in more detail below.

- Co-stance: Translanguaging co-stance refers to the enduring, dynamic process in which teachers and researchers collaboratively, respectfully and openly discuss and negotiate their philosophical, ideological or belief systems regarding bilingualism and translanguaging to better inform their pedagogical framework. Specifically, a translanguaging co-stance starts with trusting relationship building and highlights equitable forms of dialogue and listening. This not only helps teachers and researchers develop a language-as-asset stance to problematize (and even challenge) the dominant monolingual structures in TESOL [and other learning contexts], but also deepens their understanding of the complexity of classroom contexts and how to develop contextualized translanguaging pedagogies (instead of romanticizing a one-size-fits-all approach). Moreover, a translanguaging co-stance goes beyond the static roles of 'teachers' and 'researchers' in a traditional sense and transforms them. Both teachers and researchers expand their communities of practice and are in a fluid state of being and becoming a holistic education professional who engages with research and practice.
- Co-design: Translanguaging co-design refers to the iterative process that involves both teachers and researchers co-planning units, lessons

and assessments that build upon students' full linguistic repertoires. During this process, both teachers and researchers bring their own expertise and position themselves as co-learners with students. They engage in co-planning through cyclical cycles to document opportunities, challenges and tensions arising from the process and to figure out optimal ways to maximize students' learning opportunities. They both think, observe and act critically and creatively to make strategic decisions on when and how to build translanguaging spaces. Teachers and researchers could also co-teach lessons to stay close to the students, to grapple with the 'messiness' of the classroom and to enrich their understanding of translanguaging theory and pedagogy to generate ideas for collective action.

- Co-shifts: Translanguaging co-shifts refer to the many moments that teachers and researchers engage in self and communal reflections and make flexible pedagogical designs that have room for lesson adjustments and shifts in response to their observation of student participation in language-mediated classroom activities. Through continuous, critical reflection and analysis of key events and classroom scenarios, both teachers and researchers show flexibility and willingness to change the course of the lesson, as well as the ways to support students' voices and identities. With the central goal of leveraging and sustaining students' home languages and cultures while developing their linguistic repertoire to include English features, teachers and researchers make co-shifts that go with the flow of students' translanguaging practices at all points of a bilingual continuum.

By framing the research in this volume through the lens of co-stance, co-design and co-shifts, we elucidate the potential of partnership in 'demystifying translanguaging theory and pedagogy, keeping translanguaging research grounded in classrooms, and facilitating the implementation of translanguaging pedagogies' (Tian & Shepard-Carey, 2020: 1134) across educational contexts. Furthermore, this framework works towards the subversion of conventional and/or authoritative partnerships where the researcher holds the expert status. Rather, by approaching collaboration in translanguaging pedagogies with this orientation, we see the potential of transformative agency (Haapasaari *et al.*, 2016), which sees beyond individual efforts towards change but advocates for and pushes collective change. In turn, this may build sustainable pathways for translanguaging pedagogies as everyday practice for all educators and students in classrooms. Methodologically, this framework and volume offers insight on how teachers and researchers might approach collaborative endeavors, and further negotiate the ideological and practical issues that arise. Through description of how the researchers and educators negotiated co-stances, co-designs and co-shifts, this volume aims to provide transparency on the *how* of translanguaging pedagogies and the navigation of these across complex schooling contexts, further suggesting how researchers, teacher educators and K-12 teachers might improve translanguaging pedagogies. While we suggest equitable collaboration as the ideal approach, this volume represents a range of collaborative approaches and readers will find there are many ways to approach the teacher–researcher partnerships.

Book Organization

This volume seeks to provide a multidimensional perspective of how co-stances, co-designs and co-shifts (García *et al.*, 2017; Tian & Shepard-Carey, 2020) are negotiated by researchers and practitioners and how they connect to the products and practices that manifest in these spaces. Each of the chapters in this volume draw on this framework to describe how researchers and educators collaboratively envisioned, designed and implemented translanguaging pedagogies in their settings. We limit our focus on primary and secondary (K-12) school settings because these are the environments in which many multilingual children spend their days, and as such, translanguaging pedagogies are often in tension with overt and covert hegemonic language policies and constraints of the space. The authors present a range of language and content learning contexts including dual-language immersion, English-medium, English as a foreign language (EFL), content and language integrated learning (CLIL), and science, technology, engineering, arts and mathematics (STEAM). While the majority of this volume's chapters are situated in Western and United States contexts, we incorporate perspectives across international settings with partnerships from six countries, including Australia, Austria, Canada, Malaysia, Taiwan and the United States. We hope that future research in this vein centers on contexts and researchers in the Global South. With the many contexts involved in this volume, we organized this volume by highlighting mostly bilingual education contexts in the first several chapters of this book, and then putting English-medium contexts in the latter part of the volume. This volume illustrates the variability in partnerships across contexts, yet each chapter grounds their work in collaboration and our co-stance, co-design and co-shifts framework.

We begin with Ibarra Johnson, Jurado, Orozco and Trujillo in Chapter 1. They share how three teachers from dual-language bilingual education classrooms (elementary and secondary) in New Mexico, United States reflected on their implementation of translanguaging strategies as part of a Translanguaging Participatory Action Research (PAR) project. In concert with researchers, the teachers participated in a study group to engage with translanguaging theory and pedagogies, and eventually develop a lesson plan that emphasized flexible biliteracy practices. Findings exemplified how teachers developed a co-stance that asserted translanguaging as 'natural' and integral to students' identities. Teachers in the study also narrated how their collaboration and participation inspired intentional translanguaging designs that addressed student identities, (de)colonization of curriculum, assessment practices and physical set-up of the classroom.

In Chapter 2, Rajendram reports on a collaborative researcher-practitioner study conducted in a national-type Tamil primary school in Malaysia. To counteract English-only policies that were prevalent during ESL classes, she engaged a grade 5 teacher in critical discussions aimed to promote a translanguaging co-stance, and co-designed and co-taught lessons which integrated collaborative translanguaging activities. They also made instructional co-shifts based on feedback from learners during focus group interviews with them. Findings revealed that translanguaging created many cognitive–conceptual, planning–organizational, affective–social and linguistic–discursive affordances for student learning. Furthermore, the critical researcher-practitioner discussions supported a classroom-wide implementation of a translanguaging approach to English language teaching.

In Chapter 3 Lau, Liaw and Botelho showcase findings from two collaborative action research (CAR) projects in a Canadian English–French dual-language classroom and a Chinese–English dual-language classroom in the United States. With a focus on engaging elementary learners in critical literacies and translanguaging pedagogies, the participants and researchers varied in experiences and understanding of translanguaging pedagogies. Thus, collaborative processes involved the troubling of boundaries for translanguaging practices and language allocation in settings where a minoritized language was taught. This chapter offers insights into the possibilities and challenges of CAR and the ways they can inform translanguaging teaching and research for critical learning.

Next, Cataldo-Schwarzl and Erling (Chapter 4) address the gap in multilingual approaches in teacher education in Austria by exploring translanguaging pedagogies with grade 4 and 5 teachers in a variety of classroom contexts in Vienna. Through workshops, observation and individualized support to teachers, the authors inquired about the successes and challenges in implementing translanguaging pedagogies collaboratively. Through co-design processes teachers preferred working with multilingual materials and implemented same-language student groupings. While primary grade 4 teachers more readily incorporated translanguaging pedagogies, grade 5 teachers were reluctant to incorporate translanguaging pedagogies and had seemingly more emergent translanguaging stances. Implications of this study suggest sustained involvement and reciprocal relationships with teachers, as it may instill more confidence and willingness to experiment with translanguaging pedagogies.

In Chapter 5, Hamman-Ortiz explores how her collaboration with a classroom teacher, Maestra Carmen, fostered translanguaging practices within a second-grade, two-way immersion classroom in a K-5 bilingual school located in the US Midwest. The collaboration centered on the design and implementation of a bilingual identity text project, in which students collectively composed a bilingual book to represent their bilingual learning experiences. Findings focus on the evolution of the teacher–researcher collaboration, describing the co-design decisions and co-stances that emerged from their joint inquiry and highlighting the ways that these shifted over time. The chapter concludes with a discussion of three core principles that emerged as key elements of a productive research–practice partnership involving translanguaging pedagogy: (1) deeply understanding the sociolinguistic context; (2) openness to inquiry; and (3) willingness to engage in ongoing reflection and adaptation.

Moving into an English-medium setting, Brown and Pomare-McDonald (Chapter 6) formed a teacher-researcher partnership to integrate multimodal, translanguaging learning pedagogy in a first-grade English-medium classroom in a neighborhood school located in the Southeastern United States. To challenge the English-only policies and the privileging of print-centric practices in the school, both of them embarked on a journey to collaboratively develop an asset-based co-stance approach to teaching literacy to emergent bilinguals, and to co-design reading tasks that value students' full linguistic and semiotic repertoires. As a result, co-shifts were made to some of the classroom instructional and assessment practices to better support students in their navigation of texts and content (such as the selection of culturally and linguistically relevant children's literature and multimodal authoring practices). Moving forward, they wanted to continue their partnership and saw technology as one promising area for supporting the translanguaging practices of young emergent bilinguals in reading and writing.

Chapter 7 brings us to Australia. Dobinson, Dryden, Winkler, Gardner and Mercieca walk us through their teacher–researcher participatory action research project between an Australian university and a multilingual Australian primary school. Their team, consisting of four university teacher-researchers and one primary school teacher-researcher, worked together to foster a sustainable stance which sees diverse linguistic practices as valuable resources to be built upon and leveraged in academic tasks. For over two years teacher-researchers collaboratively designed, delivered and evaluated lessons, integrating in-school and out-of-school language practices and attempting to shift to a position where practitioners can respond confidently when student feedback suggests changes in pedagogies are needed. This chapter focuses on their Year Two vocabulary teaching and learning where they attempted to incorporate basic translanguaging pedagogies, such as culturally relevant story books and collaborative learning approaches, in a series of lessons. Findings shed light on important lessons learned for successful teacher–researcher collaborations.

Next, Gupta and Lin (Chapter 8) examine how they adopted critical approaches during a collaborative process with two in-service teachers (primary and secondary) to design and implement translanguaging pedagogies in the context of content and language integrated learning (CLIL) classrooms in Taiwan. The steps taken, the challenges that emerged and the decisions made throughout co-design and implementation processes are discussed. Specifically, the authors described the disagreements and emerging understandings from the teachers surrounding translanguaging pedagogies. Additionally, the chapter discusses how teachers and researchers negotiated more involvement of students' ideas and life experiences into the lessons. With evidence from lesson observation, meeting notes and the students' artifacts, this chapter demonstrates with a critical stance, how this teacher–researcher relationship facilitated a translanguaging approach in CLIL classrooms.

Then, in Chapter 9, Vacca, Vogel, Ascenzi-Moreno, and Hoadley posit a framework of acompañamiento, an approach to teacher–researcher collaborations around technology in multilingual spaces that explicitly acknowledges vulnerability and moves along an axis of redistribution of agency in the classroom. Through this framework they share work of Participating in Literacies and Computer Science (PiLa-CS), a research–practice partnership (RPP) in New York City which brought together university researchers and middle grades teachers to involve emergent bilingual middle schoolers in units of study that integrate computer science practices and concepts. They focused on the relationships between teachers and researchers by analysis of how the teacher–researcher collaboration grappled with questions of agency while attempting to integrate computing into bi/multilingual classrooms in constructivist ways, and build on students' translanguaging intentionally. Findings from this study showed that teacher vulnerability played a key role in mediating how teachers and researchers jointly engaged with the questions of agency involved in grappling with the three components of translanguaging pedagogy: co-stance, co-design and co-shifts. Specific elements of the partnership's approach – encouraging teachers to work within pre-existing curricular and pedagogical frameworks, providing ongoing acompañamiento or in-classroom support, and responding to changes over time in teachers' attitudes – helped manage teacher vulnerability.

In Chapter 10, Fine and her team (two educators: Haeyoung and Maren) bring in perspectives from a science classroom. They worked together to co-design space for grade 6 bilingual students in an English-medium middle school in the United States to translanguage on formative assessment tasks in science. They collectively enacted four (Trans)formative Assessment Co-design (TAC) cycles with each cycle consisting of five phases (Explore, Develop, Enact, Feedback and Reflect & Modify phases) over seven months. Fine *et al.* specifically unpacked the challenges and opportunities emerging from each phase and illustrated how their translanguaging (co)stances, (co)designs and (co)shifts began to move from a theoretical ideal toward a dynamic reality in an iterative process. Findings highlighted that the TAC cycle served as a driver for their teacher–researcher collaboration to understand and embrace translanguaging as a transformative pedagogical and assessment imperative.

In another secondary science classroom, Braun, Seilstad and Kim (Chapter 11) explore a collaborative partnership within an English-medium newcomer biology class in Ohio in the United States. The authors, a team of researchers and a teacher (Braun), co-designed their project, Bilingual Biomes, to affirm and leverage the students' translanguaging practices in Braun's classroom. Throughout the project, the researchers were readily available for support and observation in the classroom, and findings showed that this support helped Braun negotiate translanguaging stances, reimagine translanguaging designs that would provide more interactive opportunities for students, and shift to allow for transliteration opportunities for students. Implications suggest that reflective and ongoing cycles of collaboration have the potential to establish more complex and compassionate pedagogical designs that encompass the full range of activities from moment-to-moment interactions to long-term language policies.

Finally, Pierson (Chapter 12) presents a case study that illustrates the collaboration between a teacher (Ms S) and the author, which aimed to support translanguaging in her English-dominant sixth-grade STEM classroom in the United States. Together, Pierson and Ms S collaboratively designed, refined and taught iterations of a nine-week ecology unit. Findings showed that establishing co-stances, engaging in co-design and navigating co-shifts helped facilitate an environment that supported students' multilingual and multimodal practices. Specifically, through this process, the teacher positioned herself as a learner, further discussing and designing lessons that allowed students to identify disciplinary reasons for using translanguaging. As such, the authors cultivated an environment where students leveraged a wider range of semiotic resources than in previous iterations of their design, integrating English, Spanish, invented terms and a variety of multimodal representations in service of sensemaking.

Final Remarks

This volume positions teacher–researcher collaboration as a way to carry out and sustain translanguaging pedagogies across a variety of classroom contexts. Again, while teacher–researcher collaboration is not the only way to advance translanguaging pedagogies, we agree with García *et al.* (2021) in that these partnerships have the potential to 'reshape' theory and practice. Hence, this volume has both conceptual and methodological contributions through the rich descriptions of pedagogies and the collaborative processes between teachers and researchers.

While numerous studies have highlighted collaboration, we believe that our volume is one of the first to center teacher–researcher collaboration as a worthwhile pathway for the advancement of translanguaging pedagogies in schools and in research. We hope that this volume is a valuable resource for educators and researchers who center the lives and experiences of multilingual students and look forward to the conversations that evolve from this volume.

Note

(1) Special thanks go to Jessica McConnell for her invaluable assistance in construing and visualizing our conceptual framework.

References

Allard, E.C. (2017) Re-examining teacher translanguaging: An ecological perspective. *Bilingual Research Journal* 40 (2), 116–130.

Allard, E.C., Apt, S. and Sacks, I. (2019) Language policy and practice in almost-bilingual classrooms. *International Multilingual Research Journal* 13 (2), 73–87.

Bang, M., Medin, D., Washinawatok, K. and Chapman, S. (2010) Innovations in culturally based science education through partnerships and community. In M. Khine and I. Selah (eds) *New Science of Learning: Cognition, Computers and Collaboration in Education* (pp. 569–592). New York, NY: Springer.

Bang, M. and Vossoughi, S. (2016) Participatory design research and educational justice: Studying learning and relations within social change making. *Cognition and Instruction* 34 (3), 173–193.

Cenoz, J. and Gorter, D. (2017) Minority languages and sustainable translanguaging: Threat or opportunity? *Journal of Multilingual and Multicultural Development* 38 (10), 901–912.

Coburn, C.E., Penuel, W.R. and Geil, K.E. (2013) *Research-Practice Partnerships: A Strategy for Leveraging Research for Educational Improvement in School Districts.* New York, NY: William T. Grant Foundation.

CUNY-NYSIEB (2021) *Translanguaging and Transformative Teaching for Emergent Bilingual Students: Lessons from the CUNY-NYSIEB Project.* New York: Routledge.

Daniel, S.M., Jiménez, R.T., Pray, L. and Pacheco, M.B. (2019) Scaffolding to make translanguaging a classroom norm. *TESOL Journal* 10 (1), e00361.

David, S.S., Shepard-Carey, L., Swearingen, A.J., Hemsath, D.J. and Heo, S. (2022) Entry points and trajectories: Teachers learning and doing translanguaging pedagogy. *TESOL Journal* 13 (1), e603.

Flores, N. (2020) From academic language to language architecture: Challenging raciolinguistic ideologies in research and practice. *Theory Into Practice* 59 (1), 22–31.

Flores, N. and Rosa, J. (2015) Undoing appropriateness: Raciolinguistic ideologies and language diversity in education. *Harvard Educational Review* 85 (2), 149–171.

Galante, A. (2020) Pedagogical translanguaging in a multilingual English program in Canada: Student and teacher perspectives of challenges. *System* 92, 102274–10. https://doi.org/10.1016/j.system.2020.102274

García, O., Flores, N., Seltzer, K., Li, W., Otheguy, R. and Rosa, J. (2021) Rejecting abyssal thinking in the language and education of racialized bilinguals: A manifesto. *Critical Inquiry in Language Studies* 18 (3), 203–228.

García, O., Johnson, S.I. and Seltzer, K. (2017) *The Translanguaging Classroom: Leveraging Student Bilingualism for Learning.* Philadelphia: Caslon.

García, O. and Kleyn, T. (eds) (2016) *Translanguaging with Multilingual Students: Learning from Classroom Moments*. New York: Routledge.

García, O. and Li, W. (2014) *Translanguaging: Language, Bilingualism and Education*. London: Palgrave Macmillan.

García, O. and Otheguy, R. (2021) Conceptualizing translanguaging theory/practice juntos. In CUNY-NYSIEB (eds) *Translanguaging and Transformative Teaching for Emergent Bilingual Students: Lessons from the CUNY-NYSIEB Project* (pp. 3–24). New York: Routledge.

García-Mateus, S. and Palmer, D. (2017) Translanguaging pedagogies for positive identities in two-way dual language bilingual education. *Journal of Language, Identity & Education* 16 (4), 245–255.

Gort, M. and Sembiante, S.F. (2015) Navigating hybridized language learning spaces through translanguaging pedagogy: Dual language preschool teachers' languaging practices in support of emergent bilingual children's performance of academic discourse. *International Multilingual Research Journal* 9 (1), 7–25.

Gorter, D. and Arocena, E. (2020) Teachers' beliefs about multilingualism in a course on translanguaging. *System* 92, 102272–10. https://doi.org/10.1016/j.system.2020.102272

Gutiérrez, K.D. (2008) Developing a sociocritical literacy in the third space. *Reading Research Quarterly* 43 (2), 148–164.

Gutiérrez, K.D. and Vossoughi, S. (2010) Lifting off the ground to return anew: Mediated praxis, transformative learning, and social design experiments. *Journal of Teacher Education* 61 (1–2), 100–117.

Haapasaari, A., Engeström, Y. and Kerosuo, H. (2016) The emergence of learners' transformative agency in a Change Laboratory intervention. *Journal of Education and Work* 29 (2), 232–262.

Leonet, O., Cenoz, J. and Gorter, D. (2020) Developing morphological awareness across languages: Translanguaging pedagogies in third language acquisition. *Language Awareness* 29 (1), 41–59.

Liu, J.E., Lo, Y.Y. and Lin, A.M. (2020) Translanguaging pedagogy in teaching English for Academic Purposes: Researcher-teacher collaboration as a professional development model. *System* 92, 102276–16. https://doi.org/10.1016/j.system.2020.102276

Machado, E. and Hartman, P. (2019) Translingual writing in a linguistically diverse primary classroom. *Journal of Literacy Research* 51 (4), 480–503.

MacSwan, J. (2017) A multilingual perspective on translanguaging. *American Educational Research Journal* 54 (1), 167–201.

MacSwan, J. (ed.) (2022) *Multilingual Perspectives on Translanguaging*. Bristol: Multilingual Matters.

Mckinley, J. (2019) Evolving the TESOL teaching-research nexus. *TESOL Quarterly* 53 (3), 875–884.

McKenney, S. and Reeves, T.C. (2018) *Conducting Educational Design Research*. Abingdon: Routledge.

Ollerhead, S. (2019) Teaching across semiotic modes with multilingual learners: Translanguaging in an Australian classroom. *Language and Education* 33 (2), 106–122.

Otheguy, R., García, O. and Reid, W. (2015) Clarifying translanguaging and deconstructing named languages: A perspective from linguistics. *Applied Linguistics Review* 6 (3), 281–307.

Otheguy, R., García, O. and Reid, W. (2019) A translanguaging view of the linguistic system of bilinguals. *Applied Linguistics Review* 10 (4), 625–651.

Paris, D. (2012) Culturally sustaining pedagogy: A needed change in stance, terminology, and practice. *Educational Researcher* 41 (3), 93–97.

Paris, D. and Alim, S.H. (2014) What are we seeking to sustain through culturally sustaining pedagogy? A loving critique forward. *Harvard Educational Review* 84 (1), 85–100.

Paulsrud, B., Tian, Z. and Toth, J. (eds) (2021) *English-Medium Instruction and Translanguaging*. Bristol: Multilingual Matters.

Rajendram, S. (2021) Translanguaging as an agentive pedagogy for multilingual learners: affordances and constraints. *International Journal of Multilingualism*, 1–28.

Rose, H. (2019) Dismantling the ivory tower in TESOL: A renewed call for teaching-informed research. *TESOL Quarterly* 53 (3), 895–905.

Sánchez, M.T., García, O. and Solorza, C. (2018) Reframing language allocation policy in dual language bilingual education. *Bilingual Research Journal* 41 (1), 37–51.

Sayer, P. (2013) Translanguaging, TexMex, and bilingual pedagogy: Emergent bilinguals learning through the vernacular. *TESOL Quarterly* 47 (1), 63–88.

Shepard-Carey, L. (2022) Creating space for translingual sensemaking: A critical discourse analysis of teacher translanguaging during small-group reading. *Classroom Discourse*. https://doi.org/10.1080/19463014.2022.2089704

Shepard-Carey, L. (2021) The inference-making of elementary emergent multilinguals: Access and opportunities for learning. *Journal of Early Childhood Literacy* 21 (4), 499–537.

Shepard-Carey, L. (2020a) Making sense of comprehension practices and pedagogies in multimodal ways: A second-grade emergent bilingual's sensemaking during small-group reading. *Linguistics and Education* 55 (1), 1–12.

Shepard-Carey, L. (2020b) *Multilingual meaning-making during reading: Collaborative inquiry into translanguaging possibilities and pedagogies for elementary emergent multilinguals*. TESOL International Association: Research. https://www.tesol.org/media/epihkwqj/story-1-by-leah-shepard-carey.pdf

Sylvester, O., García Segura, A., Ashencaen Crabtree, S., Man, Z. and Parker, J. (2020) Applying an Indigenous methodology to a North–South, cross-cultural collaboration: Successes and remaining challenges. *AlterNative: An International Journal of Indigenous Peoples* 16 (1), 45v54.

Tian, Z. (2022a) Translanguaging design in a third grade Chinese language arts class. *Applied Linguistics Review* 13 (3), 327–343.

Tian, Z. (2022b) Challenging the 'dual': Designing translanguaging spaces in a Mandarin-English dual language bilingual education program. *Journal of Multilingual and Multicultural Development* 43 (6), 534–553.

Tian, Z. and Link, H. (eds) (2019) Positive synergies: Translanguaging and critical theories in education (commentary by Ofelia García). *Translation and Translanguaging in Multilingual Contexts* 5 (1). [entire issue]

Tian, Z. and Shepard-Carey, L. (2020) (Re)imagining the future of translanguaging pedagogies in TESOL through teacher-researcher collaboration. *TESOL Quarterly* 54 (4), 1131–1143.

Tian, Z., Aghai, L., Sayer, P. and Schissel, J.L. (eds) (2020) *Envisioning TESOL through a Translanguaging Lens: Global Perspectives*. Cham: Springer International Publishing.

Wagner, J. (1997) The unavoidable intervention of educational research: A framework for reconsidering researcher-practitioner cooperation. *Educational Researcher* 26 (7), 13–22.

Zapata, A. and Laman, T.T. (2016) 'I write to show how beautiful my languages are': Translingual writing instruction in English-dominant classrooms. *Language Arts* 93 (5), 366–378.

1 Transladoras Sin Fronteras: Merging Linguistic Borderlands to Take Up Students' Translanguaging Corriente

Susana Ibarra Johnson, Mishelle Jurado, María Elena Orozco and Michele Trujillo

Many researchers challenge the translanguaging stance sociopolitically as a valid tool for language development (May, 2014). However, we find it to be indispensable for bilingual educators because it promotes bi/multilingualism and positive effects on students' bilingual identity. This chapter differs from most studies because instead of studying translanguaging in isolation we aim to show how it can be applied in the classroom and how it can affect student learning and identity. Here you will see how members of a Translanguaging Participatory Action (PAR) project implement strategies gained from individual inquiry into their classroom practice. The PAR project was created to further develop dual-language bilingual education (DLBE) teachers' knowledge(s) and experience(s) regarding their instructional practices in biliteracy and translanguaging through active participation and critical transformation through collaborative study. This chapter will focus on the empirical work of three DLBE teachers' implementation of Translanguaging Pedagogy (García *et al.*, 2017) and henceforth we will refer to this project as the Translanguaging '*Teacher–researcher collaboration*' (TTRC) (Tian & Shepard-Carey, 2020) project.

The TTRC project is situated in an urban school district in the Southwest whose student enrollment at the time of the study was 91,110, 16.6% of whom are identified as English learners (EL). The purpose of this research is to learn from in-service bilingual educators' current instructional practices in biliteracy and translanguaging through a study in which participants engaged in research about their own enactment of Translanguaging Pedagogy. The answer lay in understanding how translanguaging shapes biliteracy. The research questions we focused on were:

- What biliteracy and translanguaging practices do teachers engage during language arts instruction?
- How could teachers leverage the validity of their culture-specific ways of knowing and their translanguaging?

The TTRC project is positioned to understand how these teachers leveraged translanguaging in their DLBE classrooms. First, we will describe la corriente, our framework and the pathways to biliteracy explaining the literature we draw from to enact a flexible biliteracy approach. Second, we will explain how translanguaging shapes biliteracy by providing a brief overview of the methods, teacher's context and the testimonios of each teacher's translanguaging co-stance. Third, the teachers will provide a description of what biliteracy and translanguaging co-design practices they engaged in during language arts instruction followed by the findings from our joint understanding on how translanguaging shapes biliteracy. Lastly, we will share implications for further research and practice that merge linguistic borderlands to tap into students' translanguaging corriente.

La Corriente

La corriente represents the way students' fluid language and cultural practices flow through the classroom, even when invisible, like a pervasive water current (García *et al.*, 2017). A current is always present in a river, even if the river appears to be still and quiet. Similarly, even if students' fluid linguistic repertoire and translanguaging are not leveraged in the classroom, the corriente is always there mezclando las tierras fronterizas merging the students' linguistic borderlands. Rather than linguistic isolation the harnessed energy of a leveraged corriente creates dynamic multilingual classrooms of empowered students.

The expectation for the participating teachers in this TTRC project is to adopt a Translanguaging Pedagogy. That is, the teachers in the TTRC described in this work discover their personal *co-stances* that would influence the collective dynamic bilingual identity of their students and themselves. By valuing and expanding Translanguaging Pedagogy in the classroom context, they developed a unit/lesson instructional *co-design* that integrates students' linguistic repertoires and allows spaces for flexible *co-shifts* determined by students' linguistic needs and practices during learning (García *et al.*, 2017; Tian & Shepard-Carey, 2020). Through this collaboration our goal is to better understand our students' bilingualism and biliteracy through Translanguaging Pedagogy. Although the school district enacted the district Seal of Bilingualism and Biliteracy in 2004, there is no clear definition of biliteracy in most policy discussions, nor did we find clear articulations of a biliteracy pathway that embraced students' translanguaging corriente (García *et al.*, 2017). Thus, urgency to define biliteracy and develop a biliteracy pathway that leverages a Translanguaging Pedagogy is of utmost importance in our work.

Pathways to biliteracy

The origins of the term biliteracy was first published by Barbara Flores (2011) to explain how language-learning must be functional for the learner at the time of learning and the learner must see the significance and purpose. Furthermore, Flores (1979) describes biliteracy as 'the way a bilingual student knows one or more languages well and can read and write based on personal and social functions within the biliterate environment which surrounds the learner' (1979: 35). Traditional bilingual education classrooms most often follow either a convergent biliterate model or a separation biliterate model (García, 2009). The convergent biliterate model is generally found in transitional bilingual education classrooms, where reading and writing is performed in two languages, but usually following the reading and writing norms of the English language. The separation biliterate model is found in many DLBE classrooms, where the use of English and Spanish in literacy activities always occurs separately. For example, students read in one language and write in the same language. In contrast, the Translanguaging Pedagogy that we offer differs from the previous biliteracy models described; instead, we enact a flexible biliterate model that uses two named languages together, merging students' dynamic bilingualism into our teaching and learning.

Shifting to a Translanguaging Pedagogy is critical for our emergent bilingual (EB) students in Bilingual Multicultural Education Programs (BMEPs). Translanguaging is important in developing biliteracy because a bilingual's inner voice (the interpersonal voice) always contains features that are traditionally related as two named languages, but to a bilingual are a single, complete language repertoire (García, 2009; Otheguy *et al.*, 2019). That is, even with a monolingual written text a bi/multilingual student is always constructing meaning bilingually to make connections to themselves, their worlds and to the texts of those worlds (García *et al.*, 2017). When bilingual teachers require EB students to use only one named language as they engage with texts inter-and intrapersonal, they limit these students' opportunities to learn and further expand their linguistic repertoire.

Different perspectives and approaches to teaching biliteracy are needed in the field of bilingual education. Bilingual educators have a cause for concern with the increase of Hispanic/Latino/a/x simultaneous-bilingual children (children who develop two languages at the same time) in BMEPs to find a more appropriate pathway that leaves behind the traditional concept of sequential biliteracy acquisition (children who develop literacy in one language first then learn a second one). A move towards embracing a flexible biliteracy approach that takes up EB students' corriente and to co-shift as needed for deep comprehension of text and language development is necessary in the bilingual education field (García, 2009).

Understanding How Translanguaging Shapes Biliteracy

The PAR research recruitment of bilingual education teachers was done through a Google Survey in which the teachers responded to a list of questions that focused on their knowledge-base of biliteracy approaches and translanguaging pedagogy. The survey was sent to 169 bilingual education teachers; 44 responded to the survey with a response rate of 26%. At the end of the survey, teachers were asked if they wanted to be a part of a study group focused on biliteracy and Translanguaging Pedagogy; 15 bilingual educators enrolled. Data gathered by Susana, a District Biliteracy Specialist, from interview questions regarding teachers' knowledge and perspectives about biliteracy and translanguaging were employed to create study group topics based on *The Translanguaging Classroom: Leveraging Student Bilingualism for Learning* (García *et al.*, 2017) and research articles to establish a common understanding of Translanguaging Pedagogy. The project was formed to jointly produce knowledge and critical interpretations of readings with others to transform their pedagogy. The project was an ongoing learning process, a research approach that emphasizes co-learning, co-participation and systemic transformation (Greenwood *et al.*, 1993; Tian & Shepard-Carey, 2020).

Currently, there are very few DLBE programs that understand how to leverage translanguaging in DLBE classrooms. To implement a flexible biliteracy approach in bilingual education programs, we implemented a TTRC method through qualitative design. Further, TTRC affords a cyclical process of research, action and reflection from all participants. Teacher participants are to be experienced, reflexive and capable of participating in the entire research process generating knowledge through participants' collective efforts and actions. To address the effectiveness of the TTRC project, participants were interviewed to document their stance, how they leverage the validity of their culture-specific ways of knowing and their translanguaging. The pre-interview provided questions about biliteracy and translanguaging teaching and learning. Post-interview was in the form of Testimonios to learn about their translanguaging stance. Testimonios as a pedagogical tool lends itself to a form of teaching and learning that brings the mind, body and political tension (Bernal *et al.*, 2016) to the forefront of Translanguaging Pedagogy. Teachers were instructed to consider thoughtfully and creatively [their] histories and experiences associated with their translanguaging journey. Other research methods used were classroom observations and collection of student artifacts.

Data analysis

We engaged in three rounds of coding using a thematic analysis approach (Braun & Clarke, 2006). We chose thematic analysis because it allowed us to look broadly across our entire data set. We first separately coded our individual classroom observations and student artifacts, taking note of themes from these data. We categorized data in response to our research questions. From here, we engaged in a second round of coding, reorganizing teacher insights into broader themes, for example: literacy and language use; stigma of home language; and critical self-awareness. Finally, we continually returned to the data to hone our definitions of broader themes until we concluded with three overarching patterns: *acknowledging students' linguistic repertoire, unifying pieces of their bilingual identity* and *experiencing translanguaging in a variety of contexts and settings.*

Maestras en acción: Los testimonios

Although all three teacher collaborators taught in a Spanish-English DLBE context, the TTRC teachers' settings are quite different. Monica's DLBE Kindergarten class included both monolinguals and simultaneous bilinguals. The DLBE program is an 80/20 model where Monica conscientiously models using knowledge of one named language to help the other when reading, writing, drawing, speaking and thinking. Suzette's third-grade classroom is situated in a rural area of this urban school district whose students are largely part of a multigenerational Spanish heritage language community. Suzette revitalizes the language through culturally relevant opportunities for sociolinguistic interaction in a 50/50 DLBE model. Ximena teaches an Advanced Placement (AP) Spanish literature course in a dual language high school where most students participate in the district Seal of Bilingualism and Biliteracy. She approached her courses using a decolonial pedagogy juxtaposed with a colonized curriculum, engaging students in critical language practices that draw on their bilingual identities. You will hear their voices of how the teachers in the TTRC project developed a translanguaging co-stance.

Monica: Translanguaging es natural

Kindergarten teachers have the unique privilege of introducing to and guiding children through the new world of school. A bilingual Kindergarten teacher, for many, is also a guide into bilingual life. The concept of named languages as a fixed set of rules and words or the implications of speaking another named language with proficiency are often not firmly developed when students enter Kindergarten. Instead, their understanding of named languages, language ability, and language identity are quite fluid and will develop over the year. Translanguaging es natural for Kindergartners because of this fluidity; they will naturally use all their named language knowledge because it is not separated internally. An established translanguaging co-stance in this initial classroom experience will greatly affect the formation of their academic and bilingual identities this first year and very likely the years to come.

In my bilingual journey, I have come to understand translanguaging as the acknowledgement of all knowledge and experiences and finding not only a harmony, but an essential usefulness in their connection. Establishing a translanguaging co-stance that encourages creativity and flexibility in language drawn from multiple sources of knowledge happens naturally because of the unique qualities of Kindergartners.

Despite my cultivating such a fluidity, my class does have mandated language allocations. I, however, do not demand that the children adjust their speech accordingly throughout the school day. It would not be realistic, nor would it be fair. We are not fully immersed in the target language at the school level and these young children are just learning to use their voice to contribute to classroom conversations; I would not want to discourage their emerging voices. Besides, often I am checking for knowledge and understanding of concepts in our various subjects; named language(s) are the vehicles the children use to get there.

Suzette: Open la compuerta de la Acequia Madre

My translanguaging stance springs from a current that flows in my veins. I compartmentalized my bilingualism as it played out in various contexts: Spanish to pray and speak with my grandparents; formal Spanish and English at school and Spanglish at home. I realize now that my bilingualism is a linguistic movement within that guide my actions, emotions, and responses. This experience allowed me to embrace the Translanguaging Stance with an open heart to see students' language and culture holistically. Students shouldn't view their language as belonging to a certain context or relationship but rather a unifying piece of their identity.

Over the past two years, I have come to adopt the translanguaging co-stance to name the philosophy held in my heart for which had no name in bilingual education; bilingual students hold a unified system of language which include multiple named languages resulting from personal, societal, cultural, and educational experiences that influence their identities. As a bilingual educator, I am responsible for implementing strategies to bridge the home and school. Upon reflection of my students' profiles in bilingual schools where I have taught for the past 20 years, I yearned to bring English and Spanish together in the classroom in a structured but natural manner to diminish roadblocks to critical thinking resulting from students' specific language needs.

In the first year of the project, we studied translanguaging pedagogy. Sheltering alone does not suffice for all students to move beyond comprehension to critical thinking in the bilingual classroom. Translanguaging incited my curiosity as to how I could maintain the rigor of bilingual education whilst allowing the corriente of bilingualism to flow naturally in my classroom. It is from here that we began to co-design instruction, incorporating tranglaguaging spaces for students to engage with each other and with content, enriching discussion and writing with their complete language repertoire.

Ximena: Moving within and around their corriente of named language(s)

My stance as a veteran bilingual educator, with more than 18 years of classroom experience teaching Spanish in a variety of settings, my stance (re)fashions itself every time I learn something new. I am a knowledge-seeker who rarely, if ever, is satisfied with the status quo basura that many times demoralizes bilingual teachers. I seek, through my stance, to give the best to my students, cultivating knowledge that empowers interactions in class that provide them the language they desire and deserve; creating opportunities for them to delve into the intersectionalities of their lives.

For the last 12 years I have taught Spanish Language Arts (SpLA) in a dual language setting at the high school level. I taught 10th-grade SpLA, 11th grade AP Spanish Language and Culture, and 12th grade AP Spanish Literature and Culture. For this chapter, I am concentrating on the 12th grade AP Spanish Literature and Culture class. Our dual language program requires students to take SLA every year as well as English Language Arts (ELA) and they take two content areas (Math, Science, Social Studies) in Spanish, the rest of their classes are in English. They have a total of seven classes that provide them many opportunities to move within and around their corriente of named language(s). I intentionally mention the grade levels because it is important to note that our students have the unique opportunity to experience language in a variety of contexts and settings.

In this project, I embraced the space to discuss and learn from other teachers who were walking in their linguistic corrientes as bilingual teachers and how co-designing for translanguaging impacted my students' corriente as well as my own.

As you read los testimonios of how these teachers came to understand translanguaging, we ask you as readers to be open to hearing perspectives that may be different from your own testimonio as a bilingual educator. Monica's, Suzette's and Ximena's pedagogical practice, process and product begins with theorizing about translanguaging, and they approach their co-design with reverence for the process which transforms their classrooms in creative, innovative and nurturing ways *acknowledging* their students' corriente *in a variety of contexts and settings* to be described next.

Monica: Pedagogía a lo natural

My involvement in the TTRC project greatly impacted the way I set up the learning environment, both physically and philosophically. It validated centering my pedagogy on the natural ways my young students learn and see the world and I used this awareness to develop and co-design lessons, activities and assessment.

I found a way to find harmony among what I felt was right and natural for the children with what I was expected to implement into my teaching. I made sure that my Spanish instruction in the main subject areas included the Spanish-language materials and curriculum we were given, while making sure to strategically include and use supports in the home language when needed. Keeping the children's natural linguistic flexibility in mind, more often I began to conscientiously talk about using knowledge of one named language to help the other and modeled how it can be done when reading, writing, drawing, speaking and thinking.

The English Language Development (ELD) Block had been the part of the day towards which I felt the most resistance because I felt pressured to stick to only using one named language: English. Co-collaborating with my compañeras in the TTRC project, I reconsidered my priorities for my EB students and restructured the way I co-designed and delivered my lessons. I moved from using a mental 'Puente de palabras' list to help connect ideas from one named language to another to developing an actual physical chart in the form of a large dry-erase flip chart that children were able to access both during the actual discussion and afterwards for reference (see Figure 1.1 Puente de palabras chart). How the chart was implemented further evolved from drawing *in front of* the children into a guided drawing activity in which the children *drew in their notebooks alongside me* while we bilingually discussed concepts (e.g. las estaciones, fall, otoño, winter, invierno) we had just studied, co-creating individual, yet collaborative drawings. Figure 1.2 is an example of a collaborative drawing of the plant cycle.

As a person who draws often, I understand that drawing develops a deeper understanding of the subject matter, much more so than from observation alone. Guided drawing quickly became our new main mode

Figure 1.1 Puente de palabras chart

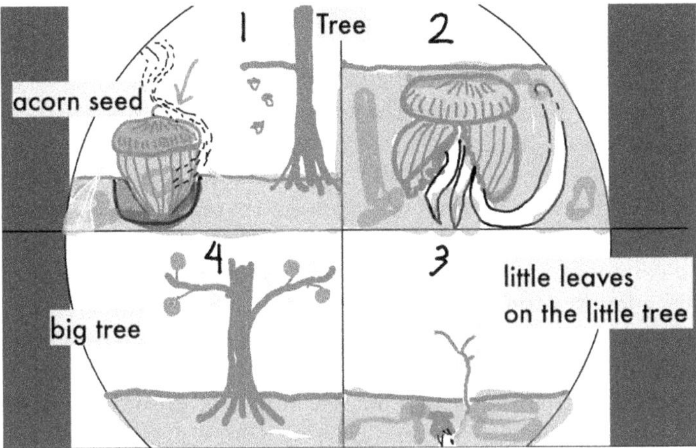

Figure 1.2 Collaborative drawing of the plant cycle

of learning during the ELD block because drawing together not only provided an opportunity for deeper understanding of content, consideration of supporting details and opportunities for me to model and students to apply new Spanish and English vocabulary words in conversation, but it also added an interactive element to an otherwise lecture-style lesson and the students were much more engaged.

When it came time for assessment, I wanted to develop something outside of the curriculum assessment tools. I thought about what I knew about young children and how they express their thoughts and ideas. Kindergartners' minds are geared towards learning words, labels and pronunciation, having just experienced that phase of development. In fact, Kindergartners are very adept at expressing themselves and understanding others through non-verbal communication; many have infant or toddler siblings who require a developed understanding of various forms of communication.

Furthermore, because the children are young and are only just learning to write and to speak in both Spanish and English, it is important to allow them a variety of ways to demonstrate their understanding of lessons. As previously discussed, drawings are the primary way that young children express their thoughts in a written form, but other elements need consideration when looking to assess a unit's worth of learning. The ways in which I modified my instruction based on my co-collaboration in the TTRC project now needed to be reflected in the ways I assessed my students. I knew that drawing would need to be combined with oral explanation and possibly other forms of expression and I looked to the children themselves to see what they naturally do when learning.

I noticed that when children were working at their tables, conversation was guaranteed. Because of their stage of development, young children tend to narrate their thoughts and to explain their actions to anyone around. It is common to hear 'I drew this because ...' or 'Esto es el ...'. In gearing up for assessment, I supplied the children with a graphic organizer upon which they were to draw the main points of the unit. I then took advantage of this verbal buzz by circulating the room with an iPad or other recording device because it is in this initial thinking phase of the assessment process that the children will express themselves most freely. The children will also listen and react to each other and have a built-in opportunity to collaborate and potentially enhance their understanding.

After a few sessions, the students are then ready to officially show their learning. By this point they will have had multiple weeks of stories, both fiction and non-fiction, videos and songs throughout the day as well as activities in which they acted out the stages of growth of plants, for example. Young children are very creative. If asked, they *can* represent roots, sprouts and leaves through creative movement and willingly show their expertise. When I am ready to assess, I select them individually and ask them to bring their graphic organizers with them. I ask them to explain what they have written and drawn, and I record their oral explanation. Later I will check it for content and language use.

Figure 1.3 Students' visual tools

Co-collaboration with the TTRC project influenced more evolutions in my form of assessment. *Individual explanations* of finished work with me as the audience progressed into *student presentations* in front of the whole class. As we approached the end of the unit, I let both the children and their parents know about the class presentation as well as my expectations and intentions. I took both pictures and video clips of their presentations to reference later for report cards. This proved to be enjoyable for the kids and effective for me, and really gave the children freedom and autonomy to develop their own visual tools and ways to demonstrate their learning using their creative, translingual and multimodal ways of meaning-making. For an example of students' visual tools used to assess their learning see Figure 1.3.

Suzette: Regar the rows del jardín

Year two of the TTRC project included analysis of students' language profile and identification of skills to develop academic and social English and Spanish. As teacher co-collaborators we discussed connections between language-specific (exclusive use of linguistic features of one named language to perform classroom tasks) and general linguistic (refers to speakers' ability to perform with language, the ability to tell a joke, to explain) task-based performances and how these terms fit into the preexisting schema of language objective and content standards. We identified differentiated language objectives using WIDA descriptors, and 'rings' for individual assistance or scaffolds (Sánchez *et al.*, 2018, to increase language production in their content areas. My co-design was a Social Studies and Language Arts thematic unit named *Encuentros of Cultural Groups in the United States and New Mexico.* I utilized the standards from English Language Arts (ELA) curriculum unit, 'Point of View' and integrated culturally relevant Social Studies content. Culturally relevant texts and culturally responsive environments are precursors to effective Translanguaging Space (Li, 2011). Columbus Day has transitioned to Indigenous Day in my state, and I wanted students to think critically about the cultures which shaped our state, make opinions about its historical events, and identify various viewpoints in historical texts. Figure 1.4 describes the translanguaging lesson design with essential questions, general linguistic and language-specific task-based performances.

In our TRRC project we designed translanguaging lessons to benefit each of our unique class language profiles. Teacher observations were a part of translanguaging lesson implementation. Feedback I received from my colleagues included adding complex language conversation structures for increasing inquiry questions from ¿quién?, ¿qué?, ¿dónde?, ¿cómo?, ¿cuándo? to deeper questions: ¿qué pasaría si, ¿cuándo debería? By creating a graphic organizer to support students in developing more in-depth questions, we activated a critical multilingual awareness where teachers give students permission to reflect on their own bilingualism and biliteracy and

<table>
<tr><td colspan="2">Essential Question:
What makes people view the same experience in different ways?
¿Por qué se ve el mismo evento desde diferentes puntos de vista?</td></tr>
<tr><td colspan="2">Task-Based Performances</td></tr>
<tr><td>General Linguistic
Students will orally compare/contrast the most important points and key details presented in two historical fiction texts about the encounter between Spanish explorers and Native Americans by jointly constructing a graphic organizer with teacher and other peers.</td><td>Language-Specific
Los estudiantes van a expresar su opinión y elaborarán una estructura organizativa que enumere las razones que apoyan su opinión.

Los estudiantes van a usar palabras y frases de enlace (ejemplo: porque, por lo tanto, al fin) para conectar la opinión con las razones y ofrecen una declaración o sección final.</td></tr>
</table>

Figure 1.4 Translanguaging lesson design

their meaning-making resources (García & Kleifgen, 2019). We modeled questions, then students wrote their own questions. Questions included: 'Were the Indigenous and Spaniards friends or enemies? Did the Indigenous people lose their culture? Were they afraid of the Europeans?' They discussed opinions, evidence and questions in guided reading groups with collaborative academic discussion protocols. Although I modeled in Spanish, students used English in their discussions. Por ejemplo, una niña preguntó, '¿Por qué mataron muchos de la gente Piro de Acoma?' Su compañera respondió, 'En mi opinión mataron mucha gente porque los indios Piro compartían muchas cosas pero luego querían más y más por eso se enojaron mucho.' In addition to content and language, students needed considerable background knowledge in argument discourse to better support them in practicing this type of organization. We created a Translanguaging Space for students to state opinions about a familiar topic. For example, we asked the students to discuss the following questions: ¿Es mejor tener un perro o un gato para una mascota? ¿Por qué?

In writing Spanish opinion essays, students and I analyzed the language of opinion writing in English and Spanish through co-created anchor charts. These daily lessons occurred at specific times during the ELA or SLA block. Students studied sentence syntax needed to demonstrate language-specific performances and practiced using frames with content-specific vocabulary. In addition, students utilized the Translanguaging Space to demonstrate general linguistic performances, increasing motivation, engagement and performance during language-specific instruction. During guided whole-group read-aloud, close readings of mentor text and modeled writing, students deconstructed Spanish text with critical multilingual rings for comprehension. They collaborated to jointly construct evidence of their comprehension, opinions, connections and evidence. I administered a pre-writing assessment (Figure 1.5)

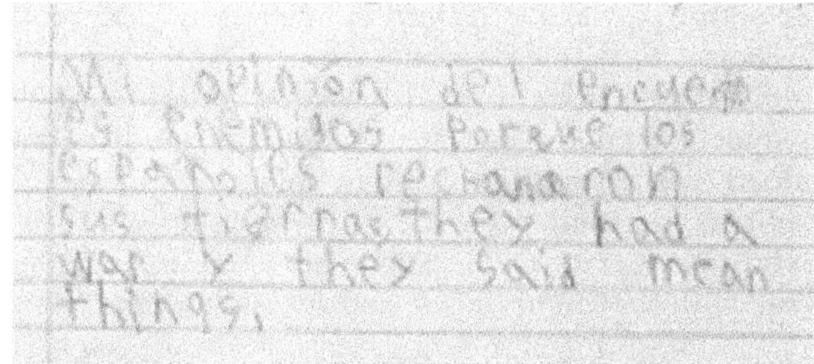

Figure 1.5 Pre-writing sample

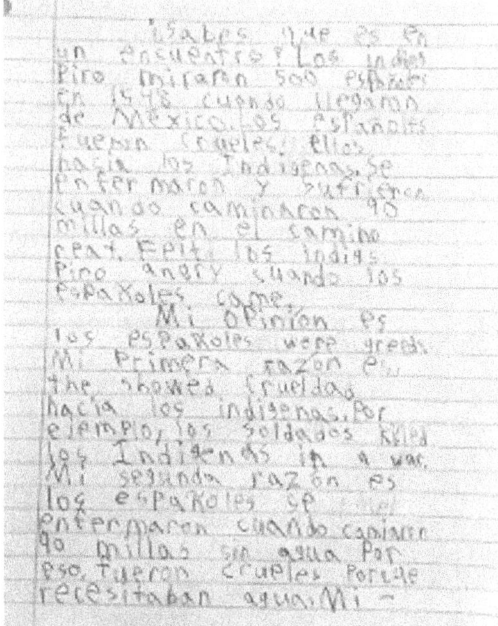

Figure 1.6 Post-writing sample

1) 'Los españoles fueron crueles. Ellos hacia los Indígena se enfermaron y sufrieron' showed la manifestación de su opinión sobre temas con frases comunes.

2) She also writes 'Mi opinión es los españoles were greedy.' Her use of the word 'greedy' demonstrates the power of experiential language. Students use this word in personal ways and although I taught 'codioso' through predictive illustrations and quotes from the mentor text depicting the serpent-like eyes of the Spaniards when seeing gold; the student's written sample recalled the meaning but processed it from Spanish to English.

3) Ella defendió sus ideas u opiniones con ejemplos y detalles y conectó sus ideas con sus razones a través de conectores, 'Los españoles se enfermaron cuando caminaron 90 millas sin agua, por eso fueron crueles.' She associated her personal point of view with the Spaniards to justify her opinion. Student writing shows cultural and sociolinguistic diversity in a Translanguaging Space provided opportunities for development of critical metalinguistic awareness.

of students' ability to write a Spanish opinion essay. The prompt was: 'Were Indigenous and Spaniards friends or enemies?'

The amount and quality of Spanish writing in the pretest was emergent. This student applied the frame 'Mi opiníon', used language from the read-aloud 'encuentro' and made inferences, 'said mean things.' The translanguaging that occurred in pre-writing samples demonstrated application of critical thinking in her complete language repertoire to write with the language she had access to at the beginning of the unit.

The post-writing assessment (Figure 1.6) of this same student sample included three detailed paragraphs.

Students were successful in determining points of view and forming opinions of a historical event both in writing and speaking. By choosing a mentor text which provided various viewpoints, students had multiple entries into the topic of Spanish Colonization in the Southwest. The Translanguaging Space brought students together by thinking critically about language use through analysis of 'El Encuentro.' This metaphorical encuentro, in a historical and classroom-culture context, was embedded into students' language repertoire in Spanish although they will remember the content and cultural relevance in their own personal translanguaging reflection to activate a critical multilingual awareness in a Translanguaging Space.

Ximena: Descolonízate: A colonized curriculum

Spanish Language Arts (SpLA) is a relatively new content area and has traditionally been taught through a Modern Language lens. Nonetheless, bilingual teachers who teach these courses at our school have spent many years learning the content of Language Arts in Spanish within a US context. While learning about SpLA I have often found myself in an English Language Arts (ELA) space to learn how to teach the content and then transfer the knowledge to my SpLA class. Teaching AP Spanish Literature is a love–hate relationship. Many years ago, I began the process of decolonizing this curriculum by infusing borderland theory by Gloria Anzaldúa and decolonial thought by reading Katherine Walsh, Walter Mignolo and Aníbal Quijano. Decolonization is the dismantling of structures that maintain the status quo via addressing unbalanced power dynamics, which are extremely present in AP curriculum (Quijano, 2007). To decolonize is more than a process of dismantling, though, as the decolonized systems are recreated, revitalized, and replaced using Indigenous Knowledge(s) and Way(s) of Being. The TTRC project validated my instructional choices and empowered me to use the process(es) in my classroom and to deliver professional development to my school community. I have always moved between my named languages to fit any given purpose or situation, and so do my students. Thus, implementing a

Translanguaging Pedagogy supported my understanding of heteroglossic ideologies, where two or more named languages coexist dynamically while creating knowledge that support our multifaceted bilingual identities. Participating in the TTRC project has moved me in the direction of building new crossroads in curriculum development, assessment and professional development.

At the beginning of the year, we intentionally explore the following concepts: intersectionality, Nepantla and Borderlands within oneself. We call these *translanguaging fronteras*. Since we move back and forth within the literature it is of essence that students understand and apply how they can connect to pieces of text that they do not always have the cultural capital to understand, so that it is more than reading words on a page. As such, every year we co-construct the meanings of these concepts to later apply them into the texts they will explore. By creating Translanguaging Spaces, it supports students to use their whole linguistic repertoires to tackle complex concepts by weaving their two or more languages to create unique poems of their own intersectionality as Border People. That is, gente nepantlera, constantly living in the in-between spaces of language, culture and conciencia crítca (Anzaldúa, 1987).

Then the use of 'I' becomes a void, as we work in a 'we' space, where we create knowledge of geographical, cultural and linguistic nuances and spaces in the literature we read. It is in this space where translanguaging supports multilingual students in the appreciation and exploration of literatura, even one that does not necessarily represent who they are as Border people. In addition, this pedagogical theory, when used purposefully and intentionally, opens the opportunity to decolonize the prescribed curriculum of AP. It is up to us to make connections to these academia-chosen texts for example, connecting to hip hop and norteña music. In our class we posit we are not the counter-narrative, we are the norm; this is something translanguaging reinforces within us. To force a community to mold themselves into dominant narratives is asking them to change who they are as Border People. It is a position as a translanguerrera to combat the lack of culturally sustaining curriculum and create spaces of Nepantla, the painful in-between spaces which can exist for people of multiple cosmologies who choose to begin a journey of self-discovery and regain lost epistemologies (Anzaldúa, 1987).

During the first few days of school, I introduce our Trenza poem. This poem takes two texts that speak to our cultural, linguistic and the conciencia crítica of our community. The texts, *To live in the Borderlands* by Gloria Anzaldúa and hip-hop song, *Soy bilingüe* by Snow Tha Product are chosen as examples of translingual texts. Both women are Mexican American and, in their texts, outline the realities of living in the Borderlands. We then begin to read Anzaldúa first as a whole class, I read the poem multiple times and students listen. After each reading, they highlight the parts that represent intersectionality, Nepantla and

Borderlands concepts. In small groups students discuss their highlights and explain why they highlighted certain passages as they relate to the concepts. In this processing space, students utilize their entire linguistic repertoire. Then, students repeat the process with a new group of classmates. In the second round they are adding to their collective creation of knowledge as everyone in each group must have highlighted and annotated texts. Then students have small group discussions about what they understand and feel with Anzaldúa's words. Lastly, I ask students to identify any rhetorical devices that Anzaldúa uses and why she would use them. Students defend the use of rhetorical devices to express the deeper meaning of the text. Students choose a portavoz for their group to report out what the consensus of the poem, about what it means to them and any questions about the language they may not understand. We apply the process to the oral text 'Soy bilingüe' by Snow Tha Product. To assess reading comprehension students, create their own texts to present orally to the class. They are required to choose 25 words from Anzuldúa's text, 25 words from Snow Tha Product's text and more than 50 words of their own to create a poem or song about their own intersectionality as Border people. Figure 1.7 gives a few examples of the finished product of student poems. By creating these Translanguaging Spaces at the beginning of the year we can draw on our own lived experiences to connect to texts from a multitude of cultural and linguistic backgrounds. Once they experience excitement with these texts because they see their reflejo in them, they appreciate the other literatura more and are more analytical towards the AP list of readings.

Yo sé quien soy

¿Quien soy yo?
Who am I?
Nací desde abajo y estoy creciendo con humildad

Believing I betrayed my Indian blood
My parents working hard to put me above
De pequeña ignoraba los consejos de mi madre, enojada
Y ahora me arrepiento ¿porque hice esas pendejadas?

Having to change my voice so my accent don't come through
Having to pronounce every syllable in Spanish so my family won't disapprove

¿Quien soy yo?
Who am I?
Yo nací desde abajo y estoy creciendo con humildad

Figure 1.7 (*Continued*)

Soy hispana, mexicana, mulata, mestiza pero todo eso no me identifica
I'm a half breed Mexican-American
A woman who can speak both English and Spanish
Con el nopal en la frente
Me juzgaron varias gentes
Yo quiero vivir sin fronteras
Porque con barreras, no avanzas ni te recuperas
People call me burra trying to steal my voice
Wanting to change my race and I'm trying to avoid
I know I'm amazing, and I know I'm fantastic, I know who the hell I am so you need to look right past it
don't judge me for my skin, judge me for my actions

¿Quien soy yo?
Who am I?
Yo nací desde abajo y crecí con humildad

I am proud to say my name and love to say it loud and clear.
I am Alexandra Ximena Jáquez Dominguez Vasquez Anaya
Yo reconozco mi sangre ancestral y sé que es lo que me hace y ojalá que mi linaje mantenga su cultura y lenguaje.
Yo, ahora vivo en Nepantla, en un espacio sin espacio.
Tomo un poco de sufrimiento a veces confusión pero al fin llegue a la conclusión que mi sanación es lo más importante.

¿Quien soy yo?
Who am I?
Nací desde abajo y crecí con humildad

It's hard to see my family scream when they hear
La migra is coming and they just disappear
It's a fight to resist the beckonings of these strangers to finally give in and become the white bread that I always found unsettling
But in the end it doesn't matter to me
Because I know who I am

And I know who I'll become
And I'll be dead before anyone changes me.

¿Quien soy yo?
Who am I?
Yo ya se quien soy, I know who I am, and con humildad i'll spread my voice.

It's More Than Just Chile-

Hold up, lemme clear my throat
I use my voice to start speaking

Figure 1.7 (*Continued*)

The truth 'bout how we always seeking
A way to understand nuestra cultura,
how the world seems to open up
when we find the greater meaning,
Como esa, no hay una misma aventura.
I hold heritage
from workers who had to pick
grapes 'til their olive-red skin,
Wounded, turned black
Straight from poverty, can't turn back
There was a battleground established
Not knowing if a shred of hope can be found
Despite that, they ran to their dreams in the United States
While running desperately from the hounds
But wait, it doesn't end there
Let me speak well on my name
As well as my background,
Even the chile don't hit the same
I'm no stranger, but I ain't a fellow either
That's when my heart starts fighting with my head
Porque ellos dicen, 'no seas de allá'
That I should feel a connection with the vision here instead
La tierra donde nacieron mis padres
la amo tanto como amo a mi misma
Sus tradiciones se me quedaron marcadas
Trabajan muy duro, por eso me pongo lista
But wait, it doesn't end there
Let me speak well on my name
As well as my background,
Even the chile don't hit the same
They ask 'what's happenin''
Laughing at me, they dare to ask if
I'm one or the other,
I'm neither, I'm simply fantastic
Es cierto, soy fenomenal
Behind my back, dicen 'la nena no sabe español'
And I say, 'Porque no me lo dicen a la cara?'
Soy Mexicana, bigger sensation than the Superbowl
I can spit both in English and Spanish
Once I prove the fact, the talkers vanish
I'm either that girl or no girl, there's no in between
I'm sure you can guess which side of me I let them see
I like to live my life, I've never settled for less

Figure 1.7 (*Continued*)

Como mujer, eso me hace 'desmadrosa'
Les gustan decir que 'está loca la chava'
The rumours are true, cierto que soy otra cosa
But wait, it doesn't end there
Had just flipped the switch like a tortilla
Unbothered con mis tacos de lengua
Movin' on con mi horchata, see ya

My Rap

Soy un león, que lucha en la vida,
Que no se rinda
Que va y busca,
Que va y agarra lo que quiera
Un rey que le gusta salsa y crema, en su comida

Hola que tal, dime como están,
Yo ni soy de aqui, ni soy de alla,
Hola que tal, dime como están,
Yo si soy de aqui, y soy de alla,
Una horchata y dos de lengua, (x2)
Yah, yah, yah,

To live in the borderlands means your alive,
To live in the borderlands means,
Haters with clean white teeth want to cut you down,
Take out the hate, bring out light (x2)

Soy un león con una actitud,
Que la gente me respetan,
No como un giezel were people walk through you,

So many problemas, para arreglar,
Familia llorando pasando desgracias
Matando sueños, acaban vidas, yo soy Juan
Y tengo 17,
Yo no ando con rodeos,
Estoy enfocado, encontrando mi vida,
Buscando respuestas,
I'm Getting hipped up talking like,

Itch I jaja con jota, haha with the j,
I speak english and spanish, I'm bilingual all day,

Figure 1.7 (*Continued*)

A boxer, a stranger, fighting back in the borderlands,
You are the battleground, whether male or female,
Punching you, hating you, throwing you out feeling like a nobody,

To survive the Borderlands you must live sin fronteras,
Be a Mexican-American eating frijoles on hotdogs

Figure 1.7 Student poems

Merging Linguistic Borderlands

More translanguaging studies need to address teachers translanguaging stance (e.g. Deroo & Ponzio, 2019; García, 2017; García, 2019; Menken & Sánchez, 2019) and students' bilingual identities with Latino/a/x/ and Chicano/a/x teachers and students in US context. Drawing from Gloria Anzaldúa's (1987) *Borderlands/La Frontera* constructs where she establishes the geographical borders between the United States and Mexico as a metaphor for all types of crossings and identities. The types of crossings Monica, Suzette and Ximena share in this chapter draw from linguistic and cultural crossings where they transformed their practice by merging linguistic borderlands to tap into their students' corriente. To do this, they acknowledge students' linguistic repertoire in their unique contexts and settings by leveraging their culture-specific ways of knowing and doing translanguaging to cultivate bilingual identities for themselves and their students.

What does it mean to merge linguistic borderlands? In DLBE classrooms teachers must negotiate language allocation and separation. This negotiation is not an easy task but to be a transladora means to negociar these artificial linguistic borderlands and move from separation biliteracy models into *Borderland Biliteracy* approaches. As transladoras we develop what is called *Borderlands Biliteracy* (Johnson & García, 2022) – a co-design that brings forth emergent bilingual students' translanguaging corriente to the surface and recognizes their corriente to co-shift as needed for deeper comprehension of text, expand language development and cultivate a bilingual identity. This TTRC project fosters and supports a Borderland Biliteracy, a flexible biliteracy approach where two named languages are used to interact with grade-level complex modalities and where translanguaging is the norm to assess in a translingual mode, activate a critical multilingual awareness and support Border People. Through these three teachers' testimonios we hear their voices and see through the teacher lens how translanguaging shapes biliteracy in many different forms during Language Arts instruction. We bring to light the different practices that Monica, Suzette and Ximena co-design with their students by *multimodal assessment en vivo*, *building el aguante* with translanguaging, and exploring *translanguaging fronteras*.

Assessing multimodal activities en vivo is key to how Monica checks her students' level of understanding. Whether through guided drawing activities to process texts or through independent work, Monica describes Kindergarteners' natural tendency to self-narrate and how moments of this 'verbal buzz' can be captured with a recording device. Children's translinguistic self-expression is often uninhibited during these types of activities. As they color and illustrate, children might self-narrate, 'Las plantas crecen de semilla a frutes.' or 'Plants need agua y sol.' Class presentations as an end-of-unit assessment provide an opportunity for her young students, with guidance, to use their creativity to invent their own resources to represent learning and understanding. Assessing en vivo and encouraging multiple modes to demonstrate knowledge is Monica's way to take into practice the natural ways her young students use language and see the world.

Building el aguante in translanguaging spaces address the challenge of maintaining oral Spanish language stamina when doing complex language conversations. Suzette knows that conversations shouldn't stop when students do not have the Spanish/English vocabulary, but rather students weave in the necessary language features into the conversation by using their linguistic repertoire to process vocabulary and review ideas they must master in Spanish or English. The stamina built during these complex conversations are important to point out since in many DLBE programs the concern is that the dominant language, English, will prevail in these conversations by subordinating Spanish language use. Suzette knows that certain knowledge and skills need to be mastered in third grade. However, by allowing her students to develop this aguante in Translanguaging Spaces they can locate from their linguistic repertoire in the named language discourse, grammar and conventions, and vocabulary to create opinions about the Spanish colonization in the Southwest with a voice that drew from their community and families experiences in Spanish.

Exploring *translanguaging fronteras,* Ximena began AP Spanish Literature with the exploration of the following fronteras: intersectionality, Nepantla, and Borderlands that form the concepts that are applied as a lens to examine the prescribed AP curriculum and assessment. Students learn as Border People about these fronteras and begin to connect to their experience, language, and literacy practices. Both Ximena and her students begin the process of descolonización of their minds and then merge both fronteras of their cultural and linguistic corriente(s) to create equitable biliteracy, bilingual, and culturally sustaining instruction and learning for her students and herself.

Somos translingüistas, transladoras y translanguerreras

In this chapter, we describe how translanguaging co-stance and co-design towards enacting Translanguaging Pedagogy addressing the bilingual maestras' culture-specific ways of knowing. These maestras are *translingüistas, transladoras y translanguerreras*. That is, they are cultural and linguistic negociadoras, understanding our students' and their holistic experiences by drawing on collective knowledge(s) and experience(s) juntos with students and each other.

Translingüistas show their understanding in translanguaging multimodal ways by drawing, performing, creating, reporting, and writing translingual text. Monica's ELD block remains a challenge for her because the ELD curriculum and its expectations for teachers and students continually change. Infusing another content area with ELD, while meeting the varied linguistic needs of all her students is also very challenging and complex, but it is a worthwhile endeavor. In this block, English vs. Spanish grammar, spelling, and vocabulary are not the main objectives, but rather are discussed and used as tools. So much more is taught in an ELD block grounded in translanguaging principles. Children learn linguistic risk-taking and are treated with respect. Children learn they have many ways to show understanding – by drawing, performance, creating, reporting and emergent writing. Most importantly, by drawing on their translingual corriente students learn to access and demonstrate knowledge in both named languages, knowing that they have the tools to express their learning in an academically equitable way-the goal of the translanguaging classroom.

Transladoras are mergers of language and of worlds, able to understand the students' experiences holistically and drawing on them juntos. As a transladora, Suzette's unit language flows naturally throughout the instruction by harnessing this natural energy to shape Spanish writers, bilingual individuals, and a community of cultural and linguistic diverse learners. To mantener los bordos, she creates self-assessments in the four language domains that motivated students to set goals and developed rubrics to demonstrate proficiency. In sharing student writing, videos, and anecdotes she creates a translanguaging classroom co-shifting their instruction to provide critical multilingual rings representative of students' languages and cultures. It is evident that by building upon sociolinguistic strengths, translanguaging allows students to develop a translinguistic wholeness: pre-write bilingually, carry on an academic conversation in English, defend their opinion in Spanish, discuss bilingually after reading a text multiple times in both named languages and finally write an essay in Spanish, successfully flowing through the language learning continuum.

Translanguerreras reconstruct linguistic and cultural interactions of the classroom and of the self. Ximena's translanguaging pedagogy and heteroglossic theory changed her forever as a bilingual teacher. It empowers her instruction, her students' language and culture, and ultimately deconstructs the academic and linguistic demands of the colonized curriculum in a way that opens more corrientes, for more students. Ximena believes that bilingual educators deben abrirse and apply this theoretical epistemology and pedagogy in their classrooms, even when it's uncomfortable, when you think it doesn't work, when it feels like it's not 'correct'. Outsiders and insiders alike will witness it working. It took time to shift thinking that has been for years imposed upon us to only use authentic monoglossic language practices in the bilingual classrooms.

Be a Crossroads

This TTRC project sheds light on how districts and schools can create a sustainable learning space(s) where teachers can better understand translanguaging in deeper ways and apply it to their practice. However, through this collaboration project we realize that there is more research needed in the following three DLBE pathway research and practice areas. First, to know the true representations of what bilingual young children can do there needs to be multiple ways to show their knowledge. For example, we need more research on how emergent bilingual learners draw from physical, aesthetic and translingual multimodal representations of students work. Second, the need to document how students can sustain conversations to build stamina for learning. In DLBE, students are required to have complex or 'academic' conversations with strict separation protocols which often limits their production. Instead, complex conversations need to happen by providing opportunities for students to leverage translanguaging to make connections, to engage in critical thinking and to promote motivation and creativity which builds el aguante to produce and practice their named languages more. Lastly, areas with scant research are: (1) How to incorporate a student's bilingual identity; (2) How to descolonizar in assessment, curriculum, and instruction in DLBE classrooms by introducing students to Border Theory, for example(Anzaldúa, 1987) and more Chicano/a/x and Latina/o/x literatura to better serve the linguistic and cultural values and beliefs through their translanguaging lens and bilingual identity. Like Anzaldúa states, 'to survive the Borderlands, you must live sin fronteras be a crossroads' (Anzaldúa, 1987: 216). We are the crossroads with our students, and our fellow translingüistas, transladoras y translanguerreras of this colaboración de cruceros.

References

Anzaldúa, G. (1987) *Borderlands/La Frontera: The New Mestiza*. San Francisco: Aunt Lute Books.

Bernal, D., Burciaga, R. and Flores Carmona, J. (eds) (2016) *Chicana/Latina Testimonios as Pedagogical, Methodological, and Activist Approaches to Social Justice* (1st edn). New York: Routledge. https://doi.org/10.4324/9781315659053

Braun, V. and Clarke, V. (2006) Using thematic analysis in psychology. *Qualitative Research in Psychology*, 3 (2), 77–101.

Deroo, M.R. and Ponzio, C. (2019) Confronting ideologies: A discourse analysis of in-service teachers' translanguaging stance through an ecological lens. *Bilingual Research Journal* 42 (2), 214–231.

Flores, B.M. (2011) The sociopsychogenesis of literacy and biliteracy. In P.L. Anders (ed.) *Defying Convention, Inventing the Future in Literary Research and Practice*. New York: Routledge.

García, O. (2009) *Bilingual Education in the 21st Century: A Global Perspective*. Chichester: John Wiley & Sons.

García, O. (2017) Translanguaging in schools: Subiendo y bajando, bajando y subiendo as afterword. *Journal of Language, Identity & Education* 16 (4), 256–263.

García, O. (2019) *Decolonizing Foreign, Second, Heritage, and First Languages: Implications for Education*. New York: Routledge.

García, O., Johnson, S.I. and Seltzer, K. (2017) *The Translanguaging Classroom: Leveraging Student Bilingualism for Learning*. Philadelphia, PA: Caslon.

García, O. and Kleifgen, J.A. (2019) Translanguaging and literacies. *Reading Research Quarterly* 55 (4), 553–571. https://doi.org/10.1002/rrq.286

Goodman, K., Goodman, Y. and Flores, B. (1979) *Reading in the Bilingual Classroom: Literacy & Biliteracy*. Rosslyn, VA: Monograph of the National Clearinghouse for Bilingual Education.

Greenwood, D.J., Whyte, W.F. and Harkavy, I. (1993) Participatory action research as a process and as a goal. *Human Relations* 46 (2), 175–192.

Johnson, S.I. and García, O. (2022) Siting biliteracy in New Mexican borderlands. *Journal of Latinos and Education*, 1–16.

Li, W. (2011) Moment analysis and translanguaging space: Discursive construction of identities by multilingual Chinese youth in Britain. *Journal of Pragmatics* 43 (5), 1222–1235.

May, S. (ed.) (2013) *The Multilingual Turn: Implications for SLA, TESOL, and Bilingual Education*. Abingdon: Routledge.

Menken, K. and Sánchez, M.T. (2019) Translanguaging in English-only schools: From pedagogy to stance in the disruption of monolingual policies and practices. *TESOL Quarterly* 53 (3), 741–767.

Otheguy, R., García, O. and Reid, W. (2019) A translanguaging view of the linguistic system of bilinguals. *Applied Linguistics Review* 10 (4), 625–651.

Quijano, A. (2007) Coloniality and modernity/rationality. *Cultural Studies* 21 (2-3), 168–178.

Sánchez, M.T., García, O. and Solorza, C. (2018) Reframing language allocation policy in dual language bilingual education. *Bilingual Research Journal* 41 (1), 37–51.

Tian, Z. and Shepard-Carey, L. (2020) (Re) imagining the future of translanguaging pedagogies in TESOL through teacher – researcher collaboration. *TESOL Quarterly* 54 (4), 1131–1143.

2 Implementing a Collaborative Translanguaging Pedagogy in an Elementary ESL Classroom in Malaysia through Teacher–Researcher Collaboration

Shakina Rajendram

Background and Context

Malaysia is a multilingual and multicultural country in Southeast Asia, where there are 137 languages and dialects spoken by a population made up of Malaysian-Malays, Malaysian-Chinese, Malaysian-Indians, Indigenous peoples and immigrants and foreign workers from Indonesia, Philippines, India, Bangladesh, Pakistan, Thailand, Vietnam, Myanmar, Cambodia, China and other countries (World Atlas, 2020). Malay is the official language of Malaysia, and English is taught in all schools from Kindergarten onwards. In addition to Malay and English, many Malaysians speak another language or dialect tied to their ethnic background, for example, Mandarin, Cantonese, Hokkien, Hakka, Tamil, Telegu, Malayalam, Hindi, Bengali and a variety of regional Malay dialects. Despite the multilingualism of the Malaysian population, and the ways in which Malaysian languages have converged and influenced one another for years (Vollman & Tek, 2020), when it comes to educational policies, Malaysian languages are kept separate from one another through the compartmentalization of languages into separate subjects, and through the establishment of schools that use different mediums of instruction.

The segregated schooling system in Malaysia is a result of the country's history of colonization by the British. During British colonial rule in

Malaysia from the late 1700s to 1957, English was the official language of government and commerce. The British established separate schooling systems for the three main ethic groups (Malays, Chinese and Indians) with different languages of instruction to keep them segregated in socio-economic roles associated with their language and ethnicity (Daniels, 2005). The co-naturalization of language and race functioned to perpetuate raciolinguistic ideologies (Rosa & Flores, 2017) which positioned the Malays, Chinese and Indians as racialized others who were inferior subjects of their English-speaking European colonizers, and whose languages did not hold any social, cultural or economic capital. Malay-medium schools were established in rural areas to provide basic education for Malays and keep them in their existing roles as farmers and fishermen. Chinese-medium schools were set up for the Chinese in rural areas, and their education was intended to preserve political ties with China (Ibrahim *et al.*, 2011). The Indians were given basic Tamil-medium education in the plantations so that they could continue to serve the British as plantation laborers. A small number of Malaysians were allowed upward socioeconomic mobility by attending English-medium British and missionary schools, and working for the new British colonial order as civil servants afterwards.

As a result of the 'pyramidal colonial education system' (Ibrahim *et al.*, 2011: 1005) created by the British, Malaysia had become economically, ethnically and politically divided, and there were severe inequities in the opportunities for socioeconomic mobility among the Malays, Chinese and Indians. Therefore, after the country's independence in 1957, language was seen as central to the newly independent Malaysia's nation-building efforts. Malay was declared as the national and official language of the country and English was relegated to the status of a second language (Hashim, 2009). Although the selection of Malay as the official language was intended to create a national post-colonial identity and unity among the various ethnic groups in Malaysia, it also established the Malays as the dominant, ruling ethnic group in the country, which has created some conflict over the years between the Malays on one hand, and the Chinese and Indians on the other. Following independence, two public school systems were also established with different mediums of instruction – *Sekolah Kebangsaan* or 'national schools' where Malay was the medium of instruction and *Sekolah Jenis Kebangsaan* or 'national-type schools' for the Malaysian Chinese and Indian communities who wanted to retain their schooling in Mandarin and Tamil respectively. Despite the provision of education in Malay, Mandarin and Tamil, proficiency in English has continued to be seen as very important for socioeconomic mobility. Many parents choose to send their children to English-medium private and international schools to secure what is perceived to be a better future for their children. This has put pressure on public school systems to develop capacity in English teaching. Over the years, the Malaysian

Ministry of Education has implemented several 'upskilling' and 'upgrading' initiatives to ensure that all English teachers would 'achieve a level of fluency in the language to match those of native speakers' (The Sun Daily, 2016: para. 1). One of these initiatives is the Native Speaker Programme which brought in over 360 'native English speakers' from the United States, Britain, Australia, New Zealand and other Western English-speaking countries to train local English teachers and improve their English proficiency (The Star, 2015: para. 1). In the name of strengthening teachers' and learners' command of English, all teachers were also required to take the Cambridge Proficiency Test (CPT), and their performance in the CPT is measured against the Common European Framework of Reference (CEFR). These policies and initiatives have put pressure on English teachers to teach monolingually because teachers who use or allow their students' first languages (L1s) in the classroom are often portrayed as being incompetent (Martin, 2005; Selamat, 2014). Against this monoglossic educational backdrop, the study reported in this chapter aimed to introduce translanguaging to an elementary English as a second language (ESL) classroom in Malaysia by implementing a collaborative translanguaging pedagogy (Rajendram, 2019) through teacher–researcher collaboration. The research questions guiding the study were:

(1) What are the affordances of a collaborative translanguaging pedagogy co-designed through teacher–researcher collaboration in an elementary ESL classroom in Malaysia?
(2) How did the teacher–researcher collaboration process facilitate these affordances?

Theoretical Framework and Literature Review: Translanguaging, Sociocultural Theory, Affordances and Collaborative Learning

The theory of translanguaging posits that multilingual learners use all the features of their unitary and integrated language repertoires in an ongoing and dynamic process of interacting and making meaning (García & Li, 2014). Research on translanguaging has demonstrated how learners draw on their diverse language resources through translanguaging to develop a deeper understanding of the subject matter they are learning; engage more fully with texts and content; bring their linguistic and cultural identities into their learning; and develop new language practices (e.g. Baker, 2011; Creese & Blackledge, 2015; García, 2009; García *et al.*, 2017; Paulsrud *et al.*, 2021; Tian *et al.*, 2020). The present study contributes to this body of research by investigating the *social* aspect of using one's translanguaging repertoire in collaborative contexts. Grounded in a translanguaging and sociocultural perspective (Vygotsky, 1978, 1986), this study views translanguaging as a shared social activity, and the translanguaging repertoire of an individual as a shared resource for collective learning. This study posits that throughout the process of translanguaging, a learner's language repertoire is negotiated in relation to the social contexts and purposes for their use of language (Kaufhold, 2018). In the same way, the sociocultural model of *affordances* relates individual agency to social context. From an affordances perspective, language learners' actions are seen as interdependent with the social context of their language learning and 'mediated by social, interactional, cultural, institutional and other contextual factors' (Van Lier, 2008: 171).

The study described in this chapter brings together translanguaging and sociocultural theory by exploring the affordances of translanguaging for individual and collective learning in the context of collaborative learning activities. Gokhale (1995: 22) defines collaborative learning as 'an instructional method in which students at various performance levels work together in small groups toward a common goal.' Extending this definition, Lin (2015: 17) explains collaborative learning as a formal group of students 'working together on specific collaborative learning tasks…to mutually construct and maintain a shared conception of knowledge.' As suggested in Lin's definition, the collaborative learning approach is based on the idea that knowledge is constructed collectively when students actively interact with each other in group settings. This approach is consistent with sociocultural theory which views learning as an inherently social process, mediated by social interactions and relationships (Lantolf & Thorne, 2006; Vygotsky, 1978, 1986). In collaborative learning activities, learners are usually responsible for planning the distribution of roles and tasks themselves. Several studies have pointed to the affordances of translanguaging in collaborative language learning. In Martin-Beltrán's study (2014), high school students in Washington, DC collaborated with their peers on multilingual literacy activities such as writing autobiographical essays on Google Docs. The use of translanguaging during peer interactions opened up spaces for the students in the study to consider multiple perspectives, and to build their linguistic and conceptual understanding. In Walker's (2018) case study, bilingual learners in German and New Zealand universities collaborated online on discussing, writing reflections and preparing reports and presentations on the topic of globalization and localization. The study demonstrated the affordances of translanguaging for expanding learners' semiotic repertoires for co-constructing meaning, and building collaborative communities among learners across countries.

In the Malaysian context, there is no research to date on the affordances of translanguaging for collaborative learning, although collaborative learning is used very widely in elementary and secondary ESL classrooms in line with recommendations made by the Malaysia Education Blueprint 2013–2025 (Ministry of Education, 2013). The Blueprint emphasizes the importance of teachers 'instilling leadership and the ability to work effectively in teams for every student,' and helping 'every student reach their full potential by taking on leadership roles, and by working in groups' (Ministry of Education, 2013: 2–5). The Blueprint also encourages students to 'learn at least three languages, allowing them to collaborate and communicate effectively with fellow Malaysians and Malaysia's neighbors' (Ministry of Education, 2013: 2–7).

The studies that have been conducted on translanguaging in the Malaysian context have focused primarily on the purposes for teachers' use of translanguaging. Ramli and Jamaluddin's (2021) observations of three Malaysian university lecturers' teaching practices suggest that all three lecturers used translanguaging to encourage more student participation in their classes. Ting and Jintang's (2020) study of teachers' translanguaging practices in a preschool in Malaysia demonstrated that teachers used translanguaging for communicative functions such as affirming students' answers, management functions such as providing cues for students to participate, and academic functions such as assessing students' knowledge of what was taught in English. Other studies have found that although English, Malay, Tamil and Mandarin are taught as separate subjects in Malaysian schools, translanguaging is a common practice among Malaysian teachers and is used for purposes such as classroom management, clarifying the meaning of lexical items or concepts, explaining grammatical structures and ensuring learners' understanding of the content (e.g. Lee, 2010; Low, 2016; Martin, 2005; Selamat, 2014). However, teachers who use translanguaging or allow their students to do so report feeling guilty and ashamed because of the negative perceptions in Malaysia towards teachers who do not teach only in English. Thus, the goal of this study was to affirm teachers' and students' translanguaging in the Malaysian context by (1) documenting the affordances of translanguaging for collaborative language learning, (2) showcasing learners' purposes for and perspectives of translanguaging during their collaborative interactions and (3) introducing translanguaging as a collaborative pedagogy with enormous potential for teachers and researchers working together, and for students learning together in the Malaysian elementary ESL classroom.

Research Design: Negotiation of Co-stances, Co-designs and Co-shifts

The study took place in a national-type Tamil primary school located in the province of Selangor, Malaysia – *Sekolah Jenis Kebangsaan Tamil Bukit Mawar* (Rose Hill National Type Tamil Primary School; all names used here are pseudonyms). At the time of the study, Rose Hill had a student enrolment of close to 1000 students and 60 teachers on staff. The majority of students and teachers in the school were Malaysian Indians. The official medium of instruction in Rose Hill is Tamil, and English and Malay are taught as compulsory subjects from Grade 1 onwards. The participants for this study were 24 students in a Grade 5 classroom (8 girls and 16 boys), and their ESL teacher, Ms Kavita. Ms Kavita, along with all 24 of the students in the classroom were Malaysian Indians who identified Tamil as their home language, and Malay and English as their second languages. As a former teacher in Rose Hill school, I had observed how most ESL teachers in the school used languages other than English themselves while teaching, but were hesitant about allowing their students to do so. Ms Kavita demonstrated an openness towards translanguaging, which made her a good candidate for our teacher–researcher collaboration. She did not enforce an English-only policy in her English classrooms and did not stop her students from speaking in Tamil or Malay during her English lessons. She would frequently use Tamil and Malay herself while teaching. While Ms Kavita was open towards translanguaging, she did not actively encourage her students' use of it, nor did she create lesson plans that strategically incorporated translanguaging from the onset of the planning process.

Tian and Shepard-Carey (2020) call for teachers and researchers to engage in collaboration and negotiation to develop a translanguaging co-stance, architect a translanguaging co-design, and make translanguaging co-shifts as the need arises. I believe that it is important for researchers to meet teachers where they are at, and to listen to their concerns and ideas before proposing anything new. Thus, the first step of the teacher–researcher collaboration in my study involved having respectful, collegial and open discussions with Ms Kavita to find out about the constraints that she faced and the reasons for her hesitation in implementing a translanguaging pedagogy on an ongoing basis. These discussions took place informally during coffee breaks, social outings, and visits with each other at home, so that trust and collegiality could be established in our relationship. Ms Kavita shared with me her concerns that if she did not teach only in English, she would be 'judged' and 'seen as not capable' by her colleagues, and by an officer from the district education office who had been visiting the school every few weeks to observe, evaluate and coach the English teachers. She also explained to me that she had heard about a professional development course for English teachers attended by her colleagues where teachers were encouraged to 'upskill' themselves by speaking 'like native speakers' and avoiding the use of the L1. When asked why she occasionally used translanguaging despite these constraints, Ms Kavita explained that this was how she herself had been taught, 'My English teacher used Tamil and Malay when teaching us, and that helped me to learn English better.' To deepen her understanding of translanguaging as a pedagogy and develop a strong co-stance, I showed Ms Kavita videos of translanguaging lessons (e.g. from the CUNY-NYSIEB YouTube channel), and presented research demonstrating the benefits of translanguaging for language learning. As a doctoral student researching translanguaging and an elementary school teacher who used a multilingual approach in my own classrooms, I had entered the collaboration as a firm advocate of translanguaging. My conversations with Ms Kavita helped me develop a more nuanced and context-specific translanguaging stance because they helped me to understand the first-hand experiences and challenges that Malaysian teachers face with implementing a translanguaging design in their classrooms. These conversations also prompted me to reflect on how translanguaging research and pedagogies could be more responsive to the practical realities of the classroom.

Having negotiated a translanguaging co-stance, the next step in the teacher–researcher collaboration was to create a translanguaging co-design. This was an iterative process that took place over six months, and involved Ms Kavita and I planning ten collaborative translanguaging lessons, most of which we co-taught, and a few that we taught separately. As Ms Kavita was required to adhere to the *Kurikulum Standard Sekolah Rendah (KSSR)* (Standard Curriculum for Primary Schools), which is the official curriculum used in all Malaysian public elementary schools, the lessons that we planned were structured around thematic units from the KSSR. Examples of these units include Malaysian Folk Tales, Money Matters, Tales from Other Lands, Stories to Learn From, Safety Issues, Digital Age, Friends from Around the World, Healthy Eating and Pollution. Students were also reading the Gulliver's Travels graphic novel (Lemke & Martin, 2014) for the Literature component of the KSSR. To help students develop 21st-century skills and competencies such as critical thinking, creativity, communication and decision-making, the Malaysian Ministry of Education recommends the use of collaborative problem solving and collaborative inquiry projects in the classroom (Ministry of Education Malaysia, 2013). In line with this, the translanguaging co-design included a collaborative learning activity requiring students to work together in small groups of 3–5 in each lesson. Table 2.1 presents an overview of two sample lessons that were part of our collaborative translanguaging pedagogy co-design.

During or after each lesson that Ms Kavita and I co-taught, I wrote field notes about students' responses to and engagement in these activities, and the interactions that were taking place in the collaborative small groups. Ms Kavita and I also had a debrief session following each lesson, where we talked about our respective experiences of the lesson, and ideas of co-shifts we could make to the next few lessons. Often, these debrief sessions (re)shaped what I had considered to be the challenges and successes in each lesson. In an electronic reflexive journal that I kept throughout the study, I wrote detailed reflections on each lesson that were based on the debrief session with Ms Kavita, my field notes and the video-recordings of the lessons. I also actively reflected on how my own positionality (i.e. a Malaysian Indian who had taught in the school for several years before the study began, a doctoral student, a researcher with a critical multilingual orientation to language education) could influence the teacher–researcher collaboration process, and my interpretations and analysis of the data.

Table 2.1 Sample collaborative translanguaging lessons based on the KSSR curriculum

<u>Lesson 1 (Gulliver's Travels Graphic Novel Study). Time: 1 hour</u>

1. Recall what learners have read in their Gulliver's Travel graphic novel so far.
2. Display the picture below of Gulliver in the middle of the storm and shipwreck, with the text removed from the captions and word balloons.

3. Distribute the handout below and ask students to work in their groups to describe what Gulliver sees during the storm (e.g. ship, water, waves, man), what Gulliver hears (e.g. thunder, waves crashing against the boat), what Gulliver touches (e.g. water, rain), and how Gulliver feels (e.g. afraid, confused, worried). Encourage students to make use of the visual elements in the picture, and their own experiences of Malaysian thunderstorms, to answer each question.

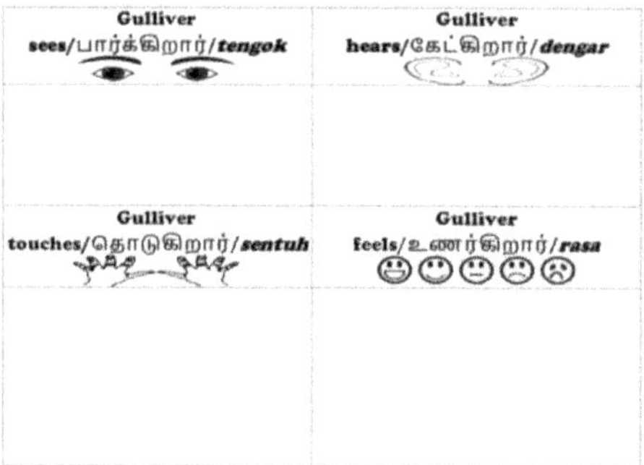

Gulliver **sees/பார்க்கிறார்/*tengok***	**Gulliver** **hears/கேட்கிறார்/*dengar***
Gulliver **touches/தொடுகிறார்/*sentuh***	**Gulliver** **feels/உணர்கிறார்/*rasa***

4. Students discuss and write their responses in the handout, <u>using any language</u>.
5. Now, tell students that they are going to fill in the caption and the word balloons in the picture, using some of the words they have come up with in the handout. Explain to them that a caption provides information about what is happening in the scene, and the word balloon captures what the character is saying. Show students how to read the pictures (from left to right, top to bottom) so that they can see the flow of events clearly.
6. Give students a few minutes to discuss with their group what could go into the caption and the word balloons. Keep encouraging them to <u>make use of all their languages</u>, and to adapt the characters and other elements of the story to fit the Malaysian context.
7. After students fill in the captions and word balloons in the picture, they role play their scene to the class.

(*Continued*)

Table 2.1 (*Continued*)

Lesson 2 (Healthy Eating). Time: 1 hour

1. Ask students to do a think–pair–share about their favourite Malaysian food, and say what the food is called in English, Malay, Tamil and other languages they know.
2. Draw students' attention to the food label in their textbooks, and ask students if they can identify the ingredients and nutritional information in the label.

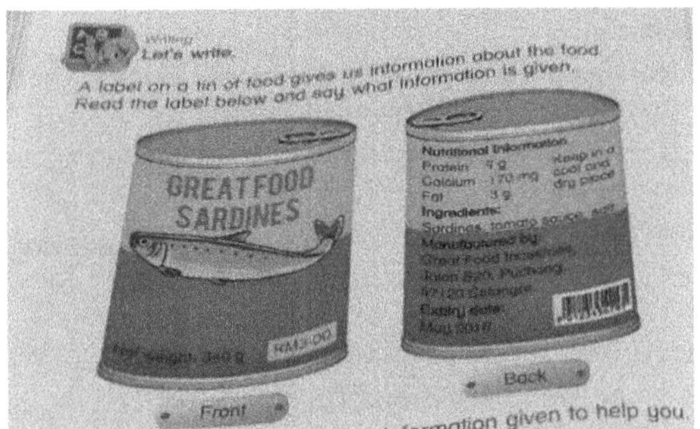

3. Discuss the importance of healthy eating, and ask students to make a list of healthy and unhealthy food they know. Encourage them to use any language in their list.

Healthy Food ***Makanan berkhasiat*** ஆரோக்கியமான உணவு	**Unhealthy Food** ***Makanan yang tidak berkhasiat*** ஆரோக்கியமற்ற உணவு

4. Working in their small groups, students come up with an idea for a healthy food product and create a poster advertising this food product. Students can incorporate any language into their poster.
5. Students present their posters to the class, and they vote for their favourite food product.

Data Collection and Analysis

As students worked together in small groups during each lesson, their interactions were audio- and video-recorded using digital voice recorders and mini wireless camcorders. Altogether, approximately 70 videos were recorded. Out of the 70 videos, 50 videos were selected to be transcribed and analyzed. The selection criteria for the videos were: (1) videos that were clear in audio and video quality to allow for more accurate transcription and (2) videos where learners were working together in small groups of 3–5 to allow for thicker descriptions of their interactions. I transcribed the recordings word-for-word using the Inqscribe transcription software, and I used the Latin alphabet when transcribing their English and Malay interactions, and the Tamil (தமிழ்) script when transcribing their Tamil interactions. The transcription conventions I used are detailed in Table 2.2. The different symbols that are used to represent Tamil and Malay are not intended to position these named

Table 2.2 Transcription conventions

Convention	Meaning
Words in Tamil script	Words in Tamil
(தமிழ்)	Words in Malay
Words in italics	
( )	Words in round parentheses provide the English translation of Tamil/Malay
< >	Words in angle brackets provide the context of the interaction or the non-verbal actions that were carried out
[ ]	Words in square brackets indicate added words that were not part of the original quote
UPPER CASE	Emphasis on a word

languages as separate entities, but rather to draw readers' attention more easily to the use of translanguaging in learners' interactions.

At different points in the study, I conducted semi-structured interviews with the 24 learners in their small groups, as learners indicated they would be more comfortable speaking to me together instead of individually. During my interviews with the learners, I asked them about their feelings and perceptions towards Ms Kavita's and their other teachers' classroom language policies; their feelings about using languages other than English during their English lessons and other subjects; their language use in school and at home; and their perceptions about the roles and functions of translanguaging during their collaborative learning. Since I speak the same three languages the learners do, all of our interviews took place multilingually.

The analysis of the classroom and interview data was conducted using sociocultural critical discourse analysis (SCDA) (Rajendram, 2019), which combines elements of sociocultural discourse analysis (SDA) (Mercer, 2004) and critical discourse analysis (CDA) (Fairclough, 1995). SDA, which is based on a sociocultural view of language, thought and social interaction, is a methodology for analyzing classroom talk which focuses less on the linguistic aspect of spoken language, and more on its functions for the pursuit of joint activity (Mercer, 2004). SDA aims to understand how language is used as a tool for collective thinking and the joint construction of knowledge among learners. CDA extends SDA by considering how issues of race, social reproduction, power and identity can shape learners' discourses within a particular sociocultural context. To bring CDA and SDA together, I drew on the three procedures of analysis associated with Fairclough's (1995) CDA framework: description, interpretation and explanation.

The SCDA of the classroom recordings and interviews were conducted in three stages, corresponding with the three analytic procedures above. In the first and second stages, I conducted an inductive analysis of the 50 transcripts using the *speech act,* which Cohen (2004: 302) defines as 'an utterance which serves as a functional unit in communication,' as the unit of analysis. I operationalized a speech act as any utterance that fulfilled a function in the interaction, such as a statement, request, question, answer, invitation, compliment, or command. Each speech was separated from the next speech act through a pause or change in function. Any word, phrase or sentence that was repeated by the speaker more than once in a row (e.g. 'What does this mean? What does this mean?') was only coded once, and words that were unintelligible were not coded. The length of the speech acts ranged from a string of words to complex sentences. Examples of speech acts are presented in Tables 2.3, 2.4, 2.5 and 2.6.

I analyzed 3868 speech acts in total by describing the *translanguaging constellation* (Duarte, 2016) that was used, and creating a code to interpret the specific function that the speech act served within the context of the collaborative translanguaging activity. This inductive analysis process was guided by the notes from my classroom observations, student artefacts that were gathered during the observations, interviews with the learners, as well as a review of studies on the functions and affordances of peer discourse during collaborative learning (e.g. Duarte, 2016; Martin-Beltrán, 2017; Neokleous, 2017; Wielander, 2016). This process generated a list of 100 functions, which were divided into four categories (cognitive–conceptual, planning–organizational, affective–social and linguistic–discursive), according to the broad affordance they served in the collaboration. Functions with similar affordances were placed into the same category. For example, 'Asking about grammar/vocabulary,' 'Helping peers to spell a word/correcting their spelling' and 'Providing the translation of a word/phrase/sentence' were grouped into the linguistic–discursive affordances category because they all focused on learning and supporting each other's knowledge of linguistic components.

In the third stage, I analyzed the interview data to explain learners' reasons for translanguaging, and their perceptions of their teachers' classroom language policies and practices. The results of the analysis in all three stages were corroborated by triangulating data from the classroom observations, debrief sessions with Ms Kavita, reflexive journal entries, and the interviews with learners.

Findings: Affordances of a Collaborative Translanguaging Pedagogy

Learners used translanguaging widely in all 50 transcripts that were analyzed. Eighty-seven percent of the 3868 speech acts that were analyzed contained a variety of translanguaging constellations such as: (1) Tamil and English, (2) Malay and Tamil, (3) Malay, English and Tamil and (4) English and Malay, which points to the diversity of language practices present in their translanguaging repertoires. The SCDA of learners' translanguaging interactions generated a list of 100 functions, which were classified into four categories based on their affordance for students' collaborative learning: cognitive–conceptual (28.2%), planning–organizational (27.5%), affective–social (24.5%) and linguistic–discursive (19.8%). A full list of the 100 functions along with illustrative examples of each is provided in Rajendram (2019). In the following sections, I expand on these four categories of affordances with a few examples from the classroom and interview data, and explain how these affordances were influenced by the teacher–researcher collaboration.

Cognitive–Conceptual Affordances: Translanguaging to Apply Cognitive Strategies and Learn New Concepts

The cognitive–conceptual affordances category included functions which provided a supportive framework for learners to share information, knowledge and ideas, engage with each other's ideas critically and constructively, and apply cognitive strategies to support each other's understanding of new concepts they were learning. Table 2.3 presents examples of the cognitive–conceptual functions that were identified through the SCDA of learners' collaborative translanguaging interactions (from most frequent to least frequent).

Through their translanguaging speech acts, learners provided suggestions related to content, expanded on and critically engaged with their peers' suggestions, solved problems together, and exercised higher-order and critical thinking skills such as evaluating their work against a list of criteria, providing an informed rationale and justification for their contributions, distinguishing between fact and opinion, taking on multiple perspectives in discussions and identifying cause-and-effect relationships. These findings support the results of prior research which has demonstrated how learners practise higher-order thinking functions such as problem-solving, negotiating and hypothesizing through translanguaging (e.g. Carroll & Sambolín Morales, 2016; Duarte, 2016). One of the factors that facilitated the use of higher-order thinking skills during learners' interactions was Ms Kavita's use of translanguaging herself. For example, during a lesson on preventing pollution, Ms Kavita used a combination of Tamil and English in her speaking and in visual aids that we had created together to explain terms such as 'cause' and 'effect' (see Figure 2.1). This helped learners to understand the meaning of those concepts, and consequently be able to engage in discussions in their own small groups about cause-and-effect relationships in environmental problems such as pollution.

An important co-shift that occurred related to the use of multilingual materials in the lessons. At the beginning of the study, Ms Kavita felt more comfortable using the KSSR grade 5 English textbook as the primary resource for her lessons. For example, during the lesson on healthy eating described in Table 2.1, she asked learners to look at a food label in their textbook and identify and explain the nutritional value of the food

Table 2.3 Cognitive–conceptual functions carried out through translanguaging (adapted from Rajendram, 2019)

Cognitive–conceptual functions	Examples of translanguaging speech acts
Making a suggestion related to the content of the task	Nisha: Okay, we take a phone, ஒரு ஜாமான் இப்ப தெரியலனா, அந்த ஜாமான் ஒரு இடம் GPS-ல் மட்டும் கண்டுப்பிடிக்கலாம் (Okay, we take a phone, if we don't know where an object is, we can use the GPS to find it) <inventing a new gadget based on an existing one>
Providing/drawing peers' attention to information in books/texts/other materials	Bavani: Here expiry date, here is *maklumat pemakanan* (Here's the expiry date, here's the nutritional information) <pointing out parts of a real food label to her peer during an activity where they have to create their own food label>
Asking for/providing factual information related to the topic	Harini: Water pollution எப்படி வரும்? (How does water pollution happen?) <while writing about the causes and effects of pollution> Tanushri: Water pollution happens when the rubbish goes into the water
Looking for answers/ideas/information in books/texts/other materials	Hema: Internet எடுத்தா, textbook-ல் இருக்கும் (If we choose the Internet, there must be something about it in the textbook) <flipping through textbook while picking a topic to create safety rules on>
Thinking out loud to brainstorm ideas/answers/course of action	Sivashakti: நான் அம்மகிட்ட எவ்வளவு கொடுப்பேன்? நூறு? (How much would I give my mother? One hundred?) <thinking out loud during a budgeting activity>
Demonstrating to peers how to answer a question/solve a problem	Vettri: Three thousand போட்டு, thousand minus பன்னு, அப்போதான் balance தெரியும் (Write three thousand, then subtract a thousand, that's how you will know the balance) <while showing his peer how to do a math calculation>
Suggesting a topic/idea for the group to work on	Tarun: நம்ம ஒரு story போடுவோம் லா, நம்ம வாழ்க்கைல நடந்தது போடுவோம் (Let's create a story, let's write about what happened in our lives) <while creating a script for a drama>
Explaining how one arrived at an answer/the logic of a solution	Kartik: நான் பாத்தேன் டா, R-ல் தேடுனேன் (I saw it, I looked for it under R) <explaining how he found the meaning of a word in the dictionary>
Discussing cause and effect relationships/pros and cons of an idea/action	Amira: Rule இல்லனா, accident நடக்குது (If there are no rules, accidents will happen) <discussing the importance of safety rules>
Analyzing/discussing a topic/issue from multiple perspectives	Kamini: நான் judge-ஆ இருந்தா, எல்லாருக்கும் ஒரே தீர்ப்புதான் (If I was the judge, I'd give the same judgement to everyone) <discussing what she would do if she was the judge in a story they're reading>

multilingually. I observed that because the label only contained terms in English as opposed to the multilingual terminology found in all food labels in Malaysia, learners struggled to understand the terms used on the label. In our debrief session, I suggested to Ms Kavita that we ask learners to bring in real food and beverage packages and labels in the next lesson,

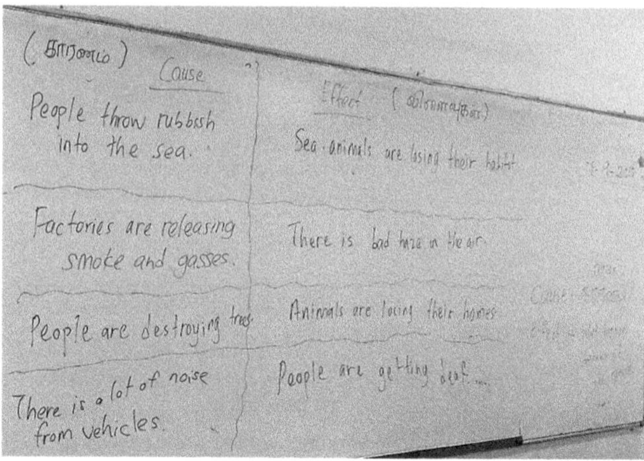

Figure 2.1 Ms Kavita's use of translanguaging to explain cause-and-effect relationships

where they would need to create a poster advertising a product. Ms Kavita agreed to this idea and conveyed the information to the learners. All of the packages and labels that learners brought from home in the subsequent lesson were multilingual (see Figure 2.2) and contained terms related to food ingredients and nutrients in different languages, for example, *maklumat pemakanan* (nutritional facts/information), சத்து (nutrition), *tenaga* (energy), *lemak* (fat), *air gula* (sugar syrup), *pati perahan laici* (lychee puree) and *pengawet* (preservatives). Learners were quick to recognize the Malay and Tamil terms on the labels as they had learned those

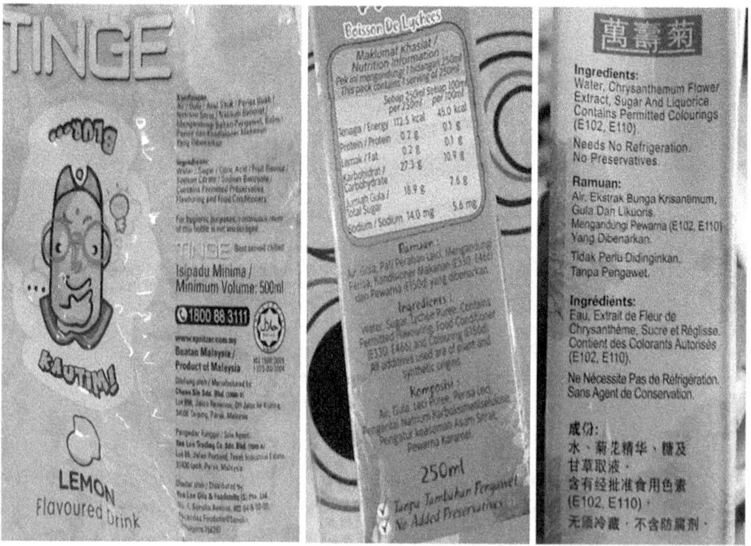

Figure 2.2 Examples of multilingual food labels that students brought from home

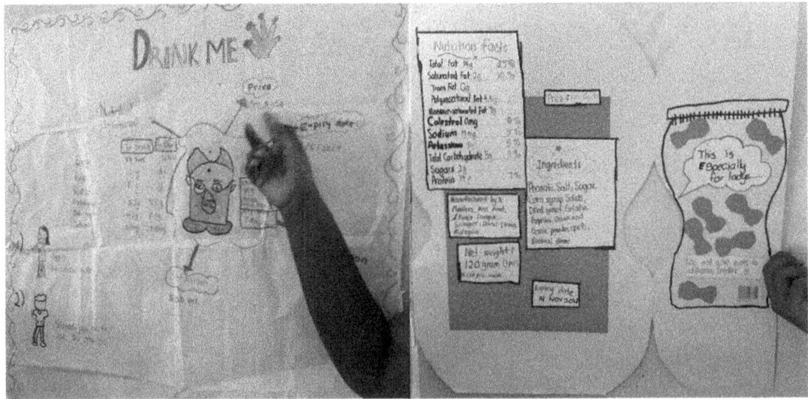

Figure 2.3 Examples of learners' food product posters

terms in their Malay, Tamil and Science lessons. They applied their knowledge of the Malay and Tamil terms to make sense of the unfamiliar English terminology on the food label in their textbook, and to use these terms correctly in the food label posters they created and presented (see Figure 2.3). This corroborates the results of studies which suggest that translanguaging helps learners to develop a fuller understanding of subjects such as math and science because it allows learners to interweave their linguistic and cultural resources with cross-disciplinary content (e.g. Karlsson *et al.*, 2018; Lewis *et al.*, 2012).

As a result of the co-shift that occurred through our teacher–researcher collaboration, Ms Kavita provided learners with bilingual Tamil–English dictionaries in every subsequent lesson, and encouraged them to refer to any other bi/multilingual textbooks and materials they had while completing tasks. The availability of these materials helped to strengthen learners' understanding of new concepts, and enabled them to draw on their background knowledge of the topics they were introduced to, thereby creating more cognitive–conceptual affordances. For example, during a lesson where learners had to read a passage on a technological device (e.g. mobile phones, laptops, tablets) and then evaluate the pros and cons of the device, learners used the bilingual dictionaries provided by Ms Kavita to find the meaning of key vocabulary from the passage, and then discuss the benefits and disadvantages of the device assigned to their group, as shown in Figure 2.4.

In another lesson requiring learners to write a paragraph in their small groups on an endangered animal, they searched their Science textbook (which was in Tamil) to find facts about their chosen animal, and created a draft of their paragraph in Tamil. Next, they used their bilingual dictionaries to translate the paragraph they had written into English. Getting factual information in Tamil from their Science book and linguistic support from their bilingual dictionaries resulted in learners being able to write paragraphs with accurate factual information, as in Figure 2.5 below.

Figure 2.4 Learner looking for vocabulary related to technology in a bilingual dictionary

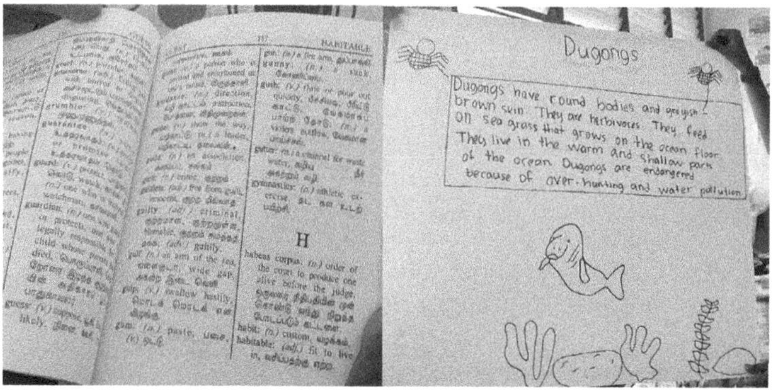

Figure 2.5 Information from bilingual dictionaries used in a paragraph on endangered animals

Planning–Organizational Affordances: Translanguaging to Collaborate Effectively

The planning–organizational affordances category included functions that helped learners to demonstrate autonomy in organizing and coordinating their collaborative work, planning tasks, distributing roles and responsibilities and ensuring effective collaboration between group members. Table 2.4 presents examples of the planning–organizational functions that were accomplished through translanguaging in learners' collaborative interactions (from most frequent to least frequent).

Prior to the study, Ms Kavita and I had observed that it was usually the learners who were more proficient in English who tended to dominate discussions and make most of the decisions during their small group work. The work was also not distributed equally, and there was very little

Table 2.4 Planning–organizational functions carried out through translanguaging (adapted from Rajendram, 2019)

Planning–organizational functions	Examples of translanguaging speech acts
Distributing/negotiating roles/responsibilities/tasks in the group	Tanuja: எல்லோருமே படிக்க போரும் எல்லாம் ஒரு ஒரு வாக்கியம் படிக்க போரொம் (All of us will read, we'll read one sentence each) <planning the presentation of their work>
Planning/organizing materials for the activity	Gayatri: *Malay Utusan* நமக்கு கிடைச்சதுனா, நல்லா இருக்கும் (If we get the *Malay Utusan* [a newspaper in the reading corner], that'll be good)
Offering to work on a specific task	Harini: நான் dialogue எழுதுறேன் (I'll write the dialogue) <when the group is preparing a drama based on a story in their textbook>
Explaining the procedures/instructions of the task	Poorna: அந்த கேள்வி கெட்டதுனா harmful எழுதனும், அந்த கேள்வி நல்லதுனா useful எழுதனும் (If the question [statement] is bad, we must write 'harmful,' if the question [statement] is good, we must write 'useful') <activity requiring them to decide whether each statement about the Internet indicates whether it is useful or harmful>
Planning how to execute/complete a task/solve a problem	Tanuja: முதல் chapter-ல படிச்சி பாக்கனும், அது என்ன வாக்கியம் எதோட ஒத்து போகுது அத முதல ஒன்று போடனும் (We need to read the first chapter, then whichever sentence matches that chapter, we'll put that as number one) <during an activity where they have to rearrange sentences according to the sequence of events in Gulliver's Travels>
Requesting for a turn/role in the task	Thiva: நீ எழுதலனா, நான் ஒன்னு எழுதுறேன் please? (If you're not writing, can I write one, please?)
Moving the task along/getting peers back on track	Divya: இப்ப இல்லை, இப்ப discuss பன்னி செய்யனும் என்ன choose பன்னலாம் (Not now, we need to discuss what we should choose first) <when her group members each start cutting out different gadgets from their worksheet before deciding which gadget the group wants to select>
Discussing/deciding on the goals/scope of the task	Risha: நம்ம ஆறு எழுதலாம் (Let's write six) <deciding on how many safety rules to write>
Offering to ask/suggesting that peers ask the teacher for clarification on the task	Amira: Teacher-கு கேட்கலாம் *jumlah*-னா என்ன (We can ask teacher what *jumlah* [amount] is)
Assigning roles/asking peers to take over tasks based on their skills/expertise	Lingkes: இது எழுதட்டும், இதோட கையெழுத்து அழகாக இருக்கும் (Let her draw, her handwriting is nice)

participation from group members who did not feel confident or proficient in English. Following the translanguaging co-design, we observed that group members who did not participate prior to the study started contributing more actively to the group work because they were able to take on 'expert' roles based on their language expertise. Additionally, the use of translanguaging in the activities played an important role in helping learners to plan and organize their collaborative work more effectively, negotiate and coordinate their tasks, and to self-regulate as a collaborative group. This in turn created greater rapport among group members. Comparing how he felt before and after the study, Premil expressed that, 'English class will be very fun with the group work, it will be very fun all to do together, can enjoy with the group, feel happy, like friends.'

In response to feedback from a few learners and a note I had made in my reflexive journal that 'the students in this class need more structure for their group work – they need to know how to collaborate, and how to collaborate well,' one of my co-planning sessions with Ms Kavita focused on the co-shifts we could make to the design of the lessons in order to provide more scaffolding of the collaborative group work, while ensuring that learners still had choice in how to organize and carry out their group work. Through our collaborative planning, we came up with suggestions of roles that each learner could take on during their tasks (e.g. note-taker, visualizer, discussion leader, teacher liaison, etc.), and we also provided learners with general recommendation of steps they might take to complete the task. We assured learners that the choice of whether or not to follow those roles and steps would be theirs. Learners appreciated having this additional scaffolding, and they took creative liberties with the roles and steps we recommended. For example, in the Gulliver's Travels lesson described in Table 2.1, four learners in a group (see Figure 2.6) each took on the roles of 'recorder,' 'translator', 'editor' and 'presentation leader.'

Learners reported during the interviews that being able to contribute to the different stages of their group work based on each of their unique expertise made them feel more united as a group, and that this showed them that 'many people [in the group] have many types of creativity.' Consistent with the feedback from learners, I noted in my reflexive journal after a debrief session with Ms Kavita that 'when groups are given autonomy with

Figure 2.6 Learners taking on different roles during their Gulliver's Travels lesson

structure, we have noticed that it leads to better collaboration, more autonomy of learning, and more creative outcomes.' The teacher–researcher collaboration contributed to these planning–organizational affordances by enabling Ms Kavita and I to provide more scaffolding supports for our students to collaborate in a more organized and effective manner, while encouraging autonomy and student leadership.

Affective–Social Affordances: Translanguaging to Weave Together Personal, Social and Cultural Identities

The affective–social affordances category included functions which focused on building rapport among learners, providing socioemotional support and affirmation to one another, taking an interest in one another's lives, and making learning more personal. This resulted in a collective sense of self-efficacy and confidence within the group. Table 2.5 presents examples of

Table 2.5 Affective–social functions carried out through translanguaging (adapted from Rajendram, 2019)

Affective–social functions	**Examples of translanguaging speech acts**
Affirming/agreeing with peers' suggestions/answers	Silvia: Suraj ஓட idea nice (Suraj's idea is nice)
Offering peers a turn/ encouraging peers to contribute their ideas or take on a task	Kishen: நான் ஒரு சொல்லிட்டேன், வேற யாராவது சொல்லுங்க (I've said one [idea], someone else say their idea)
Joking with peers/expressing amusement at peers' ideas	Suren: I know, அறிவு கெட்டவளுக்கு watch செய்யலாம் (I know, we can make a watch for people who don't know anything) Pravin: பரீட்சைக்குத் தேவை வரும் (We'll need it for our exam) <everyone laughs>
Encouraging group effort/ collaboration among group members	Tanuja: ஒரு group உ ஒன்னா செய்யனும் (We should do it together as a group)
Seeking affirmation from peers about one's own answer/idea/ work	Ashvin: அழகா இருக்கா? (Is this nice?) <showing peers his work>
Asking for peers' help/offering to help peers	Nareesh: உங்ககிட்ட நான் help பன்னட்டா? (Shall I help you?)
Asking peers about their family/ personal life	Tarun: உன் அப்பா பெயர் என்னா? (What's your dad's name?)
Correcting peers' actions/ resolving conflict	Tanuja: சண்டை வேண்டாம், okay? (No fighting, okay?) <when two group members begin to argue>
Asserting own ability or showing self-confidence	Kishen: நான் சொல்லுறேன் idea நல்லா இருக்கும் (My idea will be good)
Expressing one's emotions/ empathizing with peers	Tanuja: எனக்கு எரிச்சலா இருக்கு (I feel frustrated) Divya: ஏன் எரிச்சலா இருக்கு ? (Why do you feel frustrated?) Tanuja: கிடைக்கல (I haven't gotten it [the answer]) Harini: Discuss பன்னலாம் (Let's discuss it)

the affective–social functions that were demonstrated in learners' collaborative translanguaging interactions (from most frequent to least frequent).

The use of translanguaging enabled learners to bring their personal, social and cultural identities into the classroom, thereby making their learning a more meaningful endeavor. Throughout their collaborative interactions, learners used translanguaging to talk to each other about their shared Malaysian-Indian and Hindu customs, traditions and values. For example, they talked eagerly about their plans for Diwali, they recounted which temple their family had performed their prayers in over the weekend, they shared experiences from their older siblings' coming-of-age ceremonies, and they made references to Indian movies and television shows they enjoyed watching. Learners translanguaged, particularly in Tamil, to ask their peers about their personal lives, interests, and preferences, compliment, affirm and encourage one another, and to express their emotions. Similarly, the English as a Foreign Language (EFL) learners in Neokleous' (2017) study used their home languages to perform affective–social speech acts such as greeting, apologizing, affirming and encouraging their peers.

In one of our debrief sessions, Ms Kavita and I also observed how translanguaging helped learners to build more cohesive groups and resolve conflict among group members. Compared to lessons prior to this study where Ms Kavita used English only, we observed that when translanguaging was not just allowed but actively encouraged, learners spoke more freely with one another and there was more friendly banter and social talk both in whole-class and small-group discussions. In their interviews, learners explained that they used Tamil instead of English when they wanted to joke around with one another. Suren explained that 'When friends joke in English, no too funny, won't enjoy that much.' Consistently, I noted in my reflexive journal how the use of Tamil helped learners use humor effectively during a multilingual riddle-writing activity that Ms Kavita and I had planned together, and that I had taught:

> 'After reading a story together about a grandmother who tells her grandchildren riddles during a power outage, I asked the students to work in their groups to think of some riddles. I told them that they could think of *teka teki*s (riddles) or விடுகதை (riddles) in Malay, Tamil or English. They had a really good time with this activity and used a lot of Tamil to first tell each other riddles they already knew. Kamini's group made some clever connections between English and Tamil in their riddle, for example pronouncing 'orange' with a Tamil intonation so it sounded like the word for 'five' in Tamil. Learners' use of translanguaging during this activity fulfilled two functions: English aided comprehension by helping students understand the content of the riddles, and Tamil served a pragmatic function by making their riddles and jokes funny.'

According to Ashvin, telling jokes in Tamil also helped to relieve tension between group members, 'When we do group work, if we is *marah* (angry),

Tamil joke is like a fun, it's laughing, we are laughing already, so no more *marah* (angry).' Ashvin's response suggests that apart from being a source of amusement, joking with each other in Tamil helped to resolve conflict between group members. Consistent with Ashvin's response, another learner in the class, Ravi, explained that by translanguaging, 'ஒற்றுமையாக செய்யலாம், சண்டை இல்லாம' (we could work together without fights), and his classmate, Hema, added that 'எல்லோரும் சந்தோஷமா செய்வோம், எல்லா சேர்ந்து' (Everyone works together happily, altogether). I observed that even before our study began, Ms Kavita herself would use translanguaging for several affective–social functions such as joking with her learners. When I asked her about the reason for this, she explained that 'that way we will enjoy them more.' This finding resembles the results of Rosiers *et al.*'s (2018) study which showed that in the context of a school with a policy that did not allow learners to use other languages in the classroom, teachers still used learners' home languages for socioemotional purposes such as talking more informally to learners about their shared experiences. Despite using Tamil frequently to connect with learners, Ms Kavita expressed some trepidation in doing so because she was frequently observed and evaluated by the district education officer who encouraged her to teach only in English. After we discussed this issue to brainstorm possible solutions, we decided to show the officer examples from the interviews with learners where they spoke about enjoying Ms Kavita's lessons and feeling more connected to her and to their peers through translanguaging. Over time and through a few more discussions and classroom observations, the officer came to see what the affective–social and other affordances of translanguaging were, and she became more open to Ms Kavita's use of translanguaging in the classroom. Thus, our teacher–researcher collaboration was successful in creating greater awareness of and support for translanguaging not only among the school administrators but also officials outside the school.

Linguistic–Discursive Affordances: Translanguaging to Develop Metalinguistic Awareness and Expand One's Language Repertoire

The linguistic–discursive affordances of translanguaging comprised functions that helped learners to learn and use the target linguistic structures and discursive features to complete their tasks and scaffold their peers' linguistic knowledge in all languages. Through translanguaging, learners also developed and demonstrated the metalinguistic awareness and the metacognitive ability to use specific features of their language repertoires intentionally and strategically during their collaborative learning. Table 2.6 presents examples of the linguistic–discursive functions that were identified in the analysis of learners' collaborative translanguaging interactions (from most frequent to least frequent).

Table 2.6 Linguistic–discursive functions carried out through translanguaging (adapted from Rajendram, 2019)

Linguistic–discursive functions	Examples of translanguaging speech acts
Providing the translation of a word/ phrase/sentence	Bavani: The Malay is *maklumat pemakanan*, in English is the nutritional information (In Malay it's *maklumat pemakanan* [nutritional information], in English it's nutritional information)
Explaining grammar rules/ vocabulary usage	Tanuja: My friends is like… Divya: Friends le -s வராது, ஒரு ஆள் தானே? (There's no -s in 'friends' because it'' just one person)
Explaining the meaning of a word/ phrase/sentence	Tarun: Tropical னா சூடான இடம் ('Tropical' means a hot place)
Asking about grammar/vocabulary	Amira: Glass plural ல என்னது? (What's the plural form of 'glass'?)
Working out the meaning/usage of vocabulary using contextual cues	Harini: Bow னா என்னது? Oh, அவங்க arrows bow இருக்கு (What is bow? Oh, there's a bow in their arrows) <working out what 'bow' means based on the words and pictures on a page in Gulliver's Travels>
Providing verbal prompts/asking questions to help peers formulate their ideas	Larishan: சொல்லு, Gulliver sees…Gulliver sees என்ன? (Say this, Gulliver sees… What does Gulliver see?) <prompting his peer to come up with a sentence to describe what Gulliver sees on the island>
Requesting to use translanguaging/ encouraging peers to use translanguaging	Harini: Internet வச்சு நம்ம என்ன என்ன செய்யக்கூடாது? (What shouldn't we do on the Internet?) Riya: தமிழ்ல சொல்லலாமா? (Can I say it in Tamil?)
Assessing own linguistic knowledge	Monisha: Gold எழுதுவோம்… தமிழ்ல இன்னும் வரவே மாட்டேங்குது (Let's write 'gold'…. I don't know the word for it in Tamil yet)
Showing peers examples of target language use in books/other materials	Manickam: Kepada siapakah, இப்படி. இங்க பாரு, to whom did you give (Like this, kepada siapakah [to whom]. Look here, to whom did you give) <showing his peer examples of interrogative pronouns in their Malay and English textbooks>
Correcting one's language use based on peers' feedback	Naveen: iPhone is importable… Guna: Importable இல்ல, PORTABLE (Not importable, PORTABLE) Naveen: Ah, PORTABLE, iPhone is portable…

The linguistic–discursive talk by learners largely involved learners encouraging their peers to use Tamil or Malay when they were not able to express something in English, for example, 'தமிழில் சொல்லு' (say it [your idea] in Tamil), offering to translate for their peers, for example, 'உன்னுடைய வாக்கியம் சொல்லு, நான் Englishழில் சொல்லுவேன்' (say your sentence <in Tamil>, I'll say it in English'), and asking peers to check and correct their English use, for example, 'நான் முதலில் தமிழில் சொல்வேன், சரியா முத பார், அப்போ நான் Englishழில் சொல்வேன்' (First I'll say it <my answer> in Tamil, you see if it's right first, then I'll say it in English).

Learners confirmed during the interviews that they used translanguaging during their group work to help their friends whenever they had difficulties understanding linguistic items in English. Lingkam explained that 'ஏதாவது புரியில்லைனா, அது நாங்க தமிழில் சொல்லி புரிய வைப்போம்' (If someone does not understand something, we'll say it in Tamil and help them understand it) and his peer, Amira, confirmed that 'If some friends don't know English, we all say in Tamil, so they can understand.' A learner in another group, Kishor, suggested that his group's use of translanguaging to scaffold their peers' language learning was intentional, as they would strategically make a plan to use English and Tamil to help their friends who did not understand English, 'If somebody don't understand English, so we start, we do the plan, we plan first we talk in Tamil, then 50% English 50% Tamil. Somebody can't understand English, we talk in Tamil with them.' Students who were at the receiving end of this translanguaging support from their peers confirmed that it helped them to understand the lesson content better, learn new vocabulary, and be able to perform tasks on their own. For example, Rubin emphasized that 'இப்போ நான் என் கூட்டாளிகளுடன் Englishலெ ஒரு வார்த்தை என்ன கேட்டா, தமிழில் சொல்லவாங்க, அது அர்த்தம் டான் நான்புரிந்ஜிடுவேன்' (Now if I ask my friend what an English word is, he will explain it in Tamil, so I'll understand the meaning of the word).

The teacher–researcher collaboration contributed to the linguistic–discursive affordances by helping to ensure that the affordances of translanguaging went beyond using Tamil or Malay to scaffold English, but rather, that learners were developing *all* their language practices simultaneously. A significant co-shift that occurred during my teacher–researcher collaboration with Ms Kavita related to the use of translanguaging to help learners make explicit connections across Tamil, Malay and English. In a debrief session early on in our study, Ms Kavita and I noted that students' use of translanguaging seemed to be unidirectional, in that they translanguaged in Tamil and Malay to scaffold their peers' learning of English. We decided that we needed to show learners that the use of translanguaging could benefit not only their English learning, but also their Tamil and Malay learning. In a lesson that we re-designed following this discussion where learners had to create a role-play using interrogative pronouns such as 'who', 'whom', 'what' and 'which,' Ms Kavita and I first asked learners to create questions using the pronouns trilingually, and to make observations about the similarities and differences between how the questions were constructed in each language (see Figure 2.7).

Ms Kavita and I observed that this activity was effective in building learners' lexical, semantic and syntactical knowledge across English, Tamil and Malay. In their interviews, learners demonstrated a new awareness about how all the languages in their linguistic repertoire were connected, and could support one another. For example, Lingkam asserted

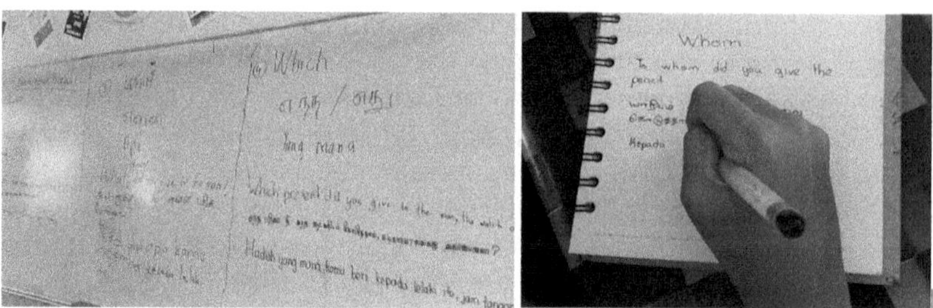

Figure 2.7 Questions constructed by learners in English, Tamil and Malay using interrogative pronouns

that 'என்னை பொறுத்தவரைக்கும், தமிழ் வந்து English க்கு உடவது, English தமிழ் க்கு உதவும்' (As far as I'm concerned, Tamil helps English, and English helps Tamil). English and Malay help to Tamil, Tamil is help English and Malay.

Conclusions and Implications for Further Research and Practice

Flores and García (2014: 256) remind us that an important prerequisite for pedagogical translanguaging is 'the teachers' willingness to engage in learning with their students, becoming an equal participant in the educational enterprise that should seek, above all else, to equalize power relations.' This study demonstrates how Ms Kavita was able to challenge the hegemonic English-only norms that are dominant in ESL contexts, and promote a pedagogy based on linguistic equity through her willingness to engage in the teacher–researcher collaboration. By moving away from didactic teacher-centered instruction and taking on a facilitative role, Ms Kavita also successfully (re)positioned students as agentic, confident and collaborative participants in charge of their learning. Reflecting on the years of English-only policies she had experienced prior to entering Ms Kavita's ESL classroom, a learner, Amira expressed that these policies had made her feel like she and her peers 'don't have freedom, சுதந்திரம் கிடைக்காத மாதிரி (like we don't have independence). நாட்டிற்க்கு சுதந்திரம் கிடைத்தது, ஆனால் நம்பளுக்கு கிடைக்கவில்லை (Our country has gained independence, but we haven't).' Another learner, Lingkam reported that every time his former teachers would tell him, 'don't talk Tamil,' he felt 'sad' because 'தெரியாது வார்த்தை வந்து கேட்கிறது பயமா இருப்போம். சில teacher எல்லாம் வந்து, கொன்ஜம் தமிழ் பேசினால் கையை அடிப்பாங்க, அடனால பயங்கித்து, பேசாம வாயை மூடித்து இருப்பென் (I will be too afraid to ask about the meaning of words we don't understand. Some teachers, if I speak even a little Tamil, they'll hit me on the hand, so I'll just shut my mouth and keep quiet because I'm too afraid)'. Lingkam's feelings about the collaborative translanguaging pedagogy he experienced in the study stood in stark contrast to how he felt about his former English lessons. He reported that anytime he did not understand a word in English, he would not hesitate to ask Ms Kavita in Tamil as he knew she would explain it to him multilingually, 'எனக்கு ஒரு வார்த்தை தெரியவில்லை என்றால், teacherவுக்கு கேட்டால், teacher தமிழில் வந்து நம்பளுக்கு வெழுங்கு சொல்லவாங்க (If I don't understand a word, if I show it to teacher, teacher will use Tamil to explain it well to me).'

Although learners expressed immense relief at being able to communicate with their teacher and peers using languages other than English in the classroom, there were certain barriers that prevented them from drawing on their full translanguaging repertoires. At the beginning of our teacher–researcher collaboration, Ms Kavita and I experienced resistance from a few learners, parents and administrators who felt that the best way to improve learners' English learning outcomes was through immersion in the classroom, and that English was the best pathway to academic success, which are common discourses in ESL contexts. Many learners were also afraid or hesitant to use Malay, despite their proficiency in the language, because of ongoing tensions and conflict between the ethnic Malay majority and Indian minority. To try and overcome these challenges, Ms Kavita and I learned that we had to take on roles that extended beyond the demarcation of 'teacher' and 'researcher.' We both became advocates and proponents of translanguaging to learners, parents, teachers and administrators. We became facilitators of critical discussions with learners about language, colonization and social justice. We also became mediators and peacekeepers who spoke to learners about the importance of intercultural understanding and tolerance. More details and examples of how these critical discussions created a space for social justice and decolonization of language learning in our classroom are provided in Rajendram (2022). Ms Kavita and I felt empowered to go outside our comfort zones in taking on these different roles because of the emotional, personal and pedagogical support we received from each other throughout our collaboration. By taking on all of these roles, Ms Kavita and I were able to create momentum in the school for a translanguaging stance and design to be adopted by other teachers in their classrooms. The implications of this research point to the importance of teacher–researcher, and also teacher–teacher collaboration in challenging English-only classroom policies in ESL and K-12 contexts and creating a school-wide openness to the importance of a translanguaging pedagogy.

During our collaboration, Ms Kavita and I faced pragmatic challenges such as having to make time during our short breaks between classes and after school to engage in planning, discussion and reflection. Ms Kavita also faced the additional pressure of having to complete the topics and activities in the prescribed textbook, and prepare students for their midterm and end-of-year examinations which were based very strictly on the standardized curriculum. For teacher collaboration to be feasible and sustainable, there should be structures or programs within the school that enable teachers to engage in co-planning, co-teaching and collaborative inquiry. Examples of these supports include providing release time for teachers to engage in professional development around translanguaging, incentivizing teachers to initiate and engage in collaborative research through access to funding and resources, and giving teachers the creative liberty to bring translanguaging into the enacted curriculum. Ms Kavita and I found that our teacher–researcher collaboration helped to alleviate a few of the pragmatic and systemic challenges she faced in implementing a translanguaging pedagogy in her classroom. For example, our lesson preparation and debriefing sessions provided a means of personalized professional development for her, and we were able to pool together existing instructional materials that we had to create resources for our translanguaging lessons.

This study contributes to research on translanguaging in the Southeast Asian context by providing evidence and examples of the contextual situatedness of translanguaging. The way that learners in Ms Kavita's class translanguaged was reflective of the social, cultural, linguistic and political contexts in which they were situated. In their translanguaging interactions, learners spoke about their social customs and traditions, made references to Malaysian, Indian and Southeast Asian culture, and enacted the values and norms of their communities. This suggests that the co-design of a translanguaging pedagogy must be attuned to the contextual particularities and nuances that may shape learners' engagement with, and response to translanguaging. As Tian *et al.* (2020: 4) emphasize, translanguaging research and pedagogies should pay attention to the contextual needs of teachers and learners, and generate 'authentic, sustainable, and contextualized knowledge' on translanguaging in language teaching and learning.

At the same time, teachers must be prepared to make important co-shifts in order to foreground learners' voices, perspectives and expertise. At different points during this study, Ms Kavita and I obtained learners' perspectives and insights through the interviews and informal conversations with them, and the perspectives that we gleaned from our learners were invaluable in informing each subsequent co-shift that we made to our lessons. The learners proved to be effective planners, guides, mentors, teachers, advisors, editors and leaders in their collaborative groups. They were also sociolinguists (Sánchez *et al.*, 2018) with the metalinguistic and metacognitive ability to use features of their repertoires selectively and strategically to support their peers for different purposes and tasks (Cenoz & Gorter, 2017; Wiley & García, 2016). These findings beckon us to consider how a translanguaging pedagogy can be designed in ESL contexts in ways that promote peer collaboration, and include learners in the co-design process, right from the onset. Teacher–learner–researcher collaboration is an important and productive avenue for further research and practice in (re)imagining the future of translanguaging pedagogies in the classroom.

References

Baker, C. (2011) *Foundations of Bilingual Education and Bilingualism* (5th edn). Bristol: Multilingual Matters.

Carroll, K.S. and Sambolín Morales, A.N. (2016) Using university students' L1 as a resource: Translanguaging in a Puerto Rican ESL classroom. *Bilingual Research Journal* 39 (3-4), 248–262.

Cenoz, J. and Gorter, D. (2017) Minority languages and sustainable translanguaging: Threat or opportunity. *Journal of Multilingual and Multicultural Development* 38 (10), 901–912.

Cohen, A.D. (2004) Assessing speech acts in a second language. In D. Boxer and A.D. Cohen (eds) *Studying Speaking to Inform Second Language Learning* (pp. 302–327). Clevedon: Multilingual Matters.

Creese, A. and Blackledge, A. (2015) Translanguaging and identity in educational settings. *Annual Review of Applied Linguistics* 35, 20–35.

Daniels, T.P. (2005) *Building Cultural Nationalism in Malaysia: Identity, Representation, and Citizenship*. New York, NY: Routledge.

Duarte, J. (2016) Translanguaging in mainstream education: A sociocultural approach. *International Journal of Bilingual Education and Bilingualism* 22 (2), 150–164.

Fairclough, N. (1995) *Critical Discourse Analysis*. London: Longman.

Flores, N. and García, O. (2014) Linguistic third spaces in education: Teachers' translanguaging across the bilingual continuum. In D. Little, C. Leung and P. Van Avermaet (eds) *Managing Diversity in Education: Languages, Policies, Pedagogies* (pp. 243–256). Bristol: Multilingual Matters.

García, O. (2009) Education, multilingualism and translanguaging in the 21st century. In A. Mohanty, M. Panda, R. Phillipson and T. Skutnabb-Kangas (eds) *Multilingual Education for Social Justice: Globalising the Local* (pp. 128–145). New Delhi: Orient Blackswan.

García, O., Johnson, S. and Seltzer, K. (2017) *The Translanguaging Classroom. Leveraging Student Bilingualism for Learning*. Philadelphia, PA: Caslon.

García, O. and Li, W. (2014) *Translanguaging: Language, Bilingualism and Education*. New York, NY: Palgrave MacMillan.

Gokhale, A.A. (1995) Collaborative learning enhances critical thinking. *Journal of Technology Education* 7 (1), 22–30.

Hashim, A. (2009) Not plain sailing: Malaysia's language choice in policy and education. *AILA Review* 22, 36–51.

Ibrahim, R., Muslim, N. and Buang, A.H. (2011) Multiculturalism and higher education in Malaysia. *Procedia Social and Behavioural Sciences* 15, 1003–1009.

Karlsson, A., Larsson, P.N. and Jakobsson, A. (2018) Multilingual students' use of translanguaging in science classrooms. *International Journal of Science Education* 41 (15), 2049–2069.

Kaufhold, K. (2018) Creating translanguaging spaces in students' academic writing practices. *Linguistics and Education* 45, 1–9.

Lantolf J.P. and Thorne, S.L. (2006) *Sociocultural Theory and the Genesis of Second Language Development*. Oxford: Oxford University Press.

Lee, H.L.J. (2010) Code switching in the teaching of English as a Second Language to secondary school students. *Malaysian Journal of ELT Research* 6 (1), 1–45.

Lemke, D. and Martin, C. (2014) *Jonathan Swift's Gulliver's Travels: A Graphic Novel*. North Mankota, MN: Stone Arch Books.

Lewis, G., Jones, B. and Baker, C. (2012) Translanguaging: Origins and development from school to street and beyond. *Educational Research and Evaluation: An International Journal on Theory and Practice* 18 (7), 641–654.

Lin, L. (2015) *Investigating Chinese HE EFL Classrooms: Using Collaborative Learning to Enhance Learning*. Heidelberg: Springer-Verlag Berlin Heidelberg.

Low, S.M. (2016) The effectiveness of classroom code-switching in Malaysian science classrooms. PhD dissertation, University of Sheffield.

Martin, P. (2005) 'Safe' language practices in two rural schools in Malaysia: Tensions between policy and practice. In A.M.Y. Lin and P.W. Martin (eds) *Decolonisation, Globalisation: Language-in-Education Policy and Practice* (pp. 74–97). Clevedon: Multilingual Matters.

Martin-Beltrán, M. (2014) 'What do you want to say?' How adolescents use translanguaging to expand learning opportunities. *International Multilingual Research Journal* 8 (3), 208–230.

Martin-Beltrán, M. (2017) Exploring peer interaction among multilingual youth: New possibilities and challenges for language and literacy learning. *International Multilingual Research Journal* 11 (3), 131–136.

Mercer, N. (2004) Sociocultural discourse analysis: Analysing classroom talk as a social mode of thinking. *Journal of Applied Linguistics* 1 (2), 137–168.

Ministry of Education Malaysia (2013) *Malaysia Education Blueprint 2013–2025 (Preschool to Post-secondary Education)*, government publication, accessed 20 February 2023. https://www.moe.gov.my/menumedia/media-cetak/penerbitan/dasar/1207-malaysia-education-blueprint-2013-2025/file

Neokleous, G. (2017) Closing the gap: Student attitudes toward first language use in monolingual EFL classrooms. *TESOL Journal* 8 (2), 314–341.

Paulsrud, B., Tian, Z. and Toth, J. (eds) (2021) *English-Medium Instruction and Translanguaging*. Bristol: Multilingual Matters.

Rajendram, S. (2019) Translanguaging as an agentive, collaborative and socioculturally responsive pedagogy for multilingual learners. PhD dissertation, University of Toronto.

Rajendram, S. (2022) 'Our country has gained independence, but we haven't': Collaborative translanguaging to decolonize English language teaching. *Annual Review of Applied Linguistics: Special Issue on Social Justice in Applied Linguistics* 42, 78–86.

Ramli, Z. and Jamaluddin, N. (2021) A case study of translanguaging in bilingual teaching and learning in public universities in Malaysia. *Turkish Journal of Computer and Mathematics Education* 12 (3), 381–389.

Rosa, J. and Flores, N. (2017) Unsettling race and language: Toward a raciolinguistic perspective. *Language in Society* 46 (5), 1–27.

Rosiers, K., van Lancker, I. and Delarue, S. (2018) Beyond the traditional scope of translanguaging: Comparing translanguaging practices in Belgian multilingual and monolingual classroom contexts. *Language & Communication* 61, 15–28.

Sánchez, M.T., García, O. and Solorza, C. (2018) Reframing language allocation policy in dual language bilingual education. *Bilingual Research Journal* 41 (1), 37–51.

Selamat, J.T. (2014) Code switching in the Malaysian ESL classroom. Master's thesis, University of Otago.

The Star Online (2015) Native English speakers to help teachers and students. *The Star Online,* newspaper article, 1 February, accessed 16 June 2021. https://www.thestar.com.my/news/nation/2015/02/01/native-english-speakers-help-teachers-and-students/

The Sun Daily (2015) Students losing out due to lack of English skill. *The Sun Daily,* newspaper article, 18 May, accessed 16 June 2021. https://www.thesundaily.my/archive/1421066-DSARCH309837

The Sun Daily (2016) Malaysian English teachers expected to reach fluency of native speakers by 2020. *The Sun Daily,* newspaper article, 30 August, accessed 16 June 2021. https://www.thesundaily.my/archive/1954788-LSARCH391476

Tian, Z., Aghai, L., Sayer, P. and Schissel, J.L. (eds) (2020) *Envisioning TESOL through a Translanguaging Lens: Global Perspectives*. Cham: Springer International Publishing.

Tian, Z. and Shepard-Carey, L. (2020) Re(imagining) the future of translanguaging pedagogies in TESOL through teacher-researcher collaboration. *TESOL Quarterly* 54 (4), 1131–1143.

Ting, S.H. and Jintang, L. (2020) Teacher and students' translanguaging practices in a Malaysian preschool. *International Journal of Early Years Education* 30 (2), 261–275.

van Lier, L. (2008) Agency in the classroom. In J.P. Lantolf and M.E. Poehner (eds) *Sociocultural Theory and The Teaching of Second Languages* (pp. 163–186). London: Equinox.

Vollman, R. and Tek, W.S. (2020) Language change and convergence in multilingual Malaysian Chinese. *Global Chinese* 6 (1), 49–67.

Vygotsky, L.S. (1978) *Mind in Society: The Development of Higher Psychological Processes*. Cambridge, MA: Harvard University Press.

Vygotsky, L.S. (1986) *Thought and Language*. Cambridge, MA: The MIT Press.

Walker, U. (2018) Translanguaging: Affordances for collaborative language learning. *New Zealand Studies in Applied Linguistics* 24 (1), 18–40.

Wielander, E. (2016) Something to talk about: Content and Language Integrated Learning in modern languages in British higher education. A case study of German at Aston University. PhD dissertation, Aston University.

Wiley, T.G. and García, O. (2016) Language policy and planning in language education: Legacies, consequences, and possibilities. *The Modern Language Journal* 100 (S1), 48–63.

World Atlas (2020) What languages are spoken in Malaysia? *World Atlas*, website, accessed 16 June 2021, https://www.worldatlas.com/articles/what-languages-are-spoken-in-malaysia.html

3 'Did you get what you want?': Negotiating Critical Translanguaging Teaching and Research in Dual Language Classrooms

Sunny Man Chu Lau, Marsha Jing-Ji Liaw and Maria José Botelho

Background

Translanguaging (TL) pedagogy proposes a political *stance* to valorize and draw on minoritized languages and identities for meaning making through purposeful teaching and assessment *designs* subject to moment-to-moment pedagogical *shifts* to address students' emerging language and learning needs (García *et al.*, 2017). School–university collaborative action research (CAR) (Park, 2006) has been central to dialogic theory building and knowledge co-construction, enabling sustainable change, situated professional learning and research–practice reciprocity in TL pedagogies (Aitken & Robinson, 2020; Lau, 2020). An ideal partnership entails parity in setting research goals and assuming research responsibilities (Rearick & Feldman, 1999), allowing researchers and practitioners to engage in the interrelated processes of co/stances, co/designs and co/shifts in CAR cycles. Complex classroom realities, however, often pose challenges to such promising partnerships (Lau & Stille, 2014). Researchers and teachers must constantly negotiate the changing power dynamics within the classroom and school contexts, mediating among the values, priorities and expectations each brings to the project.

This chapter focuses on two CAR projects conducted in an Eastern Canadian English–French classroom and a Northeast US Chinese–English dual language classroom to illustrate the unique possibilities and challenges in collaborative TL teaching and learning processes. Both projects employed TL to mobilize elementary children's meaning-making repertoires for critical literacies (CL) (Lau, 2019; Liaw, 2019). Though sharing similar initial enthusiasm for critical TL research partnerships, both the teachers and researchers in respective projects varied in their understanding of and experiences with TL and CL as well as in their priorities and expectations towards research and teaching. In these two dual-language contexts where a minority target language was involved (i.e. French and Chinese), the collaborative processes produced added challenges. Both partnerships wrestled with boundaries for TL practices and language allocation to ensure protective spaces for adequate target language models and practices (Sánchez *et al.*, 2018), resulting in constant negotiations for spaces for TL and/or monolingual practices, teaching and/or research priorities and responsibilities. In examining these complexities, the chapter offers insights into the possibilities and challenges of CAR and the ways they can inform TL teaching and research for critical learning.

Collaborative Negotiations of Stances, Designs and Shifts in Research Literature

Latest theorizations of TL recognize not only dynamic, hybrid use of language but also all semiotic resources for meaning making and communication (Li, 2018; Liu *et al.*, 2020). TL pedagogies refer to purposeful and strategic teaching and assessment methods that mobilize students' bi/multilingual practices in class regardless of the official language of instruction to maximize knowledge construction and language learning. Leveraging students' repertoires of linguistic and multimodal resources for learning allows for deeper understanding and greater socially meaningful and critical engagements (García & Li, 2014). Research literature on CL in multilingual contexts shares many theoretical positions and practices with TL – both articulating a transformative stance to reclaim diverse students' multilingual, multicultural and multimodal resources and identities to learn, examine and speak back against social injustices (Lau, 2019; Tian & Link, 2019).

García *et al.* (2017) outline four important pedagogical goals of TL: supporting students' comprehension of complex concepts and texts; developing linguistic practices in academic contexts; allowing for bilingualism and bilingual ways of knowing; and fostering bilingual identities and socioemotional development (2017: 7), all contributing to language education for social justice. To achieve these goals, TL *corriente* (2017: 21), the flows of students' emergent and dynamic bilingualism that already exists in diverse classrooms, needs to be harnessed for meaningful instruction and co-construction of knowledge. While strategic *design* in pedagogical and assessment opportunities is needed to build meaningful bridges between home and school practices, it is imperative to *shift* with the ebbs and flows of the TL *corriente* in class to make moment-by-moment modifications to planned teaching and assessment designs. As teachers allow students to practice TL, pooling and connecting school and home languages to create new linguistic features and practices, the linguistic landscape in the classroom is constantly changing. Hence, it requires teachers' willingness and *stance* that value bilingualism as a resource and a right (García *et al.*, 2017: 27) to make corresponding shifts to meaning-driven instruction and assessment in order to address students' emerging linguistic practices. TL stance, designs and shifts, ultimately, are not merely to scaffold students' learning but also to uphold students' bi/multilingual practices and ways of being and knowing.

There have been increasing studies on university–school partnerships as a venue not only for collaborative theory-building but also for teachers' capacity-building for sustained TL pedagogies (e.g. David *et al.*, 2019; Ollerhead, 2019; Vogel *et al.*, 2018). Tian and Shepard-Carey (2020) argue that teacher–researcher collaboration in TL ideally entails *co-stance*, *co-design* and *co-shifts* (2020: 1133–1134) whereby the partners engage in dynamic, two-directional processes of distributed expertise to support teaching and learning in multilingual school contexts. Co-stance represents teachers' and researchers' open and respectful negotiations of their philosophical and ideological positions and pedagogical practice that validate students' multilingualism for learning. With this co-stance, they engage in collaborative and iterative processes of planning curriculum and assessment that build on and respond to students' developing cultural and linguistic knowledge and identities. Through negotiated micro-moments of teaching and learning, co-shifts represent the team's pedagogical responses to student TL and engagement in multilingual classrooms. These three interconnected processes could potentially promote situated TL pedagogies and sustained professional learning. While a synergy exists among these interconnected processes, however, they can also amplify the complexities of collaboration, teaching and learning in the classroom as some of the research literature shows.

Most of the studies on researcher–teacher collaborations mainly report on TL teaching practices or designs and their impact on teaching and learning; not many devote attention to the complex, dynamic processes within the collaborative journey itself, including its highs and lows, benefits and challenges and teamwork and resistance. Creese and Blackledge (2010) call for TL researchers' greater attention to the local contexts in order to understand how and why certain teacher and/or student participants come to accept or reject TL pedagogies. As they argue, while it is common for bi/multilinguals to shuttle between languages, 'how to harness and build on this will depend on the sociopolitical and historical environment in which such practice is embedded and the local ecologies of schools and classrooms' (2010: 107). Focusing on the classroom ecologies allows researchers to study language and language use within a complex system of interconnected processes such as the relationships among languages, social contexts and individual users (Hornberger & Hult, 2008). Similarly, university–school partnerships for TL research should also adopt a language ecological approach to illuminate how differences in institutional structures, expectations and roles for research and practice can be constituted by (and constitutive of) material and discursive practices. Teachers', students' and schools' attitudes toward home and target languages and their societal statuses, teacher and student participants' experiences with language(s) and classroom norms for participation, all impact and shape TL practices and beliefs, which in turn impact researcher–teacher collaborations as they negotiate TL spaces and practices deemed 'appropriate' to them.

Allard's (2017) study with high school teachers in mid-Atlantic United States, for example, reveals that even though their use of TL had aided minoritized students in content-related goals and greater participation, the students themselves resented such hybrid languaging practices which they believed had got in the way of their English learning. Attending to the overall school culture, Allard found that Spanish-speaking students were often associated with gang violence, which coupled with other institutional barriers, such as the segregation of emergent bilinguals from English-dominant peers until upper levels, the lack of a unifying language policy across the courses and the overall insufficient teacher training in strategic use of TL, had contributed to the students' negative perception and reception of TL practices. Focusing on the micro-interactions in the classroom, Dagenais' (2017) pilot university–school project with English and French as a second language (FSL) teachers also reveals tension among teachers whose beliefs about fluid language practices differed. The collaborating FSL teacher, though amenable to code-switching between English and French in oral instruction, insisted on language separation when it came to written production. Dagenais explains that in western Canada where French is a minority language, language separation is often seen to protect the language and culture, an attitude also found in other multilingual contexts (see Cenoz & Gorter, 2015) where bilingualism is considered potentially detrimental to the maintenance of minority languages. In such contexts, implementation of dynamic bi/multilingual practices poses a serious dilemma for teachers, causing ambivalent, and even contradictory, attitudes toward such an approach. Liu *et al.* (2020) caution that teachers in research partnerships may not necessarily follow a linear development of changing perceptions toward TL – it is often rather *recursive* and *discursive* (2020: 14). This means teachers will often come up against dominant discourses about academic monolingualism which will cause second thoughts, confusion and conflicting beliefs about TL. Liu *et al.* urge researchers to recognize the circuitous journey that teachers may go through in research partnerships and to engage them in reading and discussing counter-discourses and empirical studies that document and amplify the educational potential of TL.

Conflicting beliefs and misunderstandings, however, are not experienced by participating teachers alone; researchers themselves could also go through changes in the collaboration process. An example is Tian's (2020) collaborative design-based research study with a Chinese teacher in a Chinese–English dual language bilingual education (DLBE) program. The focal teacher, despite her initial enthusiasm for TL, had increasing concerns about its inadvertent reinforcement for English dominance which, in her opinion, would defeat the very purpose of the DLBE program. The teacher's doubts also compelled Tian to question his assumed transformative power of TL pedagogy, helping him to gain a more nuanced understanding of TL, particularly the need to protect a pedagogical space for minoritized languages and to differentiate TL practices in response to situated needs. All in all, rich descriptions of teachers' and researchers' collaborative classroom experiences provide a fuller view of these complexities and contradictions in ideological beliefs and practices, aiding our understanding of local conditions un/favorable to the dynamic, changing processes in research collaborations. To capture the complexities in teacher–researcher collaborations, we propose representing TL processes as co/stances, co/shifts and co/designs. The slash conveys the complexity, recursiveness, messiness and, at times, disparateness of these processes while the dash (i.e. co-stance, co-design and co-shifts) (Tian & Shepard-Carey, 2020) connotes a comparatively stable process. Researchers and teachers might not start with the same stance or teaching philosophies, yet their experiences together in enacting designs might trigger shifts in their stances and/or practices, which can result in more shifts in their practices and designs, whether converging towards or diverging from TL pedagogies. Attending to these micro-interactions in research collaborations allows for new and more refined and localized understandings, theories and practices from the ground up, illuminating what is transformative about TL, to whom and under what circumstances.

Ways of Knowing and Doing in Context

In this chapter, we draw our experiences as university-based ethnographers who work with teachers in their school contexts. We seek to understand Sunny's (Author 1) and Marsha's (Author 2) recent researcher–practitioner partnerships in developing and implementing TL pedagogies for critical learning. Particularly, we inquire into how researchers and teachers negotiated co/stances, co/designs and co/shifts in TL practices and what critical engagements were possible in teachers' classrooms.

To engage with the data, we participated in critical collaborative inquiry of *teaching and learning as texts* (Botelho & Gibson-Gates, 2008; Luna *et al.*, 2004; St. Pierre, 2000; Wooldridge, 2001). The sociolinguistic construct of text recognizes policies, pedagogical practices, teaching materials, classroom interactions, reflections and memories as representations of experience that can be deconstructed and interpreted (Botelho & Felis, 2021; Denzin, 2014). For this inquiry, we revisited fieldnotes, interview transcripts and fieldwork memories. We engaged with and made more data (Ellingson & Sotirin, 2020) as we acknowledged how 'researchers, participants, material objects, historical, and cultural discourses within particular places and times' (2020: 7) are constructed. Our ongoing engagement with the data produced new data and meanings. We raised critical questions as we examined and reflected collaboratively on these researcher–practitioner collaborations that negotiated stances, curricular designs and pedagogical shifts.

Through our talk (Luna *et al.*, 2004), reading (St. Pierre, 1996) and writing (Richardson & St. Pierre, 2017) as analysis, we reviewed relevant research literature and engaged with the focus of our inquiry. These critical engagements helped us make sense of the complexities of collaboration in the L2 classrooms. Moreover, the iterative nature of this process provided us with opportunities to revisit our insights in light of our new understandings that emerged out of talk, reading and writing recursively. We agree with Jackon and Mazzei (2013) that data are 'partial and incomplete and is always in a process of a retelling and remembering' (2013: 262) as we 'plug in' (Jackson & Mazzei, 2013) a new theory or concept to think with. Engaging in the process of plugging in, we re-viewed the data through TL as some instances, practices and memories drew our attention and spurred our wonderment (Waterhouse & Arnotte, 2016). We focus on these instances and practices to take note of how they impacted TL co/stances, co/designs and co/shifts. Lastly, we draw on critical discourse analytical practices (Bloome *et al.*, 2008) to consider the ways that these negotiations of stances, designs and shifts are constructed through discourses (i.e. language use) and power relations.

Context of Sunny's research partnership: Sunny collaborated with two Quebécois elementary teachers, Beatrice and Joanie (all names are pseudonyms), from 2012 to 2016. At the beginning of the inquiry, both participants were grade 3 homeroom teachers and taught English language arts (ELA) and FSL to each other's class. Beatrice had over 20 years of teaching experience while Joanie had almost 10 with prior experience in teaching English as a second language (ESL) before becoming an FSL teacher. Both were passionate about promoting social justice education through language learning and had attempted to bring their grade 3 classes together to engage in related projects but mostly in English. They were eager to collaborate with Sunny to systematically explore how English and French could be used in more dynamic and connected ways to support the children's critical learning of social issues and to learn more about TL pedagogy in this particular context through their cross-language and cross-curricular collaborations. After the first year of their collaboration, the teachers obtained the school board approval to create a bilingual multiage classroom (grades 4 to 6) which allowed both teachers to be present at all times and that ELA, math and science were taught in English, and FSL, social studies, music/art and physical education in French. Each year, three focal students were selected representing high, average and low language competencies in both languages based on their performance in the previous year and in the initial month. Apart from student and teacher pre- and post-program interviews, bi-weekly class observations (video recorded), focal students' writing samples and other curricular artifacts were collected for analysis.

Context of Marsha's research partnership: Marsha carried out a one-year ethnographically informed CAR project with Ms Hu, a grade 5 teacher in a Chinese–English immersion classroom in New England, exploring the use of TL in Chinese language learning. Like Sunny, Marsha was not only an active observer in the classroom, but she also explored critical approaches to multimodal composing with the teacher and took part in the knowledge co-construction process with the student participants. Ms Hu, originally from Taiwan, was in her fifth year of teaching in a Chinese–English program that followed a one-way immersion model. She looped with the same group of children from fourth to fifth grade. She had a strong belief in a monolingual approach to language immersion and communicated only in Chinese with her students. After being immersed in the classroom for one month, Marsha saw an opportunity to introduce the use of TL using students' full linguistic and other semiotic repertoires to engage in critical learning. Marsha and Ms Hu co-designed a Chinese language arts curricular unit on local history. The data collection lasted from August 2016 to April 2017. Six students volunteered to participate in the project. The routine included three morning visits to the Chinese literacy class per week (either 45 minutes or 90 minutes depending on the class schedule). Marsha collected multiple data sources including audio recordings of group interactions, video clips of lesson interactions, audio of classroom dialogues and artifacts (i.e. curriculum meeting notes, lesson plans, writing samples and such).

The co-learning process between the researchers and teachers is not always ideal, given different individual, sociocultural and institutional constraints (Herrenkohl *et al.*, 2010; Moje, 2000). Similarly, Sunny's and Marsha's collaborations with teachers involved constant negotiations and, at times, tensions emerged as they tried to address different priorities, agendas and expectations for teaching and research. It was an unfolding journey of both *co/construction/deconstruction/negotiation* whereby their different understandings about pedagogies, classroom interactions as well as the theory-practice divide were recognized and challenged. We feature in the next section instances of discourse, practices and memories from Sunny's and Marsha's research partnerships that emerged through talk, writing and reading recursively about research, teaching and TL.

Negotiations

This study aims to examine how researchers and teachers negotiated co/stances, co/designs and co/shifts in TL practices and what critical engagements were made possible in teachers' classrooms. Sunny's and Marsha's researcher–practitioner collaborations involved discursive and recursive processes as they negotiated theory and practice in context, attempting to enact TL co/stances, co/designs and co/shifts together. The following negotiations foreground the complexities and discursivity of these moments.

Negotiating research and teaching

'Did you get what you want?'

Sharing a similar TL stance to support children's critical learning, Beatrice and Joanie embarked on a partnership with Sunny who aspired to CAR's core value of democratic partnership *with* teachers (Grundy, 1998) in order to respect distributed expertise and optimize change-enhancing context without imposition (Lather, 1991). Sunny strove to engage the teachers in an iterative process of strategic and collaborative planning, acting, evaluating and reflecting (Zuber-Skerritt, 1996) to find creative TL pedagogies that worked dynamically within and against the constraints of this particular context. At the early stage of their collaboration, despite having communicated this emerging and grounded approach, the two teachers continued to position the researcher as 'all-knowing', posing questions or offering comments after class observations such as 'I hope this is what you're looking for', or 'Did you get what you want?'. These remarks, despite showing the teachers' trust in Sunny's expertise, reflect their assumption about research: The researcher has complete knowledge of the study's course of development and results as well as an acceptance of their role as 'research subjects' being examined. Further, on the days when the researcher was not able to observe the class, even though the teachers had agreed to take quick notes about their class activities and interactions, they often forgot, and the same happened even after two portable audio recording devices were purchased to facilitate their ease of data recording. The teachers would remark that teaching had to come first, which suggests a distinction that the teachers had drawn between research and practice. This distinction could be difficult to reconcile given the everyday hectic classroom realities which posed constraints on time and effort for them to assume research ownership and responsibilities.

As their collaboration unfolded and relationships deepened, the boundaries between research and practice had softened but the dominant ideology continued to prevail. The team's second research grant allowed the teachers to obtain a half-day release for a research meeting once every two months to review ongoing data based on which next steps were planned. However, the teachers divulged that the administration was not always happy about their absence and worried their research participation might have disrupted the continuity of their classroom responsibilities, intimating to them the need to prioritize teaching *over* research. The discursive constructions of research as distinct from, and even interfering with, 'real' teaching had caused real (though not all valid) concerns at both personal and institutional levels. It had made it difficult for the teachers to fully identify and position themselves as co-researchers in the process.

'Research is for competent teachers'

Research practices were not expected and common at the Chinese-immersion school where Marsha started her partnership with Ms Hu. Informal conversations with the administration and teachers revealed that research was mainly understood as outside researchers coming into the school to provide their expertise to 'fix' problems identified by the administrators and teachers. The school principal accepted Marsha's invitation for a research partnership, expecting her to provide a quick fix to students' Chinese reading and writing challenges. Marsha's institutional, ethnic, and professional positionalities as both a university researcher and a Chinese–English bilingual educator matched the school's expectations. During the recruitment process, most teachers expressed concerns about research participation because they felt their practice would be put under a microscope and judged. Some were reluctant to let a researcher in their classes for fear of extra preparation needed to put their best practice forward. Eventually, only Ms Hu agreed to be a research partner. On giving her consent, Ms Hu commented, 'I'm competent, that's why you chose my class.' Although this comment could be understood as a humorous aside, the recruiting process revealed that teachers considered research participation as prestige, reserved only for those with exemplary practice.

Before Marsha's first classroom visit, she explained to Ms Hu what this research partnership entailed and encouraged her to focus on doing her daily teaching practices as usual. It was only after the researcher got a better understanding of the context and students' practices before they would collaborate on introducing TL pedagogies. During the field observations, Ms Hu often asked Marsha for feedback such as 'What do you want to see?' or 'What activities do you want my students to do for your research?' In their interactions it became clear that Ms Hu wanted to ensure the 'best data' were available to the researcher. Like the collaborating teachers in Sunny's case, Ms Hu held a similar linear view of research with the researcher 'collecting' the 'right' data that exist in the classroom to answer her questions. Additionally, positioning herself as a competent teacher 'worthy' of research, Ms Hu held onto the belief that she needed to produce the best data and to showcase the best student performances. Yet, this merit-based understanding of research engagement did compel her to be open to exploring TL approaches even though she might not totally agree with the practice, which is further explored later in the chapter.

Negotiating co/stances, co/shifts and co/designs for critical translanguaging

'The children will eventually get it'

What drew Beatrice and Joanie together before the CAR project was their shared TL stance in disrupting language separation. Joanie believed that isolating languages 'makes it much harder and disconnected and [students] won't see all the connections they can make' (Year 1 pre-program interview). In her opinion, in most Québec classrooms and its broader society, the language divide was an enduring problem: 'English is here, French is there; it's like there's a barrier between them'. (Year 1, pre-program interview). She argues that 'language is language, and even though they're different languages, we're learning about the same thing' (Year 1, pre-program interview). Further, language and literacy education should be integral to the overall education goal for critical civic engagement which, in Beatrice's words, is 'for the children's development; it's life' and for them to be 'critical thinkers'. She did not think that children are too young to learn CL as 'they understand in their own way' and it was the teachers who 'set the foundation for how [the children] identify and understand a social issue' (Year 1 pre-program interview). Similarly, Joanie highlighted the importance of the critical education of the mind and the heart: 'If you can touch their hearts now, maybe someday they'll remember it again' (Year 1 pre-program interview). She added that many teachers assumed L2 learners as incapable of grasping complex social concepts. Yet, she believed the contrary – language learning must be meaningful in order that students can learn, as she said, 'If there is no meaning, there is no retention' (Year 4 pre-program interview). Therefore, unlike most FSL teachers, Joanie opposed a grammar-focused approach believing that grammar can be learned through many other meaningful activities implicitly and that present computer applications and online programs could easily fix grammatical inaccuracies; hence, 'mechanics are secondary' to ideas and meaning construction (Year 1 pre-program interview). For both teachers, linking the curricula through TL practices was to allow for connected and extended critical inquiry into the same topic for deep understanding. As Joanie said, 'it's almost like learning it for the second time. It's like they're learning the concept in their mother tongue, then transferring [it] to the [other] language' (Year 1 pre-program interview).

This co/stance in TL for critical engagements had provided a solid foundation for their collaboration with Sunny. When it came to TL practices in class, the teachers adhered to a one teacher/one language policy – when an English storybook was read, Beatrice would lead the class discussions in English while Joanie assisted on the side posing questions or offering comments in French to stimulate further discussion, and vice versa when reading a French storybook. While the teachers used monolingual practices to provide a model for the target language, the students were allowed to code switch in oral discussions and in writing while being encouraged to use as much target language as they could. This practice created a unique environment where the teachers were utilizing each other's monolingual practices and students' dynamic bilingualism to coordinate teaching and learning activities to create linguistic connections and conceptual coherence for critical, complex learning. The teachers used bilingual recasting (i.e. rephrase students' ideas in a target language) or language brokering (i.e. interpret and rephrase students' ideas using culturally appropriate terms in a target language) so that they could continue the instruction in their own language. However, they also differentiated individual students' readiness in their target language use: While pushing more experienced students to take risks in practicing the target language, they accommodated those who lacked confidence to engage more in code-switching. This one teacher/one language coordinated TL pedagogy, like the one used in Pontier and Gort's study (2016), might not be the kind of TL practices that Sunny had envisioned at the start, but she had come to recognize the importance of language models and appreciate the priority given to meaning-driven discussions and knowledge production.

As the project entered its second year, the two teachers had shifted from teaching two grade 3 classrooms to co-teaching a grade 4–6 multiage classroom when they had to, for the first time, prepare students for the ministry and provincial uniform exams in ELA and FSL. Hence, the need to provide more structured support in both languages became apparent, especially for those students who were not experienced in either target language. With the teachers' hectic schedule, they usually could not mark the children's writing in time to share the findings in the research meetings to inform the next pedagogical steps. This could also be a result of the teachers' distinction drawn between research and teaching, that they had yet to see themselves as teacher-researchers. Because of the delay in the evaluation of the students' writing, the team had to rely mainly on the data from class discussions and individual team members' reflections to inform the next pedagogical decisions. Sunny felt the need to review students' works in a more systematic and timely manner and invited the teachers to join her at the end of year 2 to review all students' reading responses done in that year using the ministry evaluation criteria. However, they both declined as they expressed a much-needed break from the schoolwork and time reserved for family, which was understandable. Sunny in her close analysis of the children's writing found that they were very good at making personal connections but not so much in drawing comprehensive meaning from the text, making inferences based on these ideas, or justifying their understanding with references to the texts' structures and features. Further, for responses in French, even though students were allowed to use English words to replace unknown French words, their responses were short, and they struggled to express their ideas. If there had been closer attention to students' ongoing written production, it would have allowed the team to make more timely pedagogical shifts to support students' overall interpretation of the stories, comprehension of their social meaning, and the needed language structures to express their ideas.

The findings were brought back to the research meeting and some suggestions were made to strengthen the connections between class reading and discussions and writing as well as the explicit teaching of key French vocabulary and grammar structures to promote comprehension and language production. For example, the teachers agreed to both read and discuss the selected English or French story themselves first to thoroughly understand the characterization, plot, themes and other structures and features before brainstorming and co-developing discussion questions and activities together. This allowed for better thematic and linguistic connections between the English and French texts and more coherent learning goals. The teachers also started to use a more systematic approach to do their reading and discussions, highlighting key vocabulary, posing more specific questions relating to the characters, story development and key themes to invite students to make personal and textual connections while modeling how to take notes about the structures and features of the stories and create concept maps to capture their relationships. Students were also given a sampler of a reading response to understand the text components, and through modeling and collaborative writing, the teachers supported the children to synthesize ideas into a more organized reading response. Joanie also started to use the '*code de correction*' to raise students' awareness of punctuation, spelling, use of plurals and the like, and give students some follow-up exercises on key grammatical structures, which was positively received by her students. Later, she shared in a meeting that she was pleasantly surprised by the effectiveness of these strategies. There was greater accuracy in students' works and that it took her half of the time needed to mark them. Reflecting on her teaching in year 3, Joanie concluded, 'The writing I saw... I need to work more on spelling and grammar. It's funny because many of the kids' ideas were really high [...]. So, it really showed me that I need to work harder on [the mechanics] now that they have the ideas.' (Year 3 post-program interview). By the end of their collaboration, both teachers still prioritize meaning-driven over form-driven teaching, as Joanie argued that the children 'will eventually get it' because the children 'do so many activities using the same vocabulary, so they will understand and retain it really well' (Year 4 pre-program interview).

'Do we need to use English?'

Ms Hu's school followed a strict monolingual approach to Chinese language teaching, even though she is fully bilingual and biliterate. Her stance toward TL was hence different from the one adopted by Marsha who believed in flexible language use for maximized learning. Ms Hu's skepticism about TL came from her previous English language immersion experience which in her opinion was the best way to learn a language. Students were also accustomed to the school's Chinese-only policy and believed that a monolingual approach would support their L2 development. However, they would occasionally code switch to English to confirm meaning in class with Ms Hu or to engage in private conversations when out of the teacher's earshot. Marsha was advised by Ms Hu and the administrator not to speak English with the students in the classroom.

Ms Hu usually designed 'manageable' teaching activities because she could ensure that students were able to complete the tasks in Chinese and speak Chinese only. These activities were more form-focused such as sentence making, Chinese character writing, fill in the blanks, or reading and listening comprehension worksheets. Every day, she started her class with a morning sharing circle, but the discussion topics were mostly classroom-based topics such as class agenda and tasks, homework review or discipline reminders. When Ms Hu started planning her second unit, Marsha found an opportunity to introduce a more interesting topic that mobilized students' full linguistic and multimodal repertoires to engage in critical learning. They co/designed a unit on local history and a culminating project where students would create a memory snapshot of a person's daily life in 18th-century New England and a video on a particular historical event in that time period. However, the collaboration process was not easy because Ms Hu would often question the validity of TL practices, such as 'Do we need to use English?' or 'No, it's not going to work because we can't speak English' (Curriculum meeting, October 2016). Sometimes even when the researcher proposed a teaching idea which Ms Hu found useful and great for her students, she would decline and not make any concessions to the Chinese-only policy. Because of this resistance, Marsha reconsidered what TL could look like in this particular classroom. While teacher-directed TL practices was out of the question, Marsha proposed activities whereby the students could use English in a receptive way, for example, reading the Chinese translated version of *Letting Swift River Go* (Yolen & Cooney, 1995), which the students had already read in English in an earlier grade, or doing research online in English but having class discussions and assignments all done in Chinese only. This version of TL was more palatable to Ms Hu, and she was willing to try.

Students were very excited about the project and during their research session, as they browsed through English websites to explore their chosen topics, they tended to switch back to English, which worried Ms Hu since she thought such a diversion would set back their Chinese language progress and could possibly affect her teaching evaluation if her supervisor happened to pass by. Ms Hu's high level of discomfort with students' use of English had created much tension between her and Marsha, which continued throughout the research partnership. At the end of their year-long collaboration, Ms Hu acknowledged that students had made much progress in their writing and that they had become more independent in their language learning:

> 现在我觉得他们进步的很多，默默的，写作上最多的进步，然后独立性也进步很多。
>
> *I think they make a lot of progress silently (tacitly), in particular, writing has demonstrated the most progress, and their independence in learning.* (April 2017, Ms Hu's interview)

Despite students' progress, Ms Hu was disappointed that they were unable to express their opinions entirely in Chinese and using higher-level Chinese vocabulary. She would rather play safe to ensure students adhere to Chinese, even though this might mean they would engage in something less complex and engaging. Looking back, Marsha realized that her idealized stance of TL pedagogy might not have taken into consideration the institutional realities of the classroom and the pedagogical need to protect a space for the teaching and learning of this minoritized language. Even though she acted swiftly to attempt to address this issue by negotiating for students' use of multimodalities and English resources as scaffolding for their Chinese written production, Ms Hu was concerned about how the English presence in the classroom might have reduced students' target language use, and possibly put her in a precarious position with her administrators. The priorities she put on monolingual competence over meaning-construction had also created tension between her and the researcher who was eager to engage students in TL for critical learning, overlooking the need for more language teaching in context and situated linguistic structures and practices. These tensions in their collaboration process have allowed her to see the importance and difficulties in maintaining a fine balance among TL for critical learning and the need for discrete language support and a space for monolingual practice.

Discussion

The two university–school collaborations on TL pedagogies demonstrate complex, layered processes of negotiations between the teachers and researchers based on individual and sociocultural constraints and affordances (Herrenkohl *et al.*, 2010). Both teachers in Québec shared a TL stance with Sunny, understanding that language is constituting and constitutive of cultural practices and power relations and that language compartmentalization is socially imposed. This critical TL co/stance on language and education helped lay a productive foundation for their collaboration. Despite this shared belief, TL practices in the class were mainly student-led while the two teachers provided monolingual models in a coordinated way to create bridges between the two languages and concepts covered in reading, while differentiating individuals' readiness in their target language use. In the co/design process, Sunny had come to appreciate this more structured yet flexible approach in coordinating both teacher- and student-directed TL practices, ensuring that there was a protected space for L2 teaching and learning while remaining flexible and sensitive to co/shift with students' *corriente* and differentiated needs (Sánchez *et al.*, 2018). Ms Hu in New England similarly endeavored to protect the pedagogical space for Chinese in her English-Chinese bilingual classroom. The well-established language compartmentalized policy in the school ensured students to have an adequate exposure to and practice of Mandarin Chinese as L2. The students had internalized this monolingual practice and the teacher also tried her best to avoid or suppress students' *corriente*. The lack of co/stance in TL practices had created tension between the researcher and the teacher, which urged Marsha to rethink what TL pedagogies were practicable and viable in this specific context. Yet even though English was only meant for students' receptive use in reading online articles, they were excited about the activities and started using English in discussions, contributing to Ms Hu's concern about possible reprimands from the administration. In both research collaborations, the teaching and learning of a minoritized language, that is, French L2 and Chinese L2, were within anglophone school contexts and the broader English-dominant Canadian-US context. In the process, the researchers and teachers all recognized the need for a more well-defined space for target language learning (Ballinger *et al.*, 2017; Cenoz & Gorter, 2015). Both researchers also gained a more nuanced understanding of the need for contextualized TL practices that are responsive to the unique institutional demands and language status. In both contexts, the teachers' practices could be interpreted as conservative, apprehensive, or even resistant (in Marsha's case) towards TL if viewed from a strong TL standpoint which sees languages as a unitary system (García & Otheguy, 2014; Otheguy *et al.*, 2015). Yet the teachers' 'reservations' or 'apprehensions' can similarly be interpreted as being 'mindful' of language distinctions in order to support learners to effectively master a minoritized language in contexts where English dominance is prevailing and that the existing institutional structures still reward monolingualism (see detailed arguments by Cummins, 2021 and MacSwan, 2017).

The teachers in Sunny's project were passionate for CL and social justice education, and their co/shifts and co/designs, involved sometimes deconstruction and, at other times, co-construction for the team to have finally found a more structured and organized way to promote critical understanding while supporting students' development in target language structures to express complex ideas. The teachers' enthusiasm for social justice education might have caused them reluctance to engage in more explicit grammar and vocabulary instruction. Striking a balance between form-driven and meaning-driven instruction has been a main area of negotiations between the researcher and teachers. At the conclusion of the project, Joanie remarked that having seen students' improvement in idea generation and conceptual understanding, she felt more relieved to then attend to the mechanics. Such a view, though still perceiving language and thought as separate, reflects a willingness to focus on intentional development of students' L2 competencies. In Marsha's partnership, it was her eagerness to push for more meaningful and critical learning that had created tension with Ms Hu who prioritized L2 development over critical literacies. As both research projects progressed, it was the teachers in Québec and the researcher in New England who had come to appreciate the value of a more structured and explicit approach for language scaffolds and explicit teaching of language conventions and mechanics, understanding that form-driven and meaning-driven instruction are not and should not be mutually exclusive (Ellis *et al.*, 2009).

All these negotiations of different aspects of TL and critical literacies pedagogies demonstrate that TL co/stances, co/designs and co/shifts are never tidy. In some cases, the researcher and the teacher start off with a similar TL stance and end up with a more nuanced understanding of what TL looks like in their unique context, like the collaboration with Joanie and Beatrice. In other cases, like the partnership with Ms Hu, the researcher and the teacher shared different TL stances and they were not reconciled at the end but with the researcher gaining a more sympathetic understanding of the need to have a protective space for a minoritized language in an English-dominant school and society. One major challenge shared in these two university–school collaborations perhaps was the participating teachers' understanding of research. In both collaborations, the teachers' assumption about research may have been influenced by a positivist paradigm, which has a strong hold on how schools understand language and literacy learning. Researchers are deemed as experts dropping into classrooms to extract impartial data and retreat to their laboratories for data analysis and verification (Taylor & Medina, 2011). This assumption has also perpetuated a theory-practice divide that the teachers had come to internalize themselves as 'research subjects' rather than seeing themselves as classroom researchers working alongside university researchers with distributed expertise. They were there to merely provide data and, in Ms Hu's case, the best data. The research responsibilities were hence seen as residing with the university researchers, and the teachers were there to provide the data that the experts had deigned to collect. The institutional discourse on research and teaching also reinforced this compartmentalized thinking, with priority given to teaching rather than research. This positivist thinking about research presented challenges for the collaborators to truly adopt co/designs and co/shifts in the process, even though at times there was the need to push for more organized and intentional teaching of language structures for situated use.

Conclusion

Focusing on the micro-interactions (i.e. instances of discourse) and collaborative processes (or the lack thereof) between researchers and teachers, this chapter attempts to shed light on what TL co/stances, co/shifts and co/designs are possible, feasible and palatable to teachers, considering the diverse, complex and sometimes contradicting expectations and priorities teachers and researchers bring to research partnerships. Monolingual ideologies and institutional language policies constrain and surveil teachers' and students' language practices, restricting the kind of TL teachers are willing and/or convinced to adopt for teaching and learning. As Liu *et al.* (2020) argue, teachers' transformed attitude toward TL and multilingual approaches often involves a recursive and discursive process, suggesting a more prolonged partnerships with teachers to engage them, not only in practice, but also in discussion of counter-discourses against monolingual practices. However, as Jaspers (2018) cautions, even though TL might have its transformative potential, these pedagogies 'can equally become a dominating force' (2018: 12) and disallow the consideration of other issues associated with language learning. He supports his argument by making a particular reference to minoritized languages and, along with other scholars (e.g. Cenoz & Gorter, 2017), poses the question as to how the maintenance of these languages could be done through fluid language practices. Jaspers is by no means supporting linguistic purism; he is only expressing concerns that if researchers are not critical of TL as they are of monolingualism, articulations of the transformative power of TL pedagogies might feed into a 'truth regime' (2017: 13) and fail to take into consideration the complex circumstances that each context might present. Attending to the local language ecologies allows researchers to be responsive and critical of the limitations and affordances unique to the context and to learn to navigate the tensions and negotiations with individual teachers and institutions to make research and teaching more dialogic for co/stances, co/designs and co/shifts work as research partners engage with knowledge/power (Foucault, 1980) entanglements. Such negotiations and tensions, though causing discomfort, push researchers to embrace classroom realities and complexities to refine and rebuild theory grounded in practice (Herrenkohl *et al.*, 2010; Moje, 2000). The journey in each context can be different but full of co/construction/deconstruction/negotiations. These insights of the day-to-day work of teachers allow researchers to remain flexible, reflexive, and vigilant against any simplistic claims for pedagogical transformation.

References

Aitken, A. and Robinson, L. (2020) 'Walking in two worlds' in the plurilingual classroom: Learning from the case of an intergenerational project. In S.M.C. Lau and S. Van Viegen (eds) *Plurilingual Pedagogies: Critical and Creative Endeavors for Equitable Language in Education* (pp. 77–96). Berlin: Springer Nature. https://doi.org/10.1007/978-3-030-36983-5_4

Allard, E.C. (2017) Re-examining teacher translanguaging: An ecological perspective. *Bilingual Research Journal* 40 (2), 116–130. https://doi.org/10.1080/15235882.2017.1306597

Ballinger, S., Lyster, R., Sterzuk, A. and Genesee, F. (2017) Context-appropriate crosslinguistic pedagogy: Considering the role of language status in immersion education. *Journal of Immersion and Content-Based Language Education* 5 (1), 30–57. https://doi.org/10.1075/jicb.5.1.02bal

Bloome, D., Power Carter, S., Morton Christian, B., Madrid., S., Otto, S., Shuart-Faris, N. and Smith, M. (2008) *On Discourse Analysis in Classrooms: Approaches to Language and Literacy Research*. New York: Teachers College Press.

Botelho, M.J. and Gibson-Gates, C. (2008) Posing questions together: Critical collaborative inquiry in initial teacher education. *Initial Teacher Education: Enriching and Extending Partnerships* (pp. 18–23). Toronto: OISE/University of Toronto.

Botelho, M.J. and Felis, M. (2021) Teaching ethnography/ically: Entanglements of knowing/being/doing in a doctoral research course. *International Review of Qualitative Inquiry*, 1–22.

Cenoz, J. and Gorter, D. (2015) *Multilingual Education: Between Language Learning and Translanguaging*. Cambridge: Cambridge University Press.

Creese, A. and Blackledge, A. (2010) Translanguaging in the bilingual classroom: A pedagogy for learning and teaching? *The Modern Language Journal* 94 (1), 103–115.

Cummins, J. (2021) *Rethinking the Education of Multilingual Learners: A Critical Analysis of Theoretical Concepts*. Bristol: Multilingual Matters. https://doi.org/10.21832/CUMMIN3580

Dagenais, D. (2017) Tensions autour de l'enseignement des littératies plurielles en milieu minoritaire. *Éducation et francophonie* 45 (2), 5–21. https://doi.org/10.7202/1043526ar

David, S.S., Pacheco, M.B. and Jiménez, R.T. (2019) Designing translingual pedagogies: Exploring pedagogical translation through a classroom teaching experiment. *Cognition and Instruction* 37 (2), 252–275. https://doi.org/10.1080/07370008.2019.1580283

Denzin, N. (2014) *Interpretive Autoethnography* (2nd edn). Los Angeles, CA: Sage Publishers.

Ellingson, L.L. and Sotirin, P. (2020) *Making Data in Qualitative Research: Engagements, Ethics, and Entanglements*. Abingdon: Routledge.

Ellis, R., Loewen, S., Elder, C., Reinders, H., Erlam, R. and Philp, J. (2009) *Implicit and Explicit Knowledge in Second Language Learning, Testing and Teaching*. Bristol: Multilingual Matters.

Foucault, M. (1980) *Power/Knowledge: Selected Interviews and Other Writings, 1972–1977*. New York: Pantheon.

García, O., Johnson, S.I. and Seltzer, K. (2017) *The Translanguaging Classroom: Leveraging Student Bilingualism for Learning*. Philadelphia: Caslon.

García, O. and Li, W. (2014) *Translanguaging: Language, Bilingualism and Education*. London: Palgrave Macmillan.

García, O. and Otheguy, R. (2014) Spanish and Hispanic bilingualism. In M. Lacorte (ed.) *The Routledge Handbook of Hispanic Applied Linguistics* (pp. 639–658). New York: Routledge.

Grundy, S. (1998) Research partnerships: Principles and possibilities. In B. Atweh, S. Kemmis and P. Weeks (eds) *Action Research in Practice: Partnerships for Social Justice in Education* (pp. 37–46). New York: Routledge.

Herrenkohl, L.R., Kawasaki, K. and Dewater, L.S. (2010) Inside and outside: Teacher-researcher collaboration. *The New Educator* 6, 74–92.

Hornberger, N.H. and Hult, F. (2008) Ecological language policy. In B. Spolsky and F. Hult (eds) *The Handbook of Educational Linguistics* (pp. 280–296). Oxford: Blackwell.

Jackson, A.Y. and Mazzei, L.A. (2013) Plugging one text into another: Thinking with theory in qualitative research. *Qualitative Inquiry* 19 (4), 261–271.

Jaspers, J. (2018) The transformative limits of translanguaging. *Language & Communication* 58, 1–10.

Lather, P. (1991) *Getting Smart: Feminist Research and Pedagogy With/In the Postmodern*. New York: Routledge.

Lau, S.M.C. and Stille, S. (2014) Participatory research with teachers: Toward a pragmatic and dynamic view of equity and parity in research relationships. *European Journal of Teacher Education* 37 (2), 156–170. https://doi.org/10.1080/02619768.2014.882313

Lau, S.M.C. (2019) Affordances of translanguaging in critical literacy work in bilingual classrooms. *Translation and Translanguaging in Multilingual Contexts* 5 (1 [Special issue]), 67–85. https://doi.org/10.1075/ttmc.00025.lau

Lau, S.M.C. (2020) Translanguaging for critical bi-literacy: English and French teachers' collaboration in transgressive pedagogy. In S.M.C. Lau and S. Van Viegen (eds) *Plurilingual Pedagogies: Critical and Creative Endeavors For Equitable Language (In) Education* (pp. 115–135). Berlin: Springer Nature.

Li, W. (2018) Translanguaging as a practical theory of language. *Applied Linguistics* 39 (1), 9–30. https://doi.org/10.1093/applin/amx039

Liaw, J.-J.M. (2019) Negotiating critical biliteracies: Language and literacy learning in a bilingual elementary classroom (Unpublished doctoral dissertation). University of Massachusetts Amherst, Massachusetts, USA.

Liu, J.E., Lo, Y.Y. and Lin, A.M. (2020) Translanguaging pedagogy in teaching English for Academic Purposes: Researcher-teacher collaboration as a professional development model. *System* 92, 102276–16. https://doi.org/10.1016/j.system.2020.102276

Luna, C., Botelho, M.J., Fontaine, D., French, K., Iverson, K. and Matos, N. (2004) Making the road by walking and talking Making the road by walking and talking: Professional development and/as critical literacy. *Teacher Education Quarterly* 31 (1), 67–80.

MacSwan, J. (2017) A multilingual perspective on translanguaging. *American Educational Research Journal* 54 (1), 167–201. https://doi.org/10.3102/0002831216683935

Moje, E.B. (2000) Changing our minds, changing our bodies: Power as embodied in research relations. *Qualitative Studies in Education* 13 (1), 25–42.

Ollerhead, S. (2019) Teaching across semiotic modes with multilingual learners: Translanguaging in an Australian classroom. *Language and Education* 33 (2), 106–122. https://doi.org/10.1080/09500782.2018.1516780

Otheguy, R., García, O. and Reid, W. (2015) Clarifying translanguaging and deconstructing named languages: A perspective from linguistics. *Applied Linguistics Review* 6 (3), 281–307.

Park, P. (2006) Knowledge and participatory research. In P. Reason and H. Bradbury (eds) *The Handbook of Action Research* (pp. 83–93). SAGE.

Pontier, R. and Gort, M. (2016) Coordinated translanguaging pedagogy as distributed cognition: A case study of two dual language bilingual education preschool coteachers' languaging practices during shared book readings. *International Multilingual Research Journal* 10 (2), 89–106. https://doi.org/10.1080/19313152.2016.1150732

Rearick, M.L. and Feldman, A. (1999) Orientations, purposes, and reflection: A framework for understanding action research. *Teaching and Teacher Education* 15, 333–349.

Richardson, L. and St. Pierre, E.A. (2017) Writing: A method of inquiry. In N.K. Denzin and Y.S. Lincoln (eds) *The Sage Handbook of Qualitative Research* (5th edn, pp. 818–838). London: Sage Publishers.

Sánchez, M.T., García, O. and Solorza, C. (2018) Reframing language allocation policy in dual language bilingual education. *Bilingual Research Journal* 41 (1), 37–51.

St. Pierre, E.A. (1996) The responsibilities of readers: Toward an ethics of responses. *Qualitative Sociology* 19 (4), 533–538.

St. Pierre, E.A. (2000) Poststructural feminism in education: An overview. *International Journal of Qualitative Studies in Education* 13, 477–515.

Taylor, P.C. and Medina, M. (2011) Educational research paradigms: From positivism to pluralism. *College Research Journal* 1 (1), 1–16.

Tian, Z. and Link, H. (2019) Positive synergies: Translanguaging and critical theories in education. *Journal of Translation and Translanguaging in Multilingual Contexts* 5 (1 [Special Issue]).

Tian, Z. (2020) Translanguaging design in a Mandarin/English dual language bilingual education program [Doctoral dissertation, Boston College]. Boston College Electronic Thesis or Dissertation. http://hdl.handle.net/2345/bc-ir:108914

Tian, Z. and Shepard-Carey, L. (2020) (Re)imagining the future of translanguaging pedagogies in tesol through teacher-researcher collaboration. *TESOL Quarterly* 54 (4), 1131–1143. https://doi.org/10.1002/tesq.614

Vogel, S., Ascenzi-Moreno, L. and García, O. (2018) An expanded view of translanguaging: Leveraging the dynamic interactions between a young multilingual writer and machine translation software. In J. Choi and S. Ollerhead (eds) *Plurilingualism in Teaching and Learning: Complexities Across Contexts* (pp. 89–106). New York: Routledge.

Waterhouse, M. and Arnott, S. (2016) Affective disruptions of the immigrant experience: Becomings in official language education research in Canada. *International Multilingual Research Journal* 10, 121–136.

Wooldridge, N. (2001) Tensions and ambiguities in critical literacy. In B. Comber and A. Simpson (eds) *Negotiating Critical Literacies in Classrooms* (pp. 259–270). Mahwah, NJ: Lawrence Erlbaum Associates.

Yolen, J. and Cooney, B. (Illustrator) (1995) *Letting Swift River Go*. Boston: Little, Brown.

Zuber-Skerritt, O. (1996) Introduction: New directions in action research. In O. Zuber-Skerritt (ed.) *New Directions in Action Research* (pp. 3–12). London: Falmer Press.

4 Moving towards Translanguaging Pedagogies: Insights from a Teacher–Researcher Collaboration in Vienna

Lena Cataldo-Schwarzl and Elizabeth J. Erling

Background and Context

In Austria, as in most countries in Europe and beyond, linguistically heterogeneous populations increasingly define school systems, particularly in urban areas. While the European Centre for Modern Languages has been promoting multilingual and multicultural education for decades, multilingualism has until recently been relatively absent in the Austrian teacher education curriculum. Explorations of using translanguaging pedagogies to support content and language learning amongst multilingual learners – and counter the existing achievement gap – are still relatively rare. While individual efforts and projects exist, to date there has been no systematic and sustained effort to support change in teacher education programs so that teachers develop an approach to using students' multilingual repertoires as a resource for learning. It was in this context that an exploratory study on a teacher–researcher collaboration was designed involving seven in-service teachers of grade 4 primary school and grade 5 middle school in Vienna from August 2017–February 2018 (Schwarzl, 2020). The goals of the study were two-fold. First, it aimed to find out how translanguaging could be implemented in two very diverse school classes by their teachers. Second, it aimed to find out what implications for practice could be drawn from the project for teacher-education.

In the project, translanguaging-based lessons were co-designed by the researcher, who is the first author of this chapter, and the collaborating teachers of the two participating schools, and a co-shift in stance was pursued via workshops in which translanguaging theory and examples of its implementation were discussed. This approach was informed by transformative action research. Data about the project implementation were collected via an ethnographic approach, which consisted of regular observations of one class of each of the collaborating schools, and interview discussions with one teacher from each collaborating school. The observations also took place outside of class, in hallways and during breaks. The ethnographic observations followed a holistic approach in documenting reflections on discussions with the teachers and reflections on the experiences of the researcher in fieldnotes. Both the fieldnotes and the transcribed interviews were analyzed using content analysis (Kuckartz, 2018) which revealed dominant themes guided by the following research questions:

- In what ways did this collaboration succeed in facilitating teachers to implement translanguaging pedagogies? In particular, what shifts in stance and design took place?
- What were some of the challenges encountered?
- What are the implications of this collaboration for teacher education?

Before we address these questions, we provide an introduction into the role of multilingualism in the Austrian education system, focusing on how multilingualism is embedded in pre- and in-service teacher education in primary and middle schools. We then present the teacher-researcher collaboration undertaken, which offered insight into the benefits and challenges of implementing translanguaging pedagogies with in-service teachers. While the individual transformations within the project were restrained by the context, this collaboration allowed us to envision a model of holistic transformative action research that would potentially support more systemic and sustainable change in teacher education and school practice in Austria and beyond.

Multilingualism and the Austrian education system

While Austria has always been a multilingual country (Rindler Schjerve, 2003; Herzog-Punzenberger, 2017), the number of students who speak languages other than the official language of education – German – has risen in the past decade, particularly in response to the wave of migration to Europe set off by the war in Syria beginning in 2011. According to data from the Austrian National Institute of Statistics in the 2019/20 school year, about 27% of students in schools across Austria indicate that they speak other languages in addition to German at home, and that German is an additional language for them (GAL).[1] In the urban capital city, Vienna, 59% of primary school students, 77% of middle school students and 40% of academic secondary school students have GAL (Statistik Austria, 2019, 2020). These figures, however, only indicate tendencies, as data about language use have not been collected systematically and tend not to capture the complex language repertoires of many multilingual students (Erling *et al.*, 2020; Vetter & Janík, 2019).

Furthermore, Austria is one of the few OECD countries to maintain an educational system that features early tracking. After only four years of comprehensive primary school, students transition into one of two types of lower secondary school: middle school (*Mittelschule*) or general academic secondary school (*Allgemeinbildende Höhere Schule*). Middle school aims to equip students for starting apprenticeships and/or moving on to more vocationally oriented upper secondary schools, and general academic secondary schools prepare students for university (BMBWF, 2018). While there is a degree of mobility and flexibility within the system, the early tracking system in Austria has been found to contribute to an increasing gap in educational attainment (Baysu & Valk, 2012; Hanushek & Wößmann, 2006; Maaz *et al.*, 2008). Research has consistently established that early tracking results in a disadvantage for students from migration backgrounds and/or with GAL, and for students from low socioeconomic status (SES) backgrounds (Erling *et al.*, 2020, 2021; Herzog-Punzenberger & Schnell, 2019; Schreiner *et al.*, 2020). Students who are German L1 users from higher SES backgrounds are much more likely to continue to general academic secondary schools when compared to students with GAL and lower SES (39% to 31%) (Mayrhofer *et al.*, 2018). In Vienna, this trend is even more concerning, with 73% of students who are German L1 users and from higher SES backgrounds transitioning to general academic secondary schools compared to 41% of those with GAL and from lower SES backgrounds (Mayrhofer *et al.*, 2018). Moreover, there is a significant gap in performance between students in these two school types in all the core areas of the curriculum, with middle school students consistently performing below the national average. As a result, the Austrian system has been increasingly criticized for exacerbating disadvantage and failing to give lower-income multilingual and multicultural students voice and opportunity in the school system (Erkurt, 2020; Erling *et al.*, 2021).

In other contexts, it has been found that teachers cannot effectively meet the needs of multilingual and multicultural students using the limited monolingual pedagogical approaches they have been taught to use (García & Kleyn, 2016b). A wealth of contemporary research suggests that a way to support the academic achievement of multilingual students is through mobilizing their full linguistic repertoires as resources for learning (Erling & Moore, 2021; García & Sylvan, 2011; Lau & Van Viegen, 2020). Studies illustrate how translanguaging pedagogies – that is, learning activities planned by teachers in order to include students' full linguistic repertoires – can be powerful in developing confidence and legitimizing students' identities, promoting language and metalinguistic awareness, supporting the learning of the target language without necessarily disrupting students' abilities in other languages and enhancing cognition (Conteh & Meier, 2014; Duarte & Günther-van der Meij, 2018; García & Kleyn, 2016b; García & Li, 2013; Jessner & Mayr-Keiler, 2017). It has been suggested that further understanding of multilingualism and the potential of translanguaging pedagogies is required of all teachers, across the curriculum, and should be further supported in both pre-service and in-service teacher education initiatives. For example, Conteh and Meier (2014: 296) argue as follows:

> All teachers need to begin their careers with positive attitudes to language diversity, some understanding of the broader issues of multilingualism in society, and a basic toolkit of strategies for developing multilingual practices in their classrooms. As their careers progress, they need opportunities to develop more principled, theoretical knowledge of multilingualism in order to grow and develop as teachers in multilingual societies.

In line with such research, the European Centre for Modern Languages (ECML) – a European institution in which Austria has key membership – has been promoting multilingual education for decades (Dooly & Vallejo, 2020). Despite this recognition at a European level, multilingualism and translanguaging pedagogies have until recently been relatively absent in the Austrian teacher education curriculum. As in other international educational contexts, an orientation towards monolingual norms of German still sets the tone in policy and practice (Conteh & Meier, 2014; Duarte & Gogolin, 2013). This remains the case in spite of recent reforms in teacher education that have been introduced using students' multilingualism as a resource for learning as a cross-sectional competence in the undergraduate teacher education curricula for the primary and secondary school levels. Purkarthofer (2016) analyzed the undergraduate and graduate curricula for primary and lower secondary education at all universities and teacher education colleges in Austria, finding that there is more treatment of multilingualism at the undergraduate than at the graduate levels. Moreover, multilingualism is more commonly found in non-obligatory specialization courses than in the mainstream, compulsory courses. Our review of teacher education curricula at the largest Universities and University Colleges of Teacher Education in Vienna (Verbund Nord-Ost, 2017) and Graz (Verbund Süd-Ost, 2016) maintains that these findings are still relevant, though there are examples of multilingualism becoming more dominant in teacher education curricula as classrooms are becoming more linguistically diverse.

In this context, resources have been developed by national and European organizations to support teachers in better serving their students. For example, Krumm and Reich (2011) developed a 'Multilingualism Curriculum' for schools at different stages of the educational sector to highlight points in existing curricula for the integration of multilingualism in the classroom. Resources like *Trio* (Schule-mehrsprachig, 2021) have been developed, a trilingual booklet in German and two of the main migration languages in Austria – Bosnian-Croatian-Serbian (BCS) and Turkish. This resource aligns with the curriculum of primary and lower secondary school, features a number of examples of multilingual practices and activities and regularly includes varying 'guest languages'. Such policies and resources often go unused by teachers as the topics of multilingualism and translanguaging pedagogies are still not systematically covered in the compulsory teacher education curriculum. In order to enable schools to better serve their multilingual students, several independent initiatives have been developed in pre- and in-service teacher education in the last years. The authors of this chapter have been involved in such researcher–teacher initiatives, and this chapter explores some of the approaches and insights that have arisen through them.

Supporting Transformation through Translanguaging: Co-stances, Co-designs and Co-shifts

Following García *et al.* (2017), we recognize three major components of translanguaging theory required for the successful implementation of translanguaging into teaching practices and for schools' transformation: stance, design and shift. Stance refers to the development of beliefs that multilingualism and multilingual practices are resources for learning (García & Kleyn, 2016b: 20). Teachers must believe that translanguaging transforms students and their learning, helping them to become more creative and critical (García & Kleyn, 2016b; García & Li, 2013). This is an important aspect of educational change, as research in a number of international contexts – including Austria – has identified deficit perspectives of multilingual practice, particularly with regard to learners with low SES (De Angelis, 2011; Erling *et al.*, 2020; Haukås, 2016). In addition to a translanguaging stance, teachers need to design translanguaging instruction. This requires having access to a wealth of resources that are both multilingual and multimodal; setting up collaborative, student-centered learning opportunities; and directing and supporting activities that allow/encourage students to use their full linguistic and semiotic repertoire (Kleyn & García, 2019: 73). Teachers must also be prepared to respond to students' individual differences by shifting their instructional design in response to their students' interests, strengths and needs. By making shifts that facilitate individual student learning and understanding, teachers allow increasing space for students' voices in education and foster them to develop criticality and agency to challenge existing norms and hierarchies (Kleyn & García, 2019: 73). Tian and Shepard-Carey (2020) further developed this model by adding a stronger focus on collaborative partnerships, supporting a culture of dialogic planning, discussing and reciprocal learning, which they also mark in the terminology, using co-stance, co-design and co-shift. As teacher educators, we see these three aspects of supporting transformation in a collaborative process as central to our approach to teacher education and professional development. In the context of the project presented in this chapter, we rely on both the terminology used in García and Kleyn (2019) – stance, design and shift and in Tian and Shepard-Carey (2020) – co-stance, co-design and co-shift as we perceive this project on a continuum between both concepts.

Methods: Research design, data collection and analysis

In the following, we describe the collaborative researcher–teacher collaboration that sought to promote translanguaging pedagogy and transformative action among in-service teachers in two Viennese schools that were heterogeneous and multilingual – one primary and one middle school. The teacher-researcher collaboration can be viewed as an individual effort of transformative action research. We locate the collaboration in between the two above-mentioned conceptualizations of (co)-stance, (co)- design and (co)-shift, as collaboration had different forms and intensities (Tian & Shepard-Carey, 2020).

The project involved 22 students with 11 different home languages in primary school and 23 students with 12 different home languages in middle school. In total, there were seven teachers involved in the project: Three in the primary school (one regular and two assistant teachers), and four in the middle school (teachers of German, English, Mathematics, Music, Geography, Arts and a subject called 'Social Education').

Ethnographic tools and perspectives were used in this study to gain rich insights into the teachers' contexts and practices, with the researcher being immersed in the natural setting of schools for six months. The project was driven by a desire to test out the ground for implementing translanguaging pedagogies in schools, capturing teachers' voices and experiences in this process and gaining a sense of how teacher education can better prepare teachers for meeting the needs of their diverse and multilingual students. Ethnographic tools that were used for data collection included fieldnotes, observations and interviews.

Along with ethnography, the project was inspired by transformative action research, as described by García and Kleyn (2016a), to explore when and why translanguaging is taken up or resisted by teachers. Such research is done in collaboration *with* teachers (as opposed to *on* them) to explore the wider social structures that shape and constrain pedagogical practice and educational change. Like action research, the focus is to transform teaching itself, not just describe it, through a symbiotic process of teaching, learning and researching (García & Kleyn, 2016a: 49). Ideally, such research is collaborative and participatory, with researchers acting as practitioners and vice versa (although, because of teachers' time constraints, this project did not include practitioners as researchers). Lessons can be co-taught and are always co-designed with teachers and researchers (García & Kleyn, 2016a: 34). The transformative action research approach aimed for in the collaboration is situated in real educational contexts and tests out interventions in partnerships between researchers and teachers (Cobb *et al.*, 2003; Duarte & Günther-van der Meij, 2018). In this approach, visualized in Figure 4.1, the focus of research is shaped by teachers' **questions** and the perceived challenges they face in their classrooms and schools (step 1). The research then **explores** existing research to seek evidence-based solutions to the questions or problems teachers face (step 2). Armed with this knowledge, researchers and teachers then **develop** pedagogical practices that could serve as solutions to whatever perceived challenges practitioners are facing (step 3). The teachers **try** out these developed practices in the classroom, either with or without the support and presence of the researcher (step 4). Afterwards, the teachers and researchers **discuss** the impact of the practice developed – what went well and what could have gone better (step 5). Following this, if needed, the researchers and teachers revise or re-develop these

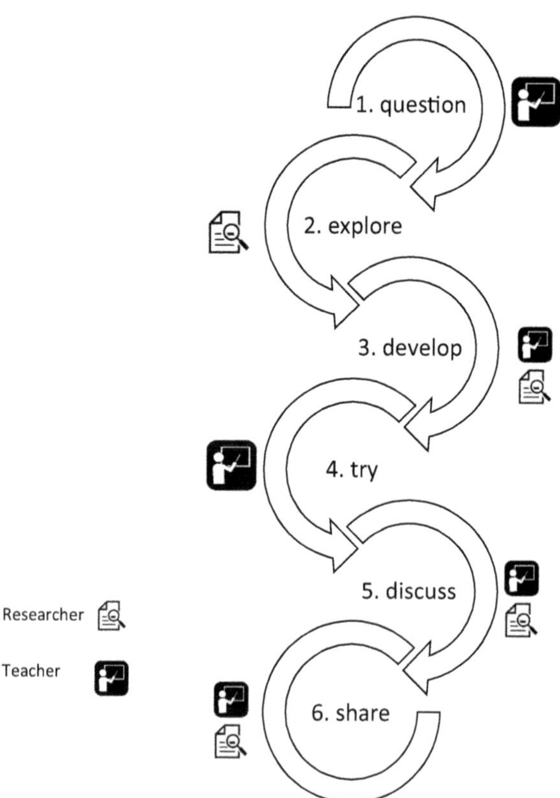

Figure 4.1 Transformative action research model

solutions, repeating steps 3, 4 and 5 as often as necessary. Finally, they **share** their outcomes with a wider audience (step 6).

This particular project consisted of introductory workshops, classroom observations and one-to-one discussion sessions and individual support with teachers, which also served as data collection events (Schwarzl, 2020). During these events, the researcher and teachers collaboratively developed activities that help to support positive practices and valuing of students' multilingual resources and identities (step 3). The teachers then tried out these activities in the classroom – sometimes with support of the researcher (step 4). After the activities were implemented, they were discussed in individual sessions if teachers desired (step 5). This approach followed the hypothesis that after this project, teachers would be able to design translanguaging-based lessons, they would have developed a translanguaging stance and they would have made some changes in their teaching as they applied translanguaging and could adapt it to their individual students' needs. However, the aspect of collaboration, highlighted in Tian and Shepard-Carey's (2020) conceptualization, could not be foregrounded as much as initially planned, as discussed further below.

School and Participant Selection

As explained above, the project involved seven in-service teachers, one of grade 4 primary school and one of grade 5 middle school in Vienna. In the primary school, one teacher covered all subjects (German, Mathematics, English, Science, Sports, Arts and Music), whereas in the middle school, there were seven teachers, covering the subjects (German, Mathematics, English, Biology, Geography, Arts, Social Sciences and Music). Convenience sampling was used to select schools for participation, with various head teachers in Viennese primary and lower secondary schools contacted via email. Primary and middle schools were chosen as a focus because they are comprehensive and more likely to reflect the linguistic and socioeconomic diversity that can be found in urban schools. The teachers' and head teachers' willingness and motivation to participate in the project were perceived as the most relevant condition for collaboration. An initial phone conversation followed when interest in the project was expressed. These phone conversations helped to plan the workshops held in both schools in late August 2017. In the following, we describe the researcher–teacher transformative action research collaboration that was designed as a project that implemented translanguaging pedagogies into daily teaching.

Ethical Considerations

A detailed project proposal for this project was approved by the Viennese Board of Education and permission to undertake the research was gained from the collaborating teachers, head teachers and parents of the children involved in their classes. All participants willingly volunteered for the project. Participation was treated in strict confidence, with the identities of teachers and schools involved being protected. Private conversations as well as more detailed descriptions of the teachers, the schools or the students involved were excluded from the analysis in order to guarantee anonymity.

Teacher Workshops: Diving into Translanguaging-Theory and Co-designing Materials

The teacher workshops served as a means to introduce the idea of translanguaging theory, to jointly explore what theory and empirical investigations have so far suggested as good practice, and to co-design materials. It aligns with the explore phase of the transformative research model (step 2 in Figure 4.1). The first workshop focused on developing a translanguaging stance and on possible ways of designing materials and lessons using translanguaging pedagogies. It presented the theory of translanguaging and examples of how teachers can integrate translanguaging into their regular teaching practice. Translanguaging activities were operationalized using Cenoz's (2017) definition of pedagogical translanguaging, i.e. translanguaging activities in the classrooms initiated by the teachers.

The implementation of translanguaging was not designed as a predefined intervention; instead, teachers were shown various ways to use translanguaging in their regular teaching practice. Teachers were not asked to follow a particular template or model, but were provided with suggestions for how to implement translanguaging into their daily practice. They were positioned as the experts for their classes and students and encouraged to adopt some of the various translanguaging approaches as needed. As teachers who design instruction based on translanguaging theory require appropriate multilingual resources (cf. García & Kleyn, 2016b: 22), teachers were provided with a collection of multilingual sources, including those in Celic and Seltzer (2011), as well as suggestions on how and in which classroom situations they could use them. In addition to *Trio*, mentioned above, other multilingual sources were provided to include additional languages. Multilingual song books and novels were obtained from (online) libraries. Suggestions for working multilingually were made, such as individual or cooperative reading, book projects, partner or group work in 'language groups' (different group compositions were recommended) or free choice of language when it comes to taking private notes or doing research. This stage of the collaboration aligns with the develop phase in the transformative action research model (step 3). Teachers were encouraged to promote oral use of family languages during their everyday teaching and to afford opportunities for students to use them.

Observations

Observations of translanguaging lessons were designed to support teachers' development of a translanguaging-stance while they were adapting their new knowledge into their practice. This aligns with the try phase of the transformative action research model (step 4). The observations also served as a means to explore the extent to which translanguaging designs, for example the implementation of collaborative and multilingual groupwork, was being implemented and adapted. Not only translanguaging lessons scheduled at a predefined date were observed, but also monolingual lessons as they 'normally' occurred. Each class was observed at least two times a week for a minimum of two to four hours a day, and in total approximately 130 hours were observed over six months. Moreover, observations were also made outside class, e.g. in the schoolyard and during breaks. The regular visits helped to establish a regular exchange of information between researcher and practitioners.

Individualized Support and Interviews

Another aspect of the project was individualized feedback and support offered to teachers through emails and one-to-one discussion sessions in which the classroom observations were discussed, which also served as the contexts for the interviews which were done with one teacher from each school who most intensively used translanguaging pedagogies in the classroom. This aligns with the **discuss** stage of the transformative action research model (step 5). Lessons were co-designed and discussed on an irregular basis (in accordance to the teachers' temporary availability) in one-to-one sessions before and/or after classroom observations. At least once or twice a month, the teachers sent their lesson plans, which helped the researcher to look for texts in different languages and think of possible ways to implement translanguaging into the topics the teachers wanted to focus on. This selection of materials and methods was then given to the teachers and sometimes discussed collaboratively, but the teachers were given the opportunity to decide whether they felt the need to discuss or to receive feedback on their selections. The interviews provided insight into how the teachers' perceived the implementation of translanguaging into their teaching practice. These discussions and interviews were documented in fieldnotes. Excerpts from these discussions are provided below, in both the German original and with an English translation.

Data Analysis

The fieldnotes and the transcriptions of the interviews were analyzed using content analysis by following Kuckartz (2018). Using this framework, the transcribed fieldnotes were first divided into interpretations and reflections, comments and observed actions. In a second step, the data from the field-observations were organized into co-stances, co-designs and co-shifts. Similarly, the interviews were transcribed in order to inductively categorize them into dominant themes. Passages, showing co-stances, co-designs and co-shifts were marked in the transcripts as well. Intensive reading led to several changes of categories from both the fieldnotes and the interviews, finally leading to the establishment of dominant themes that enabled the researcher to come up with hypotheses presented in the following sections.

Findings

In the following, we present some of the findings from this project by first reporting on some of the ways that translanguaging practices were noted with regard to co-designing translanguaging lessons and the development of co-stances and co-shifts. We then explore some of the areas in which transformation was limited.

Implementing translanguaging pedagogies

With regard to the implementation of translanguaging pedagogies, teachers preferred multilingual resources or resources in different languages. Mainly, they used *Trio* (Schule mehrsprachig, 2021), a trilingual booklet with texts predominantly in BCS, Turkish and German, but also in other languages. Multilingual texts or texts in various languages were often read and discussed together in the primary school and in the Music and Sociology lessons at the middle school. The teachers tended to directly ask and encourage some students to read the texts aloud. In the primary school class, the contents dealt with in *Trio* were often not translated into German, even if not all students could always understand them. When using other materials or communicative activities, the practice of translation/mediation was observed as a reoccurring element of translanguaging practice. The students repeatedly asked the teacher for a translation, or they were asked by the teacher if they could translate words or text passages from different languages into German.

In the interview, the primary teacher noted that the children seemed to enjoy reading multilingual texts/texts in different languages. This prompted her to develop the practice of leaving *Trio* on the students' desks encouraging them to read the magazine when they were finished with an activity. Over time, the students took out their *Trio* and read it during breaks or if they finished an activity in advance as they got used to this practice. Many students even took their *Trio* booklets home for their siblings. The interviews with the teachers show that the integration of the multilingual materials presented to them at the workshop took time and energy, but as shown in the following example, the teacher had found that to be worthwhile:

> […] wenn man sich einmal damit befasst woher man Materialien bekommt, oder wie man das gut aufbereitet, kann man das immer wieder anwenden […].
>
> […] *once you look at where you get materials from, or how you prepare them well, you can use it again and again* […]. (Primary school teacher)

This teacher also recognized that once teachers have internalized the idea of translanguaging, the practice becomes second nature and does not require much preparation.

Same home language student groupings

With regard to the pedagogical strategies implemented, the Music and the Sociology teachers at middle school paired students so that those who were more proficient in German could help each other with their exercises or explain content to each other using their multilingual repertoire. There was a group of four students, for example, who almost only spoke Turkish with each other in Biology lessons as a strategy to explain technical terms to each other, as shown in this excerpt from the fieldnotes:

> Im Zuge dieser Beobachtung konzentriere ich mich besonders auf eine Gruppe türkischsprachiger SchülerInnen. Ich kann nicht Türkisch und daher nicht beurteilen, worüber sie tatsächlich sprechen. Einige Hinweise deuten aber darauf hin, dass sie sich in dieser Biologiestunde womöglich über Inhalte oder Begriffe unterhalten, die für sie auf Deutsch offenbar schwer verständlich sind. Eine Schülerin spricht mit ihrer Sitznachbarin auf Türkisch und zeigt dabei kurz an die Tafel. Die beiden SchülerInnen wirken, als würden sie über den Text auf der Tafel diskutieren, da rasch immer eine Schülerin nach der anderen das Wort ergreift. Der Begriff 'Zwerchfell' wird, während sie miteinander Türkisch sprechen, von einer Schülerin auf Deutsch benannt. Bevor die Schülerin den Begriff ausspricht, bewegt ihr Blick sich zur Tafel, an der der Begriff steht. (Schwarzl, 2020: 129)
>
> *In the course of this observation, I am particularly concentrating on a group of Turkish-speaking students. I cannot speak Turkish and therefore cannot judge what they are actually talking about. However, there are indications that in this biology lesson they were talking about content or terms that are obviously difficult for them to understand in German. A girl speaks to the person sitting next to her in Turkish and briefly points to the blackboard. The two pupils seem to be discussing the text on the blackboard, as one student after the other quickly takes the floor. The term 'diaphragm' is used in German by a student while they speak Turkish to each other. Before the student pronounces the term, her gaze moves to the blackboard on which the term is written.* (Schwarzl, 2020: 129)

This example also shows how this group of pupils uses their shared home-language as a meaning-making resource in their everyday learning. Moreover, it indicated that the students started to use shared home-languages even if the teachers did not explicitly instruct them to do so.

Transformations in stance and design – and their limits

There were variations in how the teachers created situations in which the students could use their multilingual repertoires, and pedagogical translanguaging was observed to be increasingly emergent in only some teachers' practices. The amount of translanguaging pedagogies implemented seemed to be related to – among other things – the level and subjects that teachers were teaching and the rapport that they had with their students.

Multilingual versus monolingual teaching

In the primary school, translanguaging pedagogies were readily integrated into everyday practice and regularly observed. However, in the middle school they were only observed in certain contexts, for example in lessons of lower-stakes subjects, such as Music, Arts and Social Sciences. In the middle school, the teachers of Biology, German, Geography and Mathematics (same teacher) stuck to monolingual teaching. In their opinion, introducing translanguaging pedagogy was 'not possible' in their subjects. The Biology and the Math and Geography teacher justified this statement by stating that the multilingual sources provided were 'not suitable' for their teaching, as shown in the following excerpt from the fieldnotes:

> Der Biologielehrer und die Lehrerin für Mathematik und Geografie führen als Begründung die Materialien an, die sie für ihren Unterricht als 'unpassend' beschreiben. Näher führen sie ihre Antwort nicht aus. (Schwarzl, 2020: 122)
>
> *The biology teacher and the math and geography teacher justify that the materials were 'unsuitable' for their subjects. But they do not offer greater details on this response.* (Schwarzl, 2020: 122)

It could thus be the case that at primary school, teachers may have more room to experiment because it is lower stakes, while in secondary school in the key subjects, experimentation with translanguaging pedagogies may seem too risky, as there is more pressure to get through the curriculum.

Not only did the implementation of translanguaging pedagogies relate to the subject being taught in middle school, but also to the teachers' relationships to their classes. The findings suggest that teachers need to have good rapport with their students and confidence to experiment. For example, although the German teacher expressed interest and openness towards translanguaging pedagogy, she did not veer at all from monolingual teaching throughout the collaboration. When the researcher met her in the hallway before an observation, she mentioned that she was scared of losing control of her classroom if she could not always understand what students were saying. The classroom observations revealed that at times this teacher seemed to feel uncomfortable and insecure while the researcher was observing her teaching and this factor might have contributed to her hesitation to implement new pedagogies. She also noted that she thought that the students 'would reject that anyway', as, in her view, the class was very demanding and difficult to motivate. This attitude seemed to indicate a rejection of the translanguaging stance, which meant that the teacher was not willing to experiment with new practices.

Because of mentioned German teacher's resistance to translanguaging pedagogies, the researcher planned a multilingual lesson for her and taught it in class while the teacher was observing. In this lesson, the students were presented with the fable 'The Lion and the Mouse' in German, BCS and Turkish and they could choose in which language they wanted to read it. The joint summary of the content and the interpretation of the fable was done in German. Afterwards, the students were asked to write down or to verbally list key terms, such as 'lion' or 'mouse' in other languages. Following the lesson, the researcher and teacher discussed the methods used and how the teacher could make use of them in her following lessons. While the teacher said that she enjoyed the lesson, this experience did not encourage her to experiment with translanguaging pedagogies. While no conclusions can be made about the long-term impact of this project on this teacher, she did not appear to make any movements in her stance or design during the course of the project.

Translanguaging as a resource

The teachers who developed aspects of a translanguaging stance and design, such as the Music teacher, were surprised at how positively the students reacted to the use of translanguaging:

> [...] also ich war auch überrascht wie gut die Schüler das hinbekommen haben, das hat mich wirklich selber sehr/sehr überrascht, wie begeistert die Schüler waren. Also dass es DERARTIG gut funktioniert, das hatt' ich auch nicht erwartet.
>
> *[...] So I was also surprised how well the students did this, that really surprised me very/very much, how enthusiastic the students were. So that it would work THIS well, I didn't expect that either.* (Music teacher)

The primary school teacher also showed in one of her interviews that the use of translanguaging pedagogies can validate students' multilingual identities:

> Mhm ich glaub, die Kind:er, ähm fühlen sich vielmehr wertgeschätzt, wenn man ihre eigenen Muttersprachen immer wieder einbaut [...]
>
> *Uh, I think the children: uh, feel more valued if you integrate their mother tongues again and again [...].* (Primary school teacher)

She later noted that translanguaging pedagogies can also support the integration of all students at school and to foster them to accept and value each other – and themselves – more.

> Ich glaub, das hilft sehr viel auch für/für dieses Angenommenwerden von den Kindern, also • • dass sie sich gegenseitig auch annehmen. Und auch zu ihrer eigenen, weiß nicht, Persönlichkeit, • gehört die Sprache natürlich genauso dazu und/und, dass sie sich selbst irgendwie • • [((lachend)) wertschätzen quasi], oder selbst/selbst annehmen.
>
> *I think that helps a lot for / for the kids to feel accepted, so • • that they also accept each other. And also for their own, I don't know, personality, • the language is of course just as much a part of it and/and that they somehow • • [(laughing)] appreciate themselves, so to speak], or accept themselves themselves.* (Primary school teacher)

This teacher reflected in a discussion that she had internalized translanguaging pedagogies to a certain extent, commenting that at times it comes naturally and spontaneously to her:

> Es ist einfach, es kommt dann oft spontan, dass man halt einmal sagt, wer kann mir diese Frage oder in Mathematik dann halt dieses Textbeispiel auf• • die Sprache [((lachend)) übersetzen] und ähm, eigentlich ist das überhaupt keine Vorbereitung.
>
> *It is easy, it often happens spontaneously, that you just say, who can give me this question or in Mathematics then stop this text example • translate the language [((laughing))] and um, actually that's it at all no preparation.* (Primary school teacher)

However, this sense of translanguaging coming naturally to her also meant that she did not tend to systematically and strategically plan the integration of translanguaging pedagogies into her lessons, which limited the transformative potential of her practices.

The project revealed areas in which sustainable support is needed with regard to implementing translanguaging pedagogies. For example, in the interviews, the teachers commented that it took time for the students to get used to translanguaging pedagogy:

> [...] und die Kinder mussten sich erst dran gewöhnen, weil meine Vorgängerin das halt nicht betrieben hat und dadurch haben sie sich umstellen müssen.
>
> *[...] and the children had to get used to it, because the teacher who taught this class last year, before I came, did not do this, so they had to adapt.* (Primary school teacher)

In sum, the findings of this study indicate a certain development of translanguaging co-stances, co-designs and co-shifts throughout collaboration. Positive developments were observed in some cases with regard to teachers' practices, particularly with regard to the use of multilingual resources and the implementation of some translanguaging pedagogies, such as fostering group work in which students could work in same language groups. Although the small nature of this project's design limits the representativeness of the conclusions that can be drawn from it, the transformative potential of the project seemed to be influenced by (1) the level of education, the type of school and the subject that the teacher taught, with teachers being more prone to experiment at lower levels of schooling and in non-obligatory subjects and (2) the relationship and level of trust that the teacher had with her students.

Implications for Further Research and Practice

This project was developed as a small-scale teacher-researcher collaboration in which the researcher intended to explore with teachers the possibilities for implementation of translanguaging pedagogies in Viennese schools. Such collaborations are needed to provide teachers with the opportunity to formulate, share and develop their practical knowledge. But it is clear that a project of this nature – which relies on the resources of one researcher and where a small selection of teachers is working mostly on their own initiative with only limited institutional support – can only have limited transformative potential. Individual projects like the one presented here provide insights into where quick successes in changing practice can occur, as well as into where there are limits to the transformative potential of implementing translanguaging pedagogies.

One key take-away from this study was that translanguaging pedagogies may be easier to implement in particular grades and/or subjects. The findings suggest that translanguaging pedagogies might be best first integrated in lower grades and non-obligatory subjects so that teachers have more space and confidence for experimentation. Once they experience success in implementing translanguaging pedagogies and develop their stance and practices – with all stakeholders in education experiencing their benefits – it might then be easier to extend multilingual practice across the curriculum.

In this project, one of the obstacles was that a number of the teachers remained skeptical about the regular use of translanguaging pedagogies due to insecurity, concerns about losing control and the need to set limits (see also Schwarzl *et al.*, 2019). The study also suggests that particular considerations may need to be made for teachers who have low confidence and/or are worried about disciplinary issues in their classroom and losing control, as these will be likely to add further obstacles to implementing translanguaging pedagogies. The vision and principles outlined by García and Kleyn (2016a: 45) of supporting a multilingual ecology for the whole school and working with teachers who are open to taking risks and trying out different approaches seems to be crucial to the success of such initiatives.

Moreover, in this project, the teachers in the collaboration seemed to only develop limited translanguaging stances and designs. This is not surprising, given that studies have shown that the incorporating of translanguaging pedagogies must be accompanied by an overall school and classroom ecology that is supportive of multilingual students (Kleyn & García, 2019: 75). Moreover, the current language-in-education policy and pre-service teacher education in Austria strongly promote the use and fostering of German only (Braunsteiner *et al.*, 2018). The project therefore suggests that more long-term, holistic and systemic collaborations are needed to overcome teachers' concerns and negative beliefs. While this small-scale collaboration may not have been able to achieve this aim, it allowed us to envision how larger scale teacher-researcher collaborations might be developed following a transformational action research strategy, at a larger scale.

First of all, translanguaging pedagogies need to be more strongly integrated into pre-service teacher education initiatives across Austria. Secondly, such pedagogies need to be sustained into in-service teacher education. Such collaborations would gain more traction if they more strongly align to the transformational action research design, which was presented in Figure 4.1. Ideally in such projects, teachers would be supported to participate and would be more agentive, formulating their own agendas and questions for exploration (step 1). This would help to ensure their sustained participation and willingness to experiment with their practice. A further improvement on such collaborations would be the inclusion of pre-service teachers in such collaborations, as shown in Figure 4.2. The pre-service teachers could be involved in the exploration of evidence to underline pedagogies and resources (step 2), the development of materials (step 3) and the discussions about implementation (step 5). In some cases, the pre-service teachers could also be involved in trying out the new practices and materials (step 4), if the situation allowed for it.

Finally, in an ideal model of transformative action research, collaborations would, if possible, include videoing of teachers' classroom practice (which was not possible during this project due to restrictions from the local Board of Education). Such videos could then serve as prompts for researcher-teacher interviews and later be available for analysis in pre- and in-service teacher education programs. In addition, the possibility for teachers to further develop and share the activities and materials that they developed could be enhanced by the inclusion of pre-service teachers (step 6).

Concluding Remarks

In sum, this collaborative project in which translanguaging pedagogies were implemented and researched in a small number of schools in Vienna could achieve some transformations in teachers' stances and

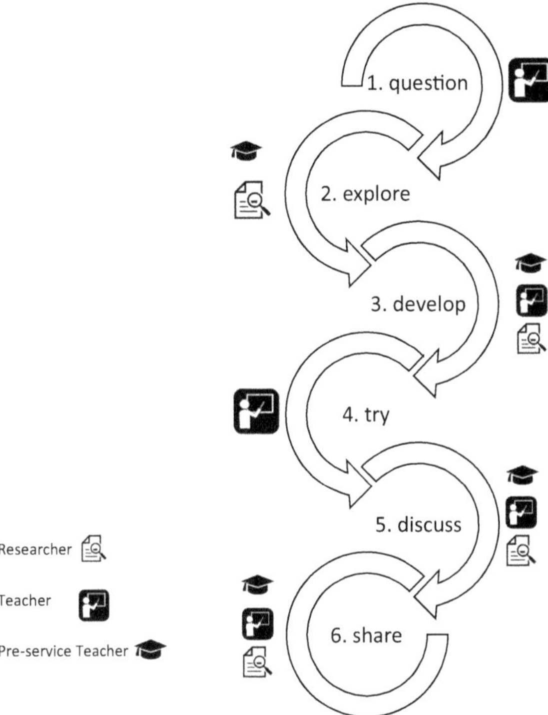

Figure 4.2 Erling's transformative action research model

designs. While in some cases skepticism towards translanguaging pedagogies could be transformed, in others, there was an outright rejection of multilingual teaching. Introducing translanguaging pedagogies in super-diverse schools in settings where there is a highly controversial view on multilingual teaching represents a strong challenge for individual projects such as the one reported on in this chapter. Transformative action research networks following the model described in this paper, and shown in Figure 4.2, could provide a holistic approach which is needed to build bridges between universities, teacher education colleges and schools. This model requires the involvement of researchers, teachers and pre-service teachers to build supportive networks of peers and to guarantee possibilities to innovate and transform, fostering a climate that is supportive and collaborative, and empowering the next generation for teaching in our diverse, multilingual societies.

Acknowledgements

A deep *thank you* to the participants of this study and to Eva Vetter, who served as a supervisor for the dissertation project the chapter was based on.

Note

(1) We refer to those who indicated that they use other languages in addition to German at home and on a regular basis as having German as an additional language (GAL).

References

Baysu, G. and De Valk, H. (2012) Navigating the school system in Sweden, Belgium, Austria and Germany: School segregation and second generation school trajectories. *Ethnicities* 12 (6), 776–799.

Braunsteiner, M., Fischer, C., Kernbichler G., Prengel, A. and Wohlhart D. (2018) Beitrag 1: Erfolgreich lernen und unterrichten in Klassen mit hoher Heterogenität. In S. Breit, F. Eder, K. Krainer, C. Schreiner, A. Seel and C. Spiel (eds) *Nationaler Bildungsbericht Österreich: Fokussierte Analysen und Zukunftsperspektiven für das Bildungswesen* (Band 2) (pp. 19–62). Bundesministerium für Bildung, Wissenschaft und Forschung, Bundesinstitut Bifie.

Celic, C. and Seltzer, K. (2011) *Translanguaging: A CUNY-NYSIEB Guide for Educators*. The Graduate Center, The City University of New York: CUNY-NYSIEB. http://www.nysieb.ws.gc.cuny.edu/files/2012/06/FINAL-Translanguaging-Guide-With-Cover-1.pdf

Cenoz, J. (2017) *Translanguaging in School Contexts: International Perspectives*. New York: Routledge.

Cobb, P., Confrey, J., Disessa, A., Lehrer, R. and Schauble, L. (2003) Design experiments in educational research. *Educational Researcher* 32 (1), 9–13. https://doi.org/10.3102/0013189X032001009

Conteh, J. and Meier, G. (eds) (2014) *The Multilingual Turn in Languages Education: Opportunities and Challenges*. Bristol: Multilingual Matters.

De Angelis, G. (2011) Teachers' beliefs about the role of prior language knowledge in learning and how these influence teaching practices. *International Journal of Multilingualism* 8 (3), 216–234. https://doi.org/10.1080/14790718.2011.560669

Dooly, M. and Vallejo, C. (2020) Bringing plurilingualism into teaching practice: A quixotic quest? *International Journal of Bilingual Education and Bilingualism* 23 (1), 81–97. https://doi.org/10.1080/13670050.2019.1598933

Duarte, J. and Gogolin, I. (2013) *Linguistic Superdiversity in Urban Areas*. Amsterdam: John Benjamins.

Duarte, J. and Günther-van der Meij, M. (2018) A holistic model for multilingualism in education. *EuroAmerican Journal of Applied Linguistics and Languages* 5 (2), 24–43.

Erkurt, M. (2020) *Generation Haram: Warum Schule lernen muss, allen eine Stimme zu geben*. Wien: Zsolnay.

Erling, E.J., and Moore, E. (2021) Socially just plurilingual education in europe: shifting subjectivities and practices through research and action. *The International Journal of Multilingualism* 18 (4), 523–533. https://doi.org/10.1080/14790718.2021.1913171

Erling, E.J., Foltz, A. and Wiener, M. (2021) Differences in English teachers' beliefs and practices and inequity in Austrian English language education: Could plurilingual pedagogies help close the gap? *The International Journal of Multilingualism* 18 (4), 570–585. https://doi.org/10.1080/14790718.2021.1913170

Erling, E.J., Radinger, S. and Foltz, A. (2020) Understanding low outcomes in English language education in Austrian middle schools: The role of teachers' beliefs and practices. *Journal of Multilingual and Multicultural Development*. https://doi.org/10.1080/01434632.2020.1829630

García, O., Johnson, S.I. and Seltzer, K. (2017) *The Translanguaging Classroom: Leveraging Student Bilingualism for Learning*. Philadelphia: Caslon.

García, O. and Kleyn, T. (2016a) A translanguaging educational project. In O. García and T. Kleyn (eds) *Translanguaging with Multilingual Students* (pp. 34–54). New York: Routledge.

García, O. and Kleyn, T. (2016b) Translanguaging theory in education. In O. García and T. Kleyn (eds) *Translanguaging with Multilingual Students* (pp. 9–33). New York: Routledge.

García, O. and Sylvan, C. (2011) Pedagogies and practices in multilingual classrooms: singularities in pluralities. *The Modern Language Journal* 95 (3) 385–400. https://doi.org/10.1111/j.1540-4781.2011.01208.x

García, O. and Li, W. (2013) *Translanguaging: Language, Bilingualism and Education* (pp. 366–369). Basingstoke: Palgrave. https://doi.org/10.1057/9781137385765

Hanushek, E. and Wößmann, L. (2006) Does educational tracking affect performance and inequality? Differences-in-differences evidence across countries. *The Economic Journal* 116, 63–76.

Haukås, Å. (2016) Teachers' beliefs about multilingualism and a multilingual pedagogical approach. *International Journal of Multilingualism* 13 (1), 1–18. https://doi.org/10.1080/14790718.2015.1041960

Herzog-Punzenberger, B. (2017) *Migration und Mehrsprachigkeit – Wie fit sind wir für die Vielfalt?* Wien: Arbeiterkammer Wien.

Herzog-Punzenberger, B. and Schnell, P. (2019) Austria: Equity research between family background, educational system and language policies. In P. Stevens and A. Dworkin (eds) *The Palgrave Handbook of Race and Ethnic Inequalities in Education* (pp. 70–105). Basingstoke: Palgrave.

Jessner, U. and Mayr-Keiler, K. (2017) Why context matters: Social inclusion and multilingualism in an Austrian school setting. *Social Inclusion* 5 (4), 87–97. https://doi.org/10.17645/si.v5i4.1139

Kleyn, T. and García, O. (2019) Translanguaging as an act of transformation restructuring teaching and learning for emergent bilingual students. In L.C. De Oliveira (ed.) *The Handbook of TESOL in K-12* (pp. 69–82). Chichester: John Wiley & Sons.

Krumm, H. and Reich, H. (2011) Curriculum Mehrsprachigkeit. oesz.at/download/cm/CurriculumMehrsprachigkeit2011.pdf

Kuckartz, U. (2018) *Qualitative Inhaltsanalyse: Methoden, Praxis, Computerunterstützung.* Basel: Beltz Juventa.

Lau, S. and Van Viegen, S. (2020) *Plurilingual Pedagogies: Critical and Creative Endeavors for Equitable Language in Education.* Berlin: Springer.

Maaz, K., Trautwein, U., Lüdtke, O. and Baumert, J. (2008) Educational transitions and differential learning environments: How explicit between-school tracking contributes to social inequality in educational outcomes. *Child Development Perspectives* 2 (2), 99–106.

Mayrhofer, L., Oberwimmer, K., Toferer, B., Neubacher, M., Freunberger, R., Vogtenhuber, S. and Baumegger, D. (2018) Indikatoren C: Prozesse des Schulsystems. In K. Oberwimmer, S. Vogtenhuber, L. Lassnigg and C. Schreiner (eds) *Nationaler Bildungsbericht Österreich: Das Schulsystem im Spiegel von Daten und Indikatoren* (Band 1) (pp. 123–190).

Purkarthofer, J. (2016) Begriffe von Mehrsprachigkeit. Sprachliche Bildung von PädagogInnen vom Kindergarten bis zur Erwachsenenbildung. https://wien.arbeiterkammer.at/service/studien/Bildung/Begriffe_von_Mehrsprachigkeit.html

Rindler Schjerve, R. (2003) *Diglossia and Power: Language Policies and Practice in the 19th Century Habsburg Empire.* Berlin: Mouton De Gruyter.

Schreiner, C., Suchań, B. and Salchegger, S. (2020) Monitoring student achievement in austria: implementation, results and political reactions. In H. Harju-Luukkainen, N. McElvany and J. Stang (eds) *Monitoring Student Achievement in the 21st Century* (pp. 65–77). Heidelberg: Springer.

Schwarzl, L. (2020) Ein mehrperspektivischer Einblick in das Translanguaging-Klassenzimmer – selbstbezogene Überzeugungen und Klassenklima im Fokus. Unpublished Dissertation Thesis. University of Vienna. http://othes.univie.ac.at/63977/

Schule mehrsprachig (2021) https://www.schule-mehrsprachig.at/trio/trio-im-unterricht

Statistik Austria (2019/2020) https://www.statistik.at/web_de/statistiken/

menschen_und_gesellschaft/bildung_und_kultur/formales_bildungswesen/schulen_schulbesuch/index.html

Tian, Z. and Shepard-Carey, L. (2020) (Re)imagining the future of translanguaging pedagogies in TESOL through teacher-researcher collaboration. *TESOL Quarterly* 54 (4), 1131–1143. https://doi.org/10.1002/tesq.614

Verbund Nord-Ost (2017) https://www.lehramt-ost.at/en/

Verbund Süd-Ost (2016) https://zentrum-paedagoginnenbildung.uni-graz.at/de/kooperationen/entwicklungsverbund-sued-ost/

Vetter, E. and Janík, M. (2019) Menschenrechte versus Effizienz? Spannungsfelder der Schulsprachenpolitik. In P. Herdina, E. Allgäuer-Hackl and E. Malzer-Papp (eds) *Mehrsprachensensibel?: Monolinguale Sprachenpolitik trifft auf mehrsprachige Praxis / Multilingual Sensibility?: Monolingual Policies meet Multilingual Practice* (pp. 125–138). Innsbruck: Innsbruck University Press

5 'Because We Are Bilingual': Transcending Binaries in Two-Way Immersion through Collaborative Bilingual Identity Texts

Laura Hamman-Ortiz

Introduction

In the United States, there are a growing number of dual language programs, bilingual education models that provide content and literacy instruction in two or more languages. One popular dual language program is two-way immersion (TWI), a model that purposefully integrates two groups of students[1] – majority and minoritized language users – to support the bilingual development of all students. Within such learning contexts, the languages of instruction are typically kept separate, allocated to distinct content areas, teachers, or times to ensure that students will 'fully' develop both instructional languages (Howard *et al.*, 2018). However, a growing body of scholarship has called for the loosening of boundaries between languages in TWI and other bilingual program models (e.g. Hamman-Ortiz, 2019; Mortimer, 2018; Palmer *et al.*, 2014; Przymus, 2016), arguing that this approach to language learning falsely presents bilingualism as double monolingualism (Heller, 1999), is rooted in racialized and deficit-framed perspectives of the language practices of minoritized language speakers (Flores & Rosa, 2015), and can limit students' opportunities for learning (Cummins, 2014).

Many of those opposed to strict language separation have proposed, instead, that teachers adopt translanguaging pedagogies (García *et al.*, 2017; Sánchez *et al.*, 2018), which are classroom practices that enable students to draw upon their full linguistic repertoire for learning. Researchers have begun to explore how translanguaging can be cultivated in TWI contexts (e.g. Bauer *et al.*, 2017; García-Mateus & Palmer, 2017; Palmer *et al.*, 2014; Somerville & Faltis, 2019), but there are still concerns that the creation of flexible languaging spaces in contexts where the two instructional languages do not hold equal status might reinforce the dominance of the majority language (Ballinger *et al.*, 2017; Cenoz & Gorter, 2017; Fortune & Tedick, 2019; Guerrero, 2021). While this is a valid concern, given the overwhelming evidence of the dynamic nature of bilingualism (Martínez *et al.*, 2017; Sayer, 2013) and the documented benefits of translanguaging as a support for student learning (Cenoz *et al.*, 2021; Garza & Arreguín-Anderson, 2018; Gort & Sembiante, 2015; Martin-Beltrán, 2014; Poza, 2018), it is incumbent upon bilingual educators and researchers to consider how translanguaging pedagogies might be strategically employed in TWI contexts.

To date, there have been few studies exploring how teacher–researcher collaborations can support the design and implementation of translanguaging pedagogies in bilingual classrooms, although there are increasing calls for research embracing such collaborations (Tian & Shepard-Carey, 2020) and compelling evidence of the efficacy of these approaches to inquiry (e.g. David *et al.*, 2019; Galante *et al.*, 2019). This chapter seeks to address this gap by reporting on a teacher–researcher collaboration that explored how translanguaging practices could be fostered within a TWI program that embraced strict language separation. The collaboration centered on the design and implementation of a bilingual identity text project, in which students collectively composed a bilingual book to represent their bilingual learning experiences. For the purposes of this chapter, I explore the evolution of the teacher–researcher collaboration, describing the co-design decisions and co-stances that emerged through our joint inquiry and highlighting the ways that these shifted over time. While not the focus of this chapter, my analysis of translanguaging design and stance also reveals some of the ways that translanguaging pedagogies supported student learning and validated students' ethnolinguistic identities. The chapter concludes with a discussion of three core principles of productive teacher–researcher collaboration to inform future research on designing translanguaging spaces.

Conceptual Framework and Literature Review

Framing translanguaging as theory and pedagogy

In recent years, translanguaging has become an influential construct for understanding the nature of bilingualism and bilingual learning. Translanguaging is a sociocognitive theory that rejects a monoglossic perspective on bilingualism (i.e. as double monolingualism) and, instead, embraces a dynamic understanding of bilingualism that is centered on the diverse ways that individuals develop and leverage their communicative repertoires (García, 2009; García & Li, 2014). Translanguaging, thus, is both a theory of the bilingual mind and bilingual practice. As a theory of the mind, translanguaging posits that bilinguals do not have two distinct language systems; rather, the inner linguistic system (or idiolect) is a holistic repertoire containing a range of communicative resources that can be employed strategically for different contexts and audiences (Otheguy *et al.*, 2015). As a theory of practice, translanguaging refers to the authentic and dynamic ways that bilingual people communicate, the '*multiple discursive practices* in which bilinguals engage in order to *make sense of their bilingual worlds*' (García, 2009: 45, emphasis in original). A substantive body of scholarship has demonstrated that translanguaging is an everyday practice for negotiating meaning, both within bilingual communities (Orellana, 2010; Zentella, 1995) and in classrooms with bi/multilingual students (Creese & Blackledge, 2010; Daniel & Pacheco, 2015; García *et al.*, 2011; Henderson & Ingram, 2018; Seltzer, 2019; Pontier & Gort, 2016).

While scholars generally acknowledge the value of translanguaging theory, there exists tension when applying translanguaging to pedagogy, especially within bilingual/immersion programs. Some contend that minoritized languages need a safe space to thrive – to be 'protected' from the majority language – and that translanguaging in these contexts can ultimately subvert programmatic goals (Ballinger *et al.*, 2017; Cenoz & Gorter, 2017). Others argue that the challenge of combating the majority language does not justify the misrepresentation of bilingualism or the reinforcement of spaces that limit students' ability to draw upon their full linguistic repertoires for learning (Cummins, 2014; de Jong, 2016). In an earlier study of a TWI classroom (Hamman, 2018), I documented this tension in practice, revealing both the potential for classroom translanguaging to support student learning and the unequal ways that majority and minoritized language speakers translanguaged during instruction. Specifically, I found that English-dominant students were more apt to draw upon their L1 during Spanish instructional time than the reverse (see Palmer, 2009 for similar findings). This evidence suggests that translanguaging pedagogy requires strategic, context-focused planning to meet its goal of 'ensuring that bilingual students, especially those who come from language minority groups, are instructed and assessed in ways that provide them with equal educational opportunities' (García *et al.*, 2017: ix).

To reconcile the tension between translanguaging theory and practice in bilingual classrooms, Sánchez and colleagues (2018) have proposed a 'both/and' perspective, proposing a *translanguaging allocation policy*, which contends that translanguaging spaces can exist alongside focused language spaces. Relatedly, García and Lin (2017) assert that, in bilingual programs, both 'strong' and 'weak' perspectives on translanguaging must co-exist, the strong view positing that 'bilingual people do not speak languages but rather, use their repertoire of linguistic features selectively', whereas the weak view 'supports national and state language boundaries and yet calls for softening these boundaries' (2017: 126). Bilingual programs, they argue, must combine these weak and strong versions of translanguaging theory, acknowledging the real and material consequences of named languages while also 'conced[ing] that the lexical and structural features that make up a bilingual student's repertoire are valid and need to be leveraged and used.' In line with these perspectives, I have called for the design of *critical translanguaging spaces* (Hamman, 2018), which are learning environments that strategically cultivate opportunities for flexible languaging while also recognizing the importance of maintaining focused spaces for the minoritized language. This conceptual lens attends to the situated sociolinguistic reality of different language learning contexts, recognizing that there is no 'one-size-fits-all' approach to translanguaging pedagogical design. The study presented in this chapter was informed by the conceptual framing of a critical translanguaging space and seeks to provide empirical evidence for what have largely been theoretical propositions for how translanguaging pedagogies might be strategically incorporated into bilingual/immersion programs.

Identity texts

To design a space for translanguaging in TWI, this study drew upon Cummins' (2001, 2006) concept of *identity text*. Identity texts are literacy projects aimed at affirming culturally and linguistically diverse students by engaging students in composing multilingual and multimodal texts that reflect their lived experiences and their full linguistic repertoires. In this way, identity texts reframe the monolingual habitus (Gogolin, 1994, 2002) present in most schools by broadening narrow understandings of literacy as print-based and dominant-language-focused. One of the first identity text projects was the *Dual Language Showcase* (Chow & Cummins, 2003; Schecter & Cummins, 2003), a teacher–researcher collaboration across two diverse elementary schools near Toronto that explored how to design literacy activities that incorporated students' home languages. The success of this project has contributed to a range of identity texts projects in Canada and around the world (see Cummins & Early, 2011 for case studies). While identity text research predates the widespread usage of the term translanguaging (Cummins, 2019), I understand these multilingual and identity-affirming projects as in alignment with the central goals of translanguaging theory and pedagogy.

Traditionally, identity text research has been carried out with minoritized language speakers. However, in a '2.0' reimagination of identity texts, Prasad (2018) shows how identity text pedagogies can also lead to productive 'encounters' among students from majority and minoritized language backgrounds. In her study, Prasad designed Collaborative Multilingual

Identity Text Projects with two teachers in France, one teaching in a newcomer classroom that served (im)migrant students and the other in a mainstream classroom serving both majority language (French-speaking) students and students from linguistically diverse backgrounds. In both sites, she found that the identity text projects repositioned minoritized language learners as 'plurilingual experts' and helped foster language awareness and an appreciation for linguistic diversity among all students. Extending Prasad's work to Spanish/English TWI contexts, the focal classroom teacher and I designed a Collaborative Bilingual Identity Text (CBIT) project to promote flexible languaging among all students in the TWI classroom as they engaged in composing a bilingual text that reflected their collective experiences.

Research Design

The CBIT project was one component of a yearlong ethnographic case study of language practices, language ideologies and identity negotiation in a second grade TWI classroom. The original research question guiding the project was: How does a collaborative bilingual identity text project impact classroom languaging and identity negotiation in a TWI classroom? For this chapter, I revisited the data with a focus on the teacher–researcher collaboration. To guide my analysis, I drew from García *et al.*'s (2017) framing of the three essential components for teachers to take up a translanguaging pedagogy: (1) adopting a translanguaging *stance* (believing a student's full linguistic repertoire is central to their identity and a resource for learning), (2) engaging in translanguaging *design* (strategically integrating students' language practices into instruction and assessment), and (3) embracing translanguaging *shifts* (flexibly drawing upon students' home languages to support learning needs as they arise). Tian and Shepard-Carey (2020) have extended this framework to teacher–research collaborations, proposing that educators and researchers must negotiate translanguaging *co-stance*, *co-design* and *co-shifts*. In line with their emphasis on negotiated processes, I adapted their framework to explore the *co-stance shifts* and *co-design shifts* that occurred as a result of collaboratively engaging in translanguaging pedagogy.

Context of the Study

The study occurred during the 2016–2017 school year at Escuela El Bosque (all names of people and places are pseudonyms), a K-5 bilingual school located in a mid-sized city in the US Midwest. Escuela El Bosque implements a school-wide TWI program that follows a 90/10 model, in which kindergarten students receive 90% of their instruction in Spanish and 10% in English, with each subsequent grade receiving 10% more instructional time in English before reaching a 50/50 split by fourth grade.

At El Bosque, the student population was predominately Latinx (63%), with the remaining students identified as White (29%), Multiracial (4%), African American (3%) and Asian or Pacific Islander (1%). In the focal classroom, the student population was more heavily English-dominant than reflected in the broader school community, with 11 students identified as native English speakers (eight White, two African American and one Hmong American) and six students (all Latinx) identified as Spanish-dominant English learners.

The classroom teacher, Maestra Carmen, was a Latinx woman in her mid-fifties who had been teaching at El Bosque for over a decade and was widely recognized for her pedagogical expertise. Prior to the CBIT project, I had spent one day each week for five months as a participant observer in the classroom, which helped me gain an understanding of existing language practices and develop a relationship with the teacher and students. During these initial months, Maestra Carmen and I also regularly engaged in informal conversations around students' language use, which informed our design of the CBIT project (described in detail in the findings section).

Researcher positionality

As a White, elective bilingual, I am aware that my interpretations of the data were influenced by my own experiences, background and biases. I believe that my previous experiences as a second-grade teacher of emergent bilingual students in Texas and Chile and instructional coach for ESL/bilingual teachers in the district provided me with some 'insider' status within Maestra Carmen's classroom. At the same time, I recognize that my positionality as a White, English-dominant researcher may have limited what I could experience in the classroom and in this teacher–researcher partnership. My own experiences with language learning also differ from those of the study participants, as I learned Spanish as a foreign/world language in secondary and tertiary education settings, not as a young child in a bilingual classroom. I acknowledge the 'social situatedness of perceiving' (Erickson, 2006: 237), recognizing that my identity and experiences shape what I perceived as relevant data and how I approached data analysis. While I made every effort to triangulate my interpretations by drawing upon a range of data sources for analysis and through member checking, all interpretations are my own.

Data generation and analysis

I prefer the term data generation in place of data collection, following Graue and Walsh (1998) who emphasize that data are not neutrally 'collected' but, instead, are generated by the researcher, who ultimately determines what counts as data (e.g. what is recorded and why). With that lens, data generation from the CBIT project involved 15 video-recorded observations of whole class writing instruction (approximately one hour each), 40 audio recordings of students' small group discussions, instructional materials, student writing artifacts at varying stages of the project, and pre-/post-project interviews with the teacher and student dyads. Additionally, at each observation, field notes were taken and expanded upon afterwards with researcher memos.

Analysis of the full data corpus followed a general qualitative approach (Miles & Huberman, 2014; Saldaña, 2013), involving multiple rounds of inductive and deductive coding framed around my three areas of inquiry: classroom language practices, articulated or embodied language ideologies and identity negotiation/performance. For this chapter, I revisited the data with new research questions that centered on collaborative sense-making processes and design decisions, asking:

> *RQ 1: What decisions shaped the initial co-design of the CBIT project? How did the design shift during implementation?*
> *RQ 2: What translanguaging co-stances did the teacher and researcher hold at the beginning of the CBIT project? How did those stances shift as a result of engaging in the project?*

To respond to these questions, I reread all field notes and memos from the CBIT project and coded data that provided insight into the design of translanguaging pedagogies ('TLANG-design') and the ideological stances that the teacher or I assumed toward translanguaging ('TLANG-stance'). Through this process, researcher memos and teacher interviews emerged as the primary data sources, as commentary upon process and stance was frequently captured in these ongoing reflections and conversations. Coded excerpts were then organized into a data matrix to facilitate the analysis of shifts in design and stance over time. At this point, a second round of coding was conducted to identify specific features of translanguaging design and stance, which were grouped into five categories: relational factors, pedagogical considerations, language practices, beliefs about bilingualism and beliefs about bilingual learning (see Table 5.1 for the second-round codebook). Emerging themes were triangulated by returning to the larger data corpus (e.g. instructional materials, field notes and student audio recordings) to evaluate if these themes manifested in other data sources. The final themes are presented chronologically in the following section (pre/during/post-project), organized within the framework of co-stance and co-design and attending to relevant shifts in each.

Table 5.1 Second round codebook

TLANG-design	TLANG-stance
Code: Relational Factors • Subcode: Trust • Subcode: Curiosity • Subcode: Openness to learn • Subcode: Vulnerability • Subcode: Tension • Subcode: Reflection on practice	**Code: Beliefs about Bilingualism** • Subcode: Balanced bilingual • Subcode: Dynamic bilingual • Subcode: Language and equity • Subcode: Language and identity
Code: Pedagogical Considerations • Subcode: Language allocation • Subcode: Student grouping • Subcode: Curricular alignment • Subcode: Timing and organization • Subcode: Responsive teaching	**Code: Beliefs about Bilingual Learning** • Subcode: 'Fully immersed' • Subcode: Linguistic hegemony • Subcode: Meaning-based • Subcode: Practice-oriented
Code: Language Practices • Subcode: Protecting language spaces • Subcode: Expanding language spaces • Subcode: Bilingual languaging • Subcode: Languaging about bilingualism	

Findings

Pre-project stances

Translanguaging co-stance #1: Commitment to equity in bilingual education

One stance that Maestra Carmen and I shared at the outset of the project was a commitment to equity in bilingual education, a stance centered on meeting the needs of language minoritized students. However, our commitment to equitable bilingual classrooms manifested through differing stances toward translanguaging in TWI. As an early career scholar of language acquisition and learning, I was deeply engaged with the emerging translanguaging scholarship and eager to explore how flexible languaging spaces could validate the lived experiences of emergent bilingual children. While I recognized the potential challenges for translanguaging in TWI contexts, I was optimistic that translanguaging pedagogy would facilitate more authentic bilingual languaging in ways that positioned language minoritized students as experts.

Maestra Carmen, on the other hand, was apprehensive about translanguaging in TWI, concerned that creating flexible language spaces would lead to increased English use in a program already struggling to maintain focused Spanish spaces. She shared these concerns during our pre-project interview, emphasizing that TWI teachers must 'respect the break of the percentage,' referencing the designated time for each language (e.g. 90% Spanish, 10% English). She explained, 'If we allowed our students to, you know, use the other language when it's supposed to be in

Spanish, or in English, either way, if we allow them to break the rule, then they're not truly immersed.' Maestra Carmen lamented the lack of adherence to strict language separation in the upper elementary classrooms, which she felt was negatively impacting students' bilingual development:

> [In the early grades] we are really working, like, 'Use your Spanish. This is English time. This is Spanish time.' But when they move onto third grade, I think with all the testing...the teachers have just given up time. So they just let them...the teachers say, 'They're bilingual.' But they're not using the languages equally.

This reflection revealed that Maestra Carmen's commitment to language separation was not driven by blind adherence to programmatic dogma; on the contrary, her concern was rooted in a critical lens on language and equity, recognizing that students were 'not using the languages equally' (i.e. were using more English than Spanish). From this perspective, translanguaging in the TWI classroom might exacerbate the challenge of combating the hegemony of English, a fear that has been echoed in other studies of dual language teachers' views toward translanguaging (e.g. Martínez *et al.*, 2017). In sum, Maestra Carmen and I both approached classroom languaging from the stance of equity for language minoritized students but differed in our understanding of the role translanguaging should play in achieving that goal.

Translanguaging co-stance #2: Curiosity and openness to learn

While we held differing views toward translanguaging in TWI, both Maestra Carmen and I were curious about what we might learn from the project and open to changing our views accordingly. For my part, I recognized that Maestra Carmen had a wealth of experience as a veteran TWI teacher and that her concerns were rooted in many years of experiencing the challenge of maintaining Spanish languaging spaces. Maestra Carmen also acknowledged that the research around language separation was shifting and that it may be time to rethink how she structured language in her classroom. This shared stance of curiosity and openness emerged during our informal lunchtime conversations in the weeks leading up to the CBIT project. During one such discussion, Maestra Carmen asked me to share my observations from spending time in her classroom, leading to a shared reflection about the tension between fluid languaging for meaning and maintaining separate language spaces to prioritize the minoritized language:

> During lunch today, Maestra Carmen asked me to share what I have learned thus far from being in her class. I commented that I have come to see her classroom as a space where students are authentically engaging in Spanish. I also shared the tension I feel between content and language learning; that is, it is evident that most students cannot fully express their ideas in their L2, which seems to limit the extent to which they can engage

> with new content learning. Yet, due to the classroom's strict language polices, students are constantly practicing and developing their L2 in ways they might not otherwise if there were a more flexible language policy. In response, Maestra Carmen shared that the principal's daughter is in the third-grade classroom, which does not have as strict of a language allocation policy, and he has noted that his daughter's Spanish seems to be getting worse this year. We reflected together upon how there is no easy solution to this challenge, as it is valuable for students to be able to fully engage in conversations about new content learning, yet we recognize that students tend to not use as much Spanish if given the option to use whatever language they want to negotiate meaning. (Researcher Memo 10/9/16)

Through such conversations, Maestra Carmen and I established a joint stance of inquiry toward translanguaging pedagogy, one that acknowledged the complexity of translanguaging in TWI – and our differing beliefs about its role – while, at the same time, embracing an openness toward broadening or changing our perspectives.

Co-design and (co-)implementation: Strategic planning and shifts

Initial co-design

In November, Maestra Carmen and I started planning the translanguaging project, beginning with informal conversations about language use and extending to more formal design sessions. During these sessions, the boundaries of teacher and researcher began to blur, as we collectively engaged in co-design, strategizing ways to align the project with existing curriculum and standards and to draw upon students' full linguistic repertoires for learning. I proposed that students work in small groups to craft bilingual identity texts that represented their shared experiences, which led Maestra Carmen to recommend aligning the project with the overarching curricular theme, My Community. After some discussion, we decided to have students create a class text framed around students' experiences of their school community (i.e. What it is like to learn at a bilingual school?) using analogies (one of the language arts standards) to describe their attitudes toward and experiences of school. We allotted three weeks in February for the project, to be carried out during the daily hour-long writing block. The planned sequence of activities involved a series of teacher-led mini-lessons, each followed by opportunities for students to engage in small groups around the topic. Mini-lesson topics included (1) brainstorming school characteristics, (2) writing analogies, (3) adding details, (4) making revisions and (5) translating the text.

While Maestra Carmen and I easily agreed upon the focus and sequence for the project, it was more challenging to negotiate the languages of instruction and interaction. I was eager to embrace a flexible languaging space for the entirety of the project whereas Maestra Carmen was adamant about privileging Spanish, even as we made space for translanguaging. We settled upon maintaining Spanish for teacher-led instruction and for all initial group work and writing tasks (i.e. brainstorming, drafting, revising), both to prioritize the Spanish language (by having students write the text first in Spanish) and in recognition that the language arts block was typically time allocated to Spanish. Then, students would transition to a more fluid languaging space when they began translating their text, a task that inherently required students to draw upon their full linguistic repertoire. We also created linguistically heterogenous groups based on students' command of English or Spanish so that they could support one another as they translated the text. Thanks to grant funding, we were able to print copies of the book for all students, and we planned a 'book reveal' event for students to share the final product with their families.

Initial implementation

As the project commenced, Maestra Carmen and I returned to the traditional roles of researcher and teacher: I positioned myself in a corner of the classroom to observe, and she began teaching the first mini-lesson. As planned, Maestra Carmen began the project fully in Spanish, explaining to students that they would be collectively composing a bilingual book, working in small groups to draft and translate the text. To begin, Maestra Carmen led students through a discussion of the word 'rasgos' (traits). She drew a brainstorm web with a picture of their school in the center and asked students to consider the traits of their school using the prompt: '¿Cómo es Escuela El Bosque?' (What is Escuela El Bosque like?). She provided the example, 'Para mí, Escuela El Bosque es amor,' (To me, Escuela El Bosque is love) and asked students to share their ideas with a partner. Following Maestra Carmen's lead, students engaged in Spanish as they brainstormed ideas with their peers. After a few minutes, Maestra Carmen brought the class back together and asked students to share their ideas as she recorded them on the anchor chart. Once several characteristics had been shared (e.g. unido, seguro, divertido), Francisco proposed 'chilero,' a word that was unfamiliar to Maestra Carmen. After several turns to clarify the meaning, she gathered that it was a synonym for 'chido' (cool) and excitedly exclaimed:

> En Guatemala, chilero es como 'chido,' como 'cool.' 'Escuela El Bosque es chilero.' Sí y voy a escribirle abajo como chido, como cool. Wow, chilero. Niños, ya sabemos otra manera para decir 'que chido.' ¿Sí? Yo en México yo diría, 'Esta bien padre.' Bien padre, voy a escribirlo aquí.
>
> **English Gloss:** In Guatemala, chilero is like 'chido,' like 'cool.' 'Escuela El Bosque es chilero.' Yes, and I am going to write below, like chido, like cool. Wow, chilero. Boys and girls, now we know another way to say 'que chido.' Right? In Mexico, I would say, 'Esta bien padre.' Bien padre, I am going to write it here.

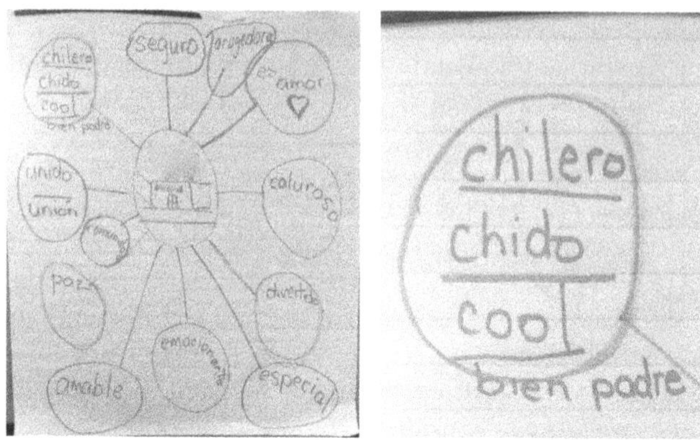

Figures 5.1(a) and 5.1(b): Characteristics of Escuela El Bosque brainstorm web

Through the affirmation of Francisco's suggestion and the addition of several related words in Spanish and English, Maestra Carmen took an important step toward broadening the languaging space of the classroom. This translanguaging shift (Sánchez *et al.*, 2017), or in-the-moment responsiveness to student languaging, not only brought English and Spanish together in the same written space (see Figures 5.1(a) and 5.1(b)) – which was not typical classroom practice – but also validated other varieties of Spanish, demonstrating to students that 'Spanish' was not a unitary entity.

Students then continued brainstorming ideas and drafting sentences in their small groups, initially engaging only in Spanish, although slowly beginning to translanguage to negotiate meaning, perhaps owing to the more fluid space that Maestra Carmen had just modeled. In one group, Tomás proposed 'te apoyan' to describe the supportive nature of the bilingual school, and then clarified the meaning to his peers in English.

	Original	**English gloss**
Tomás:	Te apoyan.	They support you.
Emma:	¿Que significa *estes?	What does that mean?
Matthew:	Como paz, amor...	Like peace, love...
Tomás:	They push you to start working. Like you learn more. That's what 'te apoyan' really means.	They push you to start working. Like you learn more. That's what 'te apoyan' really means.
Mia:	Te apoyan, sí.	They support you, yes.

In this exchange, it became clear to Tomás that his peers were unfamiliar with the Spanish verb 'apoyarse.' By drawing upon his full linguistic repertoire, Tomás was able to efficiently explain his idea to his peers, offering not a direct definition (i.e. to support someone) but the larger meaning he sought to convey.

As the group continued discussing, they began languaging more fluidly, sharing ideas in both languages, while still recording their ideas in Spanish. For example, Emma leveraged English to reference concepts learned in the recent unit on Martin Luther King Jr., which had been taught in English:

	Original	English gloss
Emma:	What's the opposite of segregation?	What's the opposite of segregation?
Mia:	Integration.	Integration.
Emma:	Write down integration.	Write down integration.
Tomás:	No, pero esto está en inglés.	No, but this is in English.
Matthew:	Es unido, es unido.	It's united, it's united.
Emma:	¡Unido! ¡Unido!	United! United!

By referencing a concept learned in English and working together to translate the idea into Spanish, students were engaging in meaningful learning *across* languages that might not have occurred under the classroom policy of language separation. Again, students did not arrive at a direct translation of an unfamiliar term but, instead, made a meaning-based cross-linguistic connection (integration/unido), which may have helped deepen their understanding of the concept.

Design shift 1: From Spanish only to bilingual languaging and languaging about bilingualism

Upon recognizing that students were drawing upon their full linguistic repertoire during group discussions – and that it seemed to be supporting their conversations – Maestra Carmen and I shifted our initial design to allow for (and encourage) translanguaging when students were collaborating. This change was made explicit to students, who began to more readily negotiate ideas across languages. For instance, after Maestra Carmen taught a mini-lesson on analogies (i.e. Escuela El Bosque es tan divertido como un partido de fútbol. / Escuela El Bosque is as fun as a soccer game.), the group discussions revealed that students were being more playful with language:

	Original	English gloss
Matthew:	Escuela El Bosque es paz como Jesus Christ.	Escuela El Bosque is peace like Jesus Christ.
Tomás:	Cheesy crust.	Cheesy crust.
Matthew:	(laughs)	(laughs)
Emma:	(laughing) Como cheesy crust.	(laughing) Like cheesy crust.

In this example, Matthew used English instead of Spanish to reference 'Jesus Christ' in his proposed analogy. In response, Tomás playfully noted how the words had sounded like 'cheesy crust,' which led to uproarious laughter from the group. Tomás was perhaps drawing attention to the fact that Matthew had shifted into English instead of using the Spanish name (Jesús Cristo) but, rather than call this out explicitly – or sanction him for breaking a language rule – he employed some lighthearted teasing to make a joke out of it, likely facilitated by the more flexible translanguaging policy that Maestra Carmen had implemented.

As the CBIT project transitioned to translation activities, Maestra Carmen realized that students needed more explicit modeling, which led to an additional softening of linguistic boundaries. In one of our planning meetings, she proposed using the bilingual children's book *¡Demasiadas peras! Too Many Pears!* (French & Whatley, 2009) as an exemplar to talk through the translation process. During the lesson that followed, Maestra Carmen explained to students that she was going to read both the English and Spanish text on each page so that they could consider the author's translation decisions. As she read, Maestra Carmen emphasized that exact translation was not always possible, which required the bilingual writer to choose the translation that they believed best fit the meaning of the sentence. This point was exemplified by a passage in which 'sirvió' (she served) was translated as 'there were.' Maestra Carmen read the page aloud, 'Sirvió peras marrones y peras verdes. There were brown pears and green pears,' and then modeled a metalinguistic think aloud:

> 'Sirvió.' Y el autor en ingles dijo, 'There were.' Y yo pienso, 'There were… había.' Sirvió…tal vez yo hubiera puesto, 'She served.' Pero el autor dijo, 'Para mí es mejor escribir 'There were brown pears.'' Vean cómo ustedes pueden negociar cómo se puede escuchar mejor en inglés.
>
> **English gloss:**
> 'Sirvió.' And the author said in English, 'There were.' And I think 'There were…había.' Sirvió…maybe I would have put, 'She served.' But the author said, 'For me it is better to write 'There were brown pears.'' See how you can negotiate how to make it sound better in English.

Through this example, Maestra Carmen demonstrated the agency of the bilingual writer in choosing the translation that best communicated their desired meaning, which revealed how translation is not an exact science but, rather, a subjective and creative activity. While Maestra Carmen maintained Spanish throughout this mini-lesson, she created a space for languaging about bilingualism that reframed the traditional presentation of bilingualism as double monolingualism, offering a more dynamic understanding of bilinguals as strategic communicators who draw upon their linguistic repertoire to creatively convey meaning to linguistically diverse audiences.

Design shift 2: From co-designers to co-teachers

Another shift that occurred during the CBIT project involved my role in the classroom. During one planning meeting, Maestra Carmen noted that students were still having difficulty translating their texts. After I proposed that she engage students in a contrastive analysis activity, Maestra Carmen asked if I would be willing to lead the mini-lesson so that she could observe what it looked like in practice. While students already referred to me as 'Maestra Laura,' I had not intended to become a participant in the study and was initially unsure if my involvement would somehow compromise the integrity of the study. However, upon reflection, I decided that, if I truly wanted to engage in collective inquiry, it made sense for me to also participate in the process of pedagogical experimentation.

Thus, I designed a contrastive analysis activity aimed at drawing students' attention to the comparative structures used in Spanish and English. I selected several examples of student sentences and created an anchor chart to explore language features used to compare (see Figure 5.2). After reading each example aloud – 'El Bosque es divertido como una fiesta. / El Bosque is fun like a party.' – I prompted students to identify the comparative words in Spanish and English, which led to the identification of forms such as 'es como' / 'is like' and 'es tan…como' / 'is as…as.' As students noted the comparative forms in each sentence, I recorded the structures in a separate column and outlined the words in red to draw attention to the similar forms across Spanish and English. While the activity was guided, students were able to identify all of the comparative forms in both languages, demonstrating their emerging cross-linguistic understandings.

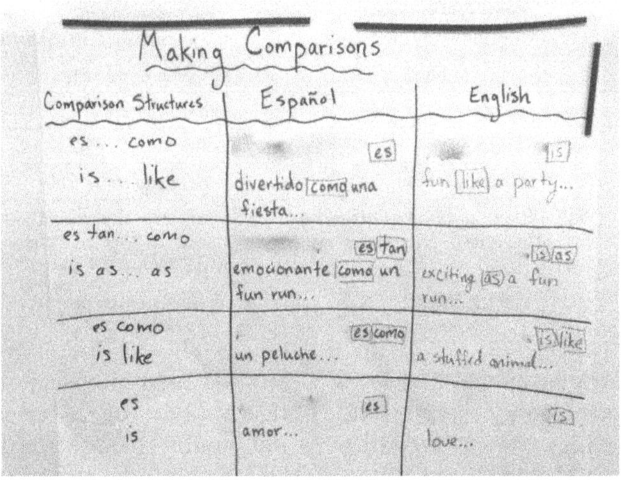

Figure 5.2 Contrastive analysis anchor chart

Once we had completed the chart, I led students through revising and translating their sentences. I selected one example and read it aloud: 'El Bosque es una comunidad porque no importa tu país de origen y no importa el color de tu piel.' As a class, we identified ways to be more precise with our language, which led to a discussion of the role of 'ni' (neither/nor) to replace the repeated phrase 'y no importa' (and it doesn't matter). Next, we translated the sentence into English, which facilitated a meaning-based discussion of languaging across Spanish and English, which Maestra Carmen also joined.

	Original	**English gloss**
LHO:	Ok, so let's start translating it. We have 'El Bosque is a community because it does not matter...' Would we say, 'it does not matter your country of origin'? Is that how we would say it in English? It sounds a little funny. It doesn't matter...what?	Ok, so let's start translating it. We have 'El Bosque is a community because it does not matter...' Would we say, 'it does not matter your country of origin'? Is that how we would say it in English? It sounds a little funny. It doesn't matter...what?
Tomás:	Your country of origin doesn't matter.	Your country of origin doesn't matter.
LHO:	So, we might switch it around and say, 'Your country of origin doesn't matter.' Is there another way we can say country of origin? Porque 'país de origin' is a pretty common phrase in Spanish, but I don't say 'country of origin' very often in English.	So, we might switch it around and say, 'Your country of origin doesn't matter.' Is there another way we can say country of origin? Because 'país de origin' is a pretty common phrase in Spanish, but I don't say 'country of origin' that often in English.
Emma:	What does that mean?	What does that mean?
LHO:	What <u>does</u> that mean?	What <u>does</u> that mean?
MC:	What is he trying to say there? What is he trying to say? Mi país de origen es México. ¿Qué estoy diciendo?	What is he trying to say there? What is he trying to say? My country of origin is Mexico. What am I saying?
Emma:	Oh, where you're born?	Oh, where you're born?
MC:	Where you are –	Where you are –
Tomás:	From.	From.
MC:	Where you come from.	Where you come from.
LHO:	Yeah! Does that sound a little more normal in English? 'Where you come from.'	Yeah! Does that sound a little more normal in English? 'Where you come from.'
Noah:	Yeah, it's a little better.	Yeah, it's a little better.

Through this exchange, Maestra Carmen and I not only supported students in learning the meaning of the phrase 'país de origin,' but also reinforced the idea that bilingualism is not double monolingualism. By pointing out that an exact translation might 'sound a little funny,' we highlighted the meaning-based ways that bilinguals negotiate understandings across languages, again modeling translation as a creative process (see Figure 5.3 for the final version of Noah's bilingual page in the class book).

Figure 5.3 Noah's page in the collaborative bilingual identity text

After the lesson, I shared with Maestra Carmen that I had gained a deeper understanding of the vulnerability that comes with being observed when trying something new. She laughed and told me the lesson had been great, although it was clear she appreciated my willingness to turn the lens (literally and figuratively) on my own pedagogy. While I had acknowledged from the start that I did not have all the answers for designing translanguaging pedagogy, the act of co-teaching helped me to actualize this stance and strengthened my relationship with Maestra Carmen throughout the remainder of the project.

Post-project stance

Co-stance #3: Bilingualism as dynamic and translanguaging as context-dependent

After the project, Maestra Carmen and I reflected together upon what we had learned. While Maestra Carmen maintained her belief in the importance of prioritizing Spanish, her perspective on translanguaging shifted dramatically toward a more dynamic stance on bilingualism. During our final interview, I asked Maestra Carmen what she believed contributed to a successful bilingual classroom, a question that had previously elicited her insistence upon language separation. During this conversation, however, Maestra Carmen proposed a much more flexible understanding of bilingual learning:

> LHO: What makes for a successful bilingual classroom?
>
> MC: Well, now that I have had the experience [of the bilingual book project], I think honoring bilingualism in the classroom, and that we have strengths in both languages. And it's okay to support one language with the other...Before I was all for separation of languages. This is how I've been working and surviving, you know, but...why? Why are we separating? And after what I saw this past year, it's just like, this is how it is, this is how it's supposed to be. You know, honoring and using, thinking, talking, writing. Because we are bilingual.

In posing the question, 'Why are we separating?' Maestra Carmen interrogated the common sense (Gramsci, 1971) undergirding TWI design: that effective bilingual learning necessitates separation of instructional languages. Instead, she argued that bilingual learners 'have strengths in both languages' that should be leveraged in the classroom to support student learning. She also revealed that she had come to view bilingualism from a more practice-oriented perspective, as something people 'do' rather than something people 'have' (García *et al.*, 2015), or, in her words, bilingualism as 'honoring and using, thinking, talking, writing.' Maestra Carmen concluded this reflection on her shifting stance by affirming students' bilingual identities, moving beyond the programmatic lens of 'native English speakers' and 'native Spanish speakers,' to recognize all students' identities of competence (Manyak, 2004) with the simple statement: 'Because we are bilingual.'

While I approached bilingualism from a dynamic perspective prior to the CBIT project, my view of translanguaging also shifted as a result of our collaboration, embracing a more context-dependent stance on translanguaging. A context-dependent stance acknowledges that the design decisions made for translanguaging in one learning environment will look different in another context. In Maestra Carmen's classroom, comprising mostly English-dominant students in an English-dominant community, the privileging of Spanish (only) spaces was essential for the efficacy of translanguaging pedagogies. While we ultimately decided to soften language boundaries to facilitate student sense-making during the project, I contend that we were able to facilitate a translanguaging space that did not become fully dominated by English because of the ways that Spanish was privileged in the classroom (although, as evident in the data presented, the project did increase the amount of English used during writing time). Maestra Carmen concurred that a context-dependent stance on translanguaging was essential for its success. In reflecting upon her language policy for the upcoming school year, she shared, 'I need to, you know, acknowledge that we are bilingual, but also honor the language that we're using, either in Spanish or in English.'

Discussion

While this chapter focused on stance and design shifts within the teacher–researcher collaboration, the analysis nevertheless afforded some important insights on translanguaging pedagogy in TWI. Specifically, the creation of a strategic translanguaging spaces through the CBIT project enabled more flexible negotiation of ideas and facilitated opportunities for students to make metalinguistic connections, a practice that has been shown to bolster students' bilingualism and biliteracy development (Henderson & Ingram, 2018). The translation activities, in particular, supported students in developing an understanding of language as a meaning-making resource (Halliday, 1978) and bilingualism as a dynamic and creative activity. Translanguaging became an important part of the writing process, even as the final product presented English and Spanish separately. In this way, the CBIT project operated within the 'middle ground' between policies of language separation and translanguaging, making space for flexible languaging-for-learning (Guzula *et al.*, 2016) to reframe monolingual ideologies, while still demonstrating what students could produce in each language independently.

In reflecting upon the teacher–researcher collaboration, I offer three principles that emerged as key elements of a productive research–practice partnership involving translanguaging pedagogy.

Principle 1: Deeply understanding the sociolinguistic context

One of the strengths of translanguaging theory is that it centers the bilingual individual, asking us to take the 'inside view' of the speaker's unique communicative repertoire and its diverse linguistic features rather than the 'outside view' of separate languages as they exist in society (Otheguy *et al.*, 2015). In the same vein, classroom translanguaging frameworks emphasize beginning pedagogical design by first considering the students and their everyday language practices (García *et al.*, 2017). While I agree with this student-centered approach to translanguaging pedagogy design, I contend that we must also attend to the unique sociolinguistic context of each classroom. Both Maestra Carmen and I had a deep understanding of her classroom's sociolinguistic context prior to beginning design of translanguaging pedagogies, knowledge that we foregrounded in our planning. For example, given that most of her students primarily used English outside of the classroom, we prioritized Spanish in both the writing process (by having students write the text in Spanish first) and in instruction (by having most lessons conducted entirely in Spanish). While we did eventually loosen the Spanish-focused stance for small group negotiations and lessons focused on translation, the privileging of Spanish throughout the project ensured that translanguaging spaces did not become fully dominated by English. Such strategic design decisions were *situated* and would look different in another sociolinguistic context. For example, Sayer's (2013) study of language practices in a second-grade bilingual classroom presented an entirely different context for translanguaging, as all of the students identified as Tejano and lived in a historically Mexican American community where flexible languaging was the norm. In such contexts, where translanguaging is central to students' everyday languaging, the maintenance of protected spaces for Spanish may not be as relevant. To put it succinctly, there is no 'one size fits all' for translanguaging pedagogy. Thus, understanding the situated sociolinguistic context of the classroom is essential prior to engaging in translanguaging design.

Principle 2: Openness to inquiry

In much of the literature, a translanguaging stance is presented as a precursor for engaging in translanguaging pedagogy (e.g. García *et al.*, 2017; Sánchez *et al.*, 2018). For example, Sánchez *et al.* (2018) explain that, to embrace a translanguaging allocation policy, teachers and leaders must 'firmly believ[e] that all students' language practices work together, not separately, and are legitimate resources for their learning' (2018: 7). However, in our teacher–researcher collaboration, Maestra Carmen did not hold a translanguaging stance prior to engaging in the CBIT project – she developed one *as a result of* participating in translanguaging pedagogies. Other studies of translanguaging pedagogy have begun to note similar findings, such as Menken and Sánchez's (2019) research with New York City public school teachers, which found that introducing teachers to translanguaging pedagogy disrupted dominant monolingual ideologies and contributed to ideological shifts toward a translanguaging stance. Similarly, Maestra Carmen shifted her views from being a proponent of strict language separation toward embracing translanguaging as an authentic practice for bilingual learning. Thus, rather than propose translanguaging stance as a precursor for translanguaging pedagogy, I contend that what is required is an openness to inquiry, a willingness to explore the potential for translanguaging practices in the TWI classroom (see Tian & Shepard-Carey, 2020 for a similar argument). Teacher–researcher collaborations might, therefore, be an important avenue for developing translanguaging stances – as a product of learning, not a precursor for it.

Principle 3: Willingness to adapt

Finally, teacher–researcher collaborations are strengthened by both parties' willingness to engage in ongoing reflection and adaptation. This principle builds upon a growing tradition in educational research toward more participatory and design-based inquiry (e.g. Bang *et al.*, 2016; Gutiérrez & Vossoughi, 2010; Penuel *et al.*, 2011; Tian, 2022), which centers the iterative nature of design. In design research, conjectures are developed, tested, and refined through 'a process featuring cycles of invention and revision' (Cobb *et al.*, 2003: 10). Applied to the design of translanguaging pedagogies, these repeated cycles of 'invention and revision' provide a useful framework for engaging in productive learning partnerships. While this study focused on only one translanguaging project and, thus, did not engage in repeated testing and refining of the same innovation, our ongoing reflection upon and revision of the project facilitated important shifts that contributed to its efficacy. Specifically, the shifts in the design of the languaging space enabled students to engage more flexibly and authentically in the task of creating a bilingual book, and shifts in the teacher/researcher roles facilitated the design of translation activities that bolstered students' metalinguistic awareness and strengthened the collaborative partnership. Importantly, both shifts emerged from our observations about what students needed to be successful in crafting a bilingual text. Thus, the design of effective translanguaging spaces and the development of strong teacher–researcher partnerships necessitates a willingness to adapt and continually refine the design, centered on how to best serve students in their developing bilingualism.

Implications for Further Research and Practice

A common challenge cited for implementing translanguaging pedagogy is teacher resistance due to their ideological stance. As García and Lin (2017) put it: 'it is difficult for teachers, steeped in monoglossic language ideologies, to accept translanguaging' (2017: 125). While it may be true that some teachers hold monoglossic language ideologies (e.g. Martínez *et al.*, 2015), this argument is an oversimplification of the challenges that teachers face in ensuring equitable learning and languaging spaces in their classrooms. Therefore, in considering the implications of this study for further research and practice, an important starting point is recognizing that classrooms are complex sociolinguistic spaces and that teachers are constantly navigating many competing ideologies and policies when they make instructional decisions. Perhaps a more productive starting point for engaging in meaningful work around classroom translanguaging is to interrogate the teacher/researcher divide, to consider how teachers and researchers can be partners in inquiry. In this study, the co-design and co-stances (Tian & Shepard-Carey, 2020) contributed to meaningful shifts in classroom languaging and beliefs about bilingual learning, yet there was certainly room for deepening the collaboration. At the end of the project, Maestra Carmen shared that she would have liked to have seen the classroom observation videos to learn more about her own practice and how students were languaging during the project. Thus, engaging teachers in the data analysis process or, at the very least, in reflection upon practice through video-elicitation interviews (Erickson &

Shultz, 1982) is an important direction for future teacher–researcher collaborations around translanguaging pedagogy.

Another implication from this study is the synergy between translation and translanguaging. In this study, the creation of a bilingual text was a meaningful way to incorporate translanguaging pedagogies into the classroom, enabling Maestra Carmen to prioritize spaces for Spanish use while also creating opportunities for students to engage in dynamic bilingual languaging and metalinguistic learning. While translation scholarship has traditionally focused on professional translators and foreign language learning in tertiary education, more recent scholarship has revealed how translation can play a role in promoting language learning in K-12 contexts (Laviosa & González-Davies, 2020). As translation scholarship increasingly reveals the benefits of translation activities for bi/multilingual learners (e.g. Jiménez *et al.*, 2015; Galante, 2021), an important future direction for those interested in translanguaging pedagogy is to consider how translation scholarship and pedagogies can inform the design of meaningful spaces for dynamic classroom languaging.

Note

(1) It is important to acknowledge that the duality implied by demarcating 'two' groups of students in two-way immersion programs has been problematized for misrepresenting students' complex linguistic experiences and identities (Hamman-Ortiz, 2019; de Jong, 2016).

References

Ballinger, S., Lyster, R., Sterzuk, A. and Genesee, F. (2017) Context-appropriate crosslinguistic pedagogy: Considering the role of language status in immersion education. *Journal of Immersion and Content-Based Language Education* 51 (2017), 30–57. https://doi.org/10.1075/jicb.5.1.02bal

Bang, M., Faber, L., Gurneau, J., Marin, A. and Soto, C. (2016) Community-based design research: Learning across generations and strategic transformations of institutional relations toward axiological innovations. *Mind, Culture, and Activity* 23 (1), 28–41. https://doi.org/10.1080/10749039.2015.1087572

Bauer, E.B., Presiado, V. and Colomer, S. (2017) Writing through partnership: Fostering translanguaging in children who are emergent bilinguals. *Journal of Literacy Research* 49 (1), 10–37.

Cenoz, J. and Gorter, D. (2017) Minority languages and sustainable translanguaging: Threat or opportunity? *Journal of Multilingual and Multicultural Development* 38 (10), 901–912.

Cenoz, J., Leonet, O. and Gorter, D. (2021) Developing cognate awareness through pedagogical translanguaging. *International Journal of Bilingual Education and Bilingualism* 25 (8), 2759–2773. https://doi.org/10.1080/13670050.2021.1961675

Cobb, P., Confrey, J., Lehrer, R. and Schauble, L. (2003) Design experiments in educational research. *Educational Researcher* 32 (1), 9–13.

Chow, P. and Cummins, J. (2003) Valuing multilingual and multicultural approaches to learning. In S.R. Schecter and J. Cummins (eds) *Multilingual Education in Practice: Using Diversity as a Resource* (pp. 32–61). London: Heinemann.

Creese, A. and Blackledge, A. (2010) Translanguaging in the bilingual classroom: A pedagogy for learning and teaching? *The Modern Language Journal* 94 (1), 103–115.

Cummins, J. (2001) *Negotiating Identities: Education for Empowerment in a Diverse Society* (2nd edn). Los Angeles: California Association for Bilingual Education.

Cummins, J. (2006) Identity texts: The imaginative construction of self through multiliteracies pedagogy. In O. García, T. Skutnabb-Kangas and M.E. Torres-Guzmán (eds) *Imagining Multilingual Schools: Languages in Education and Glocalization* (pp. 51–68). Clevedon: Multilingual Matters.

Cummins, J. (2014) Rethinking pedagogical assumptions in Canadian French immersion programs. *Journal of Immersion and Content-Based Language Education* 2 (1), 3–22.

Cummins, J. (2019) The emergence of translanguaging pedagogy: A dialogue between theory and practice. *Journal of Multilingual Education Research* 9 (1), 13.

Cummins, J. and Early, M. (eds) (2011) *Identity Texts: The Collaborative Creation of Power in Multilingual Schools*. Stoke-on-Trent: Trentham Books.

Daniel, S.M. and Pacheco, M.B. (2015) Translanguaging practices and perspectives of four multilingual teens. *Journal of Adolescent & Adult Literacy* 59 (6), 653–663

David, S.S., Pacheco, M.B. and Jiménez, R.T. (2019) Designing translingual pedagogies: Exploring pedagogical translation through a classroom teaching experiment. *Cognition and Instruction* 37 (2), 252–275. https://doi.org/10.1080/ 07370008.2019. 1580283

de Jong, E.J. (2016) Two-way immersion for the next generation: Models, policies, and principles. *International Multilingual Research Journal* 10 (1), 1931–3152.

Erickson, F. (2006) Studying side by side: Collaborative action ethnography in educational research. In G.D. Spindler and L. Hammond (eds) *Innovations in Educational Ethnography: Theory, Methods, and Results* (pp. 235–258). Mahwah, NJ: Lawrence Erlbaum Associates.

Erickson, F. and Shultz, J. (1982) *The Counselor as Gatekeeper: Social Interaction in Interviews*. Cambridge, MA: Academic Press.

Flores, N. and Rosa, J. (2015) Undoing appropriateness: Raciolinguistic ideologies and language diversity in education. *Harvard Educational Review* 85 (2), 149–171.

Fortune, T.W. and Tedick, D.J. (2019) Context matters: Translanguaging and language immersion education in the US and Canada. In M. Haneda and H. Nassaji (eds) *Perspectives on Language as Action: Festschrift in honour of Merrill Swain* (pp. 27–44). Bristol: Multilingual Matters.

French, J. and Whatley, B. (2009) *Demasiadas peras! Too Many Pears!* New York: Star Bright Books.

Galante, A., Okubo, K., Cole, C., Abd Elkader, N., Carozza, N., Wilkinson, C., Wotton, C. and Vasic, J. (2019) Plurilingualism in higher education: A collaborative initiative for the implementation of plurilingual pedagogy in an English for academic purposes program at a Canadian university. *TESL Canada Journal* 36 (1), 121–133. https://doi.org/10.18806/tesl.v36i1.1305

Galante, A. (2021) Translation as a pedagogical tool in multilingual classes. *Translation and Translanguaging in Multilingual Contexts* (January), 2352.

García, O. (2009) *Bilingual Education in the 21st Century: A Global Perspective*. Chichester: John Wiley & Sons.

García, O., Makar, C., Starcevic, M. and Terry, A. (2011) The translanguaging of Latino kindergarteners. In K. Potowski and J. Rothman (eds) *Bilingual Youth: Spanish in English-speaking Societies* (pp. 33–55). Philadelphia: John Benjamins.

García, O. and Li, W. (2014) *Translanguaging: Language, Bilingualism and Education*. New York: Palgrave Macmillan.

García, O., Flores, N. and Woodley, H.H. (2015) Constructing in-between spaces to 'do' bilingualism: A tale of two high schools in one city. In J. Cenoz and D. Gorter (eds) *Multilingual Education: Between Language Learning and Translanguaging* (pp. 199–224). Cambridge: Cambridge University Press.

García, O., Ibarra Johnson, S. and Seltzer, K. (2017) *The Translanguaging Classroom: Leveraging Student Bilingualism for Learning.* Philadelphia: Caslon.

García, O. and Lin, A.M.Y. (2017) Translanguaging in bilingual education. In O. García, A.M.Y. Lin and S. May (eds) *Bilingual and Multilingual Education (Encyclopedia of Language and Education,* Vol. 5 (pp. 117–130). Cham: Springer.

García-Mateus, S. and Palmer, D. (2017) Translanguaging pedagogies for positive identities in two-way dual language bilingual education. *Journal of Language, Identity and Education* 16 (4), 245–255. https://doi.org/10.1080/15348458.2017.1329016

Garza, E. and Arreguín-Anderson, M.G. (2018) Translanguaging: Developing scientific inquiry in a dual language classroom. *Bilingual Research Journal* 41 (2), 101–116. https://doi.org/10.1080/15235882.2018.1451790

Gogolin, I. (1994) *Der monolinguale Habitus der multilingualen Schule.* Münster: Waxmann-Verlag.

Gogolin, I. (2002) Linguistic and cultural diversity in Europe: A challenge for educational research and practice. *European Education Research Journal* 1 (1), 123–138.

Gort, M. and Sembiante, S.F. (2015) Navigating hybridized language learning spaces through translanguaging pedagogy: Dual language preschool teachers' languaging practices in support of emergent bilingual children's performance of academic discourse. *International Multilingual Research Journal* 9 (1), 7–25. https://doi.org/10.1080/19313152.2014.981775

Gramsci, A. (1971) Selections from the prison notebooks. New York: International Publishers.

Graue, M.E. and Walsh, D.J. (1998) *Studying Children in Context: Theories, Methods & Ethics.* London: Sage.

Guerrero, M. (2021) Gauging the adequacy of translanguaging allocation policy in two-way immersion programs in the US. *Journal of Latinos and Education.* Advance online publication. https://doi.org/10.1080/15348431.2021.1971086

Gutiérrez, K.D. and Vossoughi, S. (2010) Lifting off the ground to return anew: Mediated praxis, transformative learning, and social design experiments. *Journal of Teacher Education* 61 (1–2), 100–117. https://doi.org/10.1177/0022487109347877

Guzula, X., McKinney, C. and Tyler, R. (2016) Languaging-for-learning: Legitimising translanguaging and enabling multimodal practices in third spaces. *Southern African Linguistics and Applied Language Studies* 34 (3), 211–226.

Halliday, M.A.K. (1978) *Language as a Social Semiotic: The Social Interpretation of Language and Meaning.* London: Arnold.

Hamman, L. (2018) Translanguaging and positioning in two-way dual language classrooms: A case for criticality. *Language and Education* 32 (1), 21–42. https://doi.org/10.1080/09500782.2017.1384006

Hamman-Ortiz, L. (2019) Troubling the 'two' in two-way bilingual education. *Bilingual Research Journal* 42 (4), 387–407. https://doi.org/10.1080/15235882.2019.1686441

Heller, M. (1999) *Linguistic Minorities and Modernity: A Sociolinguistic Ethnography.* London: Longman.

Henderson, K.I. and Ingram, M. (2018) 'Mister, you're writing in Spanglish': Fostering spaces for meaning making and metalinguistic connections through teacher translanguaging shifts in the bilingual classroom. *Bilingual Research Journal* 41 (3), 253–271. https://doi.org/10.1080/15235882.2018.1481894

Howard, E.R., Lindholm-Leary, K., Rogers, D., Olague, N., Medina, J., Kennedy, B., Sugarman, J. and Christian, D. (2018) *Guiding Principles for Dual Language Education* (3rd edn) http://www.cal.org/twi/guidingprinciples.htm

Jiménez, R.T., David, S., Fagan, K., Risko, V.J., Pacheco, M., Pray, L. and Gonzales, M. (2015) Using translation to drive conceptual development for students becoming literate in English as an additional language. *Research in the Teaching of English* 49 (3), 248–271.

Laviosa, S. and González-Davies, M. (2020) *The Routledge Handbook of Translation and Education*. New York: Routledge.

Manyak, P.C. (2004) 'What did she say?: Translation in a primary-grade English immersion class. *Multicultural Perspectives* 6 (1), 12–18.

Martin-Beltrán, M. (2014) 'What do you want to say?' How adolescents use translanguaging to expand learning opportunities. *International Multilingual Research Journal* 8 (3), 208–230. https://doi.org/10.1080/19313152.2014.914372

Martínez, R.A., Hikida, M. and Durán, L. (2015) Unpacking ideologies of linguistic purism: How dual language teachers make sense of everyday translanguaging. *International Multilingual Research Journal* 9 (1), 26–42.

Martínez, R.A., Durán, L. and Hikida, M. (2017) Becoming 'Spanish learners': Identity and interaction among multilingual children in a Spanish-English dual language classroom. *International Multilingual Research Journal* 11 (3), 167–183. https://doi.org/10.1080/19313152.2017.1330065

Menken, K. and Sánchez, M.T. (2019) Translanguaging in English-only schools: From pedagogy to stance in the disruption of monolingual policies and practices. *TESOL Quarterly* 53 (3), 741–767. https://doi.org/10.1002/tesq.513

Miles, M.B. and Huberman, A.M. (2014) *Qualitative Data Analysis: A Methods Sourcebook* (3rd edn). Thousand Oaks, CA: Sage.

Mortimer, K.S. (2018) The hegemony of language separation: Discontents en programs de lenguaje dual en Paraguay and El Paso. *Association of Mexican American Educators Journal* 12 (2), 121–152.

Orellana, M.F. (2009) *Translating Childhoods: Immigrant Youth, Language, and Culture*. Rutgers University Press.

Otheguy, R., García, O. and Reid, W. (2015) Clarifying translanguaging and deconstructing named languages: A perspective from linguistics. *Applied Linguistics Review* 6 (3), 281–307. http://doi.org/10.1515/applirev-2015-0014

Palmer, D.K. (2009) Middle-class English speakers in a two-way immersion bilingual classroom: 'Everybody should be listening to Jonathan right now...'. *TESOL Quarterly* 43 (2), 177–202.

Palmer, D.K., Martínez, R.A., Mateus, S.G. and Henderson, K. (2014) Reframing the debate on language separation: Toward a vision for translanguaging pedagogies in the dual language classroom. *Modern Language Journal* 98 (3), 757–772. https://doi.org/10.1111/modl.12121

Penuel, W.R., Fishman, B.J., Haugan Cheng, B. and Sabelli, N. (2011) Organizing research and development at the intersection of learning, implementation, and design. *Educational Researcher* 40 (7), 331–337. https://doi.org/10.3102/0013189X11421826

Pontier, R. and Gort, M. (2016) coordinated translanguaging pedagogy as distributed cognition: A case study of two dual language bilingual education preschool coteachers' languaging practices during shared book readings. *International Multilingual Research Journal* 10 (2), 89–106.

Poza, L.E. (2018) The language of ciencia: Translanguaging and learning in a bilingual science classroom. *International Journal of Bilingual Education and Bilingualism* 21 (1), 1–19. https://doi.org/10.1080/13670050.2015.1125849

Prasad, G. (2018) Building students' language awareness and literacy engagement through the creation of collaborative multilingual identity texts 2.0. In C. Hélot, K. Van Gorp, C. Frijns and S. Sierens (eds) *Language Awareness in Multilingual Classrooms in Europe: From Theory to Practice* (pp. 207–234). Berlin: De Gruyter.

Przymus, S.D. (2016) Challenging the monolingual paradigm in secondary dual-language instruction: Reducing language-as-problem with the 2-1-L2 model. *Bilingual Research Journal* 39 (3–4), 279–295. https://doi.org/10.1080/15235882.2016.1220995

Roschelle, J. and Penuel, W. (2006) Co-design of innovations with teachers: Definition and dynamics. *The 7th International Conference on the Learning Sciences*, (August), pp. 606–612. https://doi.org/http://dx.doi.org/10.1111/j.1540-8191.2011.01373.x

Saldaña, J. (2013) *The Coding Manual for Qualitative Researchers* (2nd edn). Thousand Oaks, CA: Sage.

Sánchez, M.T., García, O. and Solorza, C. (2018) Reframing language allocation policy in dual language bilingual education. *Bilingual Research Journal* 41 (1), 37–51. https://doi.org/10.1080/15235882.2017.1405098

Sayer, P. (2013) Translanguaging, TexMex, and bilingual pedagogy: Emergent bilinguals learning through the vernacular. *TESOL Quarterly* 47 (1), 63–88.

Schecter, S. and Cummins, J. (eds) (2003) *Multilingual Education in Practice: Using Diversity as a Resource*. London: Heinemann.

Seltzer, K. (2019) Reconceptualizing 'home' and 'school' language: Taking a critical translingual approach in the English classroom. *TESOL Quarterly* 53 (4), 986–1007. https://doi.org/10.1002/tesq.530

Somerville, J. and Faltis, C. (2019) Dual Languaging as strategy and translanguaging as tactic in two-way dual language programs. *Theory into Practice* 58 (2), 164–175. https://doi.org/10.1080/00405841.2019.1569380

Tian, Z. (2022) Translanguaging design in a third grade Chinese Language Arts class. *Applied Linguistics Review* 13 (3), 327-343.

Tian, Z. and Shepard-Carey, L. (2020) (Re)imagining the future of translanguaging pedagogies in TESOL through teacher–researcher collaboration. *TESOL Quarterly* 54 (4), 1131–1143.

Zentella, A.C. (1997) *Growing Up Bilingual: Puerto Rican Children in New York*. Oxford: Blackwell.

6 Translanguaging Spaces for Student Literacy Learning: A Researcher–Teacher Partnership

Sally Brown and Margarita Pomare-McDonald

Bernardo listened to *Swarm of Bees* (Snicket, 2019), discussed it with a mixed language group of peers and created a personal response to the story. A simple evaluation of Bernardo's written language ('swarm of bees'; 'tomatos!!!' tells us very little about his comprehension. To see the remarkable in the unremarkable (Mavers, 2011), we must probe beyond the ordinary. Bernardo's drawing reveals the main character (boy) with a basket full of tomatoes and a straight-lined mouth representing the anger the boy felt. The stripes at the top (queen bee) and the gray and black dots represent the angry bees. According to Bernardo, 'His hand is up. He's 'bout to throw tomatoes.' The angry bees, mad boy and throwing of the tomatoes are at the heart of the story's plot. These are key elements that Bernardo did not include in his English written language but was able to communicate through drawing and his oral linguistic repertoire.

Introduction

Bernardo's vignette (above) causes us to pause and honestly think about the multimodal aspects of literacy learning and the ways translanguaging is at the heart of meaning-making. This is particularly important for young emergent bilinguals in English-only schools where official school work is expected to be in English and revolves around print-centric practices (Brown, 2021). A closer look at Bernardo's multimodal work paints a different picture. We can see that he has a complex understanding of the story and made intentional, agentive moves to communicate in ways that made sense. Knowing and understanding the value of multimodal, translanguaging learning pedagogy is central to the partnership formed by the researcher (Sally) and teacher (Margarita). Our researcher and teacher relationship served as a foundation for a co-stance approach to teaching literacy to emergent bilinguals. A co-stance can be referred to as an, 'enduring dynamic process in which teachers and researchers collaboratively, respectfully, and openly discuss and negotiate their philosophical, ideological, or belief systems regarding bilingualism and translanguaging to better inform their pedagogical framework' (Tian & Shepard-Carey, 2020: 1133). The collaboration combined the experiences of the researcher and teacher to co-design lessons, taking into account linguistic and cultural resources for reading books and engaging in multimodal authoring practices. We embraced a translanguaging stance as a means for moving towards educational equity for emergent bilinguals learning in the context of an English-only learning environment. Current practices and assessment tools were failing to acknowledge the literacy strengths of students learning English as a new language.

In order to examine the possibilities of translanguaging pedagogies in an early childhood classroom, the two of us initiated multimodal spaces for literacy learning. Later, Margarita extended our findings into other areas of the curriculum. This chapter presents findings related to the following research questions: (1) How do emergent bilinguals make meaning of read-alouds using available semiotic resources? (2) How can translanguaging practices be incorporated to effectively support emergent bilinguals in assessment? (3) What do the findings mean for reimagining, co-designing and co-shifting instructional practices?

Understanding the Emergent Bilinguals and Their Learning Context

School

This work took place in a neighborhood school located in the Southeastern United States, serving approximately 538 students in Pre-Kindergarten through fifth grade. The student body was racially and ethnically diverse, representing Asian/Pacific Islanders, Latinx, White, bi-racial and Black students (the majority). Over 79% of the students came from low-income families and received government-subsidized breakfast and lunch. This school was one of the district's three elementary cluster center schools that provide English to Speakers of Other Languages (ESOL) services to qualifying emergent bilinguals. These students either lived in the neighborhood or were bused from outlying areas ('The Governor's Office of Student Achievement,' n.d.).

Margarita's classroom

Margarita taught a diverse group of 21 first-grade (ages 6, 7 and 8) students whose home languages included Spanish (7), French (2), German (1), Amharic (1) and English (10). Five of the students received ESOL support services based on the district's qualification guidelines. Student ESOL support services were determined after the administration of the federal and state mandated ACCESS (Assessing Comprehension and Communication in English State-to-State for English Language Learners) test. Students were assessed in four domains: listening, reading, speaking and writing. The ACCESS test assessed a student's English proficiency. Students were also given the reading MAP (Measures of Academic Progress) three times a year. The MAP test was a standardized, computerized assessment that helps teachers, parents, students and administrators to monitor students' English academic progress and guide instruction to help with students' growth. The 11 students with home languages other than English were considered emergent bilinguals (Table 6.1).

Table 6.1 Emergent bilingual student information

Student (Pseudonym)	Age	Home language	Country of origin	English proficiency (ACCESS)	MAP reading score (BOY)
Gabriella **	7	Spanish	Guatemala	2.2	129
Matias **	7	Spanish	Honduras	1.9	121
Elena*	7	Spanish	Mexico	NA	151
Fala	6	French	Chad, Africa	NA	154
Bernardo	6	Spanish	Mexico	NA	159
Selassie	6	Amharic	Ethiopia, Africa	NA	164
Noah	6	German	USA, Military Base in Germany	NA	165
Jaime **	6	Spanish	Guatemala	3.7	152
Panambi **	7	French	Chad, Africa	3.9	157
Hugo **	7	Spanish	Mexico	2.0	144
Cesar*	6	Spanish	Mexico	NA	NA

*Moved at some point during the school year.
**Qualified for ESOL services

This term 'emergent bilinguals' is used throughout the chapter because it 'recognizes the value of the students' home languages as resources for learning and as markers of their identity as individuals who have creative ways of knowing, being, and communicating' (García & Kleifgen, 2010: 119). In this class, the teacher used several modifications to provide support and meet the needs of the students, including translators, picture cards, reading leveled texts and continued phonics instruction.

The school district used a balanced literacy approach for reading instruction consisting of four key components: Phonics, Read-Alouds, Reading Workshops and Writing Workshops. Phonics instruction followed the Wilson Foundations scripted program of explicit phonics. Read-alouds and discussions were led by the teacher with grade-level texts. Reading workshops consisted of skills-driven mini-lessons; guided reading focused on targeted (differentiated) instruction; and station rotations (centers) where students worked independently to practice using the strategies and skills learned. Writing workshops consisted of teacher-led mini-lessons using the Six Plus One Writing Traits program and daily independent practice.

According to district policy, students were placed in flexible groups based on their ability (using MAP scores) for small group centers. At the beginning of each week, the teacher introduced or reviewed the standard/topic for whole group instruction. The students gathered for whole group instruction while the teacher read a story aloud and taught a mini activity/lesson based on the focal standard. The ability grouping allowed students to work on their level through differentiated instruction provided by the teacher. During small group instruction, students worked in groups of four or five and rotated to different stations or centers: (1) Word Work – an independent language arts activity or game; (2) Technology – an online activity (i.e. reading, letter sounds, words); (3) Teacher Group – differentiated reading instruction by the teacher using leveled texts; (4) Independent Reading (on days when the researcher was not present) choosing a book on their level and writing or drawing a picture they could orally explain or Researcher Group (two days per week) – listening to a read aloud, engaging in a student-driven discussion, and creating a digital response to the text.

Teacher: Margarita

Margarita, who identifies as Black Hispanic, was a first-year teacher. Being a new teacher may be a bit misleading because she spent the last 13 years as a kindergarten paraprofessional, where she gained insight into working with diverse children. Margarita's love and passion for teaching stemmed from her childhood when she played school with her cousins during the summer. When school was out, Margarita continued learning with her cousins by playing school at home. Margarita assumed the teacher role, while her cousins became students.

Her compassion and understanding for students who speak English as a new language are personal. Both of her parents are Hispanic and bilingual. When she was younger, she spent summers in Colombia, South America (her mother's hometown). Margarita lived with her extended family members, who primarily spoke Spanish and very little English. At times, it was difficult for her to communicate with some family members who spoke very little or no English at all. Often, Margarita would sit quietly or wait to interact with other family members who spoke English. Reflecting on childhood experiences helped Margarita to understand some of the feelings, frustrations and experiences of her emergent bilinguals. For example, she understands that students can be active participants during a lesson even though they remain quiet, which is common for newcomers. This does not mean that students are not paying attention. Second, she values and accepts the various forms of communication from emergent bilinguals. Margarita learned to move fluidly between the languages in informal ways and encouraged her students to do the same. These experiences guided her work with students in the classroom. Margarita's childhood Spanish language experiences are an asset because they helped her to build a multilingual repertoire, which serves as a foundation for communicating with her Spanish speaking students and families.

Researcher: Sally

The researcher, a former early childhood teacher and current National Board Certified Teacher, conducted research at this school site for over ten years. She is a monolingual, European American college professor who considers herself a language learner. She has educational experiences in Mexico and Costa Rica that pushed her to learn some Spanish. The researcher is comfortable experimenting with her translanguaging practices as she embraces those of students. Her passion for working with emergent bilinguals comes from witnessing the inequities and challenges emergent bilinguals face daily in US schools.

The beginning of the partnership

The teacher–researcher partnership began from a professional relationship with Margarita over several years while Sally was researching at the school site. Margarita was interested in learning more about teaching emergent bilinguals, and Sally wanted to investigate multimodal literacy practices. These common interests brought us together and served the impetus that positioned us as learners along with Margarita's students. Initially, the partnership was formal with a clear focus on the research, but over time, the two of us deepened our relationship with one another. We engaged in informal conversations about our life experiences and beliefs about cultures, languages and literacies. We considered ourselves equal partners who were able to freely discuss translanguaging pedagogies from an asset-based perspective (García *et al.*, 2017). This was particularly important because the school revolved around English-only practices, and we wanted to embrace students' full linguistic and semiotic repertoires. By positioning ourselves as language learners, we were role models of fluid ways of becoming for students. These experiences cemented a bond where the two of us felt comfortable offering feedback to one another in ways that led both of us to grow as professional educators. It is important to note that the partnership was possible because Margarita's school district was open to supporting classroom research with the local university. Being able to obtain school district consent for formal research studies was a necessary component of starting the work together.

Approach to translanguaging

The translanguaging pedagogical framework embraced our beliefs in the value of all languages, whether standard or nonstandard, in addition to other modes of communication. The intermingled nature of semiotic resources used by emergent bilinguals influenced the design of the research, where home and school became one space supporting all forms of learning. Respect was given to the ways emergent bilinguals employ cross-linguistic and bi-directional language and literacy skills, meaning that students move back and forth through languages (Gort, 2012). As a result of this approach, we made instructional co-shifts based on the responses or performance of students. A co-shift represents moments where teachers and researchers communally reflect and make adjustments in lessons or activities (Tian & Shepard-Carey, 2020). Sometimes these co-shifts occurred from one lesson to another, and at other times a thoughtful reflection of data caused long-term curricular changes. For example, there were many conversations about making sure we heard the voices of students with home languages other than Spanish. This included the analysis of videotaped interactions to rethink how quiet students were participating in read-alouds and multimodal authoring practices. It is worth noting that the research was interrupted by Covid-19 when the school shut down and ultimately moved to virtual learning for the remainder of the school year. Therefore, some of the instructional changes noted will be implemented in the upcoming school year with a return to face-to-face instruction.

Translanguaging from a Multimodal Perspective

Communicating in a global society where literacy is ever-changing requires flexibility in thinking about interactions in pluralistic settings and how to best express thoughts and ideas (Fu *et al.*, 2019). Translanguaging offers an approach to support student learning in classrooms where English may be the dominant or only language, and multiple languages are assets, not deficits (Espinosa & Ascenzi-Moreno, 2021). The many complexities associated with translanguaging focus on understanding the multifaceted ways in which children move among languages, standard and nonstandard forms, to make meaning. The multimodal aspects of translanguaging are often overlooked because of the emphasis on language. But as Li Wei (2018) tells us, 'translanguaging… transcend[s] the traditional divides between linguistic and nonlinguistic cognitive and semiotic systems' (2018: 20).

Thinking about translanguaging as a communicative act helps understand the natural ways that visual and gestural elements work together with language in everyday interactions. When mixed with digital affordances, the multimodal aspects become clearer as semiotic resources are expanded (Tai & Li, 2021). Lin's (2019) work on trans/languaging and trans-semiotizing confirms the entanglement of multiple semiotic modes (including gestures and visuals) in the construction of meaning. She states, 'translanguaging is underpinned by a dynamic, dialogic, and distributed view of language,' (Lin, 2019: 8) which helps in moving away from monologic didactics. This gives rise to the spontaneous co-making of knowledge.

In addition, social semiotics provides insight into viewing translanguaging in this way. A mode, 'socially shaped, culturally available material resource' (Bezemer & Kress, 2016: 7), always appears with another mode in the meaning-making process. This may include the use of the whole body, where students' everyday semiotic resources are coupled with cultural patterns and embodied actions (Wu & Lin, 2019). Lau *et al.* (2022) push us to think about translanguaging from an expansive view that involves sensorimotor processes as well as cognition and affect. By paying attention to the larger picture or situated, ecological contexts, more can be learned about translanguaging through materiality where humans are entangled with non-human resources.

In this research, the children are using multiple modes (including multiple languages) to make sense of texts. The process of communicating their ideas about books is the central focus, and the result is considered an ensemble, the cohesive and coherent integrated communication unit (Kress, 2010). Consideration must be given to affordances and constraints of available resources if students are to create ensembles. This process includes utilizing resources from linguistic repertoires and drawings embedded with intentional use of color, emojis, digital stickers and such. The semiotic work positions students in a constant stage of 'becoming' (García & Li, 2014).

This sense of becoming occurs as students use their semiotic resources to acquire new ways of speaking, acting, languaging, knowing and doing (García & Li, 2014). This work occurs within social environments where students work with their peers to take in new information, remix it and craft outputs. Their rich social histories and desires influence students about what they want to communicate with others. Small group discussions surrounding books are one space where emergent bilinguals can acquire new language practices and integrate these into one linguistic repertoire, and thus, resulting in unique meaning-making resources.

Research in the area of translanguaging in young emergent bilinguals is continuing to evolve, especially when embedded within a multimodal framework. Leung's (2019) work with kindergartners in Hong Kong found translanguaging evidence in visual languages such as Chinese using pictorial elements as forms of communication. Children engaged in a type of translanguaging play intermixing oral language with the visual elements from the visual aspects of Chinese words. Similarly, Axelrod and Cole (2018) examined the choices young Latinx learners made when crafting responses associated with photographs. The children considered their audience and used this in their design choices. Martínez-Álvarez and Ghiso's (2017) study of Latinx first graders documented the multimodal nature of translanguaging. Photography and writing were used to showcase the children's embodied knowledge of their communities. Additional studies inform the role of translanguaging when technology affords other semiotic resources like the recording of stories, drawing tools and photography (Rowe, 2018; Rowe & Miller, 2016). The possibilities are endless when emergent bilinguals engage with multimodal resources to make meaning. Each learner uses the tools in innovative ways to represent personal understandings of texts.

Standard English alphabetic print and monolingual ideologies must be challenged if we are to move forward in educating all children. Zapata (2020) refers to a 'linguistic and modal landscape' (2020: 384) where students access all language varieties and forms of communication. This landscape can help us shift classroom structures from a print-centric practice to a multimodal one that unravels boundaries and resists the colonial practices of schools that privilege Standard English (García & Kleyn, 2016; Zapata, 2020).

Methodology

Our collaborative design process

Collaboration was an essential aspect of the project. We worked to co-design literacy lessons where all languages and forms of communication were welcomed (García *et al.*, 2017). For example, the selected literacy skills for the week were taught by both of us. On one occasion, main idea was taught in the guided reading group and during the read aloud center activity. The two different methods of teaching main idea complimented one another. This repeated practice was co-designed in advance when we discussed the literacy needs of the class. This possibility existed only because of the close partnership based on trust where we brought different aspects of expertise to planning and valued a translanguaging pedagogy. Students' voices, cultures and languages were considered in terms of book selection, languages for oral discussions and multimodal ways to share understandings of complex texts. A flexible and fluid design allowed for multiple ways of knowing as represented by various modes, including the use of digital tools. The emergent bilinguals' 'ways of knowing [were] seen as both informing *and* informed by classroom instruction' (García *et al.*, 2017: 28). For example, students were encouraged to change the language setting on their keyboards to facilitate writing in their home languages.

Data collection and analyses

Sally served as a participant-observer (Spradley, 2016) in the classroom literacy instruction two days per week for the school-year until March when traditional face-to-face schooling was interrupted by Covid. During this time, Sally read aloud books to students in the small groups arranged by Margarita. Her work was considered a center where students rotated while Margarita taught guided reading groups. Upon completion of the read aloud, the students were invited to engage in multimodal authoring practices using tablet computers. This research was part of a larger study focused on emergent bilinguals' multimodal literacy practices.

Sally documented the collaboration and work with students through field notes as a way to capture the context of the literacy events as well as any details that were not videotaped. For example, the notes documented informal interactions between Margarita and students, collaborative conversations about instruction, or non-academic interactions which offered insights into the students' attitudes or behaviors. In addition, analytic memos (Saldaña, 2021) reflected on the dynamics unfolding in the literacy learning processes of the students as well as providing insight into the co-stance, co-design and co-shifts. The small group interactions between Sally and the students were videotaped (which included student-to-student interactions), and selected excerpts were multimodally transcribed (Norris, 2019). These multimodal transcripts assisted in understanding the multimodalities involved in how students made meaning of texts. Translanguaging was one aspect of the analyses that helped show the fluid and flexible nature of language use in real-world book discussions.

The multimodal work samples of students were also collected and analyzed using the *Multilingual Composing Profile for Multimodal Texts* (Brown & Allmond, 2020). This included an examination of the oral and written forms of languages and drawings to document indicators of multifaceted intricacies of sophisticated reading comprehension abilities. The instrument was not administered as a standalone assessment but remained a fluid part of authentic instructional activities.

The dearth of multilingual, multimodal assessments for young emergent bilinguals is a real problem. Many literacy assessments for speakers of languages other than English are mere adaptations. They were not explicitly developed for multilingual learners (Espinosa, 2012). In addition, there has been a failure of traditional methods of assessment in describing the true performance of emergent bilinguals because of print-centric foci (Spence, 2010). These factors caused the researcher to create an assets-based assessment capable of capturing the rich, complex ways that emergent bilinguals showcase their understandings of texts. The goal was to capture students' existing knowledge that results in equitable and quality learning experiences based on the information gained from the assessment.

The Composing Profile was specifically designed based on the analysis of over 300 emergent bilinguals' multimodal responses to children's literature and a review of literature in the field of multimodal, multilingual writing for young learners. Codes regarding themes were compared to existing literature. Then, the themes were examined as the instrument passed through revisions in its use evaluating emergent bilinguals. These include authenticity, practicality, utilization of development patterns, descriptive outcomes, a comparison of growth over time and comprehensiveness (Rowe & Wilson, 2015).

After the revisions, the instrument was used to evaluate 93 work samples or ensembles from this classroom. The profile equally valued oral language, image construction (including the development of new literacies associated with technology use), and written language, each counting approximately one-third towards the final score. More important than the final score was tracking growth over time with students and crediting them with the resources they used to make meaning of texts. Many of these elements go unnoticed by educators. Any named language and language variety were acceptable in all aspects of the assessment. For example, it begins by asking students, 'Tell me about your work today.' This information is recorded and used to supplement the drawing (digital in this case) and written language. Google Translate, Talking Points (a communication app) and human translators were used as needed.

The collaborative analyses of the book discussions and the assessment data were used to make co-shifts and co-designs in classroom instruction as well as to change stances. Changes were made to whole and small group instruction as well as assessment practices. The findings and implications are outlined below.

Significant Findings

Drawing: A tool for adding depth to meaning-making

Prior to Sally coming into the classroom, the students did not have many opportunities to use drawing as a tool for meaning-making. Margarita was focused on teaching literacy skills in traditional ways and had not fully considered the power of drawing. She was interested in adapting her classroom literacy practices in ways that supported a translanguaging pedagogy, which is why Sally was invited into her classroom. Through informal conversations about instruction, emergent bilinguals and research, we discovered the power of multimodal forms of communication, including translanguaging, to make meaning of read-alouds. Drawing was one of those essential modes. In this case, the students were afforded digital resources for creating drawings in response to read-alouds. This meant access to coloring tools, markers, crayons, spray paint, stickers, emojis, etc. Students utilized these resources to create powerful visual images that added layers of meaning to their written and oral language.

Of the 93 work samples evaluated, 66.7% of the time, students used visual images that elaborated on their speech and writing to express understanding of read-alouds. Thirty-nine percent of the time, students' visuals contributed at least three additional pieces of information. It is important to notice this because it showed the extent to which emergent bilinguals used images as a central component of their meaning-making process. Therefore, when teachers only ask students to express themselves through writing on worksheets or journal entries, their depth of knowledge goes unnoticed. Missed information may result in a misjudgment of abilities and the assignment of deficit labels.

Let us look at an example to illustrate this point. After listening to a read aloud of *The Oldest Student* (Hubbard, 2020), Panambi (home language – French) crafted a response to the story (Figure 6.1). The story captured the real-life experiences of Mary Walker, a former slave, and how she learned to read at such an old age. Panambi was captivated by the part of the story where she remarried. Although there is no mention in the linguistic modes (oral or written), Panambi showed Mary's husband (most prominent figure) and her three children. She had two older children

Digital image	Oral description – Tell me about your work today.	Written language
	'This is when she was old and new husband and her kids.'	when his [her] husband died, and she married again *This was mainly copied from a page in the paper-based book. Panambi chose not to write any of his words.

Figure 6.1 Panambi's response to the oldest student

(represented by the two medium-sized figures) and a young child (represented by only a face and circular blanket). These details showed that he remembered the number of children and their relative sizes/ages. In addition, we can see that each of the people was represented as African American by the use of the brown marker. The facial expressions of the characters showed happiness (three) and sadness (one). Other details from the story Panambi captured visually.

This student work sample was just one of many that supported a multimodal, translanguaging approach to supporting the reading comprehension development of emergent bilinguals. Students like Panambi often shared their drawings with Margarita upon completion. They were excited and proud to share the ways they were making meaning of stories. These frequent moves by students led to co-shifts and co-design changes. Typically, we would talk during the students' lunch break in two ways. First, we discussed the in-the-moment learning experiences of the students during that particular day. We noted celebrations of accomplishments, but also discussed student needs which allowed both of us to alter planning for the following day or week. Second, the two of us engaged in larger discussions about pedagogy and lesson design from a holistic perspective. For example, how could Margarita use drawings in other areas of her instruction as a multimodal, translanguaging tool for student learning? These experiences led to co-designs shifts.

Translanguaging in small groups

Several significant themes emerged as we partnered to evaluate student work samples and transcripts for student language use. First, it was clear that student language practices were dependent upon the small group configurations. More translanguaging occurred when students had at least one peer who spoke their first language. In addition, the selection of the read text itself influenced literacy practices. The use of a book involving code-switching or specific Latinx cultural elements brought fluidity of language use across systems as ways to make meaning and communicate. Both of these aspects of teaching offered opportunities for co-designing future lessons. We engaged in ongoing conversations about the group dynamics for small group instruction to determine how best to support translanguaging practices for all students. The selection of culturally and linguistically relevant children's literature was another area of co-design where the expertise of the two of us assisted in a better use of read aloud material across the school day.

Group one consisted of four emergent bilinguals with Spanish as a home language and two English-only children. All of these students were labeled as below grade level according to their standardized MAP reading test scores. It appeared that the grouping of Spanish speakers afforded comfort in using one's home language (even though there were subtle differences between Mexican Spanish and Honduran Spanish) along with the ability to engage in extended conversations with others in Spanish. *Marta! Big & Small* (Arena, 2016), a simple text using a mixture of Spanish and English, was read to the group. Immediately, the emergent bilinguals began chorally reading the Spanish words with the researcher, which led to predicting what would come next. The Spanish emergent bilinguals made their guesses in Spanish and the English speakers in English as in the following example.

Transcript A

Sally: [Read.] *To an elephant, Marta is* … (Paused.)
Matias: It's gonna say, um, pequeño. (Quiet voice.)
Gabriella: [Smiled. Nodded yes.] Uh, huh.
Ezra: (Yelled.) Little. She's little. Just look at the page.
Sally: [Continued reading.] … pequeño. Small, very small.
Elena: I knew that was it. I hear that before. Pequeño - that means small.
Matias: Little too. They're kinda the same.
Sally: [Flipped page.] *To a turtle, Marta is* … (Paused.)
Elena: It should be Marta es, not Marta is.
Gabriella: Rapido.
Ezra: [Interrupted.] Fast. She's super-fast. That turtle is small.
Matias: Yea, I know. On la pictura ella es on a branch running.
Gabriella: Rapido, rapido.

The group picked up on the language pattern in the book along with the vivid visual cues for predicting the upcoming words. There was no regard for stigmas associated with language use as the students freely used mixtures of available resources. Each prediction and follow-up comment were valued by the group and used as a tool to make collaborative meaning. Initially, Matias was hesitant in his response 'pequeño,' but Gabriella's confirmation relieved some of his anxiety. Further confirmation was evident as the researcher read the remainder of the page, and Elena explained that it meant small. She made a connection to the language she heard at home with the Spanish she just heard from her classmates.

Matias noticed that the three words – little, small and pequeño – were synonyms and have similar meanings. This move was significant because he was internalizing a classroom reading skill (synonyms) in his way within a blend of language practices. Then, Elena's observations of printed words on the page (Marta is) and Sally's oral reading caused her to ponder the correctness of the language according to the way it was used in her home. She was aware that 'es' was the Spanish word for 'is' and that it should follow Marta to make sense. She was experimenting with how words are combined to make sentences in multiple languages. This remix was a sophisticated cognitive move involving the synthesis of two semiotic systems and her manipulation of syntax. Elena used her known languages in various ways to interact with others in her reading group (Torpsten, 2018).

Finally, Gabriella spoke up with her prediction of the word 'rapido' for 'fast.' Her prediction became intermingled with Ezra's English comment causing Gabriella to repeat her phrase to be acknowledged. Matias' final response, '... On la pictura ella es on a branch running,' provided an example of how students need opportunities to use their linguistic repertoires to make sense of books. The conversation enabled students to make meaning of the story using linguistic flexibility continually, and the result may be different if forced to communicate in English only (Osorio, 2020). The ideology guiding this situation did not view language as a problem but as an asset transformed by the context (Deroo, 2020).

Additionally, when the students found themselves in small groups where multiple languages were spoken, they took risks to learn about one another's languages. For example, Roman (English-only speaker) said to Jaime (home language – Spanish), 'Hey, will you teach me how to write this in Spanish? I want to know how you write.' In this case, the two boys collaborated using Roman's tablet to create a response to *Good Boy, Fergus!* (Shannon, 2006), a simple text showcasing the antics of a dog as he plays his way through the day. Roman already drew a picture of a boy holding a leash attached to a dog. Jaime moved closer to Roman and took control of the tablet.

Transcript B

Jaime: Okay. What do you want to say?
Roman: Well, I was thinking, thinking about, something like they went for a walk and Fergus chased a motorcycle. [Laughed.]
Jaime: You do it like this. [Began tapping letters on the keyboard and typed *el nino camna y*]
Roman: What ya typing?
Jaime: What you said. Look here. [Pointed.] It says el nino camina. That means they went walking just like you wanted.
Roman: I wanna make the words. [Took back tablet.]
Jaime: Okay.
Roman: You tell me what to do. Okay? I wanna write in Spanish.
Jaime: [Re-read the beginning of the sentence to himself.] Okay, okay. We need dog. That word is perro in Spanish. You know how to write perro?
Roman: No, what? Say it again.
Jaime: It has a P,
Roman: Perro, perro.
Jaime: Perro [Repeated word to himself slowly.], perro. P-E-R-O. Yea. Like that. You did it. Perro. Dog.

Both boys are engaged in translanguaging practices during this interaction as they tapped their linguistic repertoires to co-construct a sentence about the story. After Roman articulated his sentence in English, Jaime gathered his Spanish language knowledge to organize his thoughts. Both students used invented spelling to encode the sounds they heard by repeating words. While Jaime's initial phrase was not perfect (*el nino camna y*), Roman's meaning was conveyed. As the event continued, Roman seized control of the tablet device to type the Spanish words himself. Jaime continued to support Roman's language learning by spelling Spanish words for him. In the end, Jaime did not know the Spanish word for motorcycle, and the two decided to write the English word.

The final sentence resulted from a joint learning process where there was space and time for the students to build on one another's knowledge. The following was the result:

> **Roman's intended sentence**: They went for a walk, and Fergus chased a motorcycle.
> **Collaborative sentence**: *el nino camna y the pero veo the motrscl.* (exactly as typed on the tablet)
> **Translation**: The boy walks, and the dog sees the motorcycle.

Each learner accessed the activity in different ways, given their available resources. The goal of the lesson was fulfilled - to make meaning of the story using multiple modes. The Spanish language resources did not distract from the learning process but instead were additive for both students. These actions were only possible because of the teacher and researcher's openness to unfamiliar language practices and the creative development of new grammatical forms (Zapata & Laman, 2016).

The two transcript examples showcase the power of a teacher–researcher collaboration where new possibilities are discovered (Tian & Shepard-Carey, 2020). It was only through a close examination of transcript data, that we were able to come away with new understandings about the importance of grouping emergent bilinguals to support translanguaging. This evidence (Transcript A) provided a basis for dialogue and development of a co-stance which meant thinking differently about how educators should group students to maximize learning. In addition, we had not thought about how translanguaging might apply to English-only students, but the students in Transcript B made a case for co-designing lessons that position all students as language learners.

Newcomers: Gabriella – a mini-case study

Applying a translanguaging pedagogy is even more critical for newcomers, emergent bilinguals engaged in learning English less than six months after entering US schools. Flexibility in language practices with the inclusion of other communication modes offers newcomers opportunities to engage in English-medium environments (Hansen-Thomas *et al.*, 2021). Margarita's childhood experiences offered insight into the newcomer experience. Understanding the early quiet, observant nature of learning a language was used to deconstruct newcomer small group literacy experiences. We engaged in collaborative dialogue to make sense of one particular child's development as a reader and writer with this notion of a 'research-informed, practitioner-oriented pedagogical design' (Tian & Shepard-Carey, 2020: 1134). Sally offered insights from research and Margarita brought her childhood and teaching experiences to the discussions. As a result, there were spaces throughout the day for Gabriella to participate in unconventional ways supporting translanguaging practices.

Gabriella's experiences, a Spanish language newcomer, helps us illustrate the importance of one-word phrases, repetition and the use of gestures in the early stages of learning English. She was a Spanish-dominant student who spent much of her classroom time quietly observing others and noting the expectations associated with her US classroom. She rarely spoke in either language, whether engaged with the teacher or researcher. However, a close examination of her language use and gestures revealed Gabriella's ways of meaning-making and communicating with her peers. They were informative yet straightforward moves. Transcript C provides one example of Gabriella's participation in a book discussion and her digital response; she engaged with her small group of peers in response to a read aloud of *Little Red and the Very Hungry Lion* (Smith, 2016).

The transcript begins at the point in the story where Little Red was resting with her eyes closed under a tree, and a large lion appeared with a looming, mischievous grin. The illustration provides insight into pending events.

Transcript C

Sally: [Read the page.] *And she sat down in the shade of a shady tree. That's when Lion arrived — The Very Hungry Lion.*
Gabriella: Uh, oh. [Covered mouth with hand, gasped.]
Elena: I bet he's; he's going to get her.
Gabriella: [Nodded her head yes.]
Aliya: Something bad's gonna happen. I can tell.
Ezra: I bet he eats her kinda like, uh, Little Red Riding Hood.
Gabriella: [Smiled.] Sí. Bad, bad. [Tapped Lion's evil face on the book page.]

Although Gabriella had only a few utterances during this interaction, she demonstrated engagement and understanding of this section of the story. Upon the Sally's reading of the words, Gabriella gasped outwardly and said, 'Uh-oh.' This phrase was followed by a gesture to cover her mouth. While no words were spoken, her utterance and gesture taken together seemed to indicate a prediction that surmised the Lion was about to harm Little Red. This was central to the plot of the story. Elena verbalized this, and upon hearing her comments, Gabriella responded with an affirming nod, still indicating she understood Elena's use of English and the content of the story.

Ezra's prediction followed this action with a connection to another book, Little Red Riding Hood. Immediately after he named the story, Gabriella smiled as if she had heard those words before and connected with Little Red Riding Hood. Gabriella used the Spanish word 'sí (yes)' as a way to agree with the comments of Ezra and Aliya and then followed up by saying, 'bad, bad.' The repetition of these two words appeared to indicate that she was still communicating the impending doom of the events in the story. In addition, Gabriella touched Lion's face on the book page. The facial expression in the illustration was in line with her verbal comments.

Next, Gabriella spent time creating a digital response to the book. She worked quickly but looked up from her device several times. Her eyes moved toward the screens of others as if she was checking their work. Her creation (Figure 6.2) contained no written language, which was generally expected as a literacy practice in this grade. But what Gabriella did offer was an image of Lion when Little Red braided and twisted his hair, thus providing insight into another event in the story. Gabriella drew a happy face on the Lion, indicating how the story ended. Lion, Little Red and Aunt Rosie became friends.

All of Gabriella's literacy practices may be considered non-traditional in a school setting, but taking the time to put together utterances, one or two-word phrases, designing an image and gesturing paints a different picture. In this case, Gabriella was intentional in using available resources (English words, Spanish language, the language used by her peers, drawing tools and the paper copy of the book). This reminds us that children use their bodies for communicative purposes. Sometimes, this includes emotions like predictions about Lion's future behavior (Papen & Peach, 2020). The dynamic interplay of modes enables children to make meaning on their terms.

Figure 6.2 Gabriella's response to little red and the very hungry lion

Implications

As a result of this partnership, co-shifts were made to some of the instructional and assessment practices in Margarita's classroom to better support her emergent bilinguals in their navigation of texts and content. Discursive practices, active engagement with the same classroom of students by both of us and an examination of ongoing data collection and reflection contributed to co-stance changes and co-shifts in instructional practices. First, we worked together to navigate the school, district, and state monolingual policies in order to embrace translanguaging. Both of us had open mindsets given the vast research base about the benefits of translanguaging (Cenoz & Santos, 2020; Liu *et al.*, 2020), but needed to negotiate a space in Margarita's classroom for these practices.

The significant findings harness the power of collaboration, co-construction of knowledge and the social nature of literacy. Translanguaging occurred in small groups as students were free to draw from their rich linguistic repertoires while being supported by either the teacher or researcher (García *et al.*, 2017). How can this be extended to other classroom and assessment practices? After collaboration about the findings and numerous discussions about the emergent bilinguals, the following strategies were either implemented or planned for implementation as instruction returns to a face-to-face environment post-Covid-19.

Shifts in literacy instructional practices: Writing and technology

We are in an age where technology is an integral part of our everyday lives. Ensuring that emergent bilinguals have access to, are familiar with, and possess foundational skills is central to their academic growth and gaining real-world experiences. A more precise purpose for the use of technology emerged from this research. After observing how emergent bilinguals utilized the digital devices to showcase their understanding of texts, Margarita shifted her evolving ideas about the use of technology and saw the benefits for translingual writing and new academic content (Brown, 2021; Rowe, 2018; Rowe & Miller, 2016; Tai & Li, 2021). The vast resources like drawing tools, stickers, emojis, the availability of keyboards in multiple languages, etc., add new layers to the linguistic resources the children bring with them from home.

In the past, digital devices were relegated to reading digital stories or playing instructional games focused on phonics. No more. Margarita intentionally purchased Chromebooks to use as a medium for meaning-making, including writing, drawing, and recording students' voices. In addition, funding from Covid brought opportunities for one-on-one instruction with iPads. Margarita is currently utilizing the Pages app to engage students in writing about Benjamin Franklin. While Sally's beliefs about the power of technology remained strong, Margarita's use of technology in content areas like social studies broadened her notions of how translanguaging spaces are needed throughout the school day and not limited to the literacy block.

Further, Margarita typically waited to begin writing instruction until later in the year to allow students to master some basic skills. After months of working as a team, she realized that even young children are ready to make meaning from the beginning of the first-grade school year. There is no need to wait. As the students shared their digital authoring pieces with her, she saw all of the writing skills they were able to employ independently. Meaning resides in many modes, as evidenced by the findings in this chapter. These modes can come together to support the development of written language. Margarita plans to utilize writing prompts, sentence starters, word banks, pictures and student illustrations. She is acutely aware of the need to motivate and engage students' creativity. The co-stance on translanguaging as a transformative process that embraces creativity now pervades Margarita's mindset (Li, 2018).

We also plan to capitalize on the digital experiences emergent bilinguals gained during the Covid-19 pandemic when they had the opportunity to work with technology one-on-one at home. Emergent bilinguals can build from these experiences to complete writing assignments in multiple languages and explore their own topics and ideas. Thus, spaces were created for cultural stories where students can collaborate and co-create in unimagined ways. As a team, we plan to explore the options for co-designing technology infused lessons.

Shifts in curricular structures: Learning opportunities within groups

The school district's policy requiring ability groups for small group reading instruction left little room for us to alter the structure. This constraint impacted both of our practices during literacy instruction. We were not able to use flexible groups that provided for same language partners. After reviewing the data and talking more about how the emergent bilinguals worked together from different language groups, we saw value in mixed-group experiences and working around the system. While we did not change reading group structures, Margarita changed other small group instruction to provide authentic and meaningful learning experiences. For example, she plans to provide all students who speak Spanish with opportunities to work together with a same language partner on projects or engaging in book discussion especially in the areas of science and social studies. This may also include allowing students to process a whole group lesson in their first language, followed by an English discussion. When students struggle to 'find the English word,' Margarita will continue to encourage translanguaging by saying, 'Dije en español,' (the correct term 'Dilo en español,' which means 'Say it in Spanish'). If the emergent bilingual knows the word in Spanish, then the teacher assists in saying it in English or asking a friend to help with the translation. Thus, each discursive move affords and values a diversity of social interactions in the classroom (Zapata & Laman, 2016).

Both Sally and Margarita were challenged in their beliefs or co-stances about the ways in which the English-only students engaged in translanguaging practices with their emergent bilingual peers. It had not occurred to us that the Spanish speaking students would teach their English-only peers to speak and write Spanish. Reviews of transcripts brought this to our attention and ultimately made an impact on shifts in small groups. We realized the importance of including English-only students into the translanguaging framework by allowing them the time and space to experiment with a new language in their reading, writing, and talking. Margarita also plans to allow students to work together at various developmental levels to scaffold learning and share expertise. Students were able to bring other skills they possess to the table beyond academic skills. For example, some of her students with below grade level labels can teach higher-level students about technology or how to write in French. There is a need to make groups flexible to control their learning and select resources to make meaning. We maintain a co-stance that values students' home languages and other modes of meaning-making (Deroo, 2020; Martínez-Álvarez, 2017).

Visual strategies to enhance retelling

Throughout the research study, the teacher began utilizing retelling strategies to help students retell a story using key details (Shanahan *et al.*, 2010). The Five-Finger Retelling included (1) main character(s), (2) setting, (3) beginning or problem in the story, (4) middle or how the problem was solved, (5) ending or what happened at the end of the story. Students were encouraged to use a finger-shaped graphic organizer to write and/or draw to retell the key elements of the story It incorporated visual images, allowing emergent bilinguals access to the content. The change in design was made due to noticing the power of images in supporting the learning of emergent bilinguals. This way, students could quickly remember the five elements of retelling by looking at the poster. In addition, some students struggled to write retellings of the stories. The teacher adapted her retelling practices to include a word bank, drawing, and/or small group conferring for students to explain their ideas orally.

Selection of reading materials

Our selections of read-alouds were informed by the ongoing data analysis of the project. After noticing and discussing how students were responding to the culturally relevant books that Sally read, Margarita expanded her use of similar texts. This continuous cycle of reflective practice informed the ways we both valued languages and cultures and wanted to build upon it through thoughtful selections of reading materials used in the span of the school day (Tian & Shepard-Carey, 2020). Margarita selected familiar books, provided exposure to new knowledge, offered relatable texts that include multiple languages, and utilized culturally relevant texts.

The initial focus of our work together was the literacy block. We had not considered extending it to other curricular areas until our co-stances began to shift. This happened as a result of collaborative lunch conversations and reviewing student work samples. We noted how the emergent bilinguals translanguaged through their oral and written work around read-alouds. The fluid use of language assisted with literacy skills, so it made sense for us to expand these practices to cross-curricular opportunities as well. We should note that Sally was frequently not present during this time.

Our changes in stance pushed to Margarita to utilize particular texts to facilitate cross-curricular instruction. By integrating reading material from other content/subjects, students were exposed to a more diverse selection of literary materials across genres. For example, during science instruction, students learned about different animal classifications (i.e. mammals, reptiles, insects, amphibians) through Margarita's careful selection of animal read-alouds (explanatory and informational) as a way to develop and expand students' knowledge on new topics. This unit included books describing classifications of animals like *Crickets: World of Insects* (Green, 2006) and *Better Together: Animal Groups - Kangaroo Mob* (Kenney, 2020).

Shifts in assessment practices: Extending informal assessment options for emergent bilinguals

Retelling strategies can also be used as an informal assessment of students' understanding of the story. Emergent bilinguals may need to use drawing to elaborate or express content, as was evident in the findings. In the past, Margarita offered opportunities for students to explain written responses on assessments verbally. However, this did not include the creation of visuals or drawings. A reflection of this research regarding the rich details evident in students' drawings caused Margarita also to offer drawing as an assessment option to document what students know and can do accurately.

We provide an example to illustrate the intentional selection of books and the Five-Finger-Retelling Strategy used as an instructional and assessment strategy. After reading *The Three Bears* (Fomme, n.d.) from Epic Books (www.getepic.com), the class and Margarita used the Five-Finger Retell Strategy to discuss important details and events versus other parts of the story. This experience with a familiar story that is common across cultures was used as an impetus for a whole group read aloud of *My*

Rotten Redheaded Older Brother (Polacco, 1998). After hearing the story, students practiced the strategy in small groups. Then, to assess the students' understanding of retelling, the *Little Red Hen* (Gresser, n.d.) was read aloud. Margarita assessed the students individually as they used the graphic organizer to write or draw the key details from the story.

Gabriella (home language - Spanish), a newcomer, drew to demonstrate her understanding of the main character. She drew the Red Hen but called it a chicken. Gabriella showed her knowledge of the setting by drawing a house with flowers and words to explain it was a farm. Margarita allowed students like Gabriella to elaborate verbally and/or explain by drawing a picture for a more accurate assessment. Without the multiple modes taken together, a misjudgment of Gabriella's academic progress would likely be possibly resulting in academic failure, retention, or a deficit label. According to Cummins (2011; 2000), there are varied trajectories for students acquiring English as a new language and no scientific foundation for expecting these students to perform at grade level by the end of one year. Therefore, it is essential to not define emergent bilinguals by what they lack.

Translanguaging in early literacy, monolingual contexts

Axelrod and Cole (2018) remind us of the importance of translanguaging for young learners navigating monolingual schools and classrooms like Margarita's. Early literacy experiences need to be spaces where children can flexibly use their linguistic repertoires to make sense of stories being read, engaging in conversations, and recording their experiences through writing. Approximating meaning across language systems helps emergent bilinguals supports a developing competence of multiple languages with increasing levels of sophistication. Each child should be afforded the choice of how they use their linguistic repertoires, which may extend to how information is expressed on assessments. This research highlights the need to not only take translanguaging practices into account for instruction but also for assessing in equitable ways that maximize student learning (García *et al*., 2017).

Broader Implications: Teacher–Researcher Partnerships

Suggestions for education and research communities

Shifts in instructional practices can be challenging in the field of education (Tian & Shepard-Carey, 2020). A partnership can open spaces to think through complex theories and ideas to discover how they may translate into beneficial classroom practices that showcase the various ways meaning-making unfolds for emergent bilingual learners. Overcoming the restraints set up by school systems regarding curricular practices and the use of materials that support multiple languages can be overwhelming for an individual teacher. However, a partnership based in research can shed light on the effectiveness of translanguaging practices which can be used to convince other school officials to change assessment policies or adapt curricula for multilingual learners. A burden that seems so enormous to one teacher can be shared and tackled as a collaborative group. Partnerships need not be limited to one teacher but can involve a grade level or even the entire school. In addition, the partnership may seek funding sources to support translanguaging practices and shifts in ideologies.

Starting a partnership

Since we found our teacher–researcher partnership to be such a positive experience, we offer some suggestions to guide the establishment of a partnership around translanguaging pedagogies. First, search a local university for professors who are currently investigating topics surrounding translanguaging. This can start with a simple review of their website, and be followed up through emails expressing an interest in a collaborative venture. Propose coming together for a meeting, virtual or face-to-face, to discuss possibilities given your context. Second, invite your school administrator to the conversation. Nothing can move forward in terms of research without the school district's approval. Next, develop research questions that explore your interests in how translanguaging practices can improve the literacy learning of your multilingual students. This may require reading current literature on the topic. Finally, co-design your research plan and collaborative activities in order to get started.

Conclusion

The teacher–research partnership was informed through a co-stance (Tian & Shepard-Carey, 2020). The two of us continually engaged in conversations about the literacy and instructional practices of the emergent bilinguals featured in this chapter. Both of us were influenced by one another's insights and changing beliefs about the best ways to teach literacy to young emergent bilinguals. This relationship began with trust and continues to be a space where the two of us problematize school mandates and look for better ways to document the assets children bring to school and use them as resources for academic learning. We know that students are constantly becoming, and their identities are highly influenced by their language practices (Kuby & Rucker, 2016). Our ultimate goal is to help other educators understand and utilize a translanguaging pedagogy that influences curriculum design and instruction shifts.

Our partnership continues as we revise instructional and assessment practices for the new set of emergent bilinguals that will enter the classroom doors in the near future. Covid restrictions prevented collaborative efforts in Fall 2021 with hopes of continuation in Spring 2022. As schools reopen, we hope to continue to ponder and seek answers to new questions arising out of our collaboration. Technology is one area where the two of us see promise for supporting the translanguaging practices of young emergent bilinguals. We would like to investigate what affordances technology offers to support translanguaging literacy practices in diverse classrooms. Margarita's students now have one-on-one access to iPads, which will be the platform for pushing us into new ways of supporting emergent bilinguals' experiences with reading and writing. Our investigation may also involve looking closely at the capacity of visual literacy as a means for articulating meaning across sign systems. Finally, in order to continue our work on asset-based assessments, we plan to co-design assessments across literacy practices, not just read-alouds.

References

Arena, J. (2016) *Marta Big & Small.* New York: Roaring Book Press.

Axelrod, Y. and Cole, M. (2018) 'The pumpkins are coming... vienen las calabazas... that sounds funny': Translanguaging practices of young emergent bilinguals. *Journal of Early Childhood Literacy* 18 (1), 129–153.

Bezemer, J. and Kress, G. (2016) *Multimodality, Learning, and Communication: A Social Semiotic Frame.* Abingdon: Routledge.

Brown, S.A. (2021) Emergent bilinguals as text designers: Rendering meaning through signs. *English Teaching: Practice and Critique* 20 (2), 130–148.

Brown, S. and Allmond, A. (2020) Constructing my world: A case study examining emergent bilingual composing practices. *Early Childhood Education Journal* 49 (2), 209–221.

Cenoz, J. and Santos, A. (2020) Implementing pedagogical translanguaging in trilingual schools. *System* 92, 102273–102279. https://doi.org/10.1016/j.system.2020.102273

Cummins, J. (2011) Literacy engagement: Fueling academic growth for English learners. *The Reading Teacher* 65 (2), 142–146.

Cummins, J. (2000) *Language, Power and Pedagogy: Bilingual Children in the Crossfire.* Clevedon: Multilingual Matters.

Deroo, M. (2020) Translanguaging pedagogy to support bi/multilingual students' language learning in social studies: 'How we communicate everything'. In A. Slapac and S. Coppersmith (eds) *Beyond Language Learning Instruction: Transformative Supports for Emergent Bilinguals and Educators* (pp. 233–261). Hershey, PA: IGI Global.

Espinosa, L. (2012) Assessment of Young English language learners. *The Encyclopedia of Applied Linguistics.* Chichester: Wiley & Sons.

Espinosa, C. and Ascenzi-Moreno, L. (2021) *Rooted in Strength: The Power of Multilingualism and Translanguaging.* New York: Scholastic.

Fomme, C. (n.d.) *The Three Bears.* https://www.getepic.com/app/read/37547

Fu, D., Hadjioannou, X. and Zhou, X. (2019) *Translanguaging for Emergent Bilinguals: Inclusive Teaching in the Linguistically Diverse Classroom.* New York: Teachers College Press.

García, O., Johnson, S. and Seltzer, K. (2017) *The Translanguaging Classroom: Leveraging Student Bilingualism for Learning.* Philadelphia, PA: Caslon.

García, O. and Kleifgen, J.A. (2010) *Educating Emergent Bilinguals: Policies, Programs, and Practices for English Language Learners.* New York: Teachers College Press.

García, O. and Kleyn, T. (2016) A translanguaging education policy: Disruptions and creating spaces of possibility. In O. García and T. Kleyn (eds) *Translanguaging with Multilingual Students: Learning from Classroom Moments* (pp. 181–201). New York: Routledge.

García, O. and Li, W. (2014) *Translanguaging: Language, Bilingualism, and Education*. London: Palgrave McMillan.

Gort, M. (2012) Evaluation and revision processes of young bilinguals in a dual language program. In E. Bauer and M. Gort (eds) *Early Biliteracy Development: Exploring Young Learners' Use of their Linguistic Resources* (pp. 90–110). New York: Routledge.

Green, E. (2006) Crickets: World of insects. https://www.getepic.com/app/read/35881

Gresser, V. (n.d.) *The Little Red Hen*. https://betterlesson.com/lesson/resource/2404646/little-red-hen-pdf

Hansen-Thomas, H., Stewart, M.A., Flint, P. and Dollar, T. (2021) Co-learning in the high school English class through translanguaging: emergent bilingual newcomers and monolingual teachers. *Journal of Language, Identity & Education* 20 (3), 151–166.

Hubbard, R. (2020) *The Oldest Student: How Mary Walker Learned to Read*. New York: Schwartz & Wade.

Kenney, K. (2020) Better together: Animal groups – kangaroo mob. https://www.getepic.com/app/read/70542

Kress, G. (2010) *Multimodality: A Social Semiotic Approach to Contemporary Communication*. Abingdon: Routledge.

Kuby, C. and Rucker, T. (2016) *Go be a Writer!: Expanding the Curricular Boundaries of Literacy Learning with Children*. New York: Teachers College Press.

Lau, S.M.C., Tian, Z. and Lin, A.M. (2022) Critical literacy and additional language learning: An expansive view of translanguaging for change-enhancing possibilities. In J.Z. Pandya *et al.* (eds) *The Handbook of Critical Literacies* (pp. 381–390). New York: Routledge.

Leung, S.K. (2019) Translanguaging through visual arts in early childhood: A case study in a Hong Kong kindergarten. *Asia-Pacific Journal of Research in Early Childhood Education* 13 (1), 47–67.

Li, W. (2018) Translanguaging as a practical theory of language. *Applied Linguistics* 39 (1), 9–30.

Lin, A.M. (2019) Theories of trans/languaging and trans-semiotizing: Implications for content-based education classrooms. *International Journal of Bilingual Education and Bilingualism* 22 (1), 5–16.

Liu, J.E., Lo, Y.Y. and Lin, A.M. (2020) Translanguaging pedagogy in teaching English for Academic Purposes: Researcher-teacher collaboration as a professional development model. *System* 92, 102276–16. https://doi.org/10.1016/j.system.2020.102276

Martínez-Álvarez, P. (2017) Language multiplicity and dynamism: Emergent bilinguals taking ownership of language use in a hybrid curricular space. *International Multilingual Research Journal* 11 (4), 255–276.

Martínez-Álvarez, P. and Ghiso, M.P. (2017) On languaging and communities: Latino/a emergent bilinguals' expansive learning and critical inquiries into global childhoods. *International Journal of Bilingual Education and Bilingualism* 20 (6), 667–687.

Mavers, D. (2011) *Children's Writing and Drawing: The Remarkable in the Unremarkable*. New York: Routledge.

Norris, S. (2019) *Systematically Working with Multimodal Data: Research Methods in Multimodal Discourse Analysis*. Chichester: John Wiley and Sons.

Osorio, S.L. (2020) Building culturally and linguistically sustaining spaces for emergent bilinguals: Using read-alouds to promote translanguaging. *The Reading Teacher* 74 (2), 127–135.

Papen, U. and Peach, E. (2020) Using picture books to develop critical visual literacy in primary schools: Challenges of a dialogic approach. *Literacy* 54 (1), 3–10.

Polacco, P. (1998) *My Rotten Redheaded Older Brother.* New York: Simon & Schuster.

Rowe, L.W. (2018) Say it in your language: Supporting translanguaging in multilingual classes. *The Reading Teacher* 72 (1), 31–38.

Rowe, D.W. and Miller, M.E. (2016) Designing for diverse classrooms: Using iPads and digital cameras to compose eBooks with emergent bilingual/biliterate four-year-olds. *Journal of Early Childhood Literacy* 16 (4), 425–472. https://doi.org/10.1177/1468798415593622

Rowe, D. and Wilson, S. (2015) The development of a descriptive measure of early childhood writing: Results from Write Start! writing assessment. *Journal of Literacy Research* 47 (2), 245–292.

Saldaña, J. (2021) *The Coding Manual for Qualitative Researchers.* Thousand Oaks, CA: SAGE Publications.

Shanahan, T., Callison, K., Carriere, C., Duke, N.K., Pearson, P.D., Schatschneider, C. and Torgesen, J. (2010) Improving reading comprehension in kindergarten through 3rd Grade: IES Practice Guide. NCEE 2010-4038. *What Works Clearinghouse.*

Shannon, D. (2006) *Good Boy, Fergus!* New York: Blue Sky Press.

Spradley, J. (2016) Participant Observation. Long Grove, IL: Waveland Press.

Smith, A. (2016) *Little Red and the Very Hungry Lion.* New York: Scholastic.

Snicket, L. (2019) *Swarm of Bees.* New York: Little, Brown.

Spence, L. (2010) Generous reading: Seeing students through their writing. *The Reading Teacher* 63 (8), 634–642.

The Governor's Office of Student Achievement: G.A. School Grade Reports (n.d.) https://schoolgrades.georgia.gov/

Tai, K.W.H. and Li, W. (2021) The affordances of iPad for constructing a technology-mediated space in Hong Kong English medium instruction secondary classrooms: A translanguaging view. *Language Teaching Research.* https://doi.org/10.1177/13621688211027851

Tian, Z. and Shepard-Carey, L. (2020) (Re) imagining the future of translanguaging pedagogies in TESOL through teacher–researcher collaboration. *TESOL Quarterly* 54 (4), 1131–1143.

Torpsten, A.C. (2018) Translanguaging in a Swedish multilingual classroom. *Multicultural Perspectives* 20 (2), 104–110.

Wu, Y. and Lin, A.M. (2019) Translanguaging and trans-semiotising in a CLIL biology class in Hong Kong: Whole-body sense-making in the flow of knowledge co-making. *Classroom Discourse* 10 (3–4), 252–273.

Zapata, A. (2020) Cultivating a critical translingual landscape in the elementary language arts classroom. *Language Arts* 97 (6), 384–390.

Zapata, A. and Laman, T.T. (2016) 'I write to show how beautiful my languages are': Translingual writing instruction in English-dominant classrooms. *Language Arts* 93 (5), 366–378.

7 Towards Translingualism? Collaboration Between University and School Teacher-Researchers in an Australian Multilingual Primary School

Toni Dobinson, Stephanie Dryden, Gerard Winkler, Paul Gardner and Paul Mercieca

Introduction

At the last census in 2016, Australia reported 28.5% of its population coming from overseas (Australian Bureau of Statistics (ABS), 2016). Current estimates are that up to 25% of Australian school children speak English as an Additional Language or Dialect (EAL/D) (additional language is termed LX by Dewaele, 2018). Added to this is the 5.5% of First Nations students who are Aboriginal or Torres Strait Islander (ABS, 2016). These EAL/D children of all ages come from many different cultural and socioeconomic backgrounds, have varied English language proficiency levels and home language literacy and may not necessarily have had access to formal education in their home countries. The last decade has seen considerable changes made to the funding model for English language programs in Australia. However, funding is now directed to the broader areas of literacy and numeracy for all and mainstream teacher development rather than being directed to specialized educational needs (Lingard *et al.*, 2012).

Despite best intentions of the teachers, EAL/D students' learning needs may not be sufficiently met by mainstream subject teachers (Creagh, 2014). This problem does not originate with the teachers but with policy and curriculum documents (Ball *et al.*, 2012) especially where English is not the main focus of lessons (Kettle, 2017). While the benefits of inclusive teaching point to more opportunities for all students to interact and collaborate together, many mainstream subject teachers have concerns about how to design learning to benefit both EAL/D students and students whose L1 is English (Dobinson & Buchori, 2016; Guilfoyle & Mistry, 2013). The potential for changes to curriculum and pedagogy through changes in critical consciousness brought about by collaboration between teacher-researchers from different settings has been acknowledged by many researchers in the field (Fowler-Amato & Warrington, 2017; Gutierez & Kim, 2017; Hamza *et al.*, 2018; Jung & Brady, 2016), and may better enable the introduction of translanguaging pedagogies into the classroom. Translanguaging pedagogy encourages the use of fluid language practices across multiple named languages and varieties that enhance communication (Li, 2018) and can provide EAL/D students with greater linguistic and academic support. It has at its core the 'multilingual turn' which is an 'epistemological shift that continues to challenge the framing of monolingualism as the norm' (May, 2013: 50). However, because of translanguaging's relative newness and its strong departure from maintaining monolingual norms within the classroom (Tian & Shepard-Carey, 2020), a collaborative framework that harnesses students' translanguaging practices is recommended so that teachers are assisted to create classrooms in which pedagogic, community and social values and goals can be shared (Creese & Blackledge, 2010) along with approaches to curriculum which harness students' identities and ideologies in terms of their language (Seltzer, 2020).

In this project, university teacher-researchers worked with a primary school teacher-researcher to foster a sustainable stance which sees diverse linguistic practices as valuable resources to be built upon and leveraged in the primary classroom. For over two years teacher-researchers collaboratively designed, delivered and evaluated lessons, integrating in-school and out-of-school language practices and attempting to shift to a position where practitioners can respond confidently when student feedback suggests changes in pedagogies are needed (García *et al.*, 2017). The project provided detail and analysis essential for understanding collaborative translanguaging pedagogies in primary educational settings found to be lacking in previous research (Tian & Shepard-Carey, 2020).

Using a participatory action research approach, teacher-researchers asked:

(1) To what extent can translanguaging pedagogies be introduced into a multilingual junior primary school classroom?
(2) How do the students respond to the introduction of these pedagogies?
(3) What is the experience of teacher–researcher collaborators from different educational settings in planning, delivering and evaluating translanguaging lessons?

Translanguaging as we see it

Intentional translanguaging pedagogies (García *et al.*, 2017) encourage students to foster their full space-based translingual repertoires (Canagarajah, 2018) and adapt their communicative practices to utilize all semiotic resources at their disposal (Creese & Blackledge, 2010). Linguistic hegemony can be subverted by ensuring educational contexts become sites for identity retention in learning, with translanguaging classrooms providing emergent multilingual students with opportunities to increase their engagement (Back *et al.*, 2020), which results in the promotion of equal opportunities for all students in the classroom. However, despite the consensus of language researchers on the benefits of translanguaging (Alford, 2019; Bialystok & Barac, 2012; García & Kleyn, 2016), mainstream literacy education in Australia remains largely monolingual in orientation (Cross, 2012; Ollerhead, 2018). García *et al.* (2017) advocate for a change in this monolingual mindset through the incorporation of a *translanguaging corriente*, using the metaphor of a flowing river current to describe the fluidity of students' linguistic and cultural practices. Rather than viewing named languages as sitting on opposite and separate sides of the riverbank, they argue that the use of the translanguaging 'flow' of the river dissolves this divide, enabling bilingual students to use the entirety of that territory (Johnson *et al.*, 2019).

Allowing translanguaging corrientes in the classroom provides students with an opportunity to harness their individual linguistic repertoires (Johnson *et al.*, 2019) and offers an avenue to express and share their real-life experiences with others (Bouchereau Bauer *et al.*, 2017). The encouragement of translanguaging in this context destabilizes monolingual norms in the classroom and creates an environment where students and teachers can share their diverse cultural and linguistic knowledge. However, due to these pervasive and ingrained English-only discourses within the school environment, students may initially resist translanguaging in class, but with persistence, encouragement and collaboration with others, students can discover cultural connections and deepen their vocabulary (Tian & Shepard-Carey, 2020).

Conceptual Framework

University teacher-researchers in this study sought to investigate and describe processes and products to be found in the translanguaging classroom using García *et al.*'s (2017) framework of *stance, design, shift* to guide them. In order for teachers to encourage an overt translanguaging corriente that goes beyond just using translanguaging as a meaning-making strategy for scaffolding, they need to incorporate a translanguaging *stance* that leverages students' translanguaging corriente and makes students aware that their linguistic repertoires are valuable (Johnson *et al.*,

2019). A teacher's stance is their philosophical or ideological standpoint; their set of beliefs. What a teacher decides to include or exclude from lessons and their decision to draw upon the translanguaging corriente in their multilingual classrooms or not will depend upon their beliefs about the value of translanguaging, and their willingness to transcend the dominant paradigm of monolingualism in traditional school language practices. In short, teachers with a translanguaging stance see students' home languages in lessons as a resource and a right (Ruiz, 1984). This creates a more democratic classroom where students feel welcome to actively participate, encouraging students and teachers to contribute towards their learning (Freire, 1970; García *et al.*, 2017).

Once the teacher decides on a translanguaging *stance*, they can then *design* a translanguaging space within the classroom that incorporates cultural practices, school and home languages (Tian & Shepard-Carey, 2020). This allows for expansion beyond monocultural and monolingual understandings in the classroom and promotes student connection with home languages and cultures (García *et al.*, 2017). The teacher and the students work together to integrate these resources, recognizing the value of intentional planning of translanguaging activities and using students' voices and needs to shape lesson development. This is consolidated by ongoing teacher observation and reflection during lessons (García *et al.*, 2017). Moment by moment monitoring of the students' ability to perform tasks successfully needs to be accompanied by a willingness and flexibility to change approach and tasks at any time during the lesson. In other words, teachers should be prepared to *shift* what they do in line with the dynamic nature of the translanguaging corriente and the ability of the students to perform the set tasks. Students will then be better supported and teachers more responsive to the students' needs (Johnson *et al.*, 2019), convincing students that their L1s belong at school (García *et al.*, 2017).

While García *et al.* have provided the framework of *stance, design* and *shift*, Tian and Shepard-Carey (2020) have proposed an expansion of this framework, referring specifically to collaborative partnerships (in this case, a university and a primary school) as a *co-stance, co-design* and *co-shift*. This framework may be one potential solution for subverting monolingual ideologies in the classroom, by combining the classroom expertise of the teacher with the specialized translanguaging knowledge of the researchers, to form a collaborative space that benefits linguistically diverse students. Such collaborations have the potential to ultimately improve practice for all practitioners, providing each with the tools to access a wider skillset than would be possible working alone with less resources for solving problems (Edwards, 2010). Tian and Shepard-Carey (2020: 1133) suggest that a collaborative partnership which encourages and embeds translanguaging pedagogies into practices is 'not an individual or unidirectional process, but a collaborative, dynamic, complex process' that requires both the teacher and researcher to develop a translanguaging *co-stance, co-design* and capacity to *co-shift* when necessary. The implementation of this collaborative framework allows for translanguaging classrooms enhanced by collaborative teaching, which promote and explore the linguistic and cultural repertoires of students (Tian & Shepard-Carey, 2020).

A vital element of successful collaboration involves centering the experience and knowledge that teachers have, and combining this expertise with the strategies and ideas that researchers bring (Gutiérrez & Vossoughi, 2010). This enables teacher-researcher discussions around what is central to practice, understandings about what matters in each field, and mutual recognition of each participant's values and goals (Edwards, 2011). This can create substantial change to curriculum and pedagogy, and may also foster the growth of critical consciousness of teaching approaches (Jung & Brady, 2016). Not only can discussion and dialogue between the teacher and the researcher achieve greater understandings of the others' content knowledge and specialization (Arkoudis, 2005), it can lead to the creation of a *co-stance*, where researchers and teachers work collaboratively to create belief systems regarding translanguaging in the classroom, enabling them to work together equitably to *co-design* a pedagogical framework (Tian & Shepard-Carey, 2020). Once the *co-stance* is agreed and the teacher-researchers reach the stage of *co-design*, they can create lessons that incorporate translanguaging pedagogies which encourage the students' full linguistic repertoires and decide how to create translanguaging spaces (Tian & Shepard-Carey, 2020) that provide clear expectations and goals for students (Bell & Baecher, 2012). Finally, teacher-researchers can work together to create *co-shifts*, where they continuously reflect on the classroom environment and adapt lessons to support students in their linguistic expression (Tian & Shepard-Carey, 2020).

In the Australian context, while scholars have commented on the importance of linguistically diverse spaces for EAL/D learners (see Cross, 2012), there is little in the way of collaborative translanguaging research in Australian school settings to encourage this. An exception is research by Sue Ollerhead (2019), who outlines one method of collaborative translanguaging pedagogies in a specialized secondary classroom, where students were encouraged to translanguage for a curriculum unit on poetry. In this research, translanguaging was used to encourage deeper textual analysis through the exploration and interpretation of how poems evoke mood, with the larger aim of building vocabulary, expressiveness and literacy. While Ollerhead's translanguaging pedagogy had a similar collaborative philosophy to our project, the students were adolescents in Ollerhead's project and were therefore undertaking more complex learning and literacy tasks, whereas this chapter focuses on the development of literacy and language skills of younger learners. Both studies demonstrate how collaborative translanguaging projects in action can reposition EAL/D learners to recognize their linguistic abilities and cultivate meaning making, rather than positing deficit perspectives surrounding their language competence (Cross, 2012).

These specialist collaborations result in the significant benefit of improved understanding and enhanced responses for all parties, providing more opportunities to build on the expertise that others offer to create insightful solutions to complicated problems (Edwards, 2011). In this case, Gary's classroom teaching experience, in collaboration with Toni's experience in applied linguistics and Paul G's experience with literacy, combine to form a mutual recognition of expertise that enables each expert to investigate and scaffold different possibilities to work towards pedagogical expansion. Having two researchers and one teacher in this study brought different skill sets to the table, providing different expertise and perspectives in building the students' reading skills and engaging in intentional translanguaging tasks. Having the two areas of expertise then complemented Gary's skills, whose expertise was in the classroom ecology and in his knowledge of the students.

Method

Research design

Participatory action research (sometimes called collaborative action research) is practice-based inquiry which seeks to create knowledge, propose and implement change, improve practice and performance (Stringer, 1999). Kemmis and McTaggert (1988) suggest the key stages of action research are: (1) developing a plan for improvement, (2) implementing the plan, (3) observing and documenting the effects of the plan and (4) reflecting on the outcomes of the plan to inform further planning and action. The study described here fits these criteria and is part of a larger ongoing, longitudinal (since 2018) action research practice-based inquiry involving primary school teacher-researchers at one school in Australia and university teacher-researchers at one university in Australia. An initial needs analysis administered to the classroom teacher-researcher by the university teacher-researchers suggested that both parties would benefit from collaborative planning, teaching and evaluating of lessons at the primary school site. One series of lessons that was conducted during the project focused on integrating translanguaging pedagogies into classroom literacy practices. The setting, participants, data collection procedures and data analysis frameworks for this micro-investigation are described in the next sections.

Setting and participants

The independent public primary school where the project took place has students from over 32 different cultural backgrounds enrolled. Many of these students are from refugee and low socioeconomic status families. Participants in the study were 25 students aged between seven and eight years old in a Junior Primary Year Two class. Of the 25 students, 75% (19) were plurilingual or bidialectal, speaking Punjabi, Malayalam, Bahasa Indonesia, Korean, Arabic, Mandarin, Farsi, Krio, Japanese, Dzongkha and Aboriginal English. They came from places like India, Egypt, Iraq, Sierra Leone, China, Indonesia, Korea, Japan, Bhutan and rural and remote Australia. The remainder were monolingual students speaking English as their first and only language. Participants also included three academics (university teacher-researchers Toni, Paul G and research assistant Steph) from the fields of TESOL/applied linguistics and literacy, and the classroom teacher (school teacher-researcher Gary).

Background to the study

The study reported here is the second of a two-part study. Prior to stage one, the two university teacher-researchers planned and negotiated co-teaching roles with the school teacher-researcher, who provided knowledgeable insights of the students and classroom management. Lessons were jointly planned, co-delivered and evaluated. The school teacher-researcher informed students that they would have three teachers and then Toni and Paul G introduced themselves as teachers from the local university. Both university teacher-researchers had previously been classroom practitioners. An initial lesson schedule, in which respective teaching roles were identified, had been prepared around culturally relevant literature; the elicitation of students' knowledge and experience of migration and language to describe experience. The lesson was jointly evaluated before planning a second lesson, which was also co-delivered. Both lessons utilized collaborative learning strategies designed to encourage students to share knowledge, feelings and experiences in an ethos of mutual respect and collaboration. This ethos established a 'climate' of trust, which helped students draw on the L1 knowledge in stage two of the project. Something that also should be noted that primary school classrooms in Australia do not have specific subject input. One classroom teacher teaches all subjects in the day for one group of students.

Data collection

Qualitative data were collected between December 2019 and September 2021 from five sources: an initial interview with the school teacher-researcher; written feedback from students in the class; classroom observations; teacher-researcher planning and evaluation sessions pre and post lessons; and teacher-researcher reflection sheets. Permission to conduct the study was obtained from the Department of Education and Human Ethics at the university that funded the study.

Interview

An initial interview was conducted with the classroom teacher at the beginning of the project in order to collect background information about common practices in the classroom and the perspectives of the teacher. This was semi-structured in nature, approximately 60 minutes in length and digitally recorded. Questions asked were:

- Do you have any experience with encouraging or allowing the children to use all their languages and all their varieties of language when they are communicating in speech or writing?
- How do you feel about that?
- Would you ever encourage them to do that?
- What about in terms of writing? Do the students ever translanguage, i.e. write in English and then insert words from their L1?

Written feedback from students

Students were given a set of simple questions written in English to answer straight after Lesson 3 and Lesson 4, asking them to recall what they had learned and comment on their experiences of the lesson (see example in later section).

Participatory classroom observations

Observations of the four lessons forming the focus of this study took place between March and September 2020 while researchers were co-teaching lessons. Two lessons took place in one term of 12 weeks and two lessons in the next term of 12 weeks. Digital recorders were placed on the desks in the groups of six students while the teacher-researchers were involved in teaching the lessons. Only one teacher-researcher at any time was involved in front of room teaching so the other two were able to set up and monitor the recorders as well as observe and take field notes noting any interesting occurrences connected with students' use of translanguaging or related behaviors while students were involved with the activities. Each teacher-researcher taught the part of the lesson they felt most comfortable with and according to their strengths (e.g. Toni's strength is vocabulary teaching and pronunciation so she did this part) while Paul G is a writer so he felt very comfortable in the story telling part of the initial lesson. For example, in a 90-minute teaching slot one university teacher-researcher would take the students on the mat for a warm-up and story-telling activity (Paul G) while the other (Toni) manned the recorders, monitored the students and made field notes of any interesting behaviors on the part of the students that were relevant to the study. The other university teacher-researcher would then take over with a vocabulary building task (Toni) while the other university teacher-researcher (Paul G) manned the recorders, monitored the students and made notes about anything he felt was significant to note with regard to translanguaging or classroom behaviors.

Teacher-researcher planning and evaluation of the lessons

For all of the lessons taught, Gary, Paul G and Toni came together to discuss, plan and evaluate the lessons. They used written feedback from plenary tasks together with recorded classroom observations to inform the planning of each lesson after the initial lesson. The recorded oral interaction during translanguaging activities captured students' ability and motivation to do the tasks they set as well as their coping strategies and creative use of language. All planning and evaluation sessions were audio recorded with evaluation sessions further backed up with their written reflections on how they had experienced the collaborative teaching lessons, i.e. what they had learned from each other; what they had learned about themselves, and what they had learned from the students.

Teacher-researcher reflections

After each block of two lessons teacher-researchers wrote down what they felt they had learned about the tasks and classroom set-up; what they had learned about and from the students, what they had learned about their own teaching, and what they had learned from their co-teachers.

Data analysis

The framework of co-stance, co-design and co-shift (Tian & Shepard-Carey, 2020) described in the conceptual framework was used to guide the qualitative analysis of the data, categorize the data and address the research questions. All of the questions could be addressed using this framework. The data sets of the classroom teacher-researcher interview and the classroom observations were digitally recorded and transcribed, with the data analyzed and coded inductively paying attention to themes that aligned with the co-stance, co-design and co-shift framework. Student written feedback and teacher-researcher (both school and university) planning and evaluation sessions pre- and post-lessons were analyzed for common themes through the use of written field notes and self-reflections at the conclusion of the classes. Findings were pooled to explore, holistically, how all collaborators (university teacher-researchers, classroom teacher-researcher and students) in the lessons had changed their stances, reflected on the design of the lessons and shifted their practice based on 'moment-by-moment decisions' (García *et al.*, 2017: 28) during the lessons. Trustworthiness and triangulation of the analysis was gained by university teacher-researcher consensus (Toni, Paul G and Steph).

Lesson Descriptions and Rationales

The team decided to build up to the translanguaging pedagogies lessons slowly over several lessons; making sure that students were fully acquainted with the contexts/meanings of the words with which they would be working and also relaxed and confident about using their L1s in a setting where this was rarely encouraged. In this way Lessons 1 and 2 laid the foundations and built student self-assurance about translanguaging in Lessons 3 and 4. Central to the first two lessons was the book *The Colour of Home* by Mary Hoffman and Karin Littlewood (1992) and the introduction of adjectives of feeling to describe how the main Somalian character, Hassan, might be feeling when he has to move to a new country as a refugee. The later lessons (3 and 4) built on these first two lessons and recycled new vocabulary in different tasks and encouraged students to introduce equivalents to the new English words in their own languages. A brief summary of each of the lessons is described in Figure 7.1, with lessons one and two taught collaboratively by Gary, Toni and Paul, while lessons three and four were taught collaboratively by Gary and Toni, and assisted by Steph. Only Lessons 3 and 4 were analyzed for this chapter as they were the only lessons explicitly focused on translanguaging pedagogies. This research took place during the literacy morning slots of the lessons.

The initial lessons 1, 2 and 3 aimed to: (1) build students' background knowledge about different cultures and contexts and encourage them to personalize their own stories; (2) scaffold students' ability to understand the story read out in English; (3) introduce new vocabulary in English – passive vocabulary for understanding the story and active vocabulary to add to students' repertoire of new English words; (4) develop oral literacy; and (5) develop narrative writing skills in English. Lessons 3 and 4 aimed to: (1) revise the new English vocabulary; (2) encourage students to teach each other some new words in their own languages including equivalents to the new words they had learned in English; (3) encourage students to use their own languages where possible in the stories already written in English, and replace English words with their own L1 words; (4) subvert monolingual ideologies and empower students to feel good about their translingual identities.

Lesson One (Gary, Toni and Paul) was co-designed to acquaint students with some new adjectives for describing feelings. The context was a refugee boy (Hassan) arriving in a new country in the book *The Colour of Home* (Hoffman & Littlewood, 1992). Students collaborated on integrated skills task work using the text as a springboard. Two university teacher-researchers were involved and one primary school teacher-researcher.
Lesson Two (Gary, Toni and Paul) was co-designed to reacquaint students with the story from the *Colour of Home* and the new vocabulary of feelings that was introduced in the previous lesson through a series of collaborative integrated skills task work. Two university teacher-researchers were involved and one primary school teacher-researcher.
Lesson Three (Gary and Toni) was co-designed to introduce the idea of intentional translanguaging pedagogies to students. The vocabulary introduced previously was again recycled through the story of Hassan and students were encouraged to find equivalents to these adjectives for feelings in their own L1s and teach these equivalents to their fellow students through a series of collaborative integrated skills tasks. One university teacher-researcher was involved and one primary school teacher-researcher.
Lesson Four (Gary and Toni) was co-designed to build on Lesson Three and further embolden students to translanguage and teach their L1s to other students through a series of collaborative integrated skills tasks. One university teacher-researcher was involved and one primary school teacher-researcher.

Figure 7.1 A summary of lessons one to four

Lesson three analysis

Co-stances: Teacher-researchers – pre-lesson

It would be fair to say that Gary was very new to the idea of translanguaging as seen in his response to Toni's question in Extract 1 taken from his initial interview with her.

Extract 1 Toni's interview with Gary

#	Discount	Interview transcript
1	Toni	But would you ever encourage them [students] to do that [translanguaging]? If they don't understand something, would you say …can you speak to so and so and explain it to them… in their language…?
2	Gary	Well yeah actually I haven't probably done that enough in the classroom, because…
3	Toni	Cause they're a resource
4	Gary	Yeah that would be a great resource and I think yeah I should probably be encouraging that more.

Gary admitted being aware of the corriente or the translanguaging resource available to him in his multilingual class but not yet exploiting that resource. This was the first indication that a co-stance was being created between us, with Gary, the classroom teacher-researcher seeing the multilingual child's repertoire as a resource ('yeah that would be a great resource') rather than deficit behavior (García *et al.*, 2017) and Toni, one of the university teacher-researchers pondering how this might take place in the Junior Primary context with students of different abilities and capabilities in their L1 and LX. Gary began the journey admitting a sense of negligence on his part and there was a feeling that this was based on lack of confidence to do other than what the syllabus demands. Having a collaborator to help him try out new pedagogies seemed to help him to create a more confident, risk-taking approach and an ideological stance which was curious and valuing of translanguaging in his classroom.

Co-stances: Teacher-researchers and students – during the lesson

Students' stances towards the translanguaging tasks were tentative in Lesson 3. Teachers overestimated the students' feelings of ease with the translanguaging tasks. One student said, when asked to provide a word that matched 'misunderstood' in his own language, 'I only know two words and one of them is a bad word'. From being encouraged to use only the dominant language of English when speaking in class, and Australian Standard English when writing in class, students were suddenly given license to use their heritage/home languages. This disoriented some of them even though teachers tried to encourage and provide a rationale for why the translanguaging tasks were important.

Co-design: Teacher-researchers – pre-lesson

Once a co-stance between Gary and Toni had been identified and articulated, they set about co-designing a lesson which would draw on students' L1 and LX resources and encourage collaborative involvement in both oral and written tasks which bridge home and school cultural and linguistic practices (García *et al.*, 2017).

They scaffolded the lesson with a review of the vocabulary of feelings taught in lessons one and two by reacquainting the students with Hassan, the central character of the book *The Colour of Home*. Students would reconstruct the story in pairs, telling each other what words they could remember about Hassan's feelings. Hassan's story and the adjectives for feelings would then be discussed as a class on the mat and the words written up on the whiteboard again. Toni would then elicit words from the students which meant the same or similar to the words on the whiteboard in their home languages and students would write up their L1 word next to the English word. Next students would teach each other the words in small groups using the recording and written facility of the software Book Creator on the classroom iPads. Afterwards individual group members would report what they had learned to the class. Following that, students would write chain stories substituting the already learned LX words from lessons one and two with the new L1 words provided by the different group members. Selected groups would read out their stories with their L1 words inserted – one sentence using one L1 word for each group member. Students would be asked to report on this experience in a written plenary session in class. They would take home a grid for parents to fill in with useful L1 words connected with the themes of the stories and these would be used for the follow up Lesson 4.

Co-design: Teacher-researchers and students – post-lesson (evaluation)

Students re-engaged with Hassan's story very well. They remembered all of the taught vocabulary including the pronunciation. They were, however, a little embarrassed about using their own languages initially and they laughed at each other when L1 words were uttered. Some plurilingual students were reticent to come forward with L1 words and claimed they could not think of words to teach. The teachers did not anticipate this. Students found it hard to think of words in their own languages that meant exactly the same as the English adjectives of feeling, and students without other languages looked a little lost. One group deleted all of the L1 words they had thought of when they pressed the wrong button on the iPad. They were quite upset by this. Students also found it a bit difficult to start the chain stories but began once they were provided with teacher support.

Students became very noisy in parts and a bit unruly because the tasks were not guided enough. Some children without an additional language said they could not do the task rather than realizing that they could just listen to other students to learn some new words. Overall, there was not a lot of translanguaging incorporated into the story activity by the students, but stories were well done, and students used the new vocabulary we taught them in Lessons 1 and 2. Overall, Gary and Toni both felt that Lesson 3 had lost its way in terms of encouraging and scaffolding translanguaging tasks for the students. In their desire to make the lesson creative and multimodal, as well as focused on translanguaging, they had somehow lost sight of the main language aim and over-estimated the students' ability to work with the new technologies without explicit instruction in how to use them. The lesson had also been too 'full' so the translanguaging aim had been obscured.

The children evaluated their experiences with translanguaging pedagogies positively after Lesson 3. They said they 'felt good', 'excited', 'happy' about learning words in another language and 'proud' to be teaching words in their own language, which demonstrates that while the lesson could have been improved, the students still valued using translanguaging pedagogies. Figure 7.2 shows feedback from one student.

The majority of students indicated that they understood the tasks and were able to teach others by coloring the smiley face on the feedback sheet. After Lesson 3, when asked how he felt about working in a group, one monolingual boy said it was good because he could rely on his classmates to help him. However, one plurilingual boy also said he felt a little upset because people did not look at him when he was teaching words in his own language and another girl complained that she did not get an opportunity 'to say her country's words'.

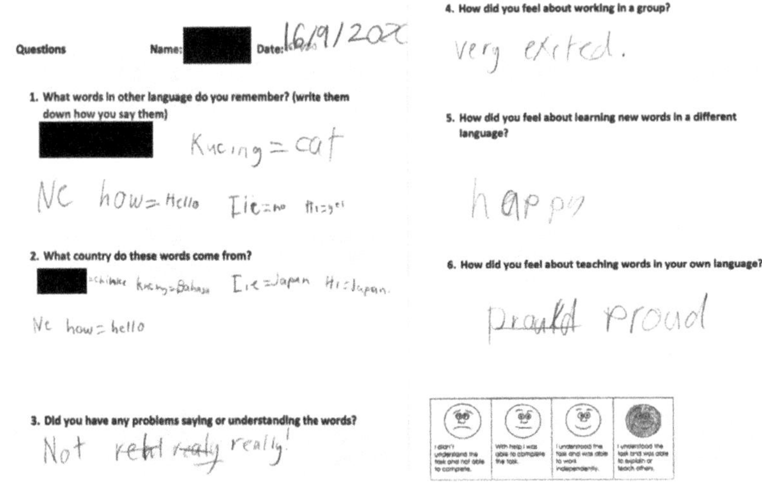

Questions Name: Date: 16/9/2020

1. What words in other language do you remember? (write them down how you say them)

Kucing = cat

Ni how = Hello Iie = no Hi = yes

2. What country do these words come from?

= Chinese Kucing = Bahasa Iie = Japan Hi = Japan.

Ni how = hello

3. Did you have any problems saying or understanding the words?

Not ~~rebl~~ ~~realy~~ really!

4. How did you feel about working in a group?

very exited.

5. How did you feel about learning new words in a different language?

happy

6. How did you feel about teaching words in your own language?

~~prauld~~ proud

I didn't understand the task and not able to complete.	With help I was able to complete the task.	I understood the task and was able to work independently.	I understood the task and was able to explain or teach others.

Figure 7.2 Example student evaluation of the lesson

Co-shift: Teacher-researchers and students

Shifting approach in response to observations of students' struggling with tasks at different stages of the lesson was not as successful in Lesson 3 as it could have been. This was probably due to a first-time lack of confidence in changing, in the moment, what had been carefully planned beforehand. Rather than returning the focus to student meaning-making teacher-researchers sometimes tried to continue on with tasks which were creative but above the level of understanding of the students in terms of procedures. When one of the groups deleted all of their L1 words on the iPads by mistake, which meant they had no material left with which to work or to report to the class, there was no contingency plan and teachers just had to leave that group of students with no record of their hard work. On a more successful note, one plurilingual boy was so inspired to learn the words in the new languages that he asked if he could look at the iPads again during the plenary session to remind himself about what he had learned. This showed his genuine engagement with the translanguaging task. Although Gary and Toni did not manage an effective co-shift in some instances, they were successful in other instances where they managed to convince monolingual students to continue with the task, because the aim of the task was equally to learn new words from others as well as teach them.

Lesson 4 analysis

Co-stances: Teacher-researchers – pre-lesson

In Lesson 4, Toni's stance and Gary's, in particular, changed considerably. They were more confident and convinced of the translanguaging tasks they would develop and the need to incorporate such tasks in lessons. Unlike in Lesson 3, they made translanguaging the main focus of the lesson; cutting down and simplifying other tasks so as not to distract from the main aim of students using their own languages meshed with their additional language of English, both in speaking and writing tasks.

Co-stances: Teacher-researchers and students – during the lesson

A monolingual Australian student started the lesson by signing a greeting in AUSLAN (Australian sign language) to another student; a sign that both multilingual and monolingual Australian students were becoming accustomed to moving between languages and dialects and growing in confidence to do so. One Punjabi student complimented the signing student saying, 'You did good dude'. The same signing student was the first to put his hand up to say he had a new word to teach the class. The word 'dar' was in the language of his Punjabi (and Hindi) friends. Along with this, about six of the students in the class had remembered to ask their parents to provide them with words and definitions in their L1s on the task sheet that Gary had given out to students as a means of connecting home and school experiences. This indicated some development of a positive co-stance towards translanguaging between teachers, students and their parents. One monolingual student, however, did approach Gary and Toni during the group tasks to tell them he did not speak another language, he just spoke 'normal', indicating that they still had some work to do in developing a multilingual co-stance with students in the dominant language group. Students were also much keener to read their stories out to the class with the English words replaced by the students' L1 words. Some came up to the front of the room in pairs. Students who had not been chosen even tried to sneak up to the front and get a turn. One local monolingual student wanted to read out the new sentence created with the new L1 word even though the word was not his word in his language.

Co-design: Teacher-researchers – pre-lesson

Gary and Toni planned Lesson 4 after evaluating Lesson 3 for student learning and engagement. They built on the lessons that were used to build up to the translanguaging lessons with Paul G. In Lesson 4 they decided to reacquaint the students with the small group stories they had written in Lesson 3 by doing a show and tell exercise with each story to begin the session. They then elicited the vocabulary that made the stories interesting and hoped that students brought up the L1 words they had inserted into the stories. Afterwards the focus would be on a few of the L1 words that students had brought from home via the activity sheet sent to their parents. Students could write the words in their own scripts and English script on flash cards and put them up on the whiteboard. They would then use these new L1 words and others that they could think of to add to the small stories written last lesson. Each student used a different color pen and write one sentence with one new word. Students would then share their chain stories on the mat, reading out the sentence that they wrote incorporating the L1 word. A follow up extension task was for students to publish the stories and make them into a movie with students reading out the story as a voice over.

Co-design: Teacher-researchers and students – during the lesson

The co-written stories were well executed by the majority of students, with all students contributing at least one sentence and students agreeing when to insert L1 words and which words to insert. Figure 7.3 shows a translingual story written by one group of students.

The children mainly substituted their L1 nouns and adjectives for other English nouns and adjectives in their stories. For example, 'magician' was replaced by the Punjabi word 'jadhugar' and 'scared' by the Hindi word 'dar'. They also included the adjectives of feelings (i.e. isolated, misunderstood, distressed, anxious) taught in the build-up lessons 1 and 2. There was rich discussion and collaboration as seen in Extract 2

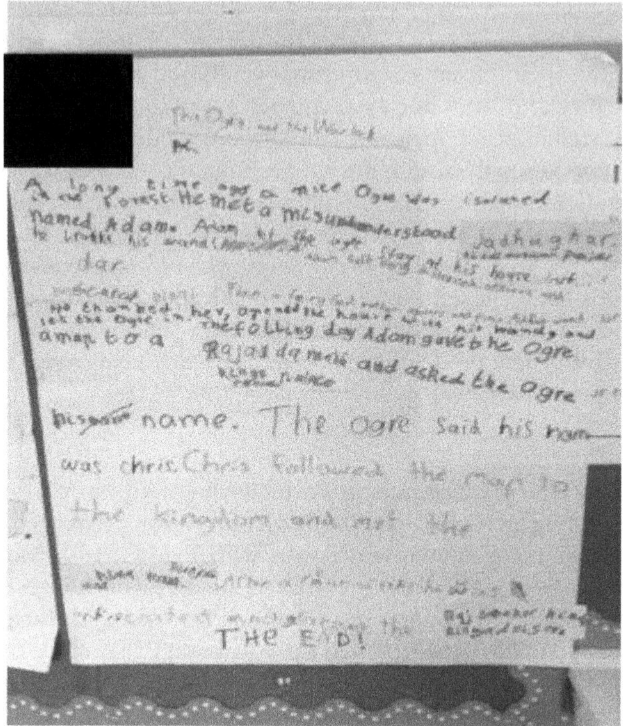

Figure 7.3 Example small story using students' L1 words

with students taking the role of teachers and encouraging and evaluating the other students' responses. Names are all pseudonyms.

Extract 2 Students discussing the new Punjabi word introduced by a student

#	Discussant	Classroom interaction transcript
1	Student Ajeet	We got the same language, this is Punjabi, we're writing this in Punjabi and Hindi, in Hindi.
2	Student Eric	How can somebody understand that? Haha!
3	Student Ajeet	At first, when you don't know anything and look at it and it's like this is impossible, and then when you start learning it, it's like dude, this is so easy.
4	Teacher	Alright, Ajeet, pick a word you want to teach everyone.
5	Student Ajeet	[Translanguages] Jadhughar … which is magician.
6	Student Balbir	Or wizard!
7	Student Ajeet	Or warlock!
8	Teacher	[Gets Ajeet to repeat the word because the others were not listening]
9	Student Ajeet	But you need to put more stress on the 'er'
10	Everyone	Jadhughar.

11	**Teacher**	And which language is that?
12	**Student Ajeet**	Punjabi. [He spells the word out with Balbir]
13	**Teacher**	Everyone repeat the word again.
14	**Student Ajeet**	I think Yuki's was the most accurate.

The monolingual student, Eric, was originally unsure about the translanguaging tasks; feeling confused and under confident to engage with the new languages and laughing both at the sound of the words and uneasily as he realizes he does not know what is being said ('How can somebody understand that? Haha!'). The plurilingual student, Ajeet, is empowered by speaking in his own language and knowing something that his other classmates do not. However, he empathizes with Eric and attempts to reassure him that understanding will come slowly. Ajeet becomes a language teacher, highlighting the correct pronunciation of the Punjabi word 'jadhughar' ('But you need to put more stress on the 'er'') and giving feedback to the group ('I think Yuki's was the most accurate'). Both Punjabi students, Ajeet and Balbir, then spell the word out for the group. All of this shows plurilingual students successfully translanguaging and bringing their monolingual classmates along with them. Given time these types of tasks can become second nature for all students and perceptions of monolingual students can be changed, especially if the plurilingual students take their roles as language teachers seriously and endeavor to include all students in new understandings in the manner shown here, i.e. supportive and non-judgmental.

Co-design: Teacher-researchers and students – post-lesson (evaluation)

Students were much more engaged this time round and understood better the task at hand. However, monitoring of the groups was very labor intensive. Keeping students on track required a lot of energy. Students recalled the new words in different languages and where they had come from very well, nonetheless, during the plenary session. Most students were able to write two to three new words in another language and their meaning. The third question in the plenary asked students if they had had any problems with saying or understanding the new words. Most students did not fill this in, possibly due to time constraints or perhaps an unwillingness to show any weaknesses. Those who did fill it in mostly said 'no' with one person replying 'no, because I learned them from my friends'. One student did admit to having problems but did not say why.

Co-shift: Teacher-researchers and students

Lesson 4 saw all participants co-shifting with more ease than Lesson 3. This may have been due to Gary and Toni being clearer in their minds about what they wanted to achieve and putting translanguaging aims foremost. With parents being more supportive this time they had a good selection of characters, settings, problems and resolutions in different home languages supplied by them and even different scripts which made moment by moment decision making easier. Students were also more flexible and seemed to grow more accustomed to the idea of speaking their own languages and teaching others. All of this led to greater confidence for all participants to change direction and co-shift from what had been planned when necessary. Students were also more comfortable with asking their fellow students for help and Gary and Toni were more relaxed about allowing them to do whatever came easiest for them in the stories.

Discussion

The collaborative teaching journey described here investigated the extent to which translanguaging pedagogies could be introduced into a junior primary multilingual classroom; the students' responses to the introduction of translanguaging pedagogies into lessons; and the experiences of teacher-researcher collaborators from different educational settings working together to deliver lessons using translanguaging pedagogies. The lessons analyzed in this chapter indicated that incorporating translanguaging elements into the lessons of even very young children is effective in creating a community of learners who use each other's backgrounds and languages as a collaborative learning resource and develop a co-stance which values the use of all students' L1s in the classroom. Moreover, co-stances of teacher-researchers can be developed and fine-tuned through the delivery and evaluation of such lessons. Students' comments in their evaluations endorsed that they felt 'proud' and 'excited' to be using their own languages in the classroom while being supported by their peers to do so.

Challenges along the way pointed to the need for careful co-design/planning of lessons and consideration of the skills sets (i.e. digital literacies) of the students. It was apparent that scaffolding of translanguaging processes needed to be systematic and unhurried, without distraction and demotivation caused by other demands of the tasks (Daniel *et al.*, 2019; Zapata & Laman, 2016). In this instance, scaffolding the translanguaging lessons using the previous two lessons to build up confidence and context worked well. While procedural challenges were present, the most difficult challenge was contesting the established dominant norms of the monolingual classroom and school. The student who felt he was speaking 'normal' because he was speaking English illustrated the novelty of hearing and speaking other languages in the classroom and served as a reminder to educators of the need to construct affectively safe and socially appropriate contexts when asking students to participate in translanguaging 'events' for the first time. His response is indicative of a monolingual hegemonic perspective where English is perceived as a normative semiotic system with an exclusive claim to meaning. It illustrates what Ramanathan (2005) called an 'assumption nexus' or a complete set of social beliefs and practices that make people believe in the superiority of a specific language and which is supported by social dynamics endorsing the 'mythical values of English' (Sultana, 2014: 17; Sultana *et al.*, 2021).

While processes needed to be intentional (Celic & Seltzer, 2013), a willingness on the part of teacher-researchers to co-shift at any moment during the lessons and go with students' own instincts for better learning was also required. The products of the lessons, in the way of student-written flash cards, the iPad small book co-constructed stories and the co-written multilingual chain stories, were valuable products of the learning, but of even more value were the collaborative processes which helped students to develop linguistic identities and have positive learning experiences. These enabled teacher-researchers to learn from each other, the students and their own reflections on the lessons. Audio recordings of the interaction, while 'chaotic and noisy', indicated genuine student engagement, creativity, and collaboration, even if they did wander off topic/task at times and require extensive guidance in their groups and pairs. Such labor-intensive practice may be daunting for the classroom teacher once the collaborative teaching project is finished, however, and there is only one person to assist with this. Once translanguaging materials and tasks are systematically embedded into the lessons and the children become more familiar with these types of tasks, teachers should find it easier to work alone in this space. Creating a multilingual ecology would decrease power differentials between the monolingual students and multilingual students. Co-stances could be reconfigured away from the current monolingual orientations (Cross, 2012; García *et al.*, 2017; Ollerhead, 2018) and mindsets once translanguaging pedagogies were normalized, legitimized and regularized.

By incorporating mutual respect and a flattened power dimension into the collaborative teaching, teacher-researchers from different settings were able to learn from each other during the planning, delivery and evaluation cycle. Reflection documents indicated that they had learned from each other, from the students and from their own practice. Gary began his journey less convinced than Toni of the need to integrate translanguaging processes into his literacy block, but he was keen (as was the principal of the school) to improve literacy learning for all the children in his care. Toni was able to see the lived reality of what had previously been only theoretical persuasion, and adapt her expectations accordingly. All researcher-teacher stances became co-constructed during the time they spent co-designing, co-teaching and co-evaluating the lessons together. As with other studies (Buxton *et al.*, 2013; Hamza *et al.*, 2018: 170), they developed a 'hybridization between the two communities of practice in terms of mutual influences'. Gary soon became an advocate for translanguaging pedagogies, observing the influence such practices had on the linguistic and cultural identities of the students and their feelings of confidence and worth. Paul G and Toni were able to see first-hand the obstacles to be overcome when transferring theory into practice in a junior primary classroom.

Implications for Successful Teacher–Researcher Collaborations

From the outset, it is imperative for researchers from 'the academy' to be cognizant of the possible trepidation of classroom practitioners to engage in a 'research relationship'. This is perhaps due to the possibility of a pre-conceived notion that academics are 'experts', who may be judgmental. It is equally important that researchers acknowledge the classroom as an educational space in which the teacher is not only the expert but also has a pre-existing communal relationship with students and research capabilities. The problematizing of these issues can be obviated at the planning-stage by establishing a research community of practice (Lave & Wenger, 1998) in which mutually constructed questions; research and lesson design; data collection methods; and classroom/research roles are negotiated and are clearly understood by all involved. The practical outcome is equalization through the hybridization of roles, in which all participants are positioned as teacher-researchers. In attempting to embed intentional translanguaging pedagogies into lessons through a collaborative teacher–researcher partnership, the following implications need to be considered:

Meeting of the minds

Without a mutual commitment and willingness to try to see pedagogies and classroom practices in the same way, translanguaging pedagogies cannot easily be embedded in every day classroom practices by teacher-researchers working collaboratively. In particular, both partners in the teaching/research project need to respect each other's expertise and be prepared to work together to expand their perspectives and develop a co-stance which values translanguaging as a resource (García *et al.*, 2017) while also taking into consideration the practical parameters of classroom teaching. Students need to be included in developing a co-stance towards shifting the monolingual mind set. On another level, whole school commitment to translanguaging pedagogies and the recognition and valuing of plurilingualism needs to be established, with parents also on board with this ideology. Without this there will not be a multilingual ecology that is sustainable.

From little things big things grow

Adjusting norms, building confidence/belief in new practices and planning for translanguaging pedagogies takes time. It cannot be achieved over night. One of the challenges of this study was time. As a practicing classroom teacher Gary was constricted by the time he had to plan and evaluate, while Toni's schedule was considerably more flexible and self-managed as an academic. In terms of the students, time is needed to build students' confidence in the new style of tasks. Having lessons which build up to the translanguaging tasks eases students in slowly and confidently. Making translanguaging pedagogies intentional (Celic & Seltzer, 2013) rather than peripheral to, or diluted by, other learning outcomes and skills, ensures that translanguaging aims remain central to the lessons. Valuing students' work in the translanguaging space by putting even the smallest effort up on the wall (i.e. the flash cards of the new words in students' L1s) emphasizes to students the importance of this activity.

If translanguaging practices are incorporated into future studies and classrooms, a multi-collaborative model could be useful to practitioners due to the way it can optimize the expertise of all teacher-researchers. A similar model might work for older students if the tasks were made more sophisticated, employing the model of three teacher-researchers co-designing, co-teaching and co-evaluating together. Like the current study, students could be asked to bring vocabulary in their own languages to class to insert into a particular task. This could also be expanded to students bringing whole texts in their own home languages related to one particular topic. Students could sit together with students of the same language to arrive at a commonly agreed translation and then tell the class. What is common across ages is getting students to bring materials and new vocabulary to classes with which to work as a group.

Conclusion

Developing approaches to teaching that fall outside the institutional norms and challenge dominant monolingual ideologies in schools cannot be achieved, as Tian and Shepard-Carey (2020) point out, without the full commitment and expertise of those educators who are full-time employed as teachers in the schools. These experts need to be given relational agency which recognizes the inter-related concepts of relational expertise and common knowledge (Edwards, 2010, 2011, 2017) while co-developing their language ideologies and practices in ways which fit the context of their classrooms and students. In the case of the study described here, the school teacher-researcher was able to use students, their parents, stories and related personalized discussions and tasks as cultural and linguistic resources to develop sustainable co-stances informed by in-depth experiences of teaching the students and working with the parents. Without the good will of classroom teachers to also become researchers on an equal footing with their university counterparts and develop co-stances, co-designed practices and confidence in co-shifting, change cannot be instigated (Tian & Shepard-Carey, 2020) and intentional translanguaging pedagogies will not easily be embedded in current learning and teaching practices in schools.

References

Australian Bureau of Statistics (ABS) (2016) 2016 Census. See www.abs.gov.au/web sitedbs/censushome.nsf/home/2016ABS, 2016 (accessed April 2021).

Alford, J. (2019) Critical literacy with EAL learners: Making the most of learners' diverse languages. In R. Henderson (ed.) *Teaching Literacies: Pedagogies and Diversity* (2nd edn, pp. 308–331). Melbourne: Oxford University Press.

Arkoudis, S. (2005) Fusing pedagogic horizons: Language and content teaching in the mainstream. *Linguistics and Education* 16 (2), 173–187. https://doi.org/10.1016/j.linged.2006.01.006

Back, M., Han, M. and Weng, S.C.A. (2020) Emotional scaffolding for emergent multilingual learners through translanguaging: Case stories. *Language and Education* 34 (5), 387–406. https://doi.org/10.1080/09500782.2020.1744638

Ball, S., McGuire, M. and Braun, A. (2012) *How Schools do Policy: Policy Enactments in Secondary Schools*. Abingdon: Routledge.

Bell, A.B. and Baecher, L. (2012) Points on a continuum: ESL teachers reporting on collaboration. *TESOL Journal* 3 (3), 488–515. https://doi.org/10.1002/tesj.28

Bialystok, E. and Barac, R. (2012) Emerging bilingualism: Dissociating advantages for metalinguistic awareness and executive control. *Cognition* 122, 67–73.

Bouchereau Bauer, E., Presiado, V. and Colomer, S. (2017) Writing through partnership: Fostering translanguaging in children who are emergent bilinguals. *Journal of Literacy Research* 49 (1), 10–37. https://doi.org/10.1177/1086296X16683417

Buxton, C.A., Kayumova, S. and Allexsaht-Snider, M. (2013) Teacher, researcher, and accountability Discourses: Creating space for democratic science teaching practices in middle schools. *Democracy and Education* 21 (2), 1–10.

Canagarajah, S. (2018) Translingual practice as spatial repertoires: Expanding the paradigm beyond structuralist orientations. *Applied Linguistics* 39 (1), 31–54.

Celic, C. and Seltzer, K. (2013) *Translanguaging: A CUNY-NYSIEB Guide for Educators*. New York, NY: CUNY-NYSIEB, The Graduate Center, The City University of New York.

Creagh, S. (2014) A critical analysis of problems with the LBOTE category on the NAPLAN test. *Australian Educational Researcher* 41, 1–23.

Creese, A. and Blackledge, A. (2010) Translanguaging in the bilingual classroom: A pedagogy for learning and teaching? *The Modern Language Journal* 94, 103–115. https://doi.org/10.1111/j.1540-4781.2009.00986.x

Cross, R. (2012) Reclaiming the territory: Understanding the specialist knowledge of ESL education for literacy, curriculum and multilingual learners. *TESOL in Context* 22 (1), 4–17.

Daniel, S.M., Jiminez, R.T., Pray, L. and Pacheco, M.B. (2019) Scaffolding to make translanguaging a classroom norm. *TESOL Journal* 10 (1), e00361. https://doi.org/10.1002/tesj.361

Dewaele, J.M. (2018) Why the dichotomy 'L1 versus LX user' is better than 'native versus non-native speaker'. *Applied Linguistics* 39 (2), 236–240. https://doi.org/10.1093/applin/amw055

Dobinson, T.J. and Buchori, S. (2016) Catering for EAL/D students' language needs in mainstream classes: Early childhood teachers' perspectives and practices in one Australian setting. *Australian Journal of Teacher Education* 41 (2), 32–52.

Edwards, A. (2010) *Being an Expert Professional Practitioner: The Relational Turn in Expertise*. Dordrecht: Springer.

Edwards, A. (2011) Building common knowledge at the boundaries between professional practices: Relational agency and relational expertise in systems of distributed expertise. *International Journal of Education Research* 50 (1), 33–39.

Edwards, A. (2017) Revealing relational work. In A. Edwards (ed.) *Working Relationally in and Across Practices: A Cultural-historical Approach to Collaboration* (pp. 1–22). Cambridge: Cambridge University Press.

Fowler-Amato, M. and Warrington, A. (2017) Teachers as designers: Social design experiments as vehicles for developing antideficit English education. *Literacy Research: Theory, Method, and Practice* 66, 358–372. https://doi.org/10.1177/2381336917719054

Freire, P. (1970) *Pedagogy of the Oppressed*. New York, NY: Continuum.

García, O., Johnson, S.I. and Seltzer, K. (2017) *The Translanguaging Classroom: Leveraging Student Bilingualism for Learning*. Philadelphia, PA: Caslon.

García, O. and Kleyn, T. (eds) (2016) *Translanguaging with Multilingual Students: Learning from Classroom Moments*. New York, NY: Routledge.

Guilfoyle, N. and Mistry, M. (2013) How effective is role play in supporting speaking and listening for pupils with English as an additional language in the foundation stage? *Education 3-13* 41 (1), 63–70.

Gutierez, S.B. and Kim, H.B. (2017) Becoming teacher-researchers: Teachers' reflections on collaborative professional development. *Educational Research* 59 (4), 444–459.

Gutiérrez, K.D. and Vossoughi, S. (2010) Lifting off the ground to return anew: Mediated praxis, transformative learning, and social design experiments. *Journal of Teacher Education* 61 (1–2), 100–117. https://doi.org/10.1177/0022487109347877

Hamza, K., Palm, O., Palmqvist, J., Piqueras, J. and Wickman, P. (2018) Hybridization of practices in teacher-researcher collaboration. *European Educational Research Journal* 17 (1), 170–186.

Hoffman, M., and Littlewood, K. (1992) *The Colour of Home*. London: Frances-Lincoln.

Johnson S.I., García, O. and Seltzer, K. (2019) Biliteracy and translanguaging in dual-language bilingual education. In D.E. DeMatthews and E. Izquierdo (eds) *Dual Language Education: Teaching and Leading in Two Languages* (pp. 119–132). Cham: Springer.

Jung, H. and Brady, C. (2016) Roles of a teacher and researcher during in situ professional development around the implementation of mathematical modeling tasks. *Journal of Mathematics Teacher Education* 19 (2–3), 277–295. https://doi.org/10.1007/s10857-015-9335-6

Kemmis, S. and McTaggert, R. (1988) *The Action Research Planner*. Melbourne: Deakin University Press.

Kettle, M. (2017) *International Student Engagement in Higher Education: Transforming Practices, Pedagogies and Participation*. Bristol: Multilingual Matters.

Lave, J. and Wenger, E. (1998) *Communities of Practice: Learning, Meaning, and Identity*. Cambridge: Cambridge University Press

Li, W. (2018) Translanguaging as a practical theory of language. *Applied Linguistics* 39 (1), 9–30. https://doi.org/10.1093/applin/amx039

Lingard, B., Creagh, S. and Vass, G. (2012) Education policy as numbers: Data categories and two Australian cases of misrecognition. *Journal of Education Policy* 27 (3), 315–333.

May, S. (ed.) (2013) *The Multilingual Turn: Implications for SLA, TESOL and Bilingual Education*. New York, NY: Routledge.

Ollerhead, S. (2018) Pedagogical language knowledge: Preparing Australian pre-service teachers to support English language learners. *Asia-Pacific Journal of Teacher Education* 46 (3), 256–266. https://doi.org/10.1080/1359866X.2016.1246651

Ollerhead, S. (2019) Teaching across semiotic modes with multilingual learners: Translanguaging in an Australian classroom. *Language and Education* 33 (2), 106–122. https://doi.org/10.1080/09500782.2018.1516780

Ramanathan, V. (2005) *The English-Vernacular Divide: Postcolonial Language Politics and Practice*. Clevedon: Multilingual Matters.

Ruiz, R. (1984) Orientations in language planning. *NABE Journal* 8 (2), 15–34.

Seltzer, K. (2020) 'My English is its own rule': Voicing a translingual sensibility through poetry. *Journal of Language, Identity and Education* 19 (5), 297–311. https://doi.org/10.1080/15348458.2019.1656535

Stringer, E.T. (1999) *Action Research* (2nd edn). Thousand Oaks, CA: Sage.

Sultana, S. (2014) English as a medium of instruction in Bangladesh's higher education: Empowering or disadvantaging students. *Asian EFL Journal* 16 (1), 11–52.

Sultana, S., Roshid, M., Haider, Z., Kabir, N. and Hasan, M. (2021) *The Routledge Handbook of English Language Education in Bangladesh*. Abingdon: Routledge.

Tian, Z. and Shepard-Carey, L. (2020) (Re)imagining the future of translanguaging pedagogies in TESOL through teacher-researcher collaboration. *TESOL Quarterly* 54 (4), 1131–1143. https://doi.org/10.1002/tesq.614

Zapata, A. and Laman, T. (2016) 'I write to show how beautiful my languages are': Translingual writing instruction in English-dominant classrooms. *Language Arts* 93 (5), 366–378.

8 Adopting Translanguaging Pedagogies in Critical Content and Language Integrated Learning (CLIL) Using Social Issues as the Context: A Teacher–Researcher Collaborative Approach

Kao Chia-Ling Gupta and Angel M.Y. Lin

Introduction

With the globalization of digital media, one's chance of being exposed to a single language is reducing. People are easily exposed to information in multiple languages, e.g. Mandarin, English, Taiwanese Hokkien and Hakka in Taiwan, and information in multiple modes, e.g. texts, audios, visuals, gestures and so forth. It is based on these two notions, *multiliteracy* and *multimodality*, that García and Li's (2014) proposal of translanguaging practices has become more widely researched and encouraged. Unlike monolingual ideologies, translanguaging pedagogies value the role of students' familiar linguistic and trans-semiotic resources throughout learners' and teachers' meaning-making processes. To design translanguaging pedagogies for one's own classroom context, García *et al.* (2017) proposed an interplay between *stances*, *design* and *shift*. This framework was further expanded by Tian and Shepard-Carey (2020), who examined teacher–researcher collaboration, and proposed a *co-stance*, *co-design* and *co-shift* framework. We used this expanded framework to guide our analysis. This chapter looks at how we adopted critical approaches (Freire, 1972; Pennycook, 1999) during a collaborative process with two in-service teachers to design and implement translanguaging pedagogies in the context of critical content and language integrated learning (CLIL) classrooms in Taiwan. The steps taken, the challenges that emerged and the decisions made will be discussed with evidence from lesson observation, meeting notes and the students' artefacts to show how, with a critical stance, this teacher–researcher relationship was shaped and reshaped.

CLIL: What, Why and How

CLIL is a 'dual focused educational approach in which an additional language is used for the learning and teaching of both content and language' (Coyle *et al.*, 2010: 1). That is, it is an approach to teaching content through a language other than the first language (L1) of learners. Thus, the aim of adopting CLIL is twofold. It not only seeks to enhance learners' foreign language competence but also to facilitate the learning of content.

The rationale behind CLIL can be explained by how Halliday (1993) linked the notions of *language* and *meaning*. Halliday treated human learning as 'a process of making meaning' (Halliday, 1993: 93), and thus language is seen 'not a domain of human knowledge (except in the special context of linguistics, where it becomes an object of scientific study); language is the essential condition of knowing, the process by which experience becomes knowledge' (Halliday, 1993: 94). In other words, language is inextricably interwoven with content, when language is regarded as a resource to construct meaning. Echoing this inseparable relationship between language and content, Mercer's (1995) Vygotskian perspective depicts language as a medium of knowledge construction.

While language and content have been theoretically and commonly considered to be integrated, how and to what extent they can be integrated into the pedagogy and curriculum design has attracted different views. Bentley (2010) has proposed a continuum with 'soft CLIL' at one end and 'hard CLIL' at the other. The former is often adopted by language teachers to integrate content into their lessons, so it is language-led, while content teachers usually practice the latter, so it is subject-led. Since CLIL has been mostly carried out by English language teachers (rather than content teachers) in Taiwan, this study took more of a soft CLIL approach. At the language-led end, soft CLIL was therefore close to the field of content-based instruction (CBI), although CLIL has been set apart from it in terms of the integration of content. As part of the CLIL approach aims for learners' acquisition of a language, the call for more attention to adopting critical approaches to relevant fields such as teaching English to speakers of other languages (TESOL) (Pennycook, 1999), English for specific purposes (ESP) (Master, 1998), English for academic purposes (EAP) (Benesch, 1993, 2001) and English language teaching (ELT) (Crookes, 2013) cannot be ignored. As this study aimed to link English language education with social responsibility for developing students' critical thinking skills and enhancing their social awareness and responsibility as a citizen in society, taking a critical approach to English language education is needed. Below we discuss what *being critical* means in this study, drawing on the literature on critical pedagogy and critical thinking.

Making Sense of *Criticality*

The conceptualization of *criticality* underlying this research approach and theoretical orientation was grounded in the works in critical thinking and critical pedagogy. Although there have been various definitions of critical thinking proposed by different researchers such as Siegel (1988), Lipman (1991), Elder and Paul (1994) and so on, it is agreed that being able to think critically means the ability of a person to act as a responsible thinker. However, being critical, if defined by critical thinking skills alone, fails to include the need for raising critical awareness of ideologies in society. As education is deemed to bring about transformation, mastering the skills alone may not directly increase students' awareness of injustices existing in the societies, let alone encourage them to take actions to create a more just society, and this is where critical pedagogy comes into play as an essential component of education.

Criticality has its root in the significant contribution of critical pedagogy. The notion of *criticality* depicted by critical pedagogy is heavily influenced by the works on voice, identity, agency and power. The pioneer associated with critical pedagogy is Paulo Freire (1972), who believes that education is a means of improving human existence, and thus, his concept of criticality distinguishes traditional banking education from problem-solving education. The former is given a term as the banking education model, which sees teaching as 'an act of depositing, in which the students are the depositories, and the teacher is the depositor' (Freire, 1972: 45). Under this notion, two identities are imposed: the teachers as the knowledgeable and the students as the ignorant. This act is challenged by Freire, so problem-solving education is proposed focusing on the creation of a dialogical relation, which reveals the reality of the world by enacting student agency. Hence, the meaning of education conceptualized by Freire and supported by his belief that every individual has the potential to develop criticality, identifies teachers and students as the agents who co-construct meaning through dialogic interactions.

The important role of *criticality* lies in not only designing and implementing CLIL, but also in shaping the teacher–researcher relationship. When it comes to researchers in teacher education, it is observed to be taking on a dominant and authoritative role (Doyle, 1990), in that researchers aim to observe and verify how teachers could teach effectively. Conversely, teachers as practitioners see researchers as often without or with limited prior teaching experience, thereby forming a distant relationship (Gitlin, 1990). To reframe the teacher–researcher relationship and to

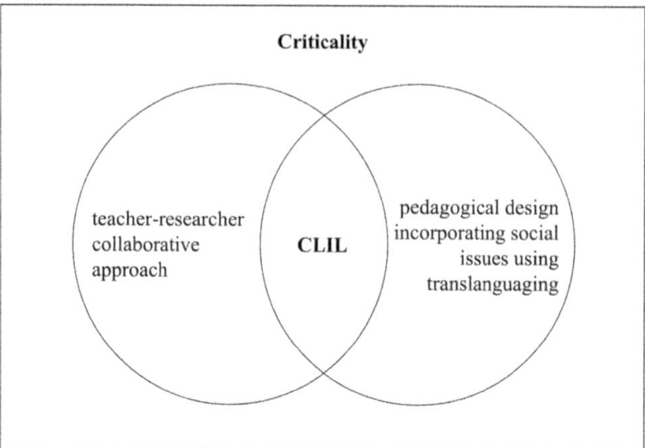

Figure 8.1 Framing criticality in this research

uncover insights often ignored by objective quantitative studies, Gupta (2020) adopted ethnography, building on which we further apply a critical lens on this collaborative research to refrain from conducting educational research with a process 'that for the most part silences those studies, ignores their personal knowledge, and strengthens the assumption that researchers are the producers of knowledge' (Gitlin, 1990: 444). Hence, we incorporate criticality to avoid the dominance of our role as researchers who intervene and to build trust with the teachers who question researchers' limited knowledge and practice in the actual classroom scenarios. In this way, we aim to create an egalitarian space and establish rapport for teacher–researcher collaboration, rather than seeing the relationship as merely the researchers and the researched. Figure 8.1 summarizes how we integrate *criticality* into framing and examining the teacher–researcher collaboration throughout this study, as well as into designing and implementing CLIL that incorporated social issues for students to reflect on the society. However, past research has shown a gap between students' performance when they discussed issues in their L1 and the target language (Luk & Lin, 2015), potentially pointing to the challenge students with beginning English proficiency level may encounter when learning about and discussing social issues. Hence, this study drew on translanguaging pedagogies to implement critical CLIL, and the nature of translanguaging, will be discussed next.

Three Strands of Translanguaging and Their Expansion

Informed by *multiliteracy* and *multimodality*, translanguaging pedagogies should be practised with three strands: *stance*, *design* and *shifts* (García *et al.*, 2017). First, *stance*, or a set of beliefs, concerns how a teacher views his or her students' full language repertoires – whether it is seen as a part of the students and as their resource of meaning-making in the class. With such a belief that students' linguistic backgrounds should be respected, appreciated and encouraged, a teacher could then create an instructional *design* that incorporates students' different linguistic and cultural resources. Finally, in the face of any unplanned scenarios in class, e.g. due to the variety in students' language performances, there exist *shifts* taken by teachers as the spontaneous decisions that go beyond *stance* and *design* to respond to students' sometimes unforeseen linguistic needs. Furthering this framework was Tian and Shepard-Carey's (2020) co-stance, co-design and co-shift framework. As a collaborative study that explored in detail the processes of how we worked together with the teachers in an egalitarian setting to design and carry out a CLIL unit, this research was analyzed following the expanded framework to describe and narrate the process of collaboration.

Research Context, Participants, Procedure and Methods

This chapter reports a design-based research (DBR) study (Barab & Squire, 2004; Bell, 2004; Hoadley, 2004) conducted in Taiwan, where internationalization has been heavily emphasized since 2002; policies were outlined to enhance internationalization. To achieve this goal, bilingual education has been laid out as one of the important approaches. However, implementing CLIL by balancing content and language teaching in bilingual education is hardly an easy endeavor (Lo, 2019) and has been relatively new in Taiwan. Hence, we took advantage of teacher–researcher collaboration to develop and try out critical CLIL drawing on both theoretical and pedagogical knowledge. In this chapter, we report the findings obtained while creating CLIL materials drawn up after several iterations of development, implementation and refinement at two case schools, lasting three months between April and June 2019 at a secondary school (henceforth School S) in New Taipei City, Taiwan, and between November 2019 and January 2020 at a primary school (henceforth School P) in Taipei City, Taiwan. The participants whose consent to take part in this study was obtained were Ms Shih (a pseudonym) at School S with four years of teaching experience, and her 29 grade 7 students aged between 12 and 13; and Ms Peng (a pseudonym) at School P with seven years' teaching experience, and her 21 grade 4 students aged between 9 and 10. Table 8.1 lists the participant information.

This study underwent three main phases at Schools P and S, from preparation, implementation to conceptualization, as shown in Figure 8.2. This research began with a needs analysis to increase our familiarity with the participating teachers and students through interviews. School P was involved in three interventions for eleven lessons, each of which lasted 40 minutes. On the other hand, there were two interventions involving five lessons, each of which lasted 45 minutes at School S. An analysis of

Table 8.1 A list of participant information

	Ms Shih	Ms Peng
Participation duration	April–June 2019	November 2019–January 2020
Years of teaching experience	4	7
Location	New Taipei City, Taiwan	Taipei City, Taiwan
School	School S	School P
School level	Lower secondary	Primary
Age of students	12–13	9–10
Number of participating students	29	21

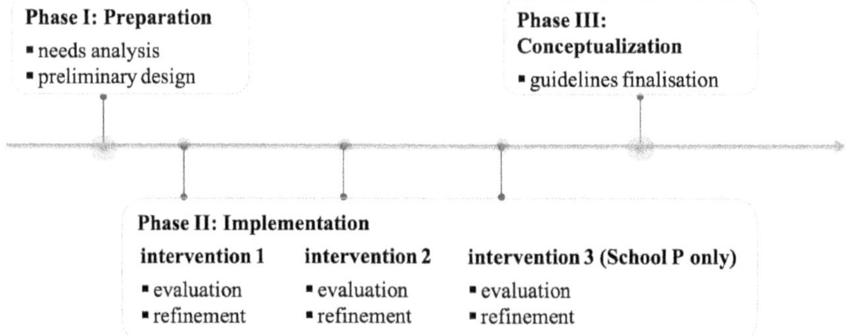

Figure 8.2 The research procedure

students' in-class performance and their learning artefacts, as well as the interviews with the teachers, was done right after the final lesson of the first unit to reflect on the learning activities, the learning materials, the students' reaction and performance, with the results guiding the creation of the following units. Similarly, we evaluated the effects of the following units and refined the design guidelines.

Research data were collected from multiple sources to enhance data credibility (Patton, 1990). The qualitative data included the interviews with the teachers and students, students' learning artefacts, lesson materials, meeting logs generated after each discussion with the teachers, classroom observation notes, audio and video clips of classroom observation, and students' written feedback received at the end of each unit. Following Ellis and Barkhuizen's (2005) steps to conduct thematic content analysis, we read through the data several times to look for patterns and generated the key codes regarding the participants' overall attitudes, the interaction between the teachers and the students, including their classroom language and colloquial language, the ways the teachers used the teaching materials and how the students responded to the lessons.

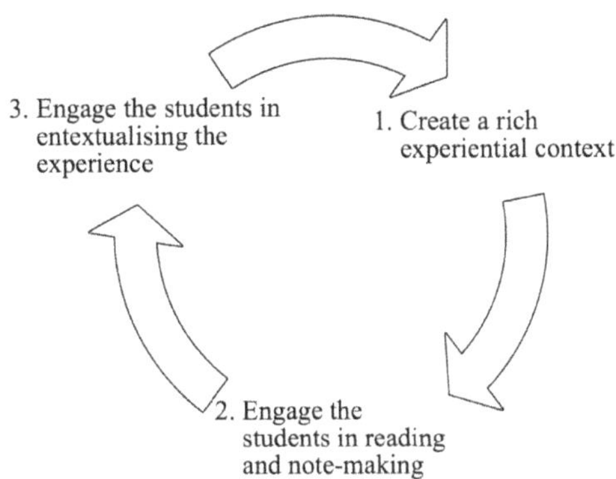

Figure 8.3 The multimodalities-entextualization cycle (MEC).
Adapted from *Language across the curriculum & CLIL in English as an additional language (EAL) contexts: Theory and practice* (Lin, 2016: 103)

The Pedagogical Framework in the Collaborative Research Process

This study developed through a collaborative research process. We worked with the participating teachers to create, design, implement, evaluate and reflect upon the CLIL units. Rather than situating this research in a hierarchical manner between the teachers and us, and between the teachers and the students, we wanted to create a dialogic space on a horizontal plane to elicit, construct and develop an understanding of adopting translanguaging pedagogies in CLIL classrooms in an EFL context, specifically in Taiwan. To guide the design of the intervention learning units, we adopted Lin's (2015, 2016) Multimodalities-Entextualization Cycle (MEC), as shown in Figure 8.3, as the curriculum genre (Christie & Martin, 2005; Rose & Martin, 2012). The emphasis on its inclusion of multilingual and multimodal resources, echoing the core principle of translanguaging pedagogies, and the fact that it can be iterated multiple times explains why it could be a useful framework to guide CLIL design. The three stages begin with creating a rich content topic-based context, followed by engaging students in reading/note-taking on the topic and finally supporting students to entextualize their experience and learning on that topic through crafting a spoken/written/multimodal text for a specific audience.

Co-developing an Understanding of Translanguaging Pedagogies

When entering the research sites and getting in contact with the participating teachers, we clearly informed the teachers of the paradigm and belief under which we were planning to conduct this research. We introduced the following key concepts or ideas and framework that underpinned this research to Ms Peng and Ms Shih: (1) CLIL, implemented not necessarily in a perfect balance between content and language but rather, a fluid point on a continuum between content and language, (2) a multilingual approach versus monolingual ideologies, e.g. English medium instruction, (3) a dialogic communicative approach (Mortimer & Scott, 2003) proposed on the basis of Bakhtin's (1986) notion that meanings are created in a dialogue which takes into account the reflection between agents, in this research, between teachers and researchers, teachers and students, and students and students, and (4) Lin's (2015, 2016) MEC as the pedagogical framework. Instead of imposing the aforementioned concepts on the participating teachers, we encouraged Ms Peng and Ms Shih to contribute their ideas, regardless of or against the key concepts as a way to refine how CLIL can be implemented and how CLIL materials can be designed, specifically the translingual practices.

At the primary and secondary school levels, neither Ms Peng nor Ms Shih showed disagreement over the idea that students' full language repertoires should be deemed an important resource. Both teachers indicated, based on their familiarity with the students and years of teaching experience, that the use of students' L1 cannot be avoided in their class. Ms Shih explained in the first interview with us in early April 2019 that School S, when hiring and interviewing teachers, required teachers to conduct their lessons in English, including non-language courses. This policy turned out to be a 'soft' one when few teachers at School S actually followed such a policy. Excerpt 8.1 shows Ms Shih's words translated from Mandarin into English, extracted from our first interview. It seems she stood against the monolingual approach from the viewpoints of *efficiency* and *effectiveness*, thereby recognizing that students' L1 facilitates students' understanding.

Excerpt 8.1

Ms Shih: Our school's feature, well, at first it features that it's a bilingual school. Yes, but in practice, we are not following such a practice.

Researcher: How does the school expect the teachers to implement the bilingual teaching practice?

Ms Shih: There are no specific ways of doing it, but when recruiting teachers, our school required teachers of all subjects to teach in English.

Researcher: All subjects? including non-language courses?

Ms Shih: Yes, except Chinese, except Chinese teachers. Right, so for all the other teachers, at first, the school required us to teach in English, when interviewing us. But eventually, most of the teachers did not do so; some biology teachers at the senior secondary level tried doing it, yeah, but we are discussing the lower secondary level. (Researcher: Right.) Then no, we are not doing it.

Researcher: So, when recruiting teachers, the school stated this regulation, but it did not strongly ask the teachers to enforce such a practice.

Ms Shih: The school cannot do it forcefully anyway because some teachers did seem to have tried but found that the kids did not understand, at least for lower secondary school kids. In that case, the results did not seem quite satisfactory.

(Interview 1 with Ms Shih at School S)

Ms Shih, as well as the other teachers at School S, expressed concern over the feasibility of the sole use of English. While the concept of translanguaging pedagogy was not explicitly introduced to the teachers, we somewhat reached consent that we would bring more linguistic resources into the CLIL lessons. At this stage, neither Ms Peng nor Ms Shih was consciously aware of translanguaging pedagogies, although both had an understanding that students' L1 was essential in class. It seemed we have developed a co-stance (Tian & Shepard-Carey, 2020) to a certain extent, in that we agreed the use of students' L1 was vital and helpful, an agreement drawn from both our theoretical grounding and Ms Shih's actual practice of teaching. Next, we negotiated the integration of such practices into the CLIL units that touched on social issues.

Co-designing and Implementing Translanguaging Pedagogies

Following the MEC pedagogical framework, the teachers and researchers designed two and three CLIL units at School S and School P, respectively. Through close discussions in various modes, e.g. face-to-face discussions, text-messages on a communication application, emails, voice calls on a communication application, we aimed to form a collaborative and supportive relationship. Each co-design (Tian & Shepard-Carey, 2020) process underwent the following three stages: (1) deciding on a topic, the process of which often involved negotiation about whether the topic was relevant to the original class agenda and students' daily life, and how it could provide opportunities for students to engage in the use of the target language; (2) selecting appropriate materials which were accessible to students regarding language demand and were inclusive of different perspectives while going through the MEC; and (3) confirming the form of students' end product, be it a poster, an oral presentation, a piece of written work that shows students' performance in L2 knowledge and content knowledge. Our development of an awareness of co-designing and implementing translanguaging pedagogies, however, did not fall into any particular stage but was seen as an ongoing process throughout the three stages. The procedure is illustrated in Figure 8.4.

Throughout the three stages, we consciously incorporated students' L1 lifeworld experience into different elements in CLIL lessons, such as

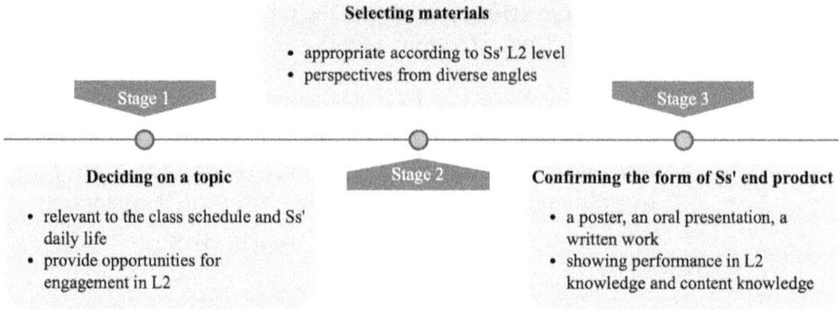

Figure 8.4 The procedure for designing CLIL lessons

the content on PowerPoint slides, the reading materials, the handouts, the teachers' talks, etc. Below is an example of how we, based on our agreement obtained from dialogic conversations, capitalized on students' L1, Mandarin. Figure 8.5 shows the first five slides extracted from a unit conducted in a Social Studies class at School P. The topic was *Urban Renewal*.

Figure 8.5 An extract of the first five PowerPoint slides presented at a CLIL lesson discussing urban renewal

Students were expected to discuss this issue from the viewpoints of a resident, a city leader and a developer. The creation of these five slides followed the first stage of the MEC, *create a rich experiential context* 'to arouse students' interest, and immerse the students in the content topic field using multimodalities…' (Lin, 2015: 85). Hence, Ms Peng began by presenting her grade 4 students with two images (purposefully blurred in this chapter to avoid copyright infringement) taken from news reports. These two images show groups of people holding some banners and boards with Chinese words on them. Students were invited to examine these two images and to answer five questions based on their observation and ideas. During Activity 1.1, students needed to utilize their deduction skills and English language skills in terms of answering the Wh-questions. The difficult words were translated into Chinese in parenthesis to facilitate students' understanding and their completion of the activity. Next, designed as a parallel task, which was operated 'on the principle of *repetition with variation*' (Lin, 2016: 123), Activity 1.2 began with a video of a news clip and was followed by a discussion over it by answering the five Wh-questions. Similar to how Activity 1.1 was carried out, Activity 1.2 did not limit the multimodal material or students' medium of discussion to only the target language. We designed the activities in this way for both pedagogical and contextual reasons (Dafouz & Smit, 2016) – to help students with a limited proficiency of English understand the aims of the activities and to recognize issues pertaining to students' daily life.

After each implementation of a unit, we held an evaluation meeting with the teachers to reflect on what we have observed that could have been done differently to improve the next design and implementation. We also identified some challenges throughout this journey. One of the major challenges was found when the teachers had to handle students' questions in content knowledge, specifically for Ms Shih, who was teaching grade 7 students. The following remark given by Ms Shih, translated from Mandarin into English, showed how she felt overwhelmed.

> During the students' debate, I found it somewhat difficult to 'cope with' students' ideas because their ideas were formed from diverse angles. I don't think I was supposed to tell them whether their ideas were right or wrong, or to provide them with a standard answer. I guess I have not done a thorough study about that area or had any deep understanding of it. What I know may be quite superficial. That is why my focus was easily lost when students presented their ideas, and so was the centre of the debate.
>
> (Evaluation 1 with Ms Shih)

During the lessons where students' L1 was allowed, it seemed that although Ms Shih was pleased to see her students' great engagement in developing and sharing ideas, she was hardly able to handle students' ideas from a wide range of aspects. Hence, during the evaluation meeting, we proposed that the teacher welcome a teacher–student relationship that sought to co-construct ideas in the class. This proposed stance would echo Freire's (1972) opposition to the banking model of education by redefining the roles of a teacher and a student. While it was true that CLIL integrates both content and language, and although a teacher is mostly trained in either track, it no longer means the teacher should be the only person delivering knowledge in the classroom.

Students' Development of Ideas under Translanguaging Pedagogies

This section reports a selected episode of translingual practice by Ms Peng, who conducted her second CLIL unit entitled 'Building houses for the homeless' in her grade 4 Social Studies class. Following it is an artefact in the target language showing arguments about the value as an artificial intelligence (AI) developer created by a group of students in a CLIL unit on *humans and technology* at School S. We shall present the artefact along with a discussion in L1 between the student presenters and audience over their arguments. The following selected episode and students' artefact will be used to discuss the effectiveness of our co-design of materials and how we have come to accept such a design and how we interpreted these results.

At School P during the first lesson of the second CLIL unit on people experiencing homelessness, which took four lessons, Ms Peng and her class translanguaged between their L1 and English, as shown in Excerpt 8.2. To facilitate understanding, the utterances in Mandarin Chinese have been translated into English, shown in bold and placed between square brackets.

Excerpt 8.2

1	Ms Peng:	Ok, today we are going to talk about *the homeless*. Does anyone know 'home'? 什麼意思 [**What does it mean?**]
2	Student 1	家 [**Home.**]
3	Ms Peng:	'-less'是什麼 [**What's '-less'?**] 比較少，或者是沒有，所以沒有家 [**meaning less or without, so without a house**] 'homeless.' 沒有家 [**Without a house**] 'homeless.' How about 'build'? 我們上次有學過 [**Last time we learned about the word**] 'building,' right?
4	Student 1:	對，建房 [**Yes, constructing houses**]
5	Ms Peng:	We are going to construct 我們要去蓋房子，蓋房子，為了誰呀 [**We are going to build houses. Build houses, for whom?**]
6	Students:	為了人，為人民 [**For humans. For citizens.**]
7	Ms Peng:	Ok, before we talk about this one, (Student 2: 為了錢 [**For money.**]) how is the weather today?
8	Students:	Rainy!
9	Ms Peng:	It's rainy, and?

10 **Students:** Cold.
11 **Ms Peng:** It's cold. Very good.
12 **Student 3:** And it's…
13 **Ms Peng:** It's…what? (Student 3: 熱 [**Hot.**]) It's sunny? Are you sure? Ok, so if you can speak in English, please try your best.
14 **Students:** Ok!
15 **Ms Peng:** Ok, so what can you see from the picture? Please raise your hand.
16 **Student 4:** It's sleeping.
17 **Ms Peng:** He is sleeping. Ok, (your group) gets one point. Anyone else?
18 **Student 5:** A people.
19 **Ms Peng:** A people. Only one people? (Student 6: Peoples) People. A person or people. Very good. (Student 7: 'People' 是人們 [**means a group of people**]) 對，'People' 是人們 [**That's right, a group of people.**]

(Implementation of the 2nd CLIL unit, *Building houses for the homeless,* the 1st lesson)

As demonstrated in the extract above, when Ms Peng asked questions in English, she noticed at first the students' slight resistance in speaking and answering her questions. However, the teacher's several and constant emphases on and encouragement in using as much English as they could gradually lead to students' increased engagement in English, although the students' responses were mostly single words or short sentences (utterances 8, 10, 12, 14, 16 and 18) in the target language. Ms Peng took the initiative to create a friendly environment by explicitly stating that students were encouraged to use English without imposing any restrictions regarding the languages used in her class (utterance 13). In addition, although students answered some of Ms Peng's questions in Mandarin (utterances 2, 4 and 6), Ms Peng did not seem to intend to help students translate those utterances into the target language; she did not provide clear feedback regarding whether the students' responses in Mandarin were correct. Instead, Ms Peng kept the lesson flowing and the discussion going, almost as if she had treated both languages as equally important media of interaction and knowledge-making, a concept and stance we had agreed upon earlier.

As a practitioner of CLIL (and not solely ELT) during our collaboration, Ms Peng seemed to be more comfortable with using students' L1. At first, she regretted that the 'hard' concepts, e.g. floor area ratio, causes of homelessness including social and structural forces, were eventually not seamlessly or orally taught in the target language, and that the students were not assessed on those concepts in the target language; she deemed this goal impossible according to her students' current proficiency level in English. Thus, she questioned how much of the target language could be acquired when translanguaging pedagogies were adopted. On the other hand, we contributed what we have obtained in our classroom observation to our discussions, pointing out that it was the attitude of using English, as opposed to the accuracy of using a language, that we were more concerned about during CLIL lessons. A co-shift was made when she agreed and came to accept her wide use of translanguaging by delineating the CLIL approach with her consciously chosen attitude toward her students' output in English. Instead of limiting students' expressions to English, she made it clear to the class that it was acceptable to use Mandarin while encouraging any output in the target language if students were willing to. Her delineation translated from Mandarin into English is expressed below. This retrospective comment demonstrates Ms Peng's understanding of CLIL, thus affecting her attitude of treating the students' output in both Mandarin and English in the class.

> When English learning is not among the learning objectives, I do not tend to praise my students' output in English. But in the case of CLIL, I respond with 'Wow! Perfect! Excellent!' in appreciation of their effort. And I tend to intensify that specific atmosphere in which the other students would follow their classmates and start speaking in English. Even though there was room for improvement in their sentence patterns, content, or pronunciation, that's fine. I simply aim to create the ambience of speaking in English by increasing their willingness. That's why I always give exceedingly high praise whenever they use English. To me, the lessons that adopt CLIL differs from the others in terms of how English is positioned.
>
> (Evaluation 3 with Ms Peng)

Ms Shih took up a similar stance; she encouraged students' use of English instead of adopting the English-only approach. The following example of an artefact and dialogue is extracted from the final lesson of a CLIL unit, during which students were required to entextualize their learning on the given topic. In that lesson, students were divided into groups to discuss and present their ideas about the value of a human, a robot or an AI developer in society. After each group presentation, the student audience was allowed to raise questions for clarification or further explanation from the presenting groups. Figure 8.6 is a poster created by one group representing an AI developer. It shows students' effort in fulfilling one of the language learning objectives of that CLIL unit: Using appropriate vocabulary and sentence patterns to describe what one can do (one's abilities) with the target sentence pattern '[A] can [VERB].' Although there are occasional grammatical errors, Ms Shih did not intentionally interrupt the group presentation but seemed to be focusing on students' delivery of their ideas.

Excerpt 8.3 shows the corresponding follow-up discussion between the presenting group (P) representing an AI developer and the student audience (A) based on P's presentation and their artefact (Figure 8.6).

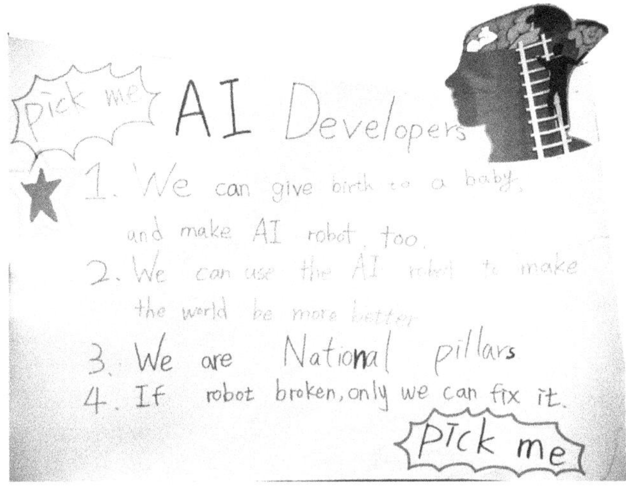

Figure 8.6 A poster listing the value of an AI developer in society as discussed by one group

Excerpt 8.3

1 T: Are there any questions? 如果有不清楚的，也可以問喔 **[You may also raise questions for clarification.]**

2 A1: 機器人也會發展出會殺人的慼情 **[Robots may also develop a desire to kill people.]**

3 P1: 有可能 **[Yes, *may*]**

4 P2: 他們的意識是我們控制的，我們控制的，我們可以植入我們想要他們做什麼 **[*We* get to control their consciousness. It's controlled by us. *We* get to embed in them what we want them to do.]**

5 A2: 你知道嗎？當你把它輸進去以後，接下來就不是你控制的了 **[You know what, once implanted, it's no longer something you can control.]**

(A discussion observed in a CLIL unit, *Humans and technology*, the final lesson)

Although the whole-class discussion was carried out in students' L1, an important theme was brought up, students demonstrating their critical thinking skills. According to the presenting group, those who create AI robots make the world a better place (Point 2 in the artefact, Figure 8.6). However, this argument was challenged by one of their peers who mentioned that it was not guaranteed all AI robots bring peace (utterance 2). To support his argument, one of the presenting students explained that it was the AI developers who had control over how they wanted their AI robots to work and to be (utterance 4). The concept of *control* was then challenged (utterance 5). Students were later engaged in discussions about who controls who/what. At this stage, Ms Shih showed no signs of any willingness to take part in the decision of students' opinions regarding which ones were right or wrong. She made sure that she remained neutral and reminded her students of the purpose of holding such discussions. During the debriefing after completing this unit, Ms Shih mentioned that her students surprisingly responded quite well in the lesson and seemed involved and engaged in discussions. One key reason could be that the language used for carrying out the discussion was not limited to English. Luk and Lin (2015) also found a difference in students' performance when they discussed issues in their L1 and the target language.

The episodes above have demonstrated how inviting students, though with limited English proficiency, to discuss important social issues, e.g. the homeless and technology in CLIL lessons was feasible with translanguaging pedagogies. The students were able to show their critical thinking skills by expressing and negotiating their ideas. While it remained elusive as to what extent using translanguaging could support students' acquisition of the target language, seeing that the students' negotiation of meaning was mainly conducted in L1, our observation showed students' active engagement in expressing opinions with enhanced awareness of social issues. If done without drawing on students' full linguistic repertoire, in Ms Shih's words, 'it would turn the classroom into a silent space.' Both teachers adopted translanguaging pedagogies with an explicit attitude toward the necessity of drawing on all linguistic resources available. This stance has provided a meaningful context for students to learn the target language with reduced resistance to English and increased intrinsic motivation (Deci & Ryan, 1985) in learning English, ultimately treating English not as a foreign language or an 'outsider' but as a tool that can be leveraged. That is, the class showed their interest in participating in the learning tasks for their own sake knowing that answering a question would not earn any points.

Conclusion

Set in the CLIL context which has dual goals in both content learning and language learning, this study tried to examine how translanguaging pedagogies can be implemented with the participating teachers in a teacher–researcher collaborative and dialogic approach (He & Lin, 2018) to facilitate the implementation of critical CLIL, which aimed to enhance students' awareness of social issues by treating language education as integral to society (Sato *et al.*, 2017). This critical stance also reframed the teacher–researcher and the teacher–student relationship by transcending it from a hierarchical pane to an egalitarian one. Instead of forming our collaboration on a hierarchical pane, we have created a dialogic space where both the participating teachers and the researchers were fully aware of and recognized the heterogeneity lying within our relationship. We acknowledged where we were coming from and what we could contribute to this collaborative work; the teachers contributed much of their knowledge and suggestions based on their years of experience gained during on-site teaching and their great familiarity with their classes of students, while the researchers provided theoretical support which could be turned to or taken as references drawing on a range of studies previously conducted in different contexts and different methods.

Finally, to implement critical CLIL, which aimed for facilitating students in rethinking and conveying in different perspectives the issues taken for granted, we adopted translanguaging pedagogies during the lessons. The findings have shown how translanguaging pedagogies have facilitated the implementation of critical CLIL in the following ways. Although Ms Peng and Ms Shih may not be explicitly aware of the research terminology of *translanguaging* in the first place since we as researchers mainly introduced the concept, the rationale, and the methods without digging into the 'jargon' per se to the teachers, they in fact practiced translanguaging in a purposeful manner (Canagarajah, 2011) throughout the implementation to (1) facilitate students' understanding, ensuring that students are following and achieving the aims of each class activity; (2) provide students with explicit language support, e.g. key vocabulary and sentence patterns and translations of difficult words and implicit language support, i.e. their constant and purposeful decisions to speak in two languages without directing students' attention to such a behavior; (3) create a 'safe space' where students' ongoing development of ideas weigh more than their fixed and finalized ideas to develop and form their opinions regarding social issues through dialogue; and (4) develop an atmosphere where students are comfortable using the target language to express ideas without fearing getting marks reduced as a result of producing 'incorrect' English, thereby recognizing English as an alternative option/tool, in addition to their L1, to deliver ideas. The findings have shown that fulfilling these purposes of using translanguaging is essential in adopting a critical CLIL approach. These findings obtained from this study which sought the incorporation of a critical lens into the CLIL approach could provide pedagogical implications, especially in employing bilingual education in classrooms of emergent bilinguals to pave the way for development and implementation of CLIL in EFL contexts.

References

Bakhtin, M.M. (1986) *Speech Genres and Other Late Essays*. Austin, TX: University of Texas Press.

Barab, S. and Squire, B. (2004) Design-based research: Putting a stake in the ground. *The Journal of the Learning Sciences* 13 (1), 1–14.

Bell, P. (2004) On the theoretical breadth of design-based research in education. *Educational Psychologist* 39 (4), 243–253.

Benesch, S. (1993) Critical thinking: A learning process for democracy. *TESOL Quarterly* 27 (3), 545–548.

Benesch, S. (2001) *Critical English for Academic Purposes: Theory, Politics, and Practice.* Mahwah, NJ: Lawrence Erlbaum Associates.

Bentley, K. (2010) *The TKT Course CLIL Module.* Cambridge: Cambridge University Press.

Canagarajah, S. (2011) Codemeshing in academic writing: Identifying teachable strategies of translanguaging. *The Modern Language Journal* 95 (3), 401–417.

Christie, F. and Martin, J.R. (eds) (2005) *Genre and Institutions: Social Processes in the Workplace and School.* New York: Continuum.

Coyle, D., Hood, P. and Marsh, D. (2010) *Content and Language Integrated Learning.* Cambridge: Cambridge University Press.

Crookes, G.V. (2013) *Critical ELT in Action: Foundations, Promises, Praxis.* New York: Routledge.

Dafouz, E. and Smit, U. (2016) Towards a dynamic conceptual framework for English-medium education in multilingual university settings. *Applied Linguistics* 37 (3), 397–415.

Deci, E.L. and Ryan, R.M. (1985) *Intrinsic Motivation and Self-determination in Human Behavior.* New York, NY: Plenum Press.

Doyle, W. (1990) Themes in teacher education research. In W.R. Houston (ed.) *Handbook of Research in Teacher Education* (pp. 3–24). New York: Macmillan.

Elder, L. and Paul, R. (1994) Critical thinking: Why we must transform our teaching. *Journal of Developmental Education* 18 (1), 34.

Ellis, R. and Barkhuizen, G.P. (2005) *Analysing Learner Language.* Oxford: Oxford University Press.

Freire, P. (1972) *Pedagogy of the Oppressed.* Translated by Myra Bergman Ramos. New York: Herder and Herder.

García, O., Johnson, S. and Seltzer, K. (2017) *The Translanguaging Classroom: Leveraging Student Bilingualism for Learning.* Philadelphia, PA: Caslon.

García, O. and Li, W. (2014) *Translanguaging: Language, Bilingualism and Education.* London: Palgrave Macmillan.

Gitlin, A.D. (1990) Educative research, voice, and school change. *Harvard Educational Review* 60 (4), 443–46.

Gupta, K.C.L. (2020) Researcher-teacher collaboration in adopting critical content and language integrated learning (CLIL): Processes, challenges and outcomes. *Trabalhos em Linguística Aplicada* 59 (1), 42–77.

Halliday, M.A. (1993) Towards a language-based theory of learning. *Linguistics and Education* 5 (2), 93–116.

He, P. and Lin, A.M.Y. (2018) Becoming a 'language-aware' content teacher: Content and language integrated learning (CLIL) teacher professional development as a collaborative, dynamic, and dialogic process. *Journal of Immersion and Content-Based Language Education* 6 (2), 162–188.

Hoadley, C.M. (2004) Methodological alignment in design-based research. *Educational Psychologist* 39 (4), 203–212.

Lin, A.M.Y. (2015) Conceptualising the potential role of L1 in CLIL. *Language, Culture and Curriculum* 28 (1), 74–89.

Lin, A.M.Y. (2016) *Language across the Curriculum & CLIL in English as an Additional Language (EAL) Contexts: Theory and Practice.* Singapore: Springer.

Lipman, M. (1991) *Thinking in Education.* Cambridge: Cambridge University Press.

Lo, Y.Y. (2019) Development of the beliefs and language awareness of content subject teachers in CLIL: Does professional development help? *International Journal of Bilingual Education and Bilingualism* 22 (7), 818–832.

Luk, J. and Lin, A.M.Y. (2015) Voices without words: Doing critical literate talk in English as a second language. *TESOL Quarterly* 49 (1), 67–91.

Master, P. (1998) Positive and negative aspects of the dominance of English. *TESOL Quarterly* 32 (4), 716–727.

Mercer, N. (1995) *The Guided Construction of Knowledge: Talk Amongst Teachers and Learners*. Clevedon: Multilingual Matters.

Mortimer, E.F. and Scott, P. (2003) *Meaning Making in Secondary Science Classrooms*. Philadelphia, PA: Open University Press.

Patton, M. (1990) *Qualitative Evaluation and Research Methods* (2nd edn). Newbury Park, CA: Sage.

Pennycook, A. (1999) Introduction: Critical approaches to TESOL. *TESOL Quarterly* 33 (3), 329–348.

Rose, D. and Martin, J.R. (2012) *Learning to Write, Reading to Learn: Genre, Knowledge and Pedagogy in the Sydney School*. Bristol: Equinox.

Sato, S., Hasegawa, A., Kumagai, Y. and Kamiyoshi, U. (2017) Content-based instruction (CBI) for the social future: A recommendation for critical content-based language instruction (CCBI). *L2 Journal* 9 (3), 50–69.

Siegel, H. (1988) *Educating Reason: Rationality, Critical Thinking, and Education*. New York: Routledge.

Tian, Z. and Shepard-Carey, L. (2020) (Re) imagining the future of translanguaging pedagogies in TESOL through teacher–researcher collaboration. *TESOL Quarterly* 54 (4), 1131–1143.

9 Acompañamiento: Centering Vulnerability and Agency in Co-Designing Computing and Translanguaging Curriculum with Teachers

Ralph Vacca, Sara Vogel, Laura Ascenzi-Moreno and Christopher Hoadley

Cultivating spaces where translanguaging can authentically occur requires an attention to broader issues of colonial ideologies, power and students' agency in leveraging their full available semiotic resources (Vogel & García, 2017). Similarly, approaches to computing education have increasingly sought to center students' agency in leveraging their diverse ecologies, cultures and language practices (e.g. Brennan, 2013; Ryoo *et al.*, 2020). In connecting translanguaging to computing education, there is both an opportunity to better support bi/multilingual, language-minoritized students, as well as find connections between curricular innovations that seek to prioritize the centering of student agency. However, key to bringing these pedagogies together is understanding how teachers can be supported in negotiating shifts in student agency.

Adopting a translanguaging approach requires teachers to let go of a desire to exercise control over students' languaging, and to position themselves as co-learners alongside students. While translanguaging emphasizes a dynamic view of language that differs from code switching/mixing theories, the degree to which implementation in the classroom focuses on meaning-making, challenging linguistic hierarchies and constructing original and complex discursive practices varies (Allard, 2017). Too often translanguaging can be positioned as a scaffold in which students are merely encouraged to use home language practices to gain competencies in the language of school (García, 2017). One key aspect to embracing the transgressive potential of translanguaging is constructing translanguaging spaces where, 'children are given agency to act linguistically by being both creative and critical, and where teachers encourage those actions' (García & Li, 2014: 74). Because translanguaging theory aims to decenter monolingualism and how it permeates the educational process, it can be a broader transformative force for shifting educators' ideologies and change student-teaching relationships to be more multidirectional (García & Li, 2014).

In adopting new technologies and ways of teaching and learning with them, questions also surface about who the experts are, potentially challenging traditional teacher–student power dynamics. In particular, constructionist approaches in computing education that seek to center student agency push teachers to consider individual and personal endpoints that go beyond coding know-how but also focus on creative expression (Blikstein & Moghadam, 2018), and connections to student interests, culture and expressive capacities (Ascenzi-Moreno *et al.*, 2020).

For any transformative potential to be realized, the field must come to understand how re-negotiations of student and teacher agency occur. Enacting these shifts presents challenges for teachers, who can experience great vulnerability as they manage negotiating power and agency in the classroom. Teacher vulnerability can vary in its effects, sometimes entailing a significant amount of emotional labor and possible teacher isolation, but also providing a gateway for transformation once teachers gain a better understanding of realities and negotiate possible alternatives (Zembylas, 2002).

Managing such vulnerabilities can be an important aspect of successful teacher–researcher collaborations. Co-designing curriculum can also be a powerful approach in that it situates the teacher as an active agent negotiating aspects of the designed student learning experience, not just implementing predefined ones. While emerging work has highlighted ways in which technology-mediated experiences can serve as another space for student translanguaging (Radke *et al.*, 2020; Vogel *et al.*, 2019), there is a need for more detailed accounts on how teacher–researcher collaborations can be set up to support the renegotiation of agency that occur in pairing technology with translanguaging.

In this chapter we posit a framework of acompañamiento, an approach to teacher–researcher collaborations around technology in multilingual spaces that explicitly acknowledges vulnerability and moves along an axis of redistribution of agency in the classroom. Through a dynamic relational trajectory that met each teacher where they were ready in terms of integrating constructivist and translanguaging approaches, acompañamiento acknowledges how strategies of intense in-classroom support and context-dependent goal setting can help manage the vulnerability that can arise as agency is re-negotiated in the classroom. Specifically, we explore the questions: (1) How did teachers understand the role of student agency in connecting computing and translanguaging? (2) How did the teachers and researchers feel support was provided in negotiating student agency?

We share the work of Participating in Literacies and Computer Science (PiLa-CS), a research–practice partnership (RPP) which brought together university researchers and middle grades teachers to involve emergent bilingual middle schoolers in units of study that integrate computer science practices and concepts. The project focuses primarily on understanding how translanguaging and computer science (CS) education could support each other, how students translanguage when engaged in computer science learning and how teachers can take up these approaches. However, in this chapter we specifically examine the relationships between the researchers and the educators as they relate to co-design.

Through an analysis of interviews with four middle school teachers and four researchers we sought to understand how our teacher–researcher collaboration grappled with questions of agency while attempting to integrate computing into bi/multilingual classrooms in constructivist ways, and build on students' translanguaging intentionally. We found that teacher vulnerability played a key role in mediating how teachers and researchers jointly engaged with the questions of agency involved in grappling with the three components of translanguaging pedagogy: co-stance, co-design and co-shifts (García, 2017; Tian & Shepard-Carey, 2020). In particular, we found that through a dynamic relational trajectory that meets each teacher where they were ready in terms of integrating constructivist and translanguaging approaches, *acompañamiento* is an approach to teacher–researcher collaborations that acknowledges and addresses the vulnerability that can arise as agency is re-negotiated in the classroom. Specific elements of the partnership's approach – encouraging teachers to work within pre-existing curricular and pedagogical frameworks, providing ongoing acompañamiento or in-classroom support and responding to changes over time in teachers' attitudes – helped manage teacher vulnerability. These findings suggest possibilities as well as notes of caution for future researcher–practitioner partnerships and projects that aim to support more transformational approaches to co-designing computer science and translanguaging. In particular this study worked across varying middle school contexts with different dual language expectations, highlighting the importance of adapting to different degrees of teacher vulnerability in negotiating teacher and student agency in computer science and translanguaging learning experiences.

Agency in Translanguaging and Technology

Translanguaging and agency

Student agency has been defined as the capacity for a student to act purposively towards individual goals, change the established pattern of classroom interactions and actively evaluate learning practice for the specific context (Arnold & Clarke, 2014). When students exercise agency in classrooms, they direct their own pathways and may draw from a wider range of linguistic, semiotic and cultural resources – including those often marginalized in schools – to make meaning and express themselves. Adopting translanguaging-supportive pedagogy directly challenges both how emergent bilinguals are viewed and the extent to which monolingual biases and restrictions in teaching and learning are circumvented by teachers.

In some instances emergent multilinguals, who are learning the language of instruction, may be perceived as lacking in cognitive resources necessary for competence and full participation (Healy & Powell, 2013). In these instances, teachers may conceive of their students solely within the bounds of their classification as English Language Learners (ELLs) and other policy-based terms, leading them to discourage emergent bilinguals from using language practices other than those perceived as dominant, deepening inequity and stifling agency (Brooks, 2016). Despite prevalent deficit-thinking, student agency is never absent in classrooms: as Seltzer notes in her study of students' metacognitive discussions about language (Seltzer, 2019), even in the most traditional monolingual environments, students exhibit agency with respect to their communicative practices, even if these are not noticed, supported or 'listened to' by teachers.

Student agency is also closely tied to teacher agency. For instance, the concept of 'co-learning,' a necessary component of translanguaging pedagogy, is understood as a sharing of power between students and teacher to shape classroom language, activities and goals. To enact translanguaging pedagogy, teachers intentionally signal the value of students' entire language repertoires and spark engagement through curation of materials and design of physical classroom environments and activities, and in doing so, need to shift plans when students' ideas and language practices seem to take activity in another direction. Ascenzi-Moreno (2017) found that as teachers shift to break free of rigid classifications of their emergent bilingual students, they may be able to exhibit greater agency in shaping curriculum, which in turn opens up spaces for students – who may already exhibit agency, but may not been seen or valued – to more freely direct their learning in personally meaningful ways.

Constructivist computing education and agency

Researchers and practitioners in CS education, too, have grappled with the role of student agency. CSforAll is part of a broad effort across the world to make computing and coding a core educational experience. Such efforts go beyond simply learning to code and often connect to goals that center student agency, including creative expression (Blikstein & Moghadam, 2018), social justice (Kafai *et al.*, 2020) and creating an informed citizenry and improving general technological literacy (Vogel *et al.*, 2017).

Early moves toward computing education ran the gamut from instructivist, behaviorist forms of instruction to what were termed 'constructionist' learning environments (Papert, 1980, 1993). These environments build on a constructivist stance by emphasizing learner agency to situate construction of ideas in the construction of artifacts (whether physical or digital) to support an individual's learning. Historically, technology use in constructionist learning environments was sometimes cast as a 'Trojan mouse' (Jackson, 2016; Lipponen, 2002) in which teaching students to build things with computers could change teachers' relationship to control in the classroom and push more progressive educational values (Linn & Pea, 1994; Papert, 1993). Research has documented ways that computing in education is more transformative when it is adopted by those with constructivist leanings (Becker & Riel, 2000), although just because teachers or designers espouse constructivist ideals doesn't mean they possess the skills to design and enact constructivism through technology in the classroom – evidence suggests that technologies can play a role in building these skills (Ronen Fuhrmann *et al.*, 2008). For example, in research by Eglash *et al.* (2009), the concept of design agency is used to describe the ways African-American children engage in creative explorations of the cultural practice of cornrow hairstyling through computational geometry. Tools such as the LOGO programming language (Papert, 1980) and its successor, Scratch (Maloney *et al.*, 2010) support student construction of interactive artifacts through coding, both as a form of creative expression and as a 'mind tool' for understanding other domains such as math, science, etc. (Papert, 1980, 1993). Depending on how they are used, these tools can impact aspects of both learner and teacher agency, requiring new forms of negotiation (Linn & Pea, 1994).

Supporting Teachers Negotiating Agency

If agency becomes a lynchpin from which translanguaging can be transgressive and technology can be liberating, then how we structure teacher–researcher collaborations to support negotiating agency is an important question to ask. In this section, we describe how vulnerability can help us understand how to support shifts in agency within the classroom. We frame vulnerability as concerns of 'not knowing' expressed as emotional experiences that connect to teachers' willingness/openness, as well as inefficaciousness/protectiveness (Lasky, 2005).

Many teachers would agree with Palmer's conclusion that teaching is a 'daily exercise in vulnerability' (1998: 17). Understood as a mood born from discomfort, not knowing and 'losing control of the processes and tasks they felt responsible for as teachers,' vulnerability is seen as a complex process that depends on teachers' identity, beliefs and perceptions of their own competence (Kelchtermans, 2005; Lasky, 2005) as well as on the broader institutional and sociocultural context and discourse surrounding them. While teachers commonly operate in demanding and uncertain environments that can prompt vulnerability, curricular innovations can often trigger new kinds of vulnerability. For instance, curricular innovations that seek to change the involvement of students as active agents in their own learning, may prompt a shift from an authoritarian hierarchical view of teaching to one which necessitates vulnerability (Palmer, 1998: 17). Teachers' vulnerability is commonly perceived as an emotion to be avoided and minimized (Bullough, 2005), but it might be mobilized for supporting teachers' professional growth.

In exploring teacher vulnerability, Lasky (2005) describes two kinds of vulnerability – open and protective. Teachers are most likely to experience open vulnerability when they feel safe and confident enough to risk opening themselves to the possibility of embarrassment and emotional stress for the sake of relationship building and student learning. Conversely, teachers are likely to experience protective vulnerability when they are anxious and fearful and they tend to avoid or move away from any event that could cause a threat. When teachers experience open vulnerability, they are likely to have positive attitudes and orientations to ongoing professional developments that may lead to pedagogical and self-transformation.

When teachers feel agency, they can move from one kind of vulnerability to another, and potentially makeshifts in pedagogies (Zembylas, 2002). Teacher agency is shaped by larger contextual factors. Teachers who experience agency within their work feel in control of their choices and that their choices are based upon their own goals, interests and motivations (Vähäsantanen, 2015). Teacher agency has been well-studied in the context of school reform initiatives and innovation. Sannino (2010) found that teachers with a high degree of agency and beliefs which conflict with a given innovation, may use their agency to offer resistance. By contrast, when the goals a teacher values correspond with the goals of an initiative, teachers' sense of agency can increase (Marshall & Drummond, 2006). How teacher learning is positioned in school also provides a framing for understanding teacher agency. Learning for practicing teachers is often associated with professional development to become familiar with new school policies or programs provided by school leaders or by outside experts. This approach can 'limit what can be learned' (Molle, 2013) and position teachers as *mere implementers* of curriculum rather than agents who craft and analyze student learning (Ascenzi-Moreno & Seltzer, 2021). Most importantly, if PD bypasses teachers' own questions, observations and ideas, the opportunity for teachers to consider the complexity of student learning, examine their own practices and craft new ones, is lost.

Context for our Teacher–Researcher Collaboration

Computer science learning and bilingual students

In 2015, spurred by grassroots activism from industry, non-profits, parent and educator groups and localities, then-President Barack Obama announced the US government would be making a substantial investment in promoting CS education for all children (CS4All). The reasons for promoting universal CS education are many, and contested, but stakeholders have envisioned futures where all students – including those that have been marginalized in the field (women, Black and Latinx students, students with disabilities) – mobilize computing to solve problems, express themselves, participate in civic life and economies, understand and shape the impacts that digital tools have on the world (Vogel *et al.*, 2017). There is little data on the participation of bi/multilingual students in computer science education, but equity audits conducted in a handful of districts in the southwest found that some high schools required particular levels of English proficiency before students labeled as 'English Learners' could participate in computing, and that students sometimes perceived stigmatizing messages from school staff about who could be successful in CS education (Hopkins *et al.*, 2021).

The New York City Department of Education founded its CS4All initiative in 2015, setting out the ambitious goal to expose all 1.1 million school children to 'meaningful units' of computer science at least once during each of four grade bands (K-2, 3-5, 6-8 and 9-12). Given that 13% of students in the district are bi/multilingual learners who receive services to learn English, and over 40% of them speak languages other than English at home (NYCDOE, 2019), considering equity from the perspective of students' language backgrounds has been a priority for the city's CS4All leaders.

Approach to collaboration

To support bi/multilingual learners' participation in computer science learning in NYC, we founded the Participating in Literacies and Computer Science (PiLa-CS) Research Practice Partnership (RPP) involving university-based researchers in bilingual education and computer science education; city-wide administrators implementing CS4All; and teachers and principals in three middle schools willing to infuse computer science into their bilingual programs. RPPs attempt to encompass five dimensions outlined by Henrick *et al.* (2017): building trust and cultivating partnership relationships, conducting rigorous research to inform action, supporting practice goals in the practice-focused organizations, producing knowledge that can inform educational improvement more broadly and building the capacity of all partners to engage in deeper partnerships. Within this framework, the PiLa-CS partnership worked to advance research related to how emergent bilingual students translanguage in the context of computer science education, how translanguaging pedagogy could support the students in simultaneously learning CS and expanding their linguistic repertoire and, most centrally for this chapter, co-designing ways for the teachers to implement a translanguaging pedagogy in their classrooms in service of CS education.

Co-design is a set of scaffolded methods that allows teachers to reflect on their own knowledge so as to fully engage in the design process (DiSalvo, 2016). When combined with a translanguaging lens (García & Li, 2014), co-design necessitates thinking deeply about students' particular language practices and contexts (García *et al.*, 2017), and curriculum designers' individual growth trajectories and curricula. Of particular importance in co-design is the mediating role of relational expertise (Dindler & Iversen, 2014), power (Bratteteig & Wagner, 2012) and trust (Vakil *et al.*, 2018), in how notions and enactments of co-design change over time. Our focus is on how enactments of translanguaging and constructivist technology pedagogy are mediated by these relational dimensions of the teacher–researcher partnership.

We took up a definition of translanguaging pedagogy defined by García *et al.* (2016). It involves a three-part framework of (1) the educators' stance towards student language practices, (2) their design of lessons and classroom norms or activities and (3) their in-the-moment shifts or responses to students' use of language form the basis of this approach. Tian and Shepard-Carey (2020) point out that collaboration between teachers and researchers is one way to help instantiate translanguaging pedagogy, in which teachers and researchers not only co-design but also develop a co-stance and support co-shifts. Although our project predates the Tian and Shepard-Carey article, we use their framework to describe how our project collaborated on inventing ways to bring translanguaging pedagogy and computer science education together. It is worth emphasizing that the PiLa-CS project goals were *not* to develop disseminable, 'canned' curricula for bilingual CS education; rather, in keeping with the translanguaging philosophy of embracing the highly variable linguistic repertoires students bring and utilizing them as assets for learning, we aimed to help each teacher develop enactments that would serve as models for future practice, sites for research and a nexus for capacity building as described by Henrick et al. (2017).

The partnership began with formulation of the grant proposal while finding practice partner schools, first through principals and later individual teachers within those schools. Once funded, the project began a rhythm of working together over two and a half school years (the project experienced some interruptions and re-thinking due to the COVID-19 pandemic). Starting with a summer kickoff meeting, the project had release time and after school time budgeted for co-design activities of researchers and teachers. One or two school-year release days were used for a combination of exploring theories of translanguaging, conducting unit co-design and reviewing student work and classroom transcripts. One of the project's graduate student members and/or faculty would typically participate in computer science units, both in co-designing/co-facilitating those units and later in doing observation and data collection. Each summer thereafter, a three-day summer institute was conducted in which a combination of future planning, co-analysis and reflection on data, and further exploration of theories of translanguaging and syncretic literacies were undertaken. Initially, project communication relied heavily on one-to-one communication between grad students and the project teachers, but we later added a monthly meeting of all teachers, conducted face-to-face at one of the schools during the teachers' on-duty professional development after school period. Most teachers heavily involved researchers in not only design of these CS-infused units, but also in supporting implementation and iterating on them in each school year. Often, researchers helped with mid-unit adjustments to the projects and provided technical expertise and support. Training on using technologies such as the Scratch programming environment and other tools such as the Common Online Data Analysis Platform (CODAP) data analysis tools was relatively informal and ongoing. Annual meetings with principals and participation in other school and district events (e.g. a parent night, a city-wide student tech festival) rounded out the collaboration loci.

Data collection and analysis

With the purpose of better understanding how the teacher–researcher collaboration supported the connection between translanguaging and computing education, semi-structured interviews were conducted with four middle school teachers and four researchers (see Table 9.1) involved in the RPP in the final stages of their two and half school year grant implementation. The four teachers come from three public schools in the Washington Heights neighborhood of Manhattan in New York City. Forty-eight percent of area residents are foreign-born, with two-thirds of them from the Dominican Republic. The neighborhood is within the NYC DOE's District 6, which had the highest share of students classified as ELLs in the City (nearly 29%) (New York State, 2015). While all of the teachers had no formal implementation of translanguaging in the classroom in place, a few teachers did prioritize student expression and comfort over strict language use in the classroom.

A grounded analysis of the data was conducted using a constant comparison (Lincoln & Guba, 1985; Maykut & Morehouse, 1994), yielding three broad themes describing how teachers' initial feelings of vulnerability transitioned to feelings of being supported, and how aspects of the support helped teachers negotiate aspects of student and teacher agency, as they related to translanguaging and computing education.

Table 9.1 Teachers and researchers

	Role	Pseudonym	Core expertise	Background/School context
T1	Teacher	Mario	Bilingual; Math	Mid-career teacher (6–15 years); Former IT professional; New to translanguaging
T2	Teacher	Kate	Bilingual; Science	Veteran teacher (15+ years); Experience with teaching coding and computer modeling; Trained as a medical doctor in the Dominican Republic
T3	Teacher	Alba	Bilingual; Language Arts	Early-career teacher (under 5 years); New, but open, to new technologies; New to translanguaging, but already flexibly using named languages in the classroom
T4	Teacher	Gina	Bilingual; English as New Language (ENL)	Mid-career teacher (6–15 years); New to technology; New to translanguaging, but comfortable welcoming students' home languages into
R1	Researcher	Charlie	Educational technology; computer science	University professor in Educational Technology
R2	Researcher	Miriam	Bilingual; Computing education	Doctoral candidate in Bilingual Education; Experience conducting translanguaging research in K-12 setting; Former bilingual teacher and digital media educator.
R3	Researcher	Dora	Bilingual education	University professor in Teacher Education; Former bilingual teacher and literacy coach; Experience conducting translanguaging research in K-12 setting;
R4	Researcher	Rafael	Linguistics	Graduate student, former ENL teacher.

What We Learned

Feeling vulnerable

Teachers and researchers reflected on feelings of vulnerability as it related to the curricular design and implementation. In particular, participants felt vulnerability around how gaps in expertise, and variations in school ideologies and context would be managed. For instance, when prompted to reflect on their biggest fears going into the project, teacher Gina (T4) shared, 'I felt like I have no idea how I'm going to implement this in the classroom. So, that was my biggest fear.' When prompted to elaborate on what aspect of the implementation seemed daunting, Gina explained, 'I was thinking about how I was gonna learn all this new stuff.'

Even teacher Kate (T2) who had taken an unrelated coding course prior to engaging in the project, reflected on managing these feelings of 'not being an expert' at the onset and pondering the extent to which the research team would help them 'know what they need to know to support these kids when they're using Scratch.' Echoing this sentiment, teacher Alba (T3), reflected:

> I didn't think they were gonna be so available to help. I was worried… just not having time and knowing what to do if something didn't like work. Or if I didn't have the answer to questions on how to do something.

While the focus of gaps in expertise mainly centered on technical expertise, a few teachers did connect concerns around 'not knowing' with language. For instance, Alba (T3) reflected on her own language expertise sharing, 'my Spanish is different, and I don't know how to say so many of the computer terms.' Gina (T4) also referenced expertise in language when asked about any initial concerns in designing computing curriculum:

> Most of our students are either from Dominican Republic, Yemen, and we have two from… Actually, two came from Senegal and one from, I believe, Ghana. So there's always this thinking around how to bring in different cultures, and how to connect it to what they're learning.

Beyond individual expertise, teachers also mentioned apprehensions related to their school context. For instance, teacher Mario (T1) shared his thoughts on how his dual language school complicated implementing his understanding of the translanguaging approach, which was a focal point of the teacher–researcher collaboration.

> Translanguage is being able to use any language you want to express your ideas, which was a conflict because my school is a dual language school. If the class is in Spanish, you have to speak in Spanish. If the class is in English, you have to speak in English. It was a new concept to us, and we're still trying to understand it and its value.

If we frame vulnerability as a mood born from discomfort in 'not knowing' and 'losing control of the processes and tasks they felt responsible for as teachers' (Kelchtermans, 2005; Lasky, 2005), initial discomforts on the side of teachers emerged from perceived gaps in their own expertise and conflicts with their own school contexts that might complicate a translanguaging approach to CS education.

Negotiating student agency

While teachers mentioned various pedagogical strategies they'd used in their classrooms prior to their involvement in this particular teacher–researcher collaboration, *co-learning alongside students* and *embracing autonomy and creative expression* emerged as key to how vulnerability around their own expertise was addressed.

All teachers reflected on their shift towards becoming co-learners and embracing not having to be the technology expert. For instance, Alba (T3) shared that she 'learned to be okay with not knowing how to do certain things. It's okay. There's this way it gets figured out. And it's part of... you know...the whole process.' When prompted to share a key piece of advice she would give teachers after looking back on her own experience, teacher Kate (T2) shared 'don't be intimidated.... I don't consider myself an expert at all, you know. We are learning, the kids are learning, you need to be comfortable of not knowing.' This emotional comfort with not knowing is paired with reflections on the role of students as teachers and teachers as co-learners. For instance, teacher Kate (T2) shared, 'I rely more on the students like we're learning together so that's something.' Another teacher Gina (T4) described how students at times became positioned as teachers in the classroom, even mimicking some of the teacher's approaches to instruction. She shared:

> She [student] learned certain blocks that I wasn't sure how to use. And she actually did the step by step process with me. She used the vocabulary first, next, then last, when we went over it. And she taught it to me first, how to do it. And then, she actually did the gradual release. And she said, 'Okay, now you do it. I taught you how to do it twice, and now you're going to do the final call.' So she actually followed my teaching lesson.

This rebalancing of agency in the classroom was not just reflected in how some teachers became co-learners alongside students, but also in how students became more independent as they sought to creatively express themselves through both the computational tool and the freedom to translanguage. One researcher Rafael (R4) described his experience in the classroom with students connecting student independence and creative expression within the translanguaging context. He shared:

> And it's very interesting. At first, the class, you know the kids are a little more quiet and hushed and they had their little like cliques, you know, like, especially as a language learner right... you're going to stick with like the people you speak the language with. As the unit progressed, it was really interesting. So if you could imagine like in any given moment, like... You have kids getting up with their laptops moving towards, like the other kids workstation asking questions... like exchanging ideas like "oh that's really cool you got your sprites and move a certain way. How did you do that?" And there was this language happening right, this is kind of like this communication happening, this is how the Google translate thing came around. One kid found it and it spread like wildfire. Look, you can use this as like a voice like if. Cause some kids knew I think about the audio capability like you use the mic on your laptop, but then one understood and found that.... oh, you can use Google translate and it does the dictation kind of like in a robotic-ish voice. They found out about you could change the languages on the fly in Scratch right so um and they just went to town... It is this... genuine learning, giving them

> agency to kind of exercise like how did they want their story to look, you know what types of techniques, are they learning Scratch from their own experiences from each other, as a group...

In several instances the teachers drew connections between becoming co-learners alongside students and their translanguaging efforts. For instance, teacher Kate (T2) reflected on the relationship between student agency in the classroom, creative expression and translanguaging. She shared:

> They're comfortable either talking English or Spanish or, you know, if they don't remember a word, they'll say it in whatever language, they're comfortable with, you know, it's okay. You know, they have that freedom to express themselves, which is which is sounds good. You see them really into what they're making using different languages. Changing the language in the tool. Asking each other.

For example, in one classroom teachers recommended that students remix a Scratch project by choosing a different author or book character to interview – but students exerted their agency to adapt the work to their own interests (see Vogel *et al.*, 2019 for more details). Students selected figures from sports such as Stephen Curry, or pop culture, like Nicki Minaj and the reggaeton artists, Bad Bunny and Ozuna. One student decided she wanted users of her project to interview her favorite bachata singer, Romeo Santos. This required her to draw on what she knew about this artist to ask him informed questions, and to import photos from the internet.

This notion of 'freedom' and its connection to use of language was expressed by all of the teachers. Gina (T4) uses 'free' here to talk about language, use later elaborating on the impact on their effort and motivation

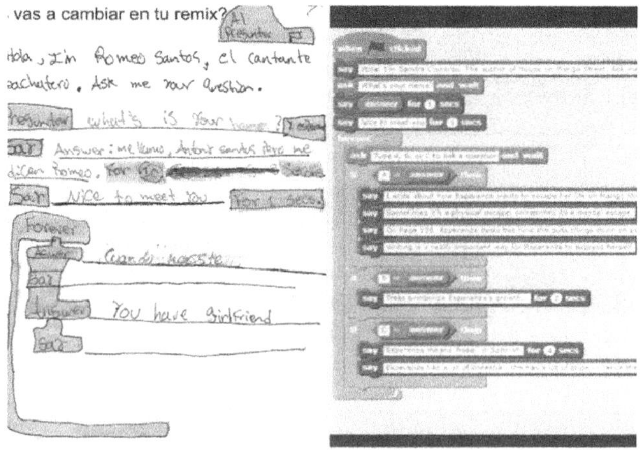

Figure 9.1 The remix plan a student drew on paper (left) before coding in Scratch software (right)

overall. She shared that students are, 'free to communicate the way they want, whatever they want whatever is best' and went on to share:

> I thought they were going to limit to themselves, sometimes they tend to do that with their writing, where they tend to say, 'This is how much English I know, this is all I can give you.' But they wouldn't do that, when it came to Scratch. They got really creative with it. Because, now we actually doing it... We'll read a story and where they've been told, 'Okay. Now, we're going to recreate what we read, into Scratch.' And that, they want to get [through stories], they just go straight into Scratch.

The shift in in-classroom agency was itself a source of vulnerability as teachers reflected on their own stances on student agency. For instance, Gina elaborated that the shifts in her classroom came after initial fears about what independence might look like in the classroom:

> I'm going to say that one of the strengths that I think that I bring now, is allowing my students to be more creative and be more independent. And I feel like before ... before I was kind of in fear of whether I was going to be able to have them do these things on their own and be more independent.

Echoing this connection, Alba (T3) described how the freedom to explore and create connected to communication and translanguaging:

> You see them really get into it. They have this idea of what they're trying to make. Right. And they're using whatever it takes to ... you know. To get there. If they don't remember a word, they'll say it in whatever language they're comfortable with. They can use animations or words in their language.

This connection between engagement, creative expression, autonomy and translanguaging was echoed by how teacher Mario (T1) described the learning in his classroom.

> They are engaged. I would say their engagement is the strongest part of my lessons, because once you teach them something, they will try different blocks, and they will work together and be persistent trying to make it work by debugging the program and so on. It's the fact that you're not forcing them to speak English, it makes them feel more comfortable, it makes them safe and now they're more motivated to speak in the classroom because when they have to speak English and they don't know that much English, they just don't say anything. Now they are actually talking, which is good.

Shared among the various reflections were threads connecting student agency to classroom dynamics where students were free to share their budding expertise with technology in more flexible ways, where teachers became co-learners and creative expression became synergistic with translanguaging efforts.

Support

The teacher–researcher collaboration was characterized by teachers and researchers as one that was both *flexible* and *shared*. This sense that the collaboration was flexible related to how researchers adapted to teachers' initial stances around agency in the classroom, and in turn how curricular implementation might look in the classroom. In contrast to approaches that seek to support teachers in adopting existing curriculum and the underlying pedagogical ideologies underlying such curriculum, the approach taken in this collaboration provided a differentiated approach, affording different endpoints for each teacher. Gina (T4) described this differentiated approach, as, 'So, they never made it, Okay, you have to recreate your curriculum, just to fit this in. Let's work with what you already have in place.' Basically, fitting it into what you're doing.' In differentiating the endpoints, teachers reflected on the sense of feeling 'respected' and researchers reflected on their embrace of a 'co-learning stance.' Teacher Mario (T1) in particular reflected on how his initial stance was both noticeably different, yet supported.

> We're very respectful of each other's philosophy and we're very respectful of teaching stuff, because for example, I'm a math person. I am very direct and very logical. The way I teach Scratch is completely different than everybody else who teaches Scratch.

In describing his approach to teaching coding as 'completely different than everybody else,' Mario was potentially referring to his approach of teaching students about the function of each category of programming blocks in the Scratch library in a linear fashion week-to-week. Researchers were at first discouraged by Mario's approach, which seemed inconsistent with constructivist pedagogies, but decided to take up a co-learning stance upon seeing just how participatory and engaged students were during times the teacher opened up moments for students to try out the code blocks he taught. Researchers continued visiting and debriefing with this teacher, pointing out examples of how his students ran with and went beyond the particular code blocks and functions he had taught for the day. Over time, Mario built in more space and time for students to explore and create projects of their own design, and became a vocal champion for free problem-solving time for his students – though he continued his block-by-block approach as well.

Across all of the collaborations, researchers aimed to work with teachers to go beyond thinking about translanguaging pedagogy as simply encouraging students to use any language at any time, or using it solely as a scaffold for English. However, the researchers made note of how the collaboration required them to make shifts to accommodate differences in how teachers sought to connect computing education and translanguaging goals. As an example, researcher Dora (R3) shared how the team negotiated translanguaging pedagogy within the programmatic goals of a dual language bilingual program, which aimed to support students to practice both English and Spanish. For this, in language arts Scratch projects where students were asked to depict Q-and-A style interviews between an interviewer of their choice and an authors, teachers and researchers expected students to write in both languages. While students had the agency to make choices of characters, this promoting of two languages in all projects could feel forced.

> ...so there was one group who had Shakira interview a character [from] House on Mango Street ... and Shakira spoke English and Spanish and asked her questions. So it was a little imposed...as opposed to how we would have wanted it to be.

Researchers found it difficult to root activities in programmatic goals while staying true to philosophies in translanguaging that center how authentic communication can happen across and beyond named languages. Activities varied in how they aligned with the translanguaging stances of the researchers. Here Dora (R3) draws a contrast with a different designed activity in the ENL class that aligned with a more open-ended focus that allowed for a more fluid translanguaging:

> [Gina] created such an open ended kind of family stories type of activity that kids could bring in their resources. The kids were like .... your translanguaging is accepted here. In fact we want you to do it.

This flexibility afforded the collaboration a way to meet teachers where they were at in terms of both their expertise and stance, mediating the kind of co-designed curricular units that were devised. Yet, despite adapting to teacher skills, philosophy and goals, teachers still felt trepidation as they planned lessons that centered the connection of computing education with translanguaging. One key aspect of the collaboration was the regular and flexible one-to-one in-classroom support. This helped teachers feel comfortable in planning student experiences that, while adapted to their own needs, still caused them to feel vulnerable about implementation. As one teacher Alba (T3) shared:

> We would plan these lessons, but the whole time I'm thinking. I'm so glad I'm not gonna be doing this alone. Like, oh... (breathes) there's this person that is going to help me out, you know, be there with me. That... that was really helpful.

This sense that feelings of vulnerability in trying new curriculum that might challenge existing norms on students' agency in the classroom were shared were touched on by all of the teachers. Here, teacher Mario (T1) describes the kind of support provided by one of the researchers Miriam (R2):

> She is always available when you need her. She will come to you to ask. If I need help planning, for example, I will call [Miriam], 'Listen, can we plan next week,' and she will find the time to help you, her being an

> excellent point person. I don't know if she has the flexibility, but she's been able to be flexible to come to our school when we need help and she will help us plan and give us feedback on whatever. She will come and help us in any way that we need help.

When prompted to further elaborate on how this level of support made him feel, Mario shared, 'like we were an actual team. If it didn't go how we want it to, we would both deal with it.' This kind of dependability extended into how unforeseen situations emerged. During the research project, COVID impacted the teachers in many ways including being tasked with teaching remotely. Within this context, the teachers expressed how they relied on the flexible support provided. One teacher, Kate (T2) shared:

> My gosh, it was challenging in the beginning, I was like, How am I going to do this? And, um, but fortunately [Miriam] was by my side... And you know, we introduced Scratch to them online completely and the kids really you know they got it. They, the kids, basically took over. And did you know which was great. It was great.

However, there were tensions that emerged with such an adaptive approach in that by negotiating goals instead of adhering strictly to predetermined curriculum, the researchers felt the need to actively balance their stance with those of the teachers. In reflecting on her experience as a researcher, Miriam (R2) describes how her relationships to different teachers varied and reflects on the challenges of creating space for teachers to exert their own ideas:

> So really for me, negotiating that line of, like, am I a coach, am I a co designer, am I like... a co teacher, am I just a buddy? Because sometimes after class, ... I'm just there and I'm hanging out and I'm listening. So there's just a lot of different hats. ...just negotiating these roles like how far do I push, how far do I step back, when do I let them take ownership, when do I step in, because it's very fluid ....it's sort of like just an ongoing relationship. And I want to talk to them as people, and if I get a cool idea will I step back and just be like... no... like... you do what you were going to do.

Furthermore, in sharing how co-shifts occurred by being in the classroom alongside teachers, issues of sustainability became very evident. One teacher, Gina (T4), reflected on their current challenge after four years participating in the collaboration. She shared:

> Sometimes I tend to second guess what I'm doing, because I wonder what misconceptions my students are going to have when they're working in Scratch. So, I'm always trying to think of, what are they going to do here? What if they get stuck on this section? Am I going to be able to help them, not having [Miriam] in the room? Or when I used to have [Rafael] help me. I think that's my biggest challenge.

Connected to this issue of sustainability was real reflection on the role of capacity building around computer science that should be afforded teachers as part of the collaboration. Researcher Charlie (R1) shared:

> We have some teachers who really want like I don't want to say predigested curriculum, but more hand holding, especially if they have a great discomfort about computer science or Scratch. And so there's there's a role that we're fulfilling that maybe we need to pay more deliberate attention to of… really teaching computer science directly to the teachers. And that's sort of an ambiguous role at the moment it comes up spontaneously in the middle of some of these things.

Expanding on these concerns around the sustainability and the tensions presented by engaging in such a close collaboration, researcher Miriam (R2) shared:

> Part of a goal of this project could also be sustainability, and I think I remember, there were moments, where I was just like…. ah… I'm doing too much. We want the teacher voice to come through and I felt like a lot of what I was doing was maybe just stifling it. Over time I've kind of let go of that idea….. That idea of feeling guilty for being too heavy handed I think was something that I was able to shed over time because I realized that they did want me in their classroom and we are co designers and that's different from being a coach. Like if I was their CS coach I would really want to help them become independent. But in this case it's like, sure independence is part of it and they're learning a lot of great skills along the way, but they only have so much to give to this project, they're really busy, they have full schedules and it's not their full- their attention isn't solely on this project, and so, if sometimes I'm helping out more than I would, that's part of it, if we want the units to happen.

The approach taken in this teacher–research collaboration is in line with many best practices on co-designing with teachers such as truly co-designing goals and sharing power (Penuel *et al.*, 2007; Penuel, 2019). The team reflected on how this adaptive approach to the collaboration had challenges around sustainability, but benefits in terms of creating room for teachers to find their own balance of student agency in their classrooms as they implemented new curriculum.

Discussion

Renegotiating agency to mediate vulnerability

Pedagogical innovations bring to the forefront numerous challenges. Those include grappling with the extent to which teachers need to develop new forms of expertise, such as bi/multilingualism to enact translanguaging pedagogy or technical expertise for computing education. These assumptions around expertise can trigger forms of teacher vulnerability, where teachers experience fears or anxieties around being able to meet what is being asked or demanded of them. As described earlier, the move towards open vulnerability versus protective vulnerability is largely dependent on individual characteristics of teachers themselves, sociocultural context (Lasky, 2005), as well as the degree to which teachers feel a sense of agency in shifting their pedagogies (Zembylas, 2002).

In supporting teachers to address gaps in expertise and support a sense of agency in shifting their pedagogies, a common approach is to focus primarily on teacher skills development at the onset so as to raise teacher expertise and possibly ameliorate teacher vulnerability and their negative perceptions around risk and implementation. However, such an approach that primarily front-loads skills development is not without tradeoffs. First, this approach relies on a certain degree of initial teacher buy-in around the need to develop such expertise, and may create significant conflicts with the limited time teachers have during planning. This prerequisite of buy-in may also result in narrowing the kind of teachers that are recruited, focusing on teachers that already have certain skills, or have already formed strong stances on technology and translanguaging. Lastly, an approach that primarily front-loads skills development should acknowledge that many 'curricular innovations' often take such an approach, offering pre-packaged curriculum alongside a pathway to skills development to support implementation. This approach relies on schools sustaining particular programmatic implementations for the time it may take a teacher to develop expertise – not a trivial feat in often-changing school policy environments.

A different approach might instead concurrently center renegotiation of teacher and student agency in the classroom alongside efforts to build expertise. In this approach, teachers challenge their own assumptions on being the sole experts, become co-learners and in turn create space for students to exercise their agency through teaching and sharing. In addition, teachers can create room for creative expression that encourages students to utilize different resources in ways that may not adhere to a predetermined form or approach. In this study, the RPP sought to orient towards a more constructivist classroom space whereby students could exhibit a greater degree of agency in their learning. The impetus for the re-negotiation of student agency stemmed from taking up translanguaging and constructivist approaches to computing education. However, for teachers, it was also motivated by feelings of vulnerability and was enabled in part by the support of the research team. In addressing the research question, how did teachers understand the role of student agency in connecting computing and translanguaging, as we noted in the findings, teachers in the projects engaged in two notable shifts: moving towards co-learning, and creating space for student autonomy and creative expression.

In teachers' descriptions of their experiences of co-learning with students, they shared about creating space for students to share their own growing expertise about the tools, to express themselves with the tools and to translanguage in the process – integrating language from their full repertoires, as well as cultural interests and social resources. What developed wasn't just teachers' ability to see students' linguistic repertoires as resources, but also to see students' agentive capacity as a resource for creative expression, and as a catalyst for teacher co-learning. In co-learning approaches both teacher and students are sharing, learning and adapting to each other's needs, learning styles, desires and funds of knowledge (Rosiers, 2016; Li, 2014). This in turn, created a transformative approach to translanguaging in which students were not just empowered to mix languages or use their home language as a scaffold, but to also express themselves as teachers in the classroom, creative artists, storytellers, and expressive in yet another language, computational logic. In the end, teachers reflected and valued that students were not only gaining competencies in one discipline or another, but were meaningfully engaged and interactive with each other throughout the learning process. In connecting constructivist computing approaches with translanguaging, additional opportunities to consider student agency surface, perhaps creating what David *et al.* (2021) referred to as an 'entry point' that serves to introduce new pedagogical routines that support translanguaging design, shifts or stances.

While translanguaging pedagogy can have many expressions, we note that its alignment to the original intent of countering monoglossic ideologies can vary. For example, when translanguaging pedagogy is expressed as a scaffold, while supporting students by providing access to curriculum, the monoglossic and Eurocentric approaches to education in that curricula are preserved. We argue that when translanguaging is paired with a more constructivist and organic view of both the subject and of students, translanguaging pedagogy can be better aligned to the transgressive goals (Vogel, 2021). In centering learner agency, much the same way the freedom to translanguage transgresses language boundaries and hierarchies, the student experience itself can transgress epistemological boundaries on who is the expert, and vice-versa. The connection between constructivist computing approaches and translanguaging is further extended through a view on language that includes broader semiotic resources such as block programming and multimedia expressivity (Vogel *et al.*, 2020).

Future work should further explore how the more transgressive goals of translanguaging may be reinforced alongside constructivist computing pedagogy by centering student agency. It might also continue to investigate how to support teachers acting as co-learners alongside students, and supporting student creative expression and independent learning.

Acompañamiento: Support that centers teacher vulnerability and student agency

These findings additionally illustrate how researchers in the project co-learned with teachers and made shifts of their own to welcome more kinds of stances and designs than they had expected. Through a dynamic relational trajectory that meets each teacher where they are, acompañamiento is an approach to teacher–researcher collaborations that acknowledges and addresses the vulnerability that can arise as agency is re-negotiated in the classroom. In addressing our second research question (How did the team feel support was provided in negotiating student agency?) we found support centered mainly around two practices that embodied this acompañamiento approach: co-designing goals not just implementation, and co-shifting as partners to share vulnerability.

In co-designing goals not just implementation, the teacher–researcher collaboration becomes more attentive to power and adapting to contexts. To not allow that flexibility is to treat teachers more as informants rather than partners. Asking researchers to possibly shift their own goals to accommodate teacher needs and goals puts in action a dynamic relational trajectory that mediates vulnerability by meeting each teacher where they were ready in terms of integrating and expanding on constructivist and translanguaging approaches. However, this strategy may present challenges to how we consider standardized curriculum in that inherent in curriculum are embedded stances that both make assumptions and limit how teachers can and should move through different trajectories of change.

Vulnerability was also managed through co-shifting as partners to share vulnerability. In many instances implementation in the classroom is left to teachers, while planning and debriefing is part of the teacher–researcher collaboration. In co-shifting as partners, intense in-classroom support not only served to distribute available expertise in the classroom as new curriculum was implemented, it also served as a way to share the vulnerability of trying something new and renegotiating student agency in the classroom.

Limitations to such an approach include strong considerations around how sustainable a dependable in-class support approach can be during and after the collaboration, as well as how an adaptive support that prioritized co-designing goals might impede uniform progress towards a shared research and pedagogical goal. Future work should further explore the ways in which these bottom-up shifts in in-classroom agency can support broader shifts that Penuel (2019) called 'infrastructuring' that addresses school policies, resources and cultures. For instance, infrastructure shifts that might enable a more sustainable acompañamiento approach would be the use of computer-science or language coaches, allocating professional development time not just to skills development but in debriefing lessons and discussing co-shifts with colleagues.

Conclusion

The move to integrate CS with other disciplinary subjects in our collaborative project can serve as an example for how different expressions of translanguaging are possible when paired with a constructivist approach to pedagogy. The examples provided in this chapter illustrate that when teachers are faced with teaching a new discipline (CS) and integrating that new discipline into their existing work, technology can open up a space for teacher vulnerability and the negotiation of both student and teacher agency. What we learned from listening to PiLa-CS members is that the pairing of technology and translanguaging may illuminate larger issues, namely the potential of translanguaging to be transgressive depending on how it is positioned in relationship to curricula and, in turn, how this relationship between curriculum and translanguaging may have on the nature of collaborative projects between teachers and researchers.

While translanguaging is often situated as an approach to scaffolding new language to support students to access content and express their understanding, translanguaging pedagogy as articulated by García *et al.* (2016) and García and Li (2014) intends to do more: to shift the learning and teaching space by countering monoglossic ideologies that shape curriculum, teacher–student relationships and programming. Taking up a constructivist implementation of technology (and specifically tools that emerge from constructivist traditions such as Scratch), may have provided an additional push for teachers to challenge assumptions around in-class expertise and move towards making more and different kinds of space for student agency in the classroom. Such negotiation is key if translanguaging pedagogy is to truly promote students' meaningful expression and autonomy.

But to get to this transformative vision requires teacher professional development that goes beyond imparting teachers with specific skills and knowledge. In our work, we found that managing teacher vulnerability was necessary for promoting learning and shifts in teacher paradigms and frameworks. Vulnerability was managed through a dynamic relational trajectory that met each teacher where they were ready in terms of integrating constructivist and translanguaging approaches paired with intense in-classroom support, and moved along towards a redistribution of agency in the classroom. Limitations to such an approach include strong considerations around how sustainable a dependable in-class support approach can be during and after the collaboration, as well as how an adaptive support might impede uniform progress towards shared research and pedagogical goals.

As researchers and educators investigate how translanguaging might prompt teachers to support students' agency to make communicative choices and express themselves, they might attend to research from computing education that explores how constructionist orientations to computing can support student agency and expressivity. They will find many parallels: translanguaging approaches connect student agency to broader sociopolitical tensions such as language hegemony and cultural marginalization, and computing education research explores how student agency can challenge assumptions in computing fields that have historically marginalized certain groups. We hope this chapter provides some insights into how a teacher–researcher collaboration might be arranged and adapted to connect translanguaging and computing education in ways that are mutually beneficial and reinforcing to the empowerment of both students and teachers.

Acknowledgements

This material is based upon work supported by the National Science Foundation under Grant Nos. 1738645 and 1837446 and the George Lucas Educational Foundation. Any opinions, findings, and conclusions or recommendations expressed in this material are those of the author(s) and do not necessarily reflect the views of the funders. We'd also like to thank our teacher partners for collaborating, and administrative leadership for their support.

References

Allard, E.C. (2017) Re-examining teacher translanguaging: An ecological perspective. *Bilingual Research Journal* 40 (2), 116–130.

Arnold, J. and Clarke, D.J. (2014) What is 'agency'? Perspectives in science education research. *International Journal of Science Education* 36 (5), 735–754.

Ascenzi-Moreno, L. (2017) From deficit to diversity: How teachers of recently-arrived emergent bilinguals negotiate ideological and pedagogical change. *Schools: Studies in Education* 14 (2), 276–302.

Ascenzi-Moreno, L. and Seltzer, K. (2021) Always at the bottom: Ideologies in assessment of emergent bilinguals. *Journal of Literacy Research* 53 (4), 488–490.

Ascenzi-Moreno, L., Güilamo, A. and Vogel, S. (2020) Integrating coding and language arts: A view into sixth graders' multimodal and multilingual learning. *Voices from the Middle* 27 (4), 47–52.

Becker, H.J. and Riel, M.M. (2000) *Teacher Professional Engagement and Constructivist-Compatible Computer Use.* Teaching, Learning, and Computing: 1998 National Survey. Report #7. ERIC.

Blikstein, P. and Moghadam, S.H. (2018) Pre-college computer science education: A survey of the field.

Bratteteig, T. and Wagner, I. (2012, August) Disentangling power and decision-making in participatory design. In *Proceedings of the 12th Participatory Design Conference: Research Papers-Volume 1* (pp. 41–50). New York: Association for Computing Machinery.

Brennan, K. (2013) Best of both worlds: Issues of structure and agency in computational creation, in and out of school [Thesis, Massachusetts Institute of Technology]. http://dspace.mit.edu/handle/1721.1/79157

Brooks, M.D. (2016) How and when did you learn your languages? bilingual students' linguistic experiences and literacy instruction. *Journal of Adolescent and Adult Literacy* 60 (4), 383–93.

Bullough Jr, R.V. (2005) Being and becoming a mentor: School-based teacher educators and teacher educator identity. *Teaching and Teacher Education* 21, 143–155.

David, S.S., Shepard-Carey, L., Swearingen, A.J., Hemsath, D.J. and Heo, S. (2021) Entry points and trajectories: Teachers learning and doing translanguaging pedagogy. *TESOL Journal* 13 (1), e603.

Dindler, C. and Iversen, O.S. (2014, October) Relational expertise in participatory design. In *Proceedings of the 13th Participatory Design Conference: Research Papers-Volume 1* (pp. 41–50). New York: Association for Computing Machinery.
DiSalvo, B. (2016) Participatory design through a learning science lens. In *Proceedings of the 2016 CHI Conference on Human Factors in Computing Systems* (pp. 4459–4463). New York: Association for Computing Machinery.
Dye, J.F., Schatz, I.M., Rosenberg, B.A. and Coleman, S.T. (2000) Constant comparison method: A kaleidoscope of data. *The Qualitative Report* 4 (1/2), 1–9.
Eglash, R. and Bennett, A. (2009) Teaching with hidden capital: Agency in children's computational explorations of cornrow hairstyles. *Children Youth and Environments* 19 (1), 58–73.
García, O. and Li, W. (2014) *Translanguaging: Language, Bilingualism and Education*. London: Palgrave Pivot. https://doi.org/10.1057/9781137385765
García, O., Johnson, S.I. and Seltzer, K. (2016) *The Translanguaging Classroom: Leveraging Student Bilingualism for Learning*. Philadelphia: Caslon Publishing.
García, O. (2017) Translanguaging in schools: Subiendo y bajando, bajando y subiendo as afterword. *Journal of Language, Identity and Education* 16 (4), 256–263.
Healy, L. and Powell, A.B. (2013) Understanding and overcoming 'disadvantage' in learning mathematics. In M.A.K. Clements, A.J. Bishop, C. Keitel, J. Kilpatrick and F.K.S. Leung (eds) *Third International Handbook on Mathematics Education* (pp. 69–100). New York: Springer.
Henrick, E.C., Cobb, P., Penuel, W.R., Jackson, K. and Clark, T. (2017) Assessing research-practice partnerships: Five dimensions of effectiveness (ERIC ED610463). William T. Grant Foundation.
Hopkins, M., Weddle, H., Bjorklund Jr, P., Umansky, I.M. and Blanca Dabach, D. (2021) "It's created by a community": Local context mediating districts' approaches to serving immigrant and refugee newcomers. *AERA Open* 7, 23328584211032234.
Jackson, G.A. (2016) Evaluating learning technology. *The Journal of Higher Education* 61 (3), 294–311. https://doi.org/10.1080/00221546.1990.11780712
Kafai, Y., Proctor, C. and Lui, D. (2020) From theory bias to theory dialogue: Embracing cognitive, situated, and critical framings of computational thinking in K-12 CS education. *ACM Inroads* 11 (1), 44–53.
Kelchtermans, G. (2005) Teachers' emotions in educational reforms: Self-understanding, vulnerable commitment and micropolitical literacy. *Teaching and Teacher Education* 21 (8), 995–1006.
Lasky, S. (2005) A sociocultural approach to understanding teacher identity, agency and professional vulnerability in a context of secondary school reform. *Teaching and Teacher Education* 21 (8), 899–916.
Li, W. (2014) Who's teaching whom? Co-learning in multilingual classrooms. In S. May (ed.) *The Multilingual Turn: Implications for SLA, TESOL, and Bilingual Education* (pp. 167–190). Abingdon: Routledge.
Lincolin, Y. and Guba, E (1985) *Naturalistic Inquiry*. Beverly Hills, CA: Sage.
Linn, M. and Pea, R. (1994) A discussion of Judah Schwartz's Chapter. In A.H. Schoenfeld and A.H. Sloane (eds) *Mathematical Thinking and Problem Solving* (pp. 8–18). New York: Routledge. https://doi.org/https://doi.org/10.4324/9781315044613
Lipponen, L. (2002) Exploring foundations for computer-supported collaborative learning. In G. Stahl (ed.) *Computer Support for Collaborative Learning: Foundations for a CSCL Community* (pp. 72–81). Boulder, CO, USA: International Society of the Learning Sciences.
Maloney, J., Resnick, M., Rusk, N., Silverman, B. and Eastmond, E. (2010) The scratch programming language and environment. *ACM Transactions on Computing Education* 10 (4), 1–15. https://doi.org/10.1145/1868358.1868363
Marshall, B. and Drummond, J.M. (2006) How teachers engage with assessment for learning: Lessons from the classroom. *Research Papers in Education* 21 (02), 133–149.

Maykut, P. and Morehouse, R. (1994) *Beginning Qualitative Research: A Philosophical and Practical Guide*. London: Falmer Press.

Molle, D. (2013) The pitfalls of focusing on instructional strategies in professional development for Teachers of English Learners. *Teacher Education Quarterly* 40 (1), 101–124.

New York City Department of Education (2019) 2018–2019 English Language Learner Demographic Report. Office of Multilingual Learners. https://infohub.nyced.org/docs/default-source/default-document-library/ell-demographic-report.pdf

New York State (2015) An economic snapshot of Washington Heights and Inwood. Office of the State Comptroller, New York City Public Information Office. https://www.osc.state.ny.us/files/reports/osdc/pdf/report-2-2016.pdf

Palmer, P.J. (1998) *The Courage to Teach*. San Francisco: Jossey-Bass.

Papert, S. (1980) *Mindstorms*. New York: Basic Books.

Papert, S. (1993) *The Children's Machine: Rethinking School in the Age of the Computer*. New York: Basic Books.

Penuel, W.R. (2019) Co-design as infrastructuring with attention to power: Building collective capacity for equitable teaching and learning through design-based implementation research. In *Collaborative Curriculum Design for Sustainable Innovation and Teacher Learning* (pp. 387–401). Cham: Springer.

Penuel, W.R., Roschelle, J. and Shechtman, N. (2007) Designing formative assessment software with teachers: An analysis of the co-design process. *Research and Practice in Technology Enhanced Learning* 2 (01), 51–74.

Radke, S.C., Vogel, S., Hoadley, C. and Ma, J. (2020) Representing percents and personas: Designing syncretic curricula for modeling and statistical reasoning. *The Interdisciplinarity of the Learning Sciences: Conference Proceedings* 3, 1365–1372. https://academicworks.cuny.edu/gc_pubs/654

Ronen Fuhrmann, T., Kali, Y. and Hoadley, C. (2008, March-April) Helping education students understand learning through designing. *Educational Technology* 48 (2), 26–33.

Rosiers, K., Willaert, E., Van Avermaet, P. and Slembrouck, S. (2016) Interaction for transfer: Flexible approaches to multilingualism and their pedagogical implications for classroom interaction in linguistically diverse mainstream classrooms. *Language and Education* 30 (3), 267–280. doi:10.1080/09500782.2015.1117097

Ryoo, J.J., Tanksley, T., Estrada, C. and Margolis, J. (2020) Take space, make space: How students use computer science to disrupt and resist marginalization in schools. *Computer Science Education* 30 (3), 337–361. https://doi.org/10.1080/08993408.2020.1805284

Sannino, A. (2010) Teachers' talk of experiencing: Conflict, resistance and agency. *Teaching and Teacher Education* 26 (4), 838–844.

Seltzer, K. (2019) Reconceptualizing 'Home' and 'School' language: Taking a critical translingual approach in the English classroom. *TESOL Quarterly* 53 (4), 986–1007.

Tian, Z. and Shepard-Carey, L. (2020) (Re)imagining the future of translanguaging pedagogies in TESOL through teacher–researcher collaboration. *TESOL Quarterly* 54 (4), 1131–1143. https://doi.org/10.1002/tesq.614

Vähäsantanen, K. (2015) Professional agency in the stream of change: Understanding educational change and teachers' professional identities. *Teaching and Teacher Education* 47, 1–12.

Vogel, S. (2021) 'Los Programadores Debieron Pensarse Como Dos Veces': Exploring the intersections of language, power, and technology with bi/multilingual students. *ACM Transactions on Computing Education (TOCE)* 21 (4), 1–25.

Vogel, S. and García, O. (2017) Translanguaging. In G. Noblit and L. Moll (eds) *Oxford Research Encyclopedia of Education*. Oxford: Oxford University Press.

Vogel, S., Hoadley, C., Castillo, A.R. and Ascenzi-Moreno, L. (2020) Languages, literacies and literate programming: Can we use the latest theories on how bilingual people learn to help us teach computational literacies? *Computer Science Education* 30 (4), 420–443.

Vogel, S., Hoadley, C., Ascenzi-Moreno, L. and Menken, K. (2019, February) The role of translanguaging in computational literacies: documenting middle school bilinguals' practices in computer science integrated units. In *Proceedings of the 50th ACM Technical Symposium on Computer Science Education* (pp. 1164–1170). New York: Association for Computing Machinery.

Vogel, S., Santo, R. and Ching, D. (2017) Visions of computer science education: Unpacking arguments for and projected impacts of CS4All initiatives. In *Proceedings of the 2017 ACM SIGCSE Technical Symposium on Computer Science Education – SIGCSE'17* (pp. 609–614). New York: Association for Computing Machinery.

Zembylas, M. (2002) Constructing genealogies of teachers' emotions in science teaching. *Journal of Research in Science Teaching: The Official Journal of the National Association for Research in Science Teaching* 39 (1), 79–103.

Zembylas, M. (2010) Teacher emotions in the context of educational reforms. In *Second International Handbook of Educational Change* (pp. 221–236). Dordrecht: Springer.

10 (Trans)formative Assessment Co-design Cycles: Translanguaging Stances and Shifts in a Science Teacher–Researcher Collaboration

Caitlin G. McC. Fine, Haeyoung Littich and Maren Getz

> *You have ideas that are important and I want to hear them. You have ideas that are important and I want to make sure you have the pieces in place to engage at the same level as everybody else in the class. Or at a higher level in some cases because you have two languages and you have two ways to think about it.*
>
> Maren

The comment above came toward the end of our *(co)design* work as Maren reflected on evidence that we might use to determine the effectiveness of our teacher–researcher collaboration. During the 2019–2020 school year, Haeyoung and Maren, two public middle school science teachers, and Caitlin, a university researcher, met weekly to work through four participatory (Trans)formative Assessment Co-Design Cycles (TAC cycles). The TAC cycle structured our work to make space for emergent bilingual learners to translanguage as they demonstrated science sensemaking on formative assessment tasks. Translanguaging is the communicative norm of (bi)multilingual communities where speakers deploy different linguistic resources, but do not necessarily adhere to the socially and politically identified boundaries of named languages (García, 2011; Otheguy *et al.*, 2015). Translanguaging pedagogies and assessment practices draw upon learners' (bi)multilingual repertoires to broaden learning opportunities. Across each cycle, we expanded our knowledge and *(co)stances* about translanguaging theory and pedagogies, developed and enacted science formative assessments, gathered student feedback, reflected on translanguaging *(co)designs*, and identified *(co)shifts* needed in our formative assessment designs to center student sensemaking. Findings indicate that TAC cycles provided a participatory framework to *(co)design* formative assessments and a supportive space for deepening, negotiating and reflecting upon our translanguaging *(co)stances* and pedagogical *(co)shifts*. This chapter emphasizes processes and products of TAC cycles and focuses on opportunities and tensions felt by our teacher–researcher collaboration.

The work our teacher–researcher collaboration set out to explore is consequential for several conversations occurring around the United States. As more states adopt the National Research Council's *Framework for K-12 Science Education* (NRC, 2012), school systems have been tasked with broadening participation in science. The *Framework* envisions instruction and assessment that interweaves students' cultural and linguistic practices throughout learning opportunities rich with science ideas, practices and cross-cutting concepts. In addition, classrooms in the US are increasingly populated by emergent bilingual learners – an asset-based term that values the multiple linguistic resources of students usually referred to as English learners (García & Kleifgen, 2010). The teaching workforce, however, continues to be dominated by white and monolingual English-speaking teachers. The TESOL community is interested in translanguaging as a pedagogical resource but questions remain regarding how teachers can interpret student work in languages they themselves do not know (Tian *et al.*, 2020). The science education community is becoming increasingly interested in how translanguaging can be leveraged to support equitable sensemaking that is coherent from the student perspective (Poza, 2016; Suárez, 2020). Participatory design-based research (Bang & Vossoughi, 2016) offers a powerful way to organize teachers' collaborative learning which could address questions about supporting the Framework's vision for science education, including translanguaging pedagogies. The TAC cycle is located at the intersection of these complexities.

Designing Formative Assessment for Linguistically Sustaining Science Instruction

This section defines our approach to formative assessment during linguistically sustaining science teaching. Scholarship about participatory design research and teacher–researcher collaboration for translanguaging provides conceptual frameworks guiding the TAC cycle. Finally, we provide an overview of the TAC cycle.

What does linguistically sustaining science instruction and assessment look like?

All students should have access to learning and communicating about science in ways that build from and sustain their linguistic resources.

Empirical research grounded in robust theories of language and learning highlights what this can look like in science classrooms. Science classrooms can be places where students acquire the disciplinary language of science (Fang & Schleppegrell, 2008; Lee *et al.*, 2013). For science to be meaningful for students, it is important to build congruence between linguistic practices of school science and scientific practices in students' homes and communities (Bang & Medin, 2010; Brown, 2019). Researchers have described what it looks like to reimagine school science as a place for everyday language as well as the various named languages and discourses students use to make sense of science (Bang *et al.*, 2017; Brown, 2019; Roseberry *et al.*, 1992; Warren & Rosebery, 2011). This line of research also explores the identity- and achievement-based ramifications for students when school science does *not* embrace students' multiple linguistic resources to support sensemaking (Brown & Spang, 2008; Brown & Ryoo, 2008).

To realize this vision of linguistically sustaining science education, research points to the need to prepare *all* science teachers for roles as agentive, engaged language planners (Langman, 2014). Science teachers should be supported to take-up a sociocultural orientation toward language and science that stresses what students can do with language as they engage in the practices of science and scientific discourse (Kelly, 2007; Windschitl *et al.*, 2018). Within this vision, translanguaging pedagogies are a critical element of linguistically sustaining science teaching, learning and assessment (García & Li, 2014). Most translanguaging research focuses on the naturally occurring translanguaging practices of science teachers and students during classroom instruction (Espinosa *et al.*, 2016; Garza & Langman, 2014; Poza, 2016). These studies point to the importance of welcoming translanguaging in order to keep student meaning-making at the center of the science lesson. Researchers found that teachers who created spaces that accepted translanguaging generally modeled translanguaging practices, encouraged and validated student contributions made using components of their full linguistic repertoire, encouraged higher-order thinking and found ways to involve all students, valuing different levels of expertise (Garza & Langman, 2014; Poza, 2016). Students most often used their multiple linguistic resources to clarify instructions, negotiate group work and verify the meaning of words, although there is evidence that they also translanguaged to make sense of core scientific ideas, such as making arguments from evidence and crafting scientific explanations (Espinosa *et al.*, 2016).

Most studies focused on translanguaging in science classrooms, however, have examined students' and teachers' language use during everyday learning activities, such as during small-group hands-on investigations or whole-class discussions. Many of these studies took place in elementary school contexts. There is a gap in our understanding of how teachers can adopt translanguaging as a science formative assessment task design principle and in our understanding of translanguaging in middle school science contexts. This study contributes to our current knowledge by describing (1) how one middle-school teacher-researcher collaboration (co)designed science formative assessment tasks that made space for translanguaging, and (2) how collaboration members interpreted assessment tasks completed multilingually to inform future instructional decisions.

Translanguaging as a critical assessment design principle

Our teacher–researcher collaboration conceptualized formative assessment as informal activities students work on individually or in small groups within the classroom to share their emerging thinking about a topic for the purpose of receiving low-stakes feedback (Black & Wiliam, 1998) and informing teachers' ongoing instructional decisions (Brookhart, 2003). Researcher-facilitated formative assessment design cycles (FADCs) are one promising way to orient teacher professional learning communities around deep engagement with formative assessment design and reflection (Furtak *et al.*, 2016). During FADCs, teachers explore student ideas, design tasks, practice using tasks, enact tasks and reflect on enactment. FADCs have been found to increase teachers' abilities to interpret students' ideas, to ask questions to elicit student thinking and to provide feedback that moves student thinking forward (Furtak *et al.*, 2016). García *et al.* (2017) stress that translanguaging classroom assessment designs should include performance-based, authentic and instructionally embedded assessment experiences. Additionally, translanguaging assessments should differentiate between general linguistic (i.e. welcoming all linguistic resources) and language-specific performances (i.e. setting clear expectations that final answers be encoded in English). Finally, they stress that translanguaging assessments should be presented in both the language of instruction and common languages represented in the classroom, with attention to sociocultural factors and students' linguistic profiles and histories. Researchers have found that some teachers reduce translanguaging on assessment for clarification purposes or as a possible scaffold (Schissel *et al.*, 2021). Others embrace translanguaging as a powerful tool to support student sensemaking (Fine & Furtak, 2020; Suárez, 2020).

Participatory design research

Our teacher–researcher collaboration worked together using participatory design research methods (Bang *et al.*, 2015; Bang & Vossoughi, 2016). In participatory design research, both community-members and researchers are designers in the entire process because community members understand community needs, past histories and local injustices better than university researchers. Space should be made within the design process for critical historicity – acknowledging the 'felt' histories of a community that are often not included in mainstream or official accounts.

This includes unpacking the tensions implicit in doing design work, including possible contradictions and messiness. Designs should consider multiple epistemologies beyond those common within research universities. Finally, design teams should expand the focus of their work to include 'how can' questions. These types of questions can help us understand both processes and products that support systemic transformations of oppressive educational systems.

Teacher–researcher collaboration for translanguaging

This study takes up the framework of translanguaging *(co)stances*, *(co)designs* and *(co)shifts* described by Tian and Shepard-Carey (2020). A translanguaging *(co)stance* refers to negotiating and (co)constructing our beliefs about bilingualism and translanguaging. Translanguaging *(co)design* refers to the work of teachers and researchers iteratively co-developing lessons and assessments that make space for translanguaging. Translanguaging *(co)shifts* refer to the reflection-inspired actions that teacher–researcher collaborations engage in as they discuss and make changes to center student sensing-making. *(Co)shifts* might also look like reflections collaborators share with each other while looking over student work or while discussing student feedback.

The (Trans)formative Assessment Co-Design (TAC) cycle

The (Trans)formative Assessment Co-Design (TAC) cycle (see Figure 10.1) was inspired by the FADC (Furtak *et al.*, 2016) in the way it organizes professional collaboration focused on teachers' formative assessment practices. Specifically, during each TAC cycle, teachers and researchers work together to explore student ideas, develop formative assessment tasks that welcome translangauging, enact the co-designed formative assessment tasks and reflect on the tasks. The TAC cycle also integrates critical elements of participatory design research (Bang & Vossoughi, 2016), and centers translanguaging *(co)stances, (co)designs* and *(co)shifts* (Tian & Shepard-Carey, 2020).

During the *Explore* phase of the TAC cycle, teacher–researcher collaborators share and reflect upon their *(co)stances* toward bilingualism. Specifically, they open space for critical historicity through discussion of the 'felt' history of community-members' efforts to support emergent bilingual learners. Additionally, collaborators explore translanguaging research and pedagogical resources and discuss implications and possibilities for their own teaching context. During the *Develop* phase, teacher–researcher collaborators work together to *(co)design* formative assessment tasks and routines that incorporate and invite translanguaging. In some cases, the collaborators modify formative assessment tasks from their science curriculum during this phase to make space for translanguaging. In other cases,

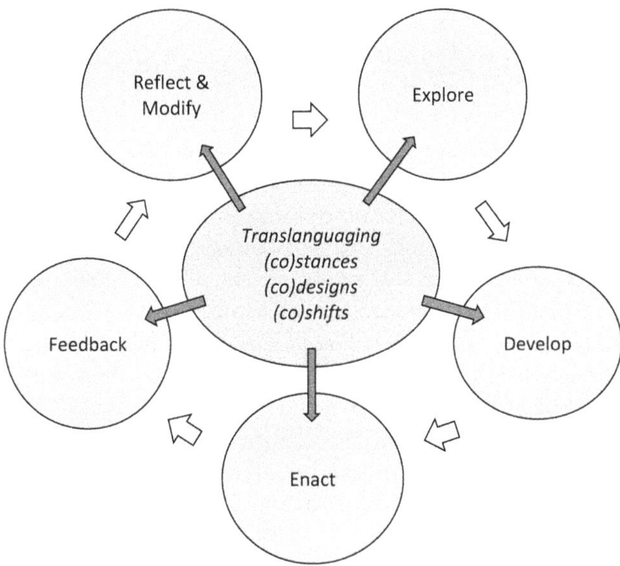

Figure 10.1 (Trans)Formative Assessment Co-Design cycle

collaborators *(co)design* formative assessments tasks from scratch that are aligned with the science content being taught and that explicitly incorporate and invite translanguaging. During the *Enact* phase, collaborators bring *(co)designed* formative assessment tasks to their classrooms, where students engage with the assessments. Teachers and researchers distribute the work of collecting feedback from students (critical stakeholders) during the *Feedback* phase. This might take the form of focus groups with students, whole-class oral discussions, or open-ended written exit tickets and questionnaires. Finally, during the *Reflect and Modify* phase teacher–researcher collaborators interpret student's completed formative assessment tasks and reflect on students' demonstrated learning as well as how collaborators might adjust the tasks for future use to better incorporate and invite translanguaging. During this phase, teachers and researchers *(co)shift* as they modify processes and products that center student sensemaking. In another study from this same body of work, we have highlighted how iterative involvement in various TAC cycles can support monolingual English-speaking teachers to develop translanguaging interpretive power and ultimately adopt more agentive stances, advocating for linguistically equitable assessment practices at the district level (Fine, 2022).

Overview of the Study

This next section describes the school context in which our study took place. We introduce the members of our teacher–researcher collaboration and the focal students involved in the TAC cycles. We also describe the data we collected as well as our data analysis processes.

Our context

Our teacher–researcher collaboration took place at Mountain View Middle School, a public middle school in a suburban district located in a large, metropolitan area of a Rocky Mountain state. The school had approximately 790 students during our teacher–researcher collaboration year. Approximately 85% of students at Mountain View received free or reduced-price lunch and 37% of students were designated as English Language Learners (ELLs) by the district. Mountain View students were culturally and linguistically heterogeneous. Approximately 70% of students identified as Hispanic, 15% identified as Black, 5% identified as White, 4% identified as Asian and 3% identified as two or more races. Languages beyond English spoken included Spanish, Swahili, Amharic, Kiswahili, Burmese and Somali.

The neighborhood in which Mountain View was located had historically been welcoming to refugee families from Guatemala, Ethiopia, the Democratic Republic of Congo, Burma and Nepal. Driving through commercial areas near the school, stores advertised their goods in English, Spanish and Nepali. Recently, the northern part of the school boundary had begun to gentrify, with the addition of large new single-family homes and community resources, such as private Montessori schools, yoga studios, coffee shops and boutique clothing stores. The increase in property value accompanying these changes had begun to push out small businesses and residents who had long called this community home. Additionally, new charter schools had begun to lure students away from Mountain View.

Our teacher–researcher collaborators

Our collaboration included Haeyoung and Maren, two sixth-grade science educators, and Caitlin, a doctoral student researcher at that time. Haeyoung is a Korean/English sequential bilingual. She moved to the US from South Korea for college and had taught sixth-grade science at Mountain View for four years. She had a BS in Biology and an MA in Curriculum and Instruction. Maren is an English monolingual teacher who grew up in the Southwest. She had 19 years of teaching experience teaching in K-5 contexts and this collaboration took place during her first year teaching middle school science. Maren had a BS in Psychology and an MA in Curriculum and Instruction with an endorsement in Culturally and Linguistically Diverse Education. Caitlin is an English/Spanish sequential bilingual with experience teaching K-5 science at a dual-language elementary school prior to pursuing her PhD in bilingual science education.

Beyond our teacher–researcher members, we consulted with a small group of students in Maren and Haeyoung's science classes as critical stakeholders. A total of 15 sixth-grade students participated in focus groups as part of each TAC cycle. Thirteen of these students were bilingual: 11 spoke Spanish and English, one spoke Nepali and English and one spoke Chuukese, a Micronesian language, in addition to English. They self-reported various levels of biliteracy.

Origin and evolution of our teacher–researcher collaboration

We came together through participation in a larger research–practice partnership focused on the adoption of Ambitious Science Teaching practices in K-8 classrooms in the district within which Mountain View was located (Windschitl *et al.*, 2018). As part of the larger partnership, Caitlin and Maren initially worked together closely for two years to support Maren's emergent bilingual elementary students' participation in small and large-group science conversations. They developed teacher-facing and student-facing discourse tools to support emergent bilingual students to share ideas about the science content. Examples of discourse tools included science talk move routines, multilingual sentence starters related to scientific practices. Maren was less worried about students sharing their ideas in English and more interested in supporting them to contribute using the linguistic resources that felt most comfortable to them.

As Maren gained experience creating a classroom culture that welcomed and valued translanguaging during general classroom activities, she often reflected that she still did not have an equitable picture of students' science learning when it came to English-only classroom assessments. Together, Maren and Caitlin decided to focus on the process of modifying, designing and interpreting science formative assessments that incorporated and welcomed translanguaging.

Between years two and three of their collaboration, Maren transferred from her elementary school to a sixth-grade science teacher position at Mountain View Middle School. As part of her transfer, she negotiated that her collaboration with Caitlin could continue. Haeyoung was already a sixth-grade teacher at Mountain View and she had participated in district-organized workshops related to the larger research–practice partnership. After Caitlin and Maren described their collaboration around translanguaging in science formative assessment, Haeyoung decided to join the teacher–researcher collaboration. She expressed her own interest in the topic and in supporting her emergent bilingual students in general, particularly because she had been an emergent bilingual in the US schooling system herself.

Data collection and analysis

Our teacher–researcher collaboration worked together over seven months between August 2019–March 2020. We worked through four TAC cycles.

Data included meeting agendas, minutes and artifacts (such as annotated iterations of formative assessments and note-catchers for practitioner-facing readings), student work samples, classroom field notes, completed student questionnaires and researcher memos. We recorded audio files of 31 teacher–researcher meetings that ranged in length from 30–90 minutes. Caitlin conducted seven semi-structured interviews with teachers and administrators and nine focus groups with consented students.

We engaged in rapid cycles of qualitative reflection within TAC cycles in order to build upon lessons learned from the current co-design cycle to inform future iterations of the TAC cycle (Gravemeijer & Cobb, 2006). This first layer of analysis was done collaboratively with teachers and researchers. Caitlin introduced a reflection protocol to help guide our conversations. The protocol allowed Maren and Haeyoung to express how the formative assessment event felt from their perspective, scaffolded a discussion of student data (including student artifacts and student focus group transcripts) and helped the co-design team develop inferences from the data that might inform future iterations of the formative assessment and/or future translanguaging routines and tools. Throughout, this level of reflective analysis was quick and focused. We discussed what it was about a particular tool/formative assessment and classroom interaction that captured what kids were able to say and do and where the tool or activity fell short. This approach, of including different perspectives within the collective qualitative analysis, was important to reduce potential hierarchies between the researcher and the teachers involved in the study.

Caitlin led retrospective inductive and deductive qualitative analyses after the teacher–researcher collaboration wrapped up for the year (Miles *et al.*, 2018). The first round of coding took place as she transcribed and read through the transcripts of all interviews, teacher–researcher meetings, memos and student focus groups. During this phase of analysis, Caitlin wrote analytic memos and kept track of emerging themes, such as challenges and opportunities the teacher–researcher collaboration worked through at each phase of the TAC cycle (Miles *et al.*, 2018). Caitlin engaged in member-checking during this phase as we worked together to prepare and present our emerging findings at two science educator conferences in October 2020 and January 2021.

The second round of coding consisted of systematically coding all interviews, teacher–researcher meeting transcripts, focus group conversations, and memos using the qualitative software package MaxQDA. Caitlin worked through this process both inductively and deductively – using codes that emerged through the first round of coding as well as codes related to the TAC cycle phases and the framework of translanguaging *co-stance*, *co-design* and *co-shifts* (Miles *et al.*, 2018). Caitlin referenced student work samples, student questionnaires and other classroom and meeting artifacts to triangulate findings. Caitlin also engaged in member-checking throughout this phase of analysis through several conversations with Maren and Haeyoung.

The TAC Cycle: A Powerful Tool to Shape Teacher–Researcher Translanguaging Assessment *(Co)stances, (Co)designs* and *(Co)shifts*

To illustrate the power of the TAC cycle to shape teacher–researcher translanguaging *(co)stances*, *(co)designs* and *(co)shifts*, the following sections describe the work we engaged in at each phase. Many opportunities and tensions emerged during our teacher–researcher collaboration. Due to limited space, here we explain several salient examples for each phase of the TAC cycle with a focus on processes and products.

The *Explore* phase

During each *Explore* phase, we spent a few meetings reading and discussing multimodal resources related to translanguaging. We reflected upon implications for assessment *(co)design* decisions and our own developing translanguaging *(co)stances*. Caitlin selected and organized resources and facilitated discussions. These resources included selections from *Translanguaging: A CUNY-NYSIEB Guide for Educators* (Celic & Seltzer, 2013) and *The Translanguaging Classroom* (García *et al.*, 2017), CUNY-NYSIEB videos, blogs about language ideologies and raciolinguistics, and research summaries of translanguaging pedagogies in science classrooms. Haeyoung and Maren appreciated allocating time during our teacher–researcher collaboration meetings to read resources independently before discussing them. During our first TAC cycle, we also conducted and discussed the CUNY-NYSIEB school-based multilingual ecology survey as well as student language-use surveys. These tools allowed us to reflect upon the linguistic landscape of the school and share our *(co)stances* and commitments to the work.

Opportunity: 'Just in time' translanguaging pedagogical resources

We could have taken a set amount of time at the beginning of our collaboration to read extensively about translanguaging and then spent the rest of our time *(co)designing* and trying out formative assessment tasks. Instead, by building the *Explore* phase into the TAC cycle, Caitlin brought translanguaging resources to the beginning of each cycle that directly related to our ongoing *(co)shifts* and *(co)design* puzzlements. For example, after Cycle 2, Maren and Haeyoung expressed frustration that some students shared amazing science ideas orally with peers in small group conversations but did not encode written responses on the formative assessment task worksheets. They wondered out loud if there was another way to capture students' science sensemaking. For the *Explore* phase of Cycle 3, Caitlin shared highlights from *Chapter 6: Translanguaging Design in Assessment* from *The Translanguaging Classroom* (García *et al.*, 2017). We specifically discussed suggestions outlined in the chapter that assessments should be performance-based and include various multimodal ways for students to express their sensemaking.

In thinking through how to make our upcoming Cycle 3 *(co)design* performance-based and multi-modal, Maren shared that she had previously used an online video creation platform with her third-grade students. Haeyoung expressed particular excitement for this approach when she shared: 'It's definitely another method of data collection since I can't listen to every single kid as I am running around everywhere.' Maren added: 'Yeah. Yeah. And then in the video they can use all their linguistic resources too. Because we can use a translator and figure it out.' We decided to focus the upcoming formative assessment around small group student-created videos that captured their oral sensemaking about the conservation of mass using physical models of molecules. Here, both Haeyoung and Maren demonstrated their *(co)stance* of keeping sensemaking activities centered around students and their multiple linguistic resources through a *(co)shift* in the way they conceptualized *(co)designed* formative assessment tasks. Ultimately, we found that the process of iteratively deepening our translanguaging knowledge across cycles and in smaller chunks allowed for 'just in time' discussions that validated subtle *(co)shifts* and informed our subsequent *(co)design* decisions.

Tension: Doing this work as lone teachers

One tension we felt was that Maren and Haeyoung were among the few teachers at Mountain View with translanguaging *(co)stances* who were enacting their stances in practice. This tension was more obvious after we completed the multilingual school ecology. During Cycle 1, Maren wondered aloud: 'I just don't know how many boundaries we are going to push … we are going to shake things up.' The lone teacher tension bubbled up at various points throughout our work together. For example, during the *Explore* phase of Cycle 2, Maren reflected on the design section of Chapter 1 of *The Translanguaging Classroom* text:

> Yes. Haeyoung and I are doing the work. But is it? I know it's not enough, but is it enough right now? Like in just one class? And I wonder if [the students] believe that we believe in their bilingualism. If only one teacher believes in it. But then they walk out to the school and everything else is in English and every other teacher…

Similarly, during Cycle 3, Haeyoung expressed frustration with her teacher colleagues who expressed asset-oriented stances about students' linguistic resources but did little to enact those stances:

> [The other teachers at this school] know consciously that a lot of people speak more than one language. And they consciously think, 'Oh, yeah – we should appreciate different cultures and different languages.' But to actually do it and being able to implement it in instruction and supporting students I think are two different things.

This constant tension points to the need for systemic initiatives that support all content-area teachers across a school or district to develop their translanguaging pedagogical knowledge and *(co)designs* if we aim to fundamentally transform teaching, learning and assessment for emergent bilingual learners.

The *Develop* phase

We spent the majority of our time in the *Develop* phase. Whereas Caitlin planned resources and facilitated the *Explore* phase, Haeyoung and Maren generally took the lead on the *Develop* phase. They had familiarity with the district's curricular resources and they knew how our *(co)designed* assessments fit into larger unit plans. We began each *Develop* phase identifying formative assessment opportunities within science resources that aligned with the district scope and sequence. We then discussed how and where to invite students to translanguage to demonstrate science sensemaking. During these meetings, we checked-in about school-based activities and district common formative assessments (CFAs). The latter was an important process that helped ensure that our *(co)designs* fit within the dynamic school and district context.

During the *Develop* phase, we relied heavily on a cloud-based shared drive to hold our formative assessment drafts. We all had equal access to add, modify, delete or comment on the *(co)designs* and we often modified *(co)designs* between meetings. The shared drive helped to decenter Caitlin as the organizer of the work and allowed the *Develop* process to be truly participatory.

Opportunity: The TAC planning template

One product of our teacher–researcher collaboration was a planning template that guided us to center translanguaging as a formative assessment *(co)design* principle (Fine *et al.*, 2023). We created the template iteratively over four TAC cycles. At each *Develop* phase, we added elements that emerged from discussions during that cycle's *Explore* phase.

During the *Develop* phase of Cycle 4, the TAC planning template (see Appendix 10.1) helped us center translanguaging as a formative assessment *(co)design* principle while also balancing district English-language expectations. For example, one section of the TAC planning template guided us to identify translanguaging objectives and/or English-language objectives. As we discussed these, Haeyoung described areas where she wanted students to try out English-language responses and areas where she wanted them to be able to use their full linguistic repertoire in an upcoming formative assessment about the movement of energy and matter through ecosystems:

> I will preferably see more English in the Identify and Model portion. And then Describe - they can use whatever. Because that's where I see more rich information. And I want them to be able to utilize what they learned in at least that initial stage of Identify and Model. But when they Describe, I want to see everything that they know.

This comment demonstrated Haeyoung's balancing of district pressure to demonstrate knowledge of English-language science vocabulary with the recognition that she might learn more about students' science conceptual knowledge by opening up space for translanguaging. The TAC planning template created space for this balancing act.

The TAC planning template also helped us see and grapple with assumptions about the usefulness of our own bilingualism for learning. For example, during Cycle 4 when we talked through teacher metalinguistic talk-moves to explicitly invite and model translanguaging, Haeyoung's talk-move rehearsal included:

> I'm just gonna give you a sentence right here. But I'm not going to write the answer in Korean just because that's one of the minor languages that none of you right now understand. But if I were to answer this in Korean or there was something like it, it would be totally fine.

Caitlin suggested that it was actually *extremely* important for Haeyoung to model Korean/English bilingualism. Caitlin highlighted that by doing so Haeyoung could empower the Burmese and Swahili speakers who did not have language partners in class to also publicly use their full linguistic repertoire for science sensemaking:

> You can even use yourself as an example. Like, 'We only provided this translation in Spanish'. But that's something that we're working on – better supporting all the linguistic resources in this school. For example, I speak Korean. No one else in this class speaks Korean. If I write in Korean, you guys probably won't understand when I'm writing. But it - [Haeyoung: It makes sense in my head.] It makes sense in my head. This is how I'm getting my thoughts out. And it makes sense to me. And it's helping me think about science.

These examples demonstrate how the TAC planning template helped us center translanguaging in our *(co)designs*. It also helped us uncover and negotiate nuance in our translanguaging *(co)stances* that inspired *(co)shifts* in how we talked to students about translanguaging.

Tension: Preparing students for district science assessments

One tension that followed us through our work was the pressure to prepare students for English-language district-level science CFAs. The CFAs took place three times a year and consisted of multiple-choice questions and a short-constructed response item. They were meant to provide teachers with timely data to inform content-specific reteach plans while giving the district a sense of overall student conceptual understanding of focal science phenomena. Initially, Haeyoung and Maren tried to leverage our *(co)designs* to prepare their emergent bilingual students for district CFAs. For example, during Cycle 1 Maren explained: 'They also need to write what they know in English. So it's not just happening in Spanish. And that they're not just translating it – not just hitting "translate." That they're actually writing what they know English.' Maren believed that this process would help her know how prepared her emergent bilingual learners were for district CFAs.

As we continued our *(co)design* work, Haeyoung and Maren demonstrated *(co)shifts* that reflected their deepening translanguaging *(co)stances*. They worried less about designing formative assessments that prepared students for district CFAs. Instead, they understood that the TAC formative assessments provided Maren and Haeyoung a more complete and nuanced understanding of emergent bilingual students' science sensemaking. For example, during Cycle 3 Maren reflected that the multimodal video recorded performance assessment using the Flipgrid application gave her a better sense of one of her emergent bilingual students' knowledge about conservation of mass than the district's English-language CFA on the same topic. Maren stated: 'I **know** Mario knows it. I have a video to prove it. Which is why I love that assessment. I want to do more of **those** assessments.' During this conversation, Maren also noted: 'And the fact that the CFA came, what, two weeks after their Flipgrid. Flipgrid came first. And the understanding was there two weeks ago.' Ultimately, Maren and Haeyoung felt frustrated by the English-medium CFAs. They found it useless to design content-focused reteach lessons around assessments that provided an incomplete picture and led to invalid inferences of what their emergent bilingual students knew and could do in science.

The *Enact* phase

During the *Enact* phase, Haeyoung and Maren enacted our translanguaging formative assessment *(co)designs*. Some assessments were in the form of exit tasks and took about 20 minutes to complete. Others were multi-day, multi-modal performance assessments. During this phase, Caitlin took fieldnotes and supported Haeyoung and Maren by rotating around the classroom to check-in with individuals and small groups. To keep student sensemaking at the center of the assessment, Caitlin often leveraged her Spanish/English bilingualism to speak with students. Haeyoung and Maren mainly interacted with students in English, although they sometimes asked Spanish/English bilingual students with higher levels of English proficiency to help translate for bilingual students who relied on Spanish to access assessment tasks.

Opportunity: Gaining a more nuanced view of students' interest in science

During the *Enact* phase, our *(co)designed* formative assessments gave us a more nuanced understanding of emergent bilingual learners' interest in science learning. For example, we began to observe that students participated in the assessments with deeper engagement and increased ownership over their work. During Cycle 1, Haeyoung explicitly invited students to translanguage on their initial model about the composition of air that

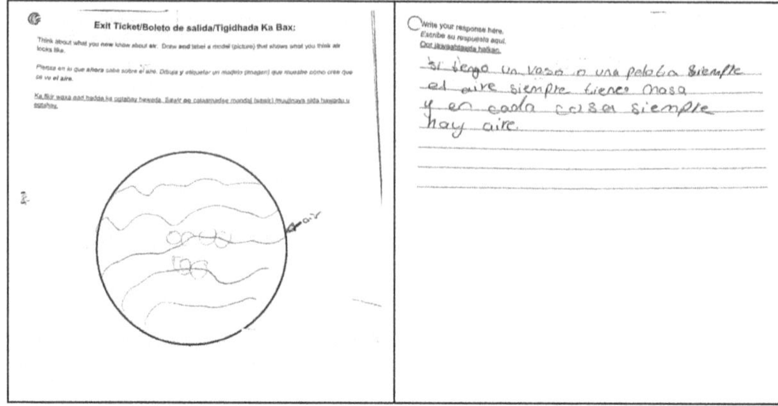

Figure 10.2 Student work sample

was informed by several recent lab investigations (NGSS MS-PS1-2: Analyze and interpret data on the properties of substances before and after the substances interact to determine if a chemical reaction has occurred). She explained to them: 'You need to at least try. Whether that's in Spanish or English, I don't care. You need to try.' She noticed that emergent bilingual students who would normally have left their assignments blank had written detailed responses (see Figure 10.2). In our meeting, Haeyoung explained: 'So I was like "Yay! There's the success rate there." Because the work habit from having this was pretty dramatic. Especially with two or three of them.'

By Cycle 3, Maren noticed that students who self-selected to sit at the back of the room early in the year started to sit in the front row and excitedly participated in both English and Spanish in whole-group consensus conversations related to the assessment tasks. She described: 'They are interrupting, like interjecting, into either a small group conversation or a whole conversation. And also, to me, they're using both languages and arguing about the content.' Maren conjectured that one possible reason for this shift in students' attitudes and participation was due to our translanguaging teacher–researcher collaboration. Specifically, she reflected that she had explicitly begun to welcome and elevate students' multilingual oral responses: 'Students' level of engagement in the classroom has changed knowing that we honor and accept all responses. That we're not forcing them to respond in one way. They feel respected as learners.'

Tension: Providing student-centered in-the-moment feedback in languages other than English

One tension that surfaced during the *Enact* phase reflected Maren and Haeyoung's deep commitment and strong agentive translanguaging *(co)stance* to keep student sensemaking at the center of formative assessment tasks through in-the-moment feedback. They identified a need to move outside of their comfort zone and communicate with students in languages other than English, but they felt stuck on how to do that. For example, during Cycle 2 Maren wondered aloud:

> How can we support them during the assessments when we don't speak Spanish? How can we just on our own support students as a monolingual English teacher and a bilingual English-Korean teacher? You know? How can we use our limited Spanish abilities to support?

On several occasions during the *Enact* phase, Maren tried to use the speech-to-text function of Google Translate on her iPad to communicate directly with bilingual learners. Unfortunately, the monolingual normed limitations of this tool (i.e. English-to-Spanish) were quickly made apparent. During Cycle 3, Maren described that the software only 'listened' in one language at a time and quickly became overwhelmed and confused as Maren and her student crossed named-languages to communicate with each other:

> So I downloaded it and I've been using it with Lupe. But what's tricky, what's hard is if there's translanguaging on there – if there's English and Spanish – it literally flips. It doesn't know what to do. Like there's two languages on here ... And we were trying. And she was so excited because you know Lupe. You know, how much she loves to communicate. And she was just looking at me. And I was just looking at her, like, 'I'm sorry, I tried!'

This experience brought home the systemic extent to which monolingual norms pervade web-based Internet languaging tools.

We discussed several *(co)designed* tools that might better support this in-the-moment communicative work. During Cycle 4, Maren brought up the idea of (co)creating multilingual teacher-facing conversation cards with common feedback phrases such as 'Can you give me an example?' or 'Can you say more about that?' so she could extend or re-direct students during the *Enact* phase. As she described the cards, she said: 'It would be great to be able to have [the multilingual] cards that I can use during discourse.' We brainstormed that we could collaboratively identify common phrases and then practice them within the teacher–researcher collaboration before using them with students. Unfortunately, since our work was cut short due to the Covid-19 pandemic, we were not able to *(co)design* and try out multilingual feedback cards.

The *Feedback* phase

The purpose of the *Feedback* phase was to hear students' perspectives on the translanguaging tools and routines integrated into the science formative assessments. We gathered student feedback in several ways. First, Caitlin conducted focus groups with consented students following each formative assessment. We co-wrote questions to attend to our collective wonderings. Second, because Haeyoung and Maren wanted to understand the student perspective from as many students as possible, we added a few short response and survey-style questions to the end of our *(co)designed* assessment tasks during Cycles 1, 3 and 4. Finally, Maren and Haeyoung engaged in informal conversations with their emergent bilingual students about the perceived usefulness of translanguaging tools and the students' suggested changes. Information from the *Feedback* phase inspired teacher-researcher *(co)shifts* during the *Reflect and Modify* phase that greatly influenced subsequent assessment *(co)design* decisions.

Opportunity: Students' reflections became central to our (co)design decisions and reinforced translanguaging (co)stances

Student feedback supported our translanguaging *(co)stance* of keeping student sensemaking at the center of our *(co)design* conversations. For example, although few students wrote in Spanish on the Cycle 1 assessment, as a result of student feedback we decided to continue to translate all science formative assessments into Spanish. This was because Spanish-English bilingual students reported finding the Spanish-language version useful to both clarify the gist of the assessment and to clarify the meaning of words they were unfamiliar with. During the Cycle 1 focus group meeting, Mario shared: 'Porque allí puedo entender más y así puedo hacer mi trabajo porque lo leí en español y entendí lo que tenía que hacer.' ['Because I can understand more and this way I can do my work because I read it in Spanish and I understood what I needed to do.'] William agreed and shared that the bilingual nature of the task was most helpful when he was checking the words, such as *representation*, that he wasn't as familiar with: 'Some of the words I didn't understand so I went back to the Spanish ones.' This was true for students who encoded their written or spoken responses in English as well as those who wrote or shared in Spanish. As Maren reflected during Cycle 3:

> I feel like even if their output is not going to be in their home language, the input supports their output. And I just feel like that's such an important piece. Because if I understood something but was missing one or two key pieces and if I could just get those key pieces, I mean, just as a learner, I just really appreciate having that opportunity.

Maren's feedback-informed reflection reinforced her commitment to continue to incorporate and invite translanguaging even if students encoded their ideas in English.

Students' reflections also included feelings of acceptance at seeing their linguistic resources incorporated in whole-class formative assessment tasks. For example, on a whole-class exit ticket for Cycle 3, one student wrote why they used translanguaging and how it made them feel: 'Sí. En mis clases porque no puedo inglés y me hizo sentir bien.' ['Yes. In my classes because I'm not great at English and it made me feel good.'] During Cycle 4, Olivia, a Spanish/English bilingual student, explained that 'it feels really cool' that a public-facing co-constructed anchor chart about living and nonliving parts of ecosystems that accompanied the performance assessment task included Spanish. She stressed how important it was that the anchor chart contained multiple languages 'because everyone could understand it. And even if they understand English, it's cool for people that speak that language.' Here Olivia spoke about her own and others' feelings of validation and acceptance when their full linguistic repertoires were represented in whole-class conversations and used in printed materials. Haeyoung reflected that these comments demonstrated the negative impact of the English-dominant language policies present in most other classrooms at the school:

> I don't know, maybe that's the environmental thing because they're so pressured, like, 'No, you have to be in ELD [English Language Development] class because you're not speaking proper English and writing and reading proper English.' So it's almost like a pressurized environment where they feel like the academic setting is the place where they only speak English. But not other languages. So – I don't now. That's how I sometimes feel what the kids feel.

In a school where students reported that few other teachers invited translanguaging, Maren and Haeyoung's formative assessment *(co)designs* and continued invitation to translanguage was a welcome and much appreciated *(co)stance*.

Tension: Including students at all phases of the TAC cycle

One process-oriented tension was also a defining characteristic of participatory design research: multigenerational design teams. For the most part, we only asked students about their thoughts on assessment *(co)designs* during specific *Feedback* sessions conducted *after* they took the formative assessments. We initially thought about scheduling teacher–researcher collaboration meetings during the time allotted for sixth-grade lunch and recess so consented students could join the entire process. However, this was not logistically possible, so we met during Haeyoung and Maren's planning period while students were learning in other classrooms.

When students supported phases of the TAC cycle beyond the *Feedback* phase, it was mainly in the role of 'approving' translations. For example, during the *Develop* phase of Cycle 1 we discussed how Maren might check in with one of her Swahili-speaking students about the Swahili translation of the upcoming formative assessment:

> **Maren:** So I will talk to her today and just say, 'Hey, when I put this question in Google Translate, does it say what I think? What it's supposed to say?'
> **Caitlin:** And then she can also help you reword it if there's something a little bit funny. Like, 'How would you say it?'
> **Maren:** Right. OK. Yeah. I'll sit down with her today.

We also spoke about inviting student feedback during the *Enact* phase by asking students to annotate the formative assessments as they completed them. Caitlin suggested: 'That could be something you do to check in with your students as they're doing it. And say "Markup your answer sheet if you think something doesn't make sense. How would you say it?"' Maren added: 'Yeah. Like, "I'm trying to get better at this."' Unfortunately, getting student input before the *Feedback* phase was the exception rather than the norm. In future work, we plan to authentically incorporate students' nuanced and multi-faceted ideas as a critical component of the entire TAC cycle.

The *Reflect and Modify* phase

During the *Reflect and Modify* phase, we first interpreted the work of students who translanguaged on their formative assessments. We then discussed student work by science ideas and sorted work samples across various 'buckets' organized by science conceptual understanding. Identifying descriptive science-idea buckets rather than adopting standards-based evaluation criteria (i.e. *advanced, proficient, partially proficient, unsatisfactory)* allowed us to identify the range and nuance of science understanding from an asset-based perspective. Finally, we discussed themes and specific examples from student feedback about the *(co)designed* translanguaging tools and routines. We then talked through how *(co)shifts* inspired by the *Reflect and Modify* phase might influence translanguaging elements of subsequent *(co)designs.*

Opportunity: Sharing our internal and external resources for sensemaking about student ideas

As we iterated through the *Reflect and Modify* phase, one important process was engaging in collective sensemaking around student work in languages other than English. This was a nuanced process and we each brought different approaches and strengths to the shared task. Here, we describe how we approached sensemaking around one student's work during Cycle 2. For this formative assessment, students drew and wrote observations about the differences between the flammability of a lit splint of wood in pure oxygen versus in atmospheric air. The NGSS Disciplinary Core Idea for this assessment was MS-PS1-2: Analyze and interpret data on the properties of substances before and after the substances interact to determine if a chemical reaction has occurred. The NGSS Science and Engineering Practices for this assessment were Analyzing and interpreting data/Obtaining, evaluating, and communicating information. The NGSS Cross-Cutting Concept for this assessment was Patterns.

One student had written: *Yo veo fuego que está pasando*? Maren began to interpret the student's idea by referencing her limited Spanish-language knowledge but she got stuck: 'I know *fire* and I know *has*.' Meanwhile, Haeyoung, with her lived experience of 'thinking like a

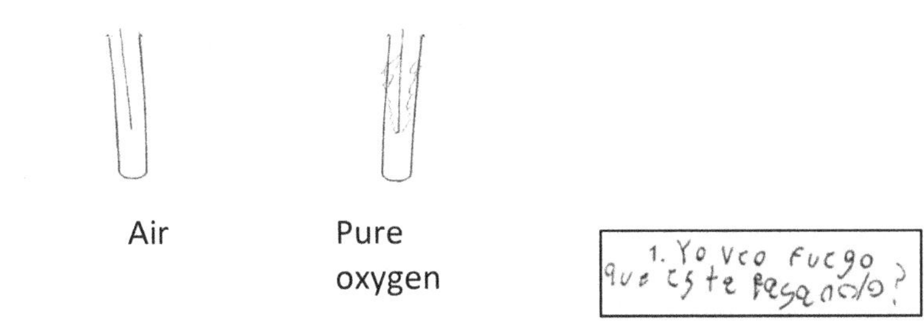

Figure 10.3 Student observation and drawing of wood splint flammability in atmospheric air versus pure oxygen

bilingual,' began interpreting this students' written work by looking at the students' drawing (see Figure 10.3) and then typing the written response into Google Translate. She suggested: 'Maybe I see fire turning back on? Kind of way ... Like, it was off but then....'

Caitlin drew on Spanish/English biliteracy and experience interpreting Spanish-language spelling and grammar approximations. She put forward that perhaps the student had written two sentences but did not use a period to indicate the break between ideas. Maren replied by saying: 'Oh. I see fire. Ok. I see fire.'

Maren also noticed that the student had written a question mark at the end of the sentence. We discussed that the second sentence might be the question 'What is going on?' Haeyoung noticed that the second sentence was written on a second line underneath the first sentence so perhaps the student used the line break as a way to indicate the sentence break without using ending punctuation or capitalization.

In reflecting on the process of engaging in collective sensemaking around translanguaging as a teacher–researcher collaboration, Maren considered: 'I just have very limited ... I know nouns, but that's it. Haha. That's it. So on my own, I wouldn't be able to know what they are saying. It would take a village. And Google Translate.' Haeyoung shared:

> I think in a way it also kind of shows each others' different interpretations. Because when I said about how maybe this kid thinks that fire can just come in and out as he wants, that's more of my way of looking at it in terms of if I'm not knowing any Spanish, I'm just purely looking at the picture. That's how I would approach it.

By working together through the *Reflect and Modify* phase, we were able to leverage our collective resources for sensemaking about students' science ideas.

Tension: Teachers need sensemaking tools too

Some of the tensions we felt in the *Reflect and Modify* phase were perennial issues teachers face. For example, we struggled with how much time to spend reflecting on student work versus modifying for future instruction. We also struggled with how to balance the pressure to assign grades for the gradebook versus allowing formative assessments to truly be formative.

One translanguaging-related tension that arose during the *Reflect and Modify* phase of our teacher–researcher collaboration was the need for a note catcher to record our sensemaking around students' science ideas and ongoing wonderings about *(co)shifts*. We sometimes felt we couldn't hold on to the rich interpretation we had done around student work samples that included translanguaging once we moved to the task of organizing students' science ideas into conceptual buckets. One workaround we came up with during Cycles 1 and 2 was to write the English translations of students' science ideas on sticky notes. We were then able to sort work by conceptual understanding and include all students' work in our discussions of upcoming science lesson modifications. This approach worked well when formative assessment tasks were paper-based.

Unfortunately, our sticky-note system was not as useful during Cycle 3. For this cycle, we engaged in sensemaking around students' oral discourse related to the conservation of mass as recorded on Flipgrid videos. Maren and Haeyoung especially found the task of interpreting students' oral recorded ideas expressed in Spanish to be challenging. Since there was nothing written on paper, they did not know what to type into Google Translate and they had trouble identifying individual words from students' oral discourse. Maren's individual interpretative work tended to focus on the visual aspects of students' videos rather than their oral discourse. In order to facilitate our *Reflect and Modify* conversation, Caitlin translated students' oral responses from Spanish to English. We talked about the usefulness of transcriptions of students' oral discourse so that all teachers could read and interpret it at their own pace.

Take-Aways and Implications for Teacher–Researcher Collaborations Centering Translanguaging in Science Formative Assessment

In this section, we summarize co-design principles for developing science formative assessments that welcome translanguaging. We outline several key take-aways for teacher–researcher collaborations interested in integrating translanguaging into science classrooms and into formative assessments through participatory design. We conclude with some thoughts about larger implications of this work and possible directions for future teacher–researcher collaboration efforts in science.

This collaboration highlighted several *(co)*design principals that should guide future endeavors focused on the design of science formative assessments for emergent bilinguals. First, teacher–researcher collaborations should engage with readings, videos, and websites that offer concrete examples of how translanguaging has been integrated into science classrooms across various contexts. These resources should be woven across *(co)*design work rather than frontloaded at the beginning of the collaboration. Second, teacher–researcher collaborations benefit from science formative assessment development tools, such as the TAC planning template (see Appendix 10.1 and Fine *et al.*, 2023). These interactive tools can guide *(co)*design conversations and considerations. They can also help teachers plan how they will enact science formative assessments in their classrooms, predict possible student responses and maintain asset-oriented stances as they interpret student work. Third, enacting science formative assessments that welcome translanguaging requires teachers to explicitly talk about translanguaging with their students and get 'meta' about language. These conversations cannot happen solely during assessment events. They must be integrated into the very fiber of the classroom community and be visible across classroom teaching and learning activities. Fourth, teacher–researcher collaborations should consult with students while they *(co)*design science formative assessment tasks. Students' reflections should be a central component of *(co)*design decisions and modifications. Finally, teacher–researcher collaborations benefit from dedicated time to analyze emergent bilinguals' work, reflect on emergent bilinguals' sensemaking and plan next instructional steps that build from emergent bilinguals' demonstrated strengths and science knowledge. This process includes discussing how *(co)*designed science formative assessment tasks support emergent bilinguals' sensemaking and what modifications might be made for future science assessment tasks and classroom lessons.

Take-aways

One important element of the TAC cycle was its iterative nature. We initially struggled to be at peace with feeling like our *(co)designs* were not perfect during the first iteration; we felt conflicted using formative assessments and science classroom materials that did not yet seem ready for primetime. We began to accept that being intentional at incorporating and inviting translanguaging into science classrooms and on formative assessments takes time. We also understood that we could never finalize science assessment tasks or science instructional materials on our own without gathering feedback from our most important stakeholders – the students themselves. We came to see our assessment *(co)designs* and science instructional materials as principled first drafts.

Ultimately, the translanguaging resources we discussed during the *Explore* phase as well as our translanguaging *(co)stances* informed our *(co)designs* and routines. Reflections on formative assessment *(co)design* enactment, related science instructional materials and on student feedback informed *(co)shifts* that in turn influenced our *(co)stances* and subsequent *(co)designs*. This process was messy and frustrating at times. It rarely felt linear, but rather like we were working together to weave multiple threads into a colorful tapestry that centered students' linguistic resources for science sensemaking.

Another important element of our teacher–researcher collaboration was the critical historicity of the school context that teachers brought to the work and their ideas about what we should be designing for. For example, Haeyoung brought knowledge of the ways in which Mountain View's multilingual ecology had shifted over the previous four years and Maren brought her knowledge of district-level policies regarding culturally and linguistically diverse education. Both Maren and Haeyoung had ideas about what was possible to *(co)design* for within their district-based context, but they were also both committed to designing science instructional materials and formative assessments for possible futures that firmly centered student sensemaking, even if those designs pushed against district structures. This commitment to make space for students to use their full linguistic repertoire in their science classrooms and on formative assessment tasks demonstrated a deeper translanguaging *(co)stance.*

Finally, the TAC cycle allowed us to broaden participation in designing and expand the type of questions we were able to explore. Instead of Caitlin bringing drafts of modified science instructional materials and formative assessment task designs to the teacher–researcher collaboration, Maren and Haeyoung were involved in *(co)design* work from the beginning. Additionally, we invited students to share their perspectives as critical stakeholders within each cycle. One tension we struggled with across cycles was how to meaningfully include students, families, and community members in *all* parts of the science assessment *(co)design* work. Future studies should explore how each component of the TAC process could be expanded to broaden 'who' participates in the science materials design process. Overall, the iterative nature of the TAC cycle led us to explore 'how can' questions that focused on the process itself which opened key opportunities and tensions.

Consequences for practice

Exploring how teacher–researcher collaborations can center translanguaging in science formative assessment and the resulting *(co)shifts* is extremely important but long-term work. Changing instructional and assessment materials as well as teachers' pedagogical practices and stances takes time. We found it helpful to reflect on our own biases and limited interpretive power by noticing how our experiences influenced our interpretation of student work. We encourage teacher–researcher collaborations to do this early and often. While we gained confidence in leveraging our own internal and external linguistic resources to interpret student work, we felt interpretations of student work were more accurate when working with a bilingual collaborator who shared linguistic resources with students. We encourage teachers to join hiring committees to advocate that schools and districts hire teachers and administrators who represent the cultural and linguistic heterogeneity of the student population.

Arguably more important than the *(co)designs* themselves were metalinguistic conversations we engaged in with students as part of the *Enact* phase where we explicitly encouraged students to leverage their full linguistic repertoires. It was important to plan out and practice these conversations as part of the instructional materials and formative assessment *Develop* phase. We encourage teacher–researcher collaborations to record science classroom metalinguistic conversations and reflect on them as a team. Ultimately, teaching emergent bilingual learners is a political act. Teacher–researcher collaborations play a vital role in pushing for equitable system changes within their multiple spheres of influence.

References

Bang, M., Brown, B., Calabrese Barton, A., Rosebery, A. and Warren, B. (2017) Towards more equitable learning in science: Expanding relationships between students, teachers, and science practices. In C. Schwarz, C. Passmore and B. Reiser (eds) *Helping Students Make Sense of the World Using Next Generation Science and Engineering Practices* (pp. 33–58). Arlington, VA: NSTA Press.

Bang, M., Faber, L., Gurneau, J., Marin, A. and Soto, C. (2015) Community-based design research: Learning across generations and strategic transformations of institutional relations toward axiological innovations. *Mind, Culture, and Activity* 23 (1), 28–41. http://doi.org/10.1080/10749039.2015.1087572

Bang, M. and Medin, D. (2010) Cultural processes in science education: Supporting the navigation of multiple epistemologies. *Science Education* 94 (6), 1008–1026. http://doi.org/10.1002/sce.20392

Bang, M. and Vossoughi, S. (2016) Participatory design research and educational justice: Studying learning and relations within social change making. *Cognition and Instruction* 34 (3), 173–193.

Black, P. and Wiliam, D. (1998) Assessment and classroom learning. *Assessment in Education* 5 (1), 7–74.

Brookhart, S.M. (2003) Developing measurement theory for classroom assessment purposes and uses. *Educational Measurement: Issues and Practice* 22 (4), 5–12.

Brown, B.A. (2019) *Science in the City: Culturally Relevant STEM Education*. Cambridge, MA: Harvard Education Press.

Brown, B.A., and Ryoo, K. (2008) Teaching science as a language: A 'content-first' approach to science teaching. *Journal of Research in Science Teaching* 45 (5), 529–553. http://doi.org/10.1002/tea.20255

Brown, B.A. and Spang, E. (2008) Double talk: Synthesizing everyday and science language in the classroom. *Science Education* 92 (4), 708–732.

Celic, C. and Seltzer, K. (2013) *Translanguaging: A CUNY-NYSIEB Guide for Educators*. New York, NY: CUNY-NYSEIB, The Graduate Center, The City University of New York.

Espinosa, C.M., Herrera, L.Y. and Montoya Gaudreau, C. (2016) Reclaiming bilingualism: Translanguaging in a science class. In O. García and T. Kleyn (eds) *Translanguaging with Multilingual Students* (pp. 160–179). New York, NY: Routledge.

Fang, Z. and Schleppegrell, M.J. (2008) Technicality and reasoning in science: Beyond vocabulary. In Z. Fang and M.J. Schleppegrell (eds) *Reading in Secondary Content Areas* (pp. 18–38). Ann Arbor, MI: University of Michigan Press.

Fine, C., Littich, H. and Getz, M. (2023) The (trans)formative assessment planning template: Explicitly welcome translanguaging during formative assessment in your science classroom. *Science Scope* 46 (31), 29–37.

Fine, C.G. McC. (2022) Translanguaging interpretive power in formative assessment co-design: A catalyst for science teacher agentive shifts. *Journal of Language, Identity & Education* 21 (3), 191–211.

Fine, C.G. McC. and Furtak, E. (2020) A framework for science classroom assessment task design for emergent bilingual learners. *Science Education* 104 (3), 393–420.

Furtak, E.M., Kiemer, K., Circi, R.K., Swanson, R., de Leon, V., Morrison, D. and Heredia, S.C. (2016) Teachers' formative assessment abilities and their relationship to student learning: Findings from a four-year intervention study. *Instructional Science* 44 (3), 1–25.

García, O. (2011) From language garden to sustainable languaging: Bilingual education in a global world. *Perspectives* 34, 5–10.

García, O., Johnson, S. and Seltzer, K. (2017) *The Translanguaging Classroom: Leveraging Student Bilingualism for Learning*. Philadelphia, PA: Caslon.

García, O. and Kleifgen, J.A. (2010) *Educating Emergent Bilinguals: Policies, Programs, and Practices for English Language Learners*. New York, NY: Teachers College Press.

García, O. and Li, W. (2014) *Translanguaging: Language, Bilingualism and Education*. London: Palgrave Macmillan.

Garza, A. and Langman, J. (2014) Translanguaging in a Latin Negotiations and mediations in a dual-Language classroom. *Association of Mexican-American Educators Journal* 8 (1), 37–49.

Gravemeijer, K. and Cobb, P. (2006) Design research from a learning design perspective. In J. Van Den Akker, K. Gravemeijer, S. McKenney and N. Nieveen (eds) *Educational Design Research* (pp. 29–63). Abingdon: Routledge.

Kelly, G. (2007) Discourse in science classrooms. In S.K. Abell and N.G. Lederman (eds) *Handbook of Research on Science Education* (2nd edn, pp. 443–470). Mahwah, NJ: Lawrence Erlbaum Associates.

Langman, J. (2014) Translanguaging, identity, and learning: Science teachers as engaged language planners. *Language Policy* 13 (2), 183–200. http://doi.org/10.1007/s10993-013-9312-9

Lee, O., Quinn, H. and Valdes, G. (2013) Science and language for English language learners in relation to next generation science standards and with implications for common core state standards for English language arts and mathematics. *Educational Researcher* 42 (4), 223–233.

Miles, M.B., Huberman, A.M. and Saldaña, J. (2018) *Qualitative Data Analysis: A Methods Sourcebook*. Thousand Oaks, CA: Sage.

National Research Council (NRC) (2012) *A Framework for K-12 Science Education: Practices, Crosscutting Concepts, and Core Ideas*. Washington, DC: National Academies Press.

Otheguy, R., García, O. and Reid, W. (2015) Clarifying translanguaging and deconstructing named languages: A perspective from linguistics. *Applied Linguistics Review* 6, 281–307. https://doi.org/10.1515/applirev-2015-0014

Poza, L.E. (2016) The language of ciencia: Translanguaging and learning in a bilingual science classroom. *International Journal of Bilingual Education and Bilingualism* 50 (January), 1–19.

Rosebery, A.S., Warren, B. and Conant, F.R. (1992) Appropriating scientific discourse: Findings from language minority classrooms. *Journal of the Learning Sciences* 2 (1), 61–94. http://doi.org/10.1207/s15327809jls0201_2

Schissel, J.L., De Korne, H. and López-Gopar, M. (2021) Grappling with translanguaging for teaching and assessment in culturally and linguistically diverse contexts: Teacher perspectives from Oaxaca, Mexico. *International Journal of Bilingual Education and Bilingualism* 24 (3), 340–356.

Suárez, E. (2020) 'Estoy explorando science': Emergent bilingual students problematizing electrical phenomena through translanguaging. *Science Education* 104 (5), 791–826. https://doi.org/10.1002/sce.21588

Tian, Z., Aghai, L., Sayer, P. and Schissel, J.L. (eds) (2020) *Envisioning TESOL Through a Translanguaging Lens: Global Perspectives*. Cham: Springer International Publishing.

Tian, Z. and Shepard-Carey, L. (2020) (Re) imagining the future of translanguaging pedagogies in TESOL through teacher – researcher collaboration. *TESOL Quarterly* 54 (4), 1131–1143.

Warren, B. and Rosebery, A.S. (2011) Navigating interculturality: African American male students and the science classroom. *Journal of African American Males in Education* 2 (1), 98–115.

Windschitl, M., Thompson, J. and Braaten, M. (2018) *Ambitious Science Teaching*. Cambridge, MA: Harvard Education Press.

Appendix 10.1: Translanguaging Formative Assessment Planning Template

Formative Assessment (FA) Task Name: ______________________
FA Source : ______________________

Science Objective(s)	(Trans)language Objective(s)	English Language Objective(s)

Students' prior experiences/expertise with this topic
Home/Community knowledge they bring to the task: ★ Classroom experiences they bring to the task: ★

FA Translanguaging Tools
<u>The FA itself</u> ❖ Task, task instructions, objectives and/or scoring tools are written in languages represented within the classroom student population ➢ ❖ A clear translanguaging objective is included in the student-facing task ➢ ❖ Task instructions indicate students may translanguage ➢ <u>Material resources</u> *(What materials can students use as they complete the FA task?)* ❖

FA Translanguaging Routines (routines employed during the FA event)
<u>Teacher pedagogical moves</u> *(Sketch-out language and practice with each other)* ❖ How we plan to talk about translanguaging with students as part of the FA task ➢ ❖ How we plan to support students' translanguaging practice (anchor charts, FA task itself, realia, etc.) ➢ <u>Planned student routines</u> ❖

How might these translanguaging tools/routines support sensemaking during the FA event?	
Teacher sensemaking about students	Student sensemaking about science

Classroom Translanguaging Tools/Routines
❖ Word wall / Project board / Anchor charts ➢ Post in multiple languages and include visuals. Students help co-create resource. ❖ Student consensus discussion take-aways/questions during instructional unit ➢ Conduct and record in multiple languages. ❖ Daily homework question ➢ Present in multiple languages. ❖ Student work ➢ Elevate / post in multiple languages. ❖ Grouping ➢ Strategic grouping so students can use all linguistic resources in small groups. ❖ Material resources ➢ Bilingual dictionaries, bilingual books, Google Translate, online resources.

11 What Teacher–Researcher Collaboration Creates: Reflections on Translanguaging Pedagogies from a Central Ohio Adolescent Newcomer Program

Derek Braun, Brian Seilstad and Somin Kim

Introduction

A disconnect often exists between educational theorists, researchers and educational practitioners. Translanguaging (García & Li, 2014) is a prime example of what happens when a new theoretical perspective emerges, prompting cycles of dialogue and evolution in the interplay between these groups. For example, educational linguists have contested the definition, scope and implications of translanguaging (Cummins, 2021; MacSwan, 2017; Mazzaferro, 2018; Otheguy *et al.*, 2015, 2019) while educational professionals have promoted translanguaging as a way to destabilize deficit-oriented and monoglossic orientations to education and literacy to promote equitable and loving educations for all, particularly historically marginalized groups, by engaging and developing students' full linguistic repertoire (García, 2020b; García *et al.*, 2016; García & Kleifgen, 2020). This volume focuses on a key question: How can a teacher–researcher collaboration position translanguaging research as a grounded practice in the classroom with positive outcomes? The phenomenon of translanguaging is explored through the lens of teacher–researcher collaborations rooted in the benefits and advantages of implementing translanguaging pedagogy in literacy and language education (Cenoz & Gorter, 2013; Creese & Blackledge, 2010; Licona & Kelly, 2020; Lin,

2013). Moreover, the purpose of this study is to investigate and highlight the potential of teacher–researcher collaborations as a means of more effectively implementing a translanguaging pedagogy. This pedagogy is supported by three pillars: stance, design and shifts. Stance requires teachers to have an understanding of and affirming approach to bi/multilingualism; design requires intentional classroom activities to support bi/multilingual students; and shifts remind teachers that principled changes will be required as classroom practices unfold (García *et al.*, 2017: 27–28). As teacher–researcher collaborations unfold, these pillars become somewhat more complex and dialogic as *co-stances, co-design* and *co-shifts* (Tian & Shepard-Carey, 2020).

Context

This chapter contributes to this framework by drawing on data collected during a multi-year collaboration beginning in November 2015 between an English Learner Biology teacher practitioner, Derek Braun, and a team of researchers, Brian Seilstad, Somin Kim, Min-Seok Choi and Afida Safriani, from The Ohio State University (OSU). At the time of the initial collaboration, the researchers were PhD students at OSU and Derek, a teacher in the local public school district working at a well-established newcomer program. Derek and Brian first met during the summer of 2015 while working together at a local refugee resettlement office. Derek, a native English speaker proficient in Spanish and Somali, was teaching ESL to newly arrived refugee adults as part of refugee employability training. Brian, also a native English speaker proficient in Arabic and French, worked as an employment specialist, which included assisting French and Arabic speaking clients with English classes, job applications and the challenges of refugee resettlement. At the time Brian was studying as a PhD student and was interested in conducting research at a newcomer ESL school where Derek was a teacher. Thus, Brian and Derek met several times in the summer of 2015 to discuss a potential research collaboration and designed a research protocol using ethnographic and discourse analytic methods. Brian worked to get IRB approval and, when this was granted in November 2015, started observing in Derek's classroom. Brian's first fieldnote from the project included this comment about Derek:

> 'A brief description about Derek: Although I do not know Derek that well, what I've come to know about him is quite encouraging. I know that he is a fluent Spanish speaker, and I've also learned that he speaks Somali, and today I asked him what he rated his level as, and he said it was intermediate. I'm curious to see him speak that and deploy that in the classroom. He's also relatively young, at about 30 years old I think, and what I see in him is sort of a symbol of what a new teacher might look like in this new generation. He is somebody who is multilingual, reasonably

well-traveled, curious about other religions yet grounded in his own, skilled in teaching, and reflective in his practices. In the discourse about the white monolingual teacher, I feel that he is a counterpoint to that.' (Fieldnotes, November 13, 2015)

In the Fall of 2015, Brian observed Derek's classroom six times, taking fieldnotes only and getting parental consent and student assent for the eventual videorecording of classroom events. In Spring of 2016, the project accelerated in that Brian invited his PhD colleagues Somin, Min-Seok and Afida to join the project as part of a Language Socialization class where the collection and analysis of longitudinal classroom events would be required. All four researchers brought multilingual abilities, Brian with Arabic and French, Somin with Korean and Spanish, Min-Seok with Korean and Afida with Indonesian. Throughout, the researchers took the stance of participant observers and would therefore work with Derek and the students to support the achievement of the language and content objectives. All were just becoming acquainted with translanguaging through their coursework at OSU. In fact, in the spring of 2016, Derek and Brian simultaneously and independently enrolled in bilingual education courses designed by Dr Mileidis Gort that incorporated a range of readings related to translanguaging (García, 2008; García & Baker, 2007; Gort, 2015). Thus, this chapter focuses on the initial period of teacher–researcher collaboration in the 2015–2016 academic year and specifically a project, The Bilingual Biomes (Seilstad *et al.*, 2019), but also reflects on the ongoing process of collaboration, with a specific focus on the framework of co-stances, co-design and co-shifts and how this has implications for students, practitioners and researchers. At time of writing, Brian and Afida have achieved their doctorates, Min-Seok and Somin are nearing the completion of their PhD programs and Derek has begun the PhD program at OSU. All continue to engage with translanguaging theory and practice in distinct ways.

The data presented in this chapter come from fieldwork in the 2015–2016 academic year in two of Derek's tenth-grade biology classes in an urban Ohio district's newcomer program serving a highly diverse student body. Newcomer programs respond to rapid demographic shifts (Vertovec, 2007) and are designed to support learners from many different home language communities as they transition to either mainstream schools or graduate from the newcomer program itself (Short & Boyson, 2004). The two biology classrooms from this study are English-centric in that English is the medium of instruction, but it is not English-only due to the multilingual character of the students, teachers and realities of everyday discourse (Pacheco, 2016).

The newcomer program serves a diverse set of students who are placed in the program due to their emerging English proficiency. The vast majority of the focal school's student body are asylum seekers, immigrants or refugees in the middle to high school-age range (i.e. 15–21 years old). The program has evolved over the years to meet the needs of the district's rapidly growing English Language Learner (ELL) population. Thus, the district's English as a Second Language (ESL) department has grown significantly from a program in the 1990s that served a small group of ELLs to a professional unit serving nearly 8000 students, or more than 15% of the districts total, across more than 100 named languages with five – Spanish, French, Nepali, Arabic and Somali – being the most common. The program utilizes secondary educators certified in specific content areas (e.g. history, math, science) as well as having Teaching English to Speakers of Other Languages (TESOL) endorsements. Derek's biology class was part of the second-year science course designed to provide the students with academic credit for graduation and prepare them for mainstream high schools. Thus, in terms of English language ability, the students were generally able to communicate in English socially with peers and instructors as well as complete appropriately moderated complex academic tasks, often by drawing on peer interactions in their home languages.

However, as ELLs, the students are faced with the arduous task of graduating from high school within the district's four-year target. In addition, many of the students have 'students with limited or interrupted formal education' (SLIFE) backgrounds and therefore face a particularly challenging path to graduation (Custodio, 2010) due to the fact that these students are essentially tasked with doing 'double the work' of acquiring the language and content necessary for mainstream schooling (Short & Fitzsimmons, 2007). These factors may explain why many adolescent newcomers struggle in schools and dropout at a higher rate than their native-born peers (Fry, 2005).

Derek's year-long biology class was taught daily, in two different morning and afternoon sections of 16 and 19 students respectively, as a two-period block class of 84 minutes and focused on two sets of objectives: (1) completing the Learning Targets as defined by the Ohio Learning Standards for the content of Biology; and (2) completing the Ohio English Language Proficiency Standards (9–12). For the research project, Min-Seok and Afida focused on the morning section and Brian and Somin the afternoon. The classroom was arranged with four different table groups in which students sat around the perimeter with the intention of creating an atmosphere of peer-to-peer interaction. The classroom also has a bilingual instructional assistant to assist in working with students one on one and in small groups.

Conceptual Framework

The researchers took the position of an equitable partnership with the focal teacher (Derek). The researchers were continually available to interact with and assist students. This partnership was the driving force behind the development of a pedagogy that values, encourages and promotes the development of students' home languages and cultures. The conceptual framework of co-stance, co-design and co-shifts informed the analysis of the data collected from the teacher–researcher collaboration.

Methodology

The research project was designed in the classroom ethnographic and discourse analytic traditions (Atkinson *et al.*, 2011; Blommaert & Dong, 2010; Bloome *et al.*, 2004). That is, the research team were in Derek's class regularly and recorded regular interactions with one or two video cameras and several microphones. Central to data collection and analysis was the teacher–researcher collaboration. The classroom teacher (Derek) participated in several aspects of data collection, through providing field notes, reflections and interviews with researchers. Interviews, times of reflections and discussions with researchers influenced and guided the classroom teacher's stance on classroom language use and language learning pedagogy. Researchers also served as subject matter experts, providing the classroom teacher with research on translanguaging and its application as a pedagogical tool in the classroom. In total, the data collected over the eight-month research period include: 20 classroom observations with fieldnotes; simultaneous audio-video recordings of the classroom supplemented by audio recordings of the teacher author (Derek) and student groups; interviews with Derek, students and instructional assistant; and artifact collection of assessments, handouts and student work. The interactional data were transcribed and organized with the support of Transana Pro. The focal data highlights points of *co-stances*, *co-design* and *co-shifts* that emerge over the eight-month data collection period.

Upon completion of the focal project, described below, students were provided the opportunity to reflect on their experience of working on the project and their classroom language practices. A survey was given to students in the form of five written questions allowing students to provide both feedback and the opportunity to reflect on their experience of working on the project and the presentation. The survey responses were also utilized by the instructor to better understand his students' language practices and reflect on his instructional methods.

Findings

Co-stance, co-design and co-shifts

In this section, we will both define and demonstrate translanguaging's co-stance, co-design and co-shifts through data presented from our collaboration.

Co-stance: Flexible language use as a norm

A translanguaging stance establishes that students' language practices and cultural understandings are a valuable source of knowledge and can enrich the experiences in the classroom (Sayer, 2013). The development of the classroom teacher's (Derek) stance evolved throughout the school year influenced by the researchers' deep commitment to incorporate students' language practices and cultural understandings into the classroom community. Throughout the teacher–researcher collaboration Derek was periodically interviewed by co-researchers, which provided an opportunity for reflection leading to further development of the co-stance. The following three excerpts, from an interview between the researcher Min-seok (MS) and the teacher author (Derek), highlight his stance and language ideology. Pseudo names for students are used for all data presented. Additional subjects throughout the paper include a bilingual teacher's assistant, Andrea, and students including Nur, José, Brandon, Kane, Halima, Israel, Friya, Danka and Padma.

Excerpt 1

MS: Have you happened to have such a conversation in another group? Like talking different languages? Because in this group two student are Spanish speakers, but in other group there might be someone who speaking different language from other than Spanish or English. Then do you happen to speak with them in English, in another language?

Derek: Another language, yeah. Somali language with some students. But my Somali language is not of high enough level that I have long extended explanations. I'll use Somali words usually in different contexts to explain short things. Yes, I do that as well.

This interaction highlights the researcher's role of providing the opportunity for Derek to reflect on his own language use in the classroom. It shows that he is leveraging the students' home language to facilitate academic tasks and provide directions for classroom activities or assignments (Licona & Kelly, 2020), which also assists in modeling and developing a classroom culture of translanguaging.

Excerpt 2

MS: You talking to her in Somali language sometimes. I saw you talking to her in Somali language, but how is the conversation different from this conversation and your understanding?

Derek: This is very content specific conversation. Sometimes with Nur it won't always just be for content. It could be class procedures or outside class, just greetings a lot of times. She likes using Somali language more so than some of the other students and I think it's a way that kind of refocuses her attention sometimes. But I will use it for content too, with her.

The teacher (Derek) and the researcher (Min-Seok) continued building on their understanding of flexible language use in the classroom throughout the interview. Derek's use of Somali language in non-academic class procedures reinforces the norms and expectations of integrating flexible language use within the classroom culture (Licona & Kelly, 2020).

Excerpt 3

MS: Does José ask you or talk to you in Spanish language or English? Because I saw him talking to you in English, but he knows you're speaking Spanish.

Derek: Yeah. I think that he mostly speaks to me in English. Yeah. Let me think. He does, I can't really think. He mostly will speak to me in English. Which is good, I mean, we're working on content in English. The worksheet is in English. So, he's just working in the language of the content, which is great to know.

MS: Did he ever change language in the middle of the talk with you in Spanish language?

Derek: I can't think specifically of him doing that. I have other students who will switch a lot. Yeah, we switch a lot.

MS: What about Brandon? Because in this conversation he is somewhat sometimes correct you or sometimes jumping when you're talking.

Derek: He does, yeah. I love that. Yeah, he's great because he is understanding that I'm speaking in not my first language and he's tracking with what I'm saying and then adding to it and correcting it. That's great. I like when he's engaged enough to be a part of-

MS: Is he engaged in the class when you're speaking or explaining in English as much as he did in this?

Derek: No, no, not as much. There'll be sometimes… Yeah, definitely… I think, it'll be safe to say he's going to be way more focused. I notice this all the time when he hears Spanish. I mean, if I'm talking to the class and I started speaking in Spanish all of a sudden, if he was like this the Spanish speakers they look. That's just natural, it gets the attention instantly. And that's kind of a natural human tendency because if they're in class all day and if you're hearing a language that's not your first language, you either are listening to it and understanding it or you can tune it out as noise in the background. I know, yeah, that he does that a lot. So if I wanted to quickly explain something for content purposes in Spanish, he listens, I think, a lot better

In the interview, researcher MS is asking questions to better understand Derek's language choices when interacting with students. In Excerpt 3 Derek identifies that it is positive for students' language learning that they have the opportunity to interact and communicate in the target language of English. As part of the overall goals of the course the instructor designs labs and activities that provide opportunities for communication and require collaboration through student interactions. The seating chart is arranged in table groups to encourage and facilitate collaboration through group projects and activities. The classroom, as well as the table groups, are multilingual which often makes for diverse language interactions. The classroom is English-centric by nature of the language objectives; however, the instructor models and opens up the space for multilingual conversations. Derek's multilingual conversations and use of translanguaging increases students' comprehensible input while explaining biology content and vocabulary. Moreover, Excerpts 1 and 2 show that he employs students' home languages as a means to simply greet students or make a connection. This demonstrates that the instructor's language learning philosophy extends beyond translanguaging as a tool for content instruction but rather is part of a framework that guides the teacher's holistic philosophy regarding multilingualism. Excerpt 3 also shows that the researcher, Min-Seok and Derek were engaged in the discussion about why the he allows and encourages a translanguaging space for students and how students respond to Derek's translanguaging practice. Throughout the interview we see the development of a teacher–researcher co-stance as philosophical and ideological ideas regarding bilingualism and translanguaging are discussed and negotiated (Tian & Shepard-Carey, 2020). This becomes the foundation and underpinnings moving forward to a translanguaging pedagogical framework that guides the development of co-design.

Co-design: Theory into practice

This section focuses on the ways in which García *et al.*'s (2016) previously presented design becomes co-design within a teacher–research collaboration. As teachers and researchers interact, the process results in a co-planning as the researchers influence the teacher to maximize students' learning opportunities. This collaboration unites the practical influences and firsthand experiences of the teacher that knows their students with the challenge of implementing creative and perhaps novel pedagogy in the co-design of lessons. As mentioned above, Derek was taking an OSU course entitled Foundations of Bilingual Education, which was fundamental in influencing his lesson design and guided the reimagining of the language goals for his classes.

More specifically, during the previous school year, Derek presented an activity in which students worked together in small groups to study a particular biome on earth (e.g. desert, tropical rainforest, tundra), create a PowerPoint presentation and present to the class. Groups were assigned by the instructor and care was taken to separate students who had the same home languages. This ran counter to a common practice to design seating charts and student groups to avoid students from only speaking in home languages. This was partly utilized as a tool for classroom management in minimizing off-task conversations and forcing students to utilize English as the common language of the classroom. In later reflection, it was realized that this perspective and approach conforms to the dominant monolingual structures in TESOL as teachers aim to maintain control and limit the use of students' home languages.

During an interview between researcher MS and teacher author (Derek) it was noted by the researcher that within several of the table groups there was often little to no social interactions taking place. The researcher had selected a focal group with the purpose of analyzing student interactions. The group consisted of four students, Jose, Brandon, Kane and Farhiya. Two students were Spanish speakers, one was a French speaker and one was a Somali speaker. In description of this group, the focal teacher (Derek) stated to the researcher, 'They're all kinda introverts and they all speak different languages.' During times of group work the students seldom communicated or interacted with each other. The following interview presents some of Derek's thoughts following researcher MS's observation and comments on the lack of interactions. The following excerpt reveals Derek's potential idea in regard to creating what he termed 'homogeneous language groups.' This then becomes the basis for the co-design of a project based on translanguaging pedagogies.

Derek: Ummm, they're [focal table group] quieter, so they're not initiators… (sigh) yeah… But I don't know, I'm interested, I'm curious to see just mixing it all up, changing it all and creating homogeneous language groups.

MS: Ohhh

Derek: Just to see… Nepali table, Spanish table, French table, and it might work out… I don't know, let me see… even.

MS: Do you have more than two French students, I thought Israel and Halima are speaking French.

Derek: Ummm, Israel and Halima, so Spanish… Swahili and Somali together, then French, Kane doesn't speak French though… he doesn't speak French[1], actually he should be with… It doesn't work out great because… they're not going to get a lot of work done.

MS: Haha, yeah, I know what you mean.

Derek: And then Nepali table… I think I have Halima twice, so yeah alright this will be interesting Spanish, Somali/ Swahili together, a lot of students speak both, they're familiar at least with Swahili. They are both, a little bit, I think. Kane… Swahili and Nepali… I don't know I'm just more curious… just for a project I want to see them work together.

MS: Oh, are you going to have a project for students?

Derek: Yeah, I've done this, uhhh, yeah, I'm working on ideas of like, uhh, when we get into the next chapter, like biomes, doing like a biomes project, and I don't know what it's going to look like, I'm still making it up, but I've been brainstorming about it.

Derek: Where they're basically going to research a biome, each group would… and it has to be… I'll make them do research to find a biome from their home country.

MS: Hmmm

Derek: So maybe this group… it's Central Americans and Mexicans, they'll have to pick a specific biome from one of their countries. And they'll pick a biome from… maybe like desert region East Africa. French, you know, they'll do like, they could pick a couple different biomes, but maybe they'll do uhh you know, West African could be like rain forest. And the Nepali group could do like, the biome of Nepali, lowland grassland or mountain biome.

This was a key conversation, leading to Derek completely re-thinking and re-designing the activity to encourage students to utilize translanguaging. In this way students could become the experts while utilizing their funds of knowledge and their full linguistic repertoires in completing the learning objectives as they teach one another about grammar and vocabulary (Moll *et al.*, 1992). Through the teacher–researchers' collaboration, the project entitled Bilingual Biomes Presentation was designed with the goal of affirming and leveraging the students' translanguaging practices. The project would require students to research and create a Google Slides presentation for a multilingual audience. The primary language of the presentation being the students' home language while utilizing a group member as an interpreter to present in English as well (Seilstad *et al.*, 2019). Students presented all text within the presentation in a bilingual format displaying both the students' home languages as well as English. The project was designed to complete a set of both content and language objectives.

Content objectives:

- Research real-world examples of how producers and consumers interact in an ecosystem.
- Use and interpret real-world data to present climate conditions of the focus biome, including monthly average precipitation and temperature.
- Describe energy flow within an ecosystem and interactions of organisms within their environment and the flow of energy within food webs.

Language objectives:

- Compose informational texts in both English and their first language (L1).
- Develop formal language skills in both their L1 and English.
- Interpret from their L1 to English.

Throughout the implementation of the Bilingual Biome Project, several challenges were encountered regarding the language requirements of the project and realistic language expectations. These challenges required a shift in expected language goals and outcomes. The teacher–researcher collaboration provided a context to negotiate these difficult challenges through the development of co-shift.

Co-shift: Flexible language decisions

Newcomer programs face a multitude of challenges. One of the principal challenges includes determining students' needs and learning gaps among the diverse set of educational backgrounds and language proficiencies. Due to a variety of reasons, students often arrive in the United States with limited or interrupted formal education. By the time many refugee students begin schooling in the US they may have spent the majority of their lives in refugee camps where access to consistent, quality education is limited. On the other hand, students may arrive in the US with relatively strong academic and home language skills that, due to the English-centric nature of US education, simply is not well-aligned with the US curriculum. One group in which this is the case are many of the Bhutanese-Nepali refugees that make up a significant portion of this study's focal newcomer program. These students often possess a wide range of Nepali language literacy skills but may have struggled with a relative lack of access or availability to formal education in the refugee camps in Nepal. Thus, SLIFE students often struggle to adjust to the demands of developing academic language and content proficiency in the US content (Custodio, 2010). More specifically, research shows that students lacking the foundational skills of home language literacy may encounter significant barriers to developing literacy in the L2 (Cummins, 1979). In contrast, 'children who are phonetically aware in their native language demonstrate word recognition skills and passage comprehension in a second language superior to that of their native-language counterparts who lack phonetic awareness in their native language' (Yopp & Stapleton, 2008: 376). These findings bolstered the teacher author's (Derek) commitment to developing and engaging both home language and English language objectives as both a strong pedagogical support to learning and an equity-based educational approach.

However, a significant challenge encountered by the classroom teacher (Derek) requiring a shift was determining the home language literacy levels of the students to set realistic expectations of what the learning objectives would be. While implementing the project Derek was confronted with the challenge that many of the Nepali students had not received significant formal education in reading and writing Nepali language. Some students were familiar with the Nepali alphabet and were able to decode the language but had not developed essential reading skills such as automaticity and fluency. One student, Friya, was able to read and write; Danika was able to decode and read with limited proficiency. However, both Kira and Padma were unfamiliar with the Nepali alphabet and had very limited L1 literacy skills. It is common that Nepali students write using the transliteration of Nepali, utilizing English (Latin) characters to write Nepali language. This question arose of whether it was acceptable to use the transliteration within the Google Slides presentation. The following dialogue took place between the teacher author (Derek) and Danika (D) when he was working with this particular group of Nepali students.

D: Look here Mister, this one is in Nepali, so I have to write here in these words right, or like that, something like, like that, we gonna write like this one [showing written words using the transliteration].
Derek: Ummm
This one, right? [pointing to Nepali script]
Derek: Yeah, you should practice your Nepali script. You should use the Nepali script.
D: This one also Nepali [pointing to the transliteration]
Derek: Do you know the sounds? pronunciation of the letters… the characters?
D: Yeah
Derek: Yeah, you should try, you should use the Nepali script, maybe though in your notes, in your notes for your presentation you could use this [pointing to the transliteration], you know as a backup.

This interaction shows that the classroom teacher (Derek) was unfamiliar with the level of literacy of the Nepali students in this group. He was resistant in permitting or encouraging students to utilize the transliteration; however, a shift in expectations of what students might be expected to achieve was necessary given the limited time frame and scope of the project and lack of L1 language support. Students were encouraged to utilize the Nepali script but also it was recognized that it was unrealistic for students to adapt to utilizing the script with which they did not have sufficient formal literacy training or support. The question arose in several additional interactions as to whether students should be permitted to utilize a transliteration within the project. The following interaction takes place between the Nepali student Padma (P), the bilingual instructional assistant Andrea (A) and the researcher co-author Brian (RA).

RA: Do you know how to write Nepali?
P: No
RA: It's a little tricky, you can write… maybe write it in English letters, that's fine
A: Right, that's what they are doing, yeah, they are translating Nepali and using the Latin alphabet.
RA: Yeah, that's fine
A: Right

When Padma was asked if she writes Nepali, she responds by saying 'no.' Without prompting or encouragement Padma had begun utilizing a transliteration for her research and Google Slides Presentation. Brian and Andrea promote and encourage the student to utilize the transliteration while creating her Google Slides presentation. On a separate occasion the same day, the following interaction takes place between the researcher author Brian (RA), Padma (P) and this time the teacher author (Derek).

RA: Do you guys read Nepali?
P: No Mister.

Derek: No? oh, Friya is good, and uhh, oh man where are they today [referring to absent students, Friya and Danika]
D: Absent
Derek: They're the linguists of the group.

Later in the day, Derek asks Padma to clarify how she created her slide in the following conversation.

Derek: Where did you get this [pointing to the transliteration]
P: Google
RA: Yeah, Google Translate, that's nice how they make the transliteration available.
P: You see Nepali [pointing to Nepali script], English-Nepali [pointing to transliteration], and English [pointing to English].

Derek was presented with the challenge of determining what were realistic goals and expectations to set for the Nepali language group. At first, it was decided students were to only use Nepali script and English for the Google Slides presentation. Later, through more closely working with the students and gaining a better understanding of the diverse range of home language literacy proficiencies, Derek shifted his perspective to allow students to utilize the transliteration of Nepali script in creating the Google Slides presentation. This shift in large part occurred through the interactions with both Andrea, the bilingual instructional assistant, and Brian, the classroom researcher. Both encouraged and promoted students to utilize the transliteration while completing the project. Throughout the teacher–researcher collaboration it was essential to be flexible and be prepared to make spontaneous decisions about engaging students in possible translanguaging moments. Co-shifts occur when both researchers and the classroom teachers are prepared to relinquish the role as 'expert' and enlist the help of bilingual students. In this moment, the student Padma made the spontaneous language decision to include in her presentation Nepali, 'English-Nepali' [transliteration], and English (Figure 11.1). The teacher–researcher collaboration made this flexible adjustment through a willingness to support this student's home language use and identity (Tian & Shepard-Carey, 2020).

Figure 11.1 student work in Google Slides presentation

Students' reflection on the project

Upon completion of this chapter's focal project, the Bilingual Biome Project, students were given a survey to provide feedback from the experience of incorporating their home languages into the formal setting of a school presentation. The survey results were both affirming and challenging to the collaboration. On the one hand, there was a certain amount of pride in co-creating and implementing this activity. The students' responses showed that, for many, it was the first time their home languages were incorporated into their US schooling experience. Many of them cited their pride and validation through the process of challenging the power and status of English as the language of education. The student survey included the following questions:

(1) What was the most difficult part of the bilingual biome group presentation project?
(2) How did you feel preparing a presentation in your home language?
(3) Did you feel the bilingual presentation project helped build your understanding of biomes?
(4) Do you feel the bilingual biome presentation helped build you language and communication skills?
(5) What would you have changed about the bilingual biome presentation project?

The results of the student survey were analyzed through discourse analysis, identifying repeated themes and phrases utilized by students. Overall, the results demonstrated that the majority of students had a positive experience using their home language in a formal class presentational setting. Many students cited that presenting in their home language made them 'good' or 'comfortable.' When responding to question 4 one student stated, 'yes the bilingual biome presentation helped build in my language and communication skills because I talk to my group in my lenguage and english to.' Another student responded to question 2 by stating, 'I felt in that presentation in my own language it was rare because I'm in USA and here we usually speak English so I felt brave.' However, not all students expressed a positive experience from the project. One student referred to as Amina responded to question 2 by stating, 'scary I feel shame because I can't read my own language so please don't remind me that.' This response highlights the difficulties and even 'shame' SLIFE students can experience in the classroom. Amina grew up in a multilingual environment having one parent as an Arabic speaker from Egypt and one as a native Somali speaker. She was born in a refugee camp in Kenya and identifies with Somali culture and language having grown up within the Somali community. She was not afforded the opportunity to attend school until only a few months prior to coming to the United States.

Discussion

The presented teacher–researcher collaboration revealed many of the positive results from the implementation of translanguaging pedagogies through both the product and the process. One resulting product from this collaboration was the co-design of this chapter's focal project, the Bilingual Biome Project. This project provided the context for students to connect and investigate environments and experiences from their home countries to class content while collaborating to create a presentation. The project both provided a positive outlet and application for home language, but also exposed some of the unfortunate realities of a lack of home language literacy support and development. This heuristic outcome was a result of reflections based upon researcher observations through which the classroom teacher (Derek) developed the idea to create 'homogeneous language groups' leading to opportunities for students to translanguage within the context of co-creating a group presentation. The results from the student reflections support and build on existing findings that translanguaging within the context and language integrated learning (CLIL) provides a more equitable environment for learning as well as affirms students' identities (Infante & Licona, 2018; Lin & He, 2017; Pierson *et al.*, 2021).

In the case of Amina, she represents the experiences of so many newcomers that arrive with large gaps and disruptions in formal education. Most commonly ESL programs do nothing or very little to identify or assess home language skills. The survey forced a moment of reflection back on the stance, design and shifts. Program design and classroom instruction must strive to provide ELLs with the opportunity to develop and practice home language literacy. One revision to the stance due to some of the criticisms is a realization that students deserve a much more prolonged and holistic pedagogical approach rooted in their home languages and engaging their full linguistic repertoire in educational experiences.

The challenges encountered with students having a wide range of Nepali literacy levels highlights the importance of design. Individual activity design, whole course creation and cross-curricular connections all require setting individual student language goals and outcomes. Determining these goals and language objectives requires a knowledge of the literacy level and previous educational experiences of each student. The experience of implementing translanguaging pedagogies led to Derek's development of a Language Passport adapted from The European Language Portfolio (ELP) that was implemented the following school year. In order to better understand students' home language proficiencies students were given a language self-assessment as part of their Language Passport. The self-assessment was adapted from the ELP developed by the Language Policy Unit of the Council of Europe. Students completed the assessment for all languages within their linguistic repertoires. Within the assessment students list each language then assess their proficiencies by rating each domain (reading, writing, speaking, listening) with a number 1–5. Level 1 equaling simple greetings and memorized phrases; level 5 equaling technical academic vocabulary and professional level language proficiency. The goal is to provide the classroom teacher with a greater understanding of students' previous language education levels and language proficiencies. The Language Passport also serves to have students reflect on their language proficiencies in promoting metalinguistic awareness in acting as a first step to encouraging and developing students' multilingualism. And of course, this doesn't ignore the reality of the shifts. Throughout, just as with the example above, there is a need to be ready to shift always from the stance of openness to affirming the students' linguistic repertoire. The type of literacy displayed by the Nepali-English transliteration points to the fact that, adolescents especially, will be creating and experimenting with new forms of expression and that teachers and school systems should do as much as they can to affirm these literacies and incorporate them into the educational experience.

Looking Forward

The collaboration between Derek, Brian and Somin continues to the present. All three remained engaged in translanguaging in their own ways. In 2016, Derek was moved from the newcomer program to a sheltered site at a mainstream high school where he continued his Bilingual Biomes activity for multiple years. Perhaps, more substantially, he designed and implemented a bilingual Spanish-English biology course in which translanguaging was a key component to help him, for example, working with Portuguese-speaking students in the course whose linguistic repertoires were a rich resource for making meaning of the target language and content.

Derek now is a PhD student at OSU in Foreign, Second, and Multilingual Education and will be a founding faculty member at Columbus City Schools' new multilingual middle school, World Language Middle School. Derek is currently researching the language learning outcomes from teaching with a problem-based learning methodology. His work continues to utilize a teacher–researcher collaboration as a holistic approach to achieve positive student outcomes through action research. Brian completed his PhD in 2018 based on research at the same adolescent newcomer program drawing heavily on translanguaging; his work has recently been published in book form with Multilingual Matters (Seilstad, 2021). Somin, for her part, has continued her PhD research at another sheltered site with a highly multilingual student body and even taught Korean in the school for several years.

Translanguaging pushes both researchers and practitioners to have ever more comprehensive and embracing stances towards supporting and developing students' full linguistic repertoires. This demands ever more complex and compassionate pedagogical designs that encompass the full range of activities from moment-to-moment interactions to long-term language policies. In turn, this demands sensitivity and attention to both the shifts happening in the classroom and society and, coming full circle, a stance towards shifting design to adapt to these shifts. Finally, this reflective and ongoing cycle has the potential to unsettle inequitable power relations and create the potential for new, unforeseen realities to emerge.

Note

(1) Kane is actually a French speaker.

References

Atkinson, D., Okada, H. and Talmy, S. (2011) Ethnography and discourse analysis. In K. Hyland and B. Paltridge (eds) *Bloomsbury Companion to Discourse Analysis* (pp. 85–100). New York, NY: Bloomsbury Publishing.

Blommaert, J. and Dong, J. (2010) *Ethnographic Fieldwork: A Beginner's Guide*. Bristol: Multilingual Matters.

Bloome, D., Carter, S.P., Christian, B.M., Otto, S. and Shuart-Faris, N. (2004) *Discourse Analysis and the Study of Classroom Language and Literacy Events: A Micro-ethnographic Perspective*. New York, NY: Routledge.

Cenoz, J. and Gorter, D. (2013) Towards a plurilingual approach in English language teaching: Softening the boundaries between languages. *TESOL Quarterly* 47 (3), 591–599.

Creese, A. and Blackledge, A. (2010) Translanguaging in the bilingual classroom: A pedagogy for learning and teaching? *Modern Language Journal* 94 (1), 103–115.

Cummins, J. (1979) Linguistic interdependence and the educational development of bilingual children. *Review of Educational Research* 49 (2), 222–251.

Cummins, J. (2021) *Rethinking the Education of Multilingual Learners: A Critical Analysis of Theoretical Concepts*. Bristol: Multilingual Matters.

Custodio, B. (2010) *How to Design and Implement a Newcomer Program*. Boston, MA: Pearson.

Fry, R. (2005) The higher drop-out rate of foreign-born teens. Pew Research Center's Hispanic Trends Project. See www.pewhispanic.org/2005/11/01/the-higher-drop-out-rate-of-foreign-born-teens/ (accessed February 2023).

García, O. (2008) *Bilingual Education in the 21st Century: A Global Perspective*. Malden, MA: Wiley-Blackwell.

García, O. (2020a) The education of Latinx bilingual children in times of isolation: Unlearning and relearning. *MinneTESOL Journal* 36 (1). https://minnetesoljournal.org/journal-archive/mtj-2020-1/the-education-of-latinx-bilingual-children-in-times-of-isolation-unlearning-and-relearning/.

García, O. (2020b) Translanguaging and Latinx bilingual readers. *The Reading Teacher* 73 (5), 557–562.

García, O. and Baker, C. (eds) (2007) *Bilingual Education: An Introductory Reader*. Clevedon: Multilingual Matters.

García, O., Johnson, S.I. and Seltzer, K. (2016) *The Translanguaging Classroom: Leveraging Student Bilingualism for Learning*. Philadelphia, PA: Caslon Publishing.

García, O. and Kleifgen, J.A. (2020) Translanguaging and literacies. *Reading Research Quarterly* 55 (4), 553–571.

García, O. and Li, W. (2014) *Translanguaging: Language, Bilingualism and Education*. London: Palgrave Macmillan.

Gort, M. (2015) Transforming literacy learning and teaching through translanguaging and other typical practices associated with 'Doing being bilingual.' *International Multilingual Research Journal* 9 (1), 1–6.

Infante, P. and Licona, P.R. (2018) Translanguaging as pedagogy: Developing learner scientific discursive practices in a bilingual middle school science classroom. *International Journal of Bilingual Education and Bilingualism* 24 (7), 913–926.

Licona, P.R. and Kelly, G.J. (2020) Translanguaging in a middle school science classroom: Constructing scientific arguments in English and Spanish. *Cultural Studies of Science Education* 15 (2), 485–510.

Lin, A.M.Y. (2013) Toward paradigmatic change in TESOL methodologies: Building plurilingual pedagogies from the ground up. *TESOL Quarterly* 47 (3), 521–545.

Lin, A.M.Y. and He, P. (2017) Translanguaging as dynamic activity flows in CLIL classrooms. *Journal of Language, Identity and Education* 16 (4), 228–244.

MacSwan, J. (2017) A multilingual perspective on translanguaging. *American Educational Research Journal* 54 (1), 167–201.

Mazzaferro, G. (ed.) (2018) *Translanguaging as Everyday Practice*. Cham: Springer.

Moll, L.C., Amanti, C., Neff, D. and Gonzalez, N. (1992) Funds of knowledge for teaching: Using a qualitative approach to connect homes and classrooms. *Theory into Practice* 31 (2), 132–141.

Otheguy, R., García, O. and Reid, W. (2015) Clarifying translanguaging and deconstructing named languages: A perspective from linguistics. *Applied Linguistics Review* 6 (3), 281–307.

Otheguy, R., García, O. and Reid, W. (2019) A translanguaging view of the linguistic system of bilinguals. *Applied Linguistics Review* 10 (4), 625–651.

Pacheco, M.B. (2016) Translanguaging in the English-centric Classroom: A Communities of Practice Perspective. Unpublished PhD dissertation, Vanderbilt University.

Pierson, A.E., Clark, D.B. and Brady, C.E. (2021) Scientific modeling and translanguaging: A multilingual and multimodal approach to support science learning and engagement. *Science Education* 105 (4), 776–813.

Sayer, P. (2013) Translanguaging, TexMex, and bilingual pedagogy: Emergent bilinguals learning through the vernacular. *TESOL Quarterly* 47 (1), 63–88.

Seilstad, B. (2021) *Educating Adolescent Newcomers in the Superdiverse Midwest: Multilingual Students in English-centric Contexts*. Bristol: Multilingual Matters.

Seilstad, B., Braun, D., Kim, S. and Choi, M.-S. (2019) Bilingual biomes: Revising and redoing monolingual instructional practices for multilingual students (10th grade). In M.A. Stewart and H. Hansen-Thomas (eds) *Engaging Research: Transforming Practices for the High School* (pp. 111–126). Alexandria, VA: TESOL Press.

Short, D.J. and Boyson, B.A. (2004) *Creating Access: Language and Academic Programs for Secondary School Newcomers*. Washington, DC: Center for Applied Linguistics.

Short, D.J. and Fitzsimmons, S. (2007) *Double the Work: Challenges and Solutions to Acquiring Languae and Academic Literacy for Adolescent English Language Learners*. New York, NY: Carnegie Corporation of New York.

Tian, Z. and Shepard-Carey, L. (2020) (Re)imagining the future of translanguaging pedagogies in TESOL through teacher–researcher collaboration. *TESOL Quarterly* 54 (4), 1131–1143.

Vertovec, S. (2007) Super-diversity and its implications. *Ethnic and Racial Studies* 30 (6), 1024–1054.

Wright, W.E., Boun, S. and García, O. (2015) Introduction: Key concepts and issues in bilingual and multilingual education. In W.E. Wright, S. Boun and O. García (eds) *The Handbook of Bilingual and Multilingual Education* (pp. 1–16). Malden, MA: Wiley-Blackwell.

Yopp, H.K. and Stapleton, L. (2008) Conciencia fonémica en Español (Phonemic awareness in Spanish). *The Reading Teacher* 61 (5), 374–382.

12 Translanguaging and Scientific Modeling in an English-Dominant STEM Classroom

Ashlyn Pierson

Pedagogies that center translanguaging can be transformative for teaching and learning by inviting and valuing students' full linguistic repertoires for meaning making (García *et al.*, 2017; Makoni & Pennycook, 2007; Otheguy *et al.*, 2015). However, in the US, ideologies and policies that privilege English over other languages are pervasive (Flores & Rosa, 2015). As a result, most US students learn in English-dominant classrooms (Shin, 2017). In such contexts, students often resist invitations to translanguage that can be perceived as socially risky (Charalambous *et al.*, 2016; Cole *et al.*, 2016; Daniel *et al.*, 2019).

In response, researchers and educators have begun to explore strategies for inviting and leveraging translanguaging in English-dominant classrooms. To date, this work has primarily focused on elementary classrooms, students' linguistic resources and literacy learning (Daniel *et al.*, 2019; Machado & Hartman, 2019; Ranker, 2009; Rowe, 2020; Zapata & Laman, 2016), although some studies have focused on secondary classrooms and students' multimodal resources (Smith *et al.*, 2020). Still, less is known about designing effective teaching practices and learning activities for supporting translanguaging in English-dominant STEM (science, technology, engineering and mathematics) classrooms (Pierson *et al.*, 2021).

This chapter presents as a case study (Yin, 2014) the collaboration between a teacher (Ms S) and the author (Ashlyn) as we aimed to support translanguaging in her English-dominant sixth-grade STEM classroom. Our collaboration was grounded in a syncretic approach to design (Gutiérrez & Jurow, 2016) that puts into relation formal scientific practices and the everyday practices of nondominant students. Below, I review literature that informed our design. Then, I illustrate the co-stance, co-design and co-shifts (García *et al.*, 2017; Tian & Shepard-Carey, 2020) that characterized our collaboration, and I describe successes and challenges related to the process and products of our collaboration.

Syncretic Approach to Design: Integrating Translanguaging and Scientific Modeling

In this teacher–researcher collaboration, our goal was to connect students' everyday translanguaging practices with disciplinary STEM practices; therefore, we drew on Gutiérrez and Jurow's syncretic approach to design (2016). This approach aims to connect and reorganize everyday practices and institutional practices to create new forms of knowledge and expertise in service of equitable learning. As an example of a syncretic approach, Gutiérrez and Jurow describe the Migrant Student Leadership Institute (MSLI), a design intended to help students develop sociocritical literacies. One activity that supported this objective was creating syncretic textual forms that could be valued in formal settings and by MSLI students and their families (Gutiérrez, 2008; Gutiérrez & Jurow, 2016) – for example, integrating the *testimonio*, a form of historicizing narrative, with expository essays and extended definitions.

In the context of STEM education, researchers have found that a syncretic approach to design can help students see their everyday practices as valuable for disciplinary learning while helping them access and transform disciplinary practices to explore personally meaningful lines of inquiry (e.g. Barajas-López & Bang, 2018; Suárez *et al.*, 2018; Radke *et al.*, 2020; Vogel *et al.*, 2019). Building on this work, we aimed to design learning activities that connected everyday translanguaging practices and scientific modeling practices. Scientific modeling is the practice of creating, using or revising multimodal models (conceptual or material representations) to reason or express ideas about a referent phenomenon (e.g. Latour, 1999; National Research Council [NRC], 2012; Nersessian, 2008). We chose to focus on translanguaging and modeling to capitalize on the multimodality inherent in both of these practices (Pierson & Grapin, 2021).

Theories of social semiotics have characterized modes as each having unique affordances for learning (Bezemer & Kress, 2008; Goodwin, 2018; Lemke, 2000; Ranker, 2009). Although most closely associated with linguistic modes, translanguaging also involves meaning making with nonlinguistic modes, such as drawing, gesture and action (Blackledge & Creese, 2017; Hua *et al.*, 2019; Li, 2018; Otheguy *et al.*, 2015; Sherris & Adami, 2019). Taken together, theories of translanguaging and social semiotics suggest that helping students leverage and build upon their full semiotic repertoires can expand the range of resources available to students for meaning making (Sherris & Adami, 2019). For example, in an English Language Arts classroom, Pacheco, Smith and colleagues (Pacheco & Smith, 2015; Smith *et al.*, 2017) found that multilingual and multimodal composing was generative for students, who iteratively used different modes (talk, text, visuals) to explore themes of heroism. In the process, students became increasingly comfortable with using and sharing their heritage languages in this classroom.

In STEM classrooms, researchers are beginning to explore designs for learning that leverage translanguaging and emphasize multimodality (Radke *et al.*, 2020; Vogel *et al.*, 2019). For instance, Radke and colleagues (2020) describe students in a bilingual classroom using a multilingual and multimodal programming environment to make sense of the effects of Hurricane María on Puerto Rico. The students leveraged their semiotic, cultural and experiential repertoires to explore stories of migration through quantitative statistical modeling. Building on this work, in this chapter I focus on a teacher–researcher collaboration that aimed to integrate translanguaging and scientific modeling to support bilingual students[1] and their monolingual peers in an English-dominant classroom.

Research Context: Translanguaging in an English-Dominant STEM Classroom

This chapter describes the collaboration between the author, Ashlyn (at the time, a PhD student focusing on science education), and Ms S (a STEM teacher with over 25 years of experience). This collaboration took place in the context of the larger SAIL + CTM project (NSF DRL#1742138). Our role was to collaboratively design, refine and a teach iterations of a nine-week ecology unit (designed to support standards from the state and standards from the Next Generation Science Standards) in order to develop and test principles that could be applied in the more formalized SAIL + CTM curriculum. The pilot implementation of this unit took place during the last quarter of 2018 (see Pierson *et al.*, 2020). This chapter focuses on data from the third quarter of 2019 because, in this quarter, we focused on connecting translanguaging and scientific modeling.

Participants: Ms S's sixth-grade STEM classroom

Ms S's sixth-grade STEM class participated in this iteration of the design (20 students). I consider this context English-dominant because state laws mandate 'English-only' instruction, and teachers and students at this school spoke almost exclusively using English. Still, 8% of the students at this school are classified as English learners (ELs). In this district, students are selected for EL screening based on a Home Language Survey, and they are classified as ELs based on the Individual Proficiency Test (IPT) and English Language Development Assessment (ELDA), which are used with state content assessments to monitor progress annually. Based on these assessments, the district determines whether a student's English proficiency 'does not enable them to succeed in school.' According to the district website, students are typically classified as ELs for four to seven years.

In Ms S's classroom, five students were classified as ELs, all of whom identified as bilingual speakers of Spanish and English (Carlos, Jennifer, Jesús, Luis and Luna). All five students regularly used English in class, and four of the five (Carlos, Jennifer, Jesús and Luis) regularly used Spanish during class when speaking to bilingual peers. The students expressed different levels of confidence about writing in English and Spanish. Two of the students (Carlos and Luna) said they did not like writing in either language. The other three students (Jennifer, Jesús and Luis) wrote in English and Spanish with varying degrees of fluidity.

Design: Nine-week ecology unit

Ms S's students participated in a nine-week ecology unit. The unit foregrounded modeling, a practice that invites students to create, use and refine multimodal representations to reason and express ideas about phenomena (Lehrer & Schauble, 2015). Throughout the unit, students created diagrammatic, physical, computational and embodied models that represented ecosystems (Figure 12.1). We chose these model types to offer students a wide range of modes for meaning making (including static and dynamic images, text, code, symbols, physical structures, actions and gestures) and to leverage the unique learning opportunities that each model

Figure 12.1 Examples of student models used during the unit: (a) diagrammatic model – ecosystem plan, (b) physical model – ecosystem jar, (c) diagrammatic model – food web, (d) embodied model – guppy ecosystem, (e) computational model – guppy ecosystem.

type afforded (see Pierson *et al.*, 2020 for specific affordances of computational modeling activities; Pierson & Brady, 2020 for specific affordances of embodied modeling activities). Within each model type, students chose the modes and languages they used.

Across all design iterations, the unit is framed by two challenges: students design a biosphere, a closed-system physical model (Figure 12.1(b)) that includes plants, snails and guppies (a typical pet fish in the US), and they program a computational model[2] (Figure 12.1(e)) that represents a larger ecosystem of plants, snails, guppies and guppies' competitors and predators. Throughout the unit, the students gather information and re-represent the guppies' environment with increasing complexity. In this iteration of the design, invitations to engage in translanguaging during modeling were embedded within modeling activities.

Data sources and analysis

Data sources include field notes (from planning and instruction), design products (including unit and lesson plans), video recordings of instruction, all student work (including photos and videos of students' models) and videos of students participating in class discussions and modeling activities. These sources allowed me to trace the *process* of teacher–researcher collaboration, the *products* of this collaboration, and students' *participation* in the designed learning activities. I analyzed these data sources as an exploratory case study (Yin, 2014) of a teacher–researcher collaboration that demonstrates one pathway for designing pedagogies that invite and support translanguaging in an English-dominant STEM classroom.

In my analysis, I narrowed my focus to lessons that explicitly invited and leveraged translanguaging during modeling activities. I began by identifying instances of co-stance, co-design and co-shifts (Tian & Shepard-Carey, 2020) in my field notes, which described collaborative planning and reflection for translanguaging and modeling. I used constant-comparative analysis (Strauss & Corbin, 1990) to connect the collaborative process represented in my field notes to existing research about teacher–researcher collaboration that can support the development of translanguaging pedagogies. Then, I used lesson plans and their enactment in classroom videos to describe the products of this co-design process, and I used student-level data (including classroom videos and student artifacts) to understand how students participated in the designed activities.

To analyze these data, I created rough content logs and multimodal transcripts (Erickson & Schultz, 1997; Gee, 2014; Norris & Jones, 2005) as a basis for turn-by-turn analysis of classroom interactions and artifacts (Hall, 1996; Pierson *et al.*, 2020). I used these content logs and transcripts to inductively identify themes in the data (Charmaz, 2006), focusing specifically on successes and challenges in terms of supporting translanguaging with both bilingual and monolingual students in this classroom context.

Table 12.1 Example transcript and analysis

Multimodal transcript		Mediated action	Themes
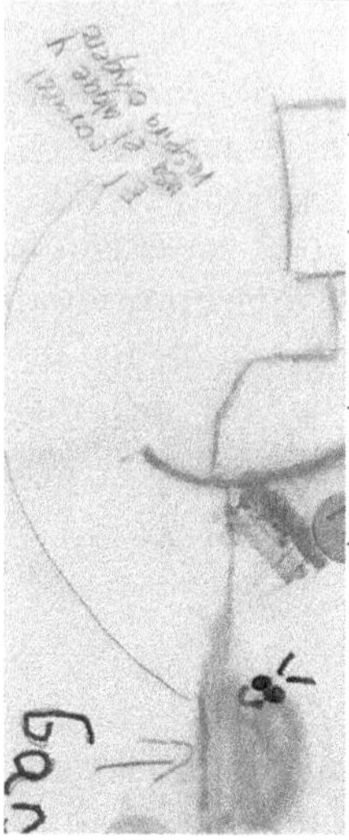	Sean: Why did you say algae?	Sean asks Luis about what he wrote on the group's model.	**Translanguaging**: Fluid use of blended English and Spanish in multilingual model. **Challenge and defense**: Challenge use of Spanish (Sean), defense of Spanish (Luis, Carlos) Challenge request for explanation (Luis, Carlos), defense of question (Sean)
	Luis: 'cause.	Luis avoids offering Sean an explanation.	
	Sean: You're pointing to a snail.	Sean clarifies his question (why write algae when pointing to a snail?)	
	Carlos: Yeah.	Carlos affirms Luis (agrees the model makes sense)	
	Luis: The snail eats the algae, right? See that's what I put (pointing to 'El caracol usa el algae y respira oxygeno' – The snail uses algae and breathes oxygen).	Luis explains the connection between the snail and the algae, translating Spanish text.	
	Sean: Well, I can't read Spanish	Sean defends his question and raises a problem with including Spanish text.	

In Table 12.1 I present an example of my analytic approach. This table is organized into columns around interactions between students and the model they were creating. In the left column, we see the students' model and interactions. In the middle column, there is an analysis of each student's goal-oriented action (Norris & Jones, 2005; Pierson *et al.*, 2020). These actions are grouped thematically into codes in the third column (Charmaz *et al.*, 2006) – in this example, students (1) engaged in translanguaging and (2) challenged or defended their participation in multilingual modeling. These themes enabled me to evaluate successes and challenges of our design processes and products.

Process: Co-Stance, Co-Design and Co-Shifts

In this section, I describe our process of teacher–researcher collaboration, focusing on co-stance, co-design and co-shifts (Tian & Shepard-Carey, 2020). Although Ms S and I are both white, monolingual English speakers, we were focused on supporting multilingual and multimodal STEM learning based on our experiences as teachers in linguistically diverse classrooms. This goal emerged from discussions in which we built a *co-stance* by negotiating 'philosophical, ideological, or belief systems regarding bilingualism and translanguaging to better inform [our] pedagogical framework' (Tian & Shepard-Carey, 2020: 1133). Our work together had previously focused on multimodal modeling, and in this iteration of the design we were interested in better supporting students' use of multilingual resources to create a more equitable learning environment for bilingual students, including students classified as ELs.

This goal developed in relation to students' participation in previous implementations of our designed unit. We noticed that, during class, bilingual students occasionally used languages other than English when they were in small groups with students who shared their linguistic backgrounds; however, these resources were not shared publicly (in class discussions or in the artifacts that the students created). We were concerned that our classroom environment was not empowering bilingual students to fully leverage their linguistic repertoires, limiting their opportunities for learning. Therefore, I suggested focusing on translanguaging to explicitly challenge the monoglossic norms in the classroom and to legitimize and value students' multilingual resources.

Our process of *co-design* involved iterative co-planning, co-teaching and reflection. Although each of these tasks was collaborative, Ms S and I were involved in them in different ways; I led planning, and Ms S led instruction. Before each quarter, I drafted and refined the lesson plans that we used during the nine-week unit (primarily based on research about science education and modeling, and, in this iteration specifically, research about translanguaging), and Ms S offered feedback and revised the plans (primarily based on knowledge of her students and her experience teaching in this context). In this way, we each contributed unique perspectives and expertise to the co-planning phase.

This iteration of the unit was refined based on research about inviting and leveraging translanguaging in English-dominant classrooms, although to date most of this work has primarily focused on literacy learning and has taken place in elementary classrooms (Daniel *et al.*, 2019; Machado & Hartman, 2019; Ranker, 2009; Rowe, 2020; Zapata & Laman, 2016). These studies have identified several promising strategies for supporting multilingual and multimodal composing, including: explicitly valuing students' language and cultures (García & Kleifgen, 2019; Rowe, 2018), modeling multilingual composing (Machado & Hartman, 2019), introducing multilingual mentor texts (Zapata & Laman, 2016), leveraging digital tools to mediate heritage-language use (Rowe, 2020; Rowe & Miller, 2016; Vogel *et al.*, 2018) and emphasizing disciplinary reasons for translanguaging (Canagarajah, 2013; García & Kleyn, 2016).

We adapted several of these approaches for Ms S's sixth-grade STEM classroom. Specifically, we focused on inviting translanguaging by (1) demonstrating that we valued students' multilingual and multimodal resources, (2) helping students identify disciplinary reasons for using multiple languages and modes in modeling and (3) creating opportunities for multimodal translanguaging during modeling activities. We recognized that students were already intuitively drawing on available semiotic resources (including embodied actions and gestures) for meaning making and expression, especially to facilitate fluid discourse (e.g. García, 2009; Williams, 2020). Therefore, our objective was not to teach students *about* translanguaging or to teach them how to *'do'* translanguaging; instead, we aimed to support students in using a wider range of linguistic and nonlinguistic resources in service of sensemaking during modeling activities.

After we created and refined lesson plans, Ms S translated the lesson plans into Google slides that we used to structure learning activities. During instruction, Ms S led most whole-class activities, occasionally asking for my input or clarification. We both worked with students during small-group and individual activities. After each class session, we reflected on successes and challenges within that day's lesson, and we discussed possible responses (for the next class session) and revisions (for the next iteration of the unit design), which I recorded in field notes. This process enabled me and Ms S to both 'grapple with the "messiness" of the classroom and to enrich [our] understanding of translanguaging theory and pedagogy' (Tian & Shepard-Carey, 2020: 1134) in a generative way.

This 'messiness' created a need for *co-shifts* in instruction; during class, Ms S and I regularly checked in with each other to see if we needed to change course during the lesson, both in order to support science learning and to support translanguaging. We made adjustments to our teaching practices and our learning activities throughout the unit in response to students' participation in our design. For example, we noticed that some of the bilingual students in the classroom felt uncomfortable writing using Spanish, either because they were unsure about spelling, they were not confident that the words they chose were 'correct' or they did not know a Spanish word for an English word they had learned in class (e.g. 'algae,' 'food chain'). In response, we decided in the moment to allow students to use Google Translate to mediate heritage language use during modeling (Rowe, 2020; Vogel *et al.*, 2018).

This instructional decision supported translanguaging in some ways; it increased bilingual students' confidence in their use of Spanish, and it opened the door for bilingual and monolingual students to explore new linguistic resources. However, it also created challenges. Initially, the experience made some students less confident in their own linguistic resources as they began to rely on Google to 'check' their translations (see Pierson *et al.*, 2021). However, over time, students' use of this tool increased their confidence in their own translations; they noticed that in some cases, Google provided translations that they recognized as incorrect for their context (for example, Google translated 'sun' to 'dom,' an abbreviation for 'Sunday,' rather than 'sol'). These experiences helped students see themselves as experts in their own linguistic resources rather than privileging Google's translations. As demonstrated in this example, our instructional shifts were not always purely positive or negative; as a result, each shift involved attending to students' responses and continued instructional adjustments. Below, I describe the products that resulted from our process of co-design and co-shifts.

Products: Syncretic Translanguaging and Modeling

This section describes the products of the teacher–researcher collaboration described above: lessons designed to invite and support translanguaging in STEM. To provide a detailed description of how these lessons were enacted in instruction, I focus on how Ms S initially introduced and invited translanguaging, though we continued to leverage these teaching practices throughout the unit.

Ms S began by helping students identify disciplinary reasons for translanguaging during the second week of the unit. To do so, she framed multiple modes as 'languages' in STEM, each with a unique disciplinary purpose. She opened the discussion by telling students that they were going to talk about language, and she asked students 'why we would talk about language in science class.' When students' responses initially focused on vocabulary, Ms S prompted students to broaden their perspective of language to include nonlinguistic modes by considering 'ways that ideas are expressed' in some of the models they had previously used in class. Students then identified reasons for using specific modes in their models. For example, referencing the students' computational models (Figure 12.1(e)), Ms S asked:

Ms S: What do you think this ((points to 3D renderer)) is representing?
Jennifer: Um the guppies and the plants and how they interact.
Ms S: Yes, how they interact? Very good...but how is this [3D renderer]- how does this kind of talk to your brain differently than this [graph]? What do you think Jesús?
Jesús: Because um like the green thing [3D renderer] um like you have to look, and like, you have to actually count it.
Ms S: ((laughs)) Right, right.
Jesús: You don't want to count all of that moving fish.

In this interaction, Jennifer and Jesús identified complementary affordances of the computational model's three-dimensional (3D) renderer and graph. By highlighting disciplinary reasons for using these and other modes (computer code, graphs, buttons and sliders), Ms S positioned diverse nonlinguistic modes ('languages') as valuable for meaning making in STEM. These discussions set the stage for Ms S to then invite students to share their diverse linguistic resources, including resources from languages other than English.

After discussing nonlinguistic modes, Ms S shifted to focusing on 'named' languages spoken by students in the class (English, Spanish and

Korean), demonstrating interest in students' linguistic resources and helping students identify disciplinary reasons for using multiple languages in STEM. To legitimize the use of languages other than English in this context, Ms S showed a video about 'untranslatable' words that highlighted unique ideas expressed across many different languages. Ms S also positioned herself as a language learner, prioritizing contributions from bilingual students and asking students to repeat and help her pronounce words that were new to her. This instructional approach created space for students to share a wider range of linguistic resources beyond academic English.

A limitation of this approach was that, as monolingual instructors, we were not always able to help bilingual students express the complexity and nuance of their contributions to this discussion. For example, Ms S asked bilingual students to share words that were 'that are hard to tell, like, someone in English what it means.' Carlos shared two words that have context-dependent meanings in Spanish:

Carlos: So part of my family is from here, and part of my family is – so my Dad and all my other uncles are from Honduras and over there we speak a little bit different from them because they say 'pajilla,' like, for different things. Like 'pajilla' is for um for drinking [a drinking straw]. While we say – well, I don't really know what we really say because I don't speak that one [form of Spanish] very much anymore.

Ms S: Do you know of any words that are hard to - like do you know any words that are hard to, so you speak Spanish –

Carlos: 'Maje.'

Ms S: 'Maje?' What does it mean?

Carlos: Um, 'brother' ((laughs))

Ms S: Okay but can you think of a word that really um it would be hard for you to describe to me what you're talking about, but I'm going to give you some examples in a minute.

In the discussion above, Carlos explained that the word for 'drinking straw' in Spanish is context-dependent. With this example, Carlos foregrounded the linguistic diversity *within* Spanish and *across* Spanish and English. Then, he shared another word – 'maje,' which means 'brother.' 'Maje' is a nuanced term, because it has a positive connotation for close friends and a negative connotation in other cases. Because we were unfamiliar with the word 'maje,' Ms S responded by asking Carlos to 'think of a word that … would be hard for you to describe to me what you're talking about,' rather than validating and helping Carlos articulate the complexity of the word 'maje.' This example illustrates a challenge of supporting translanguaging, especially for educators who do not share their students' linguistic backgrounds.

In addition to asking bilingual students to share words that are 'hard … to describe,' Ms S encouraged bilingual and monolingual students to make connections to words from the video that she showed students about 'untranslatable' terms. This encouraged all students to position themselves as language learners, and it emphasized a disciplinary reason for translanguaging: expressing complex and nuanced ideas. To connect these examples to STEM learning, Ms S also asked students to consider the affordances of various linguistic and nonlinguistic resources in their models.

In the next activity, Ms S offered students opportunities for translanguaging as they created their biosphere plans (Figure 12.1(a)). This task required students to create and present a model that represented how they could support life for at least one guppy within a closed system (a jar with a lid; Figure 12.1(b)). Ms S invited students to use multiple linguistic and nonlinguistic 'languages' in this activity. She said, 'the next thing we're going to do is to represent our biospheres, and ... you can be creative with how you show your ideas.' Directions for the assignment read: 'We need to see (1) how everything will get energy, and (2) how every living thing will get what it needs to breathe, oxygen or carbon dioxide. You can choose different languages or representations to show your ideas.' Below, I describe how students took up this invitation to participate in syncretic translanguaging and modeling.

Participation: Student Interactions and Artifacts

In this section, I focus on students' initial participation in translanguaging and modeling as they created their biosphere plans. Specifically, I compare two student groups, each of which included two bilingual students classified as ELs and one monolingual student. In both groups, inviting translanguaging created space for students to more fully leverage their semiotic repertoires; however, this shift may have also limited students' opportunities for learning and participation in other ways.

Group 1: Flexible and fluid translanguaging

Group 1 included two bilingual students (Carlos and Luis) and one monolingual student (Sean). In their biosphere plan, they represented ideas using a variety of linguistic and nonlinguistic modes (Figure 12.2). Luis added most of the text to the model, initially writing primarily in Spanish and using English for words that he had learned in class. For example, he wrote, 'El pes agara su comida de la planta y el *algae* y respira oxygeno' (the fish gets its food from the plant and the *algae* and breathes oxygen). Luis's sentence blends English and Spanish words, and it also blends Spanish and English spellings[3] (e.g. 'oxygeno' rather than 'oxygen' or 'oxígeno'), demonstrating his expressive fluidity across Spanish and English. Sean contributed English text and drawings, and Carlos focused on nonlinguistic models; he added drawings to represent components of

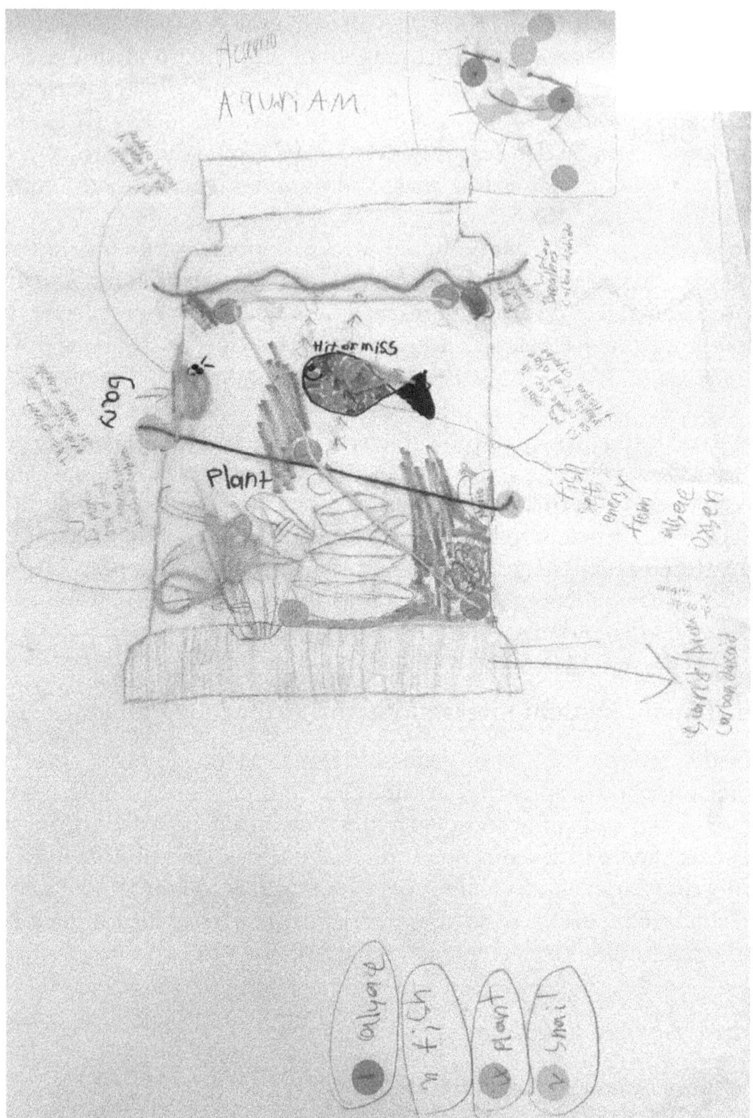

Figure 12.2 Group 1 (Luis, Carlos, Sean) – biosphere plan

their biosphere, and he added string, sticker dots and a numbering system to organize these components.

By using his full linguistic repertoire, Luis was able to represent more nuanced ideas than if he were using English alone. Luis translated his original text to English, but his hybrid text often expressed more nuanced understandings of science content than his English translations. For example, in the statement above, Luis explained how the fish use plants and algae (as food) and oxygen (to breathe). His English translation, 'fish get energy from algae oxygen,' did not distinguish between how fish use algae and how they use oxygen. This example shows that fluidly blending Spanish and English helped Luis express more nuanced understandings about ecosystems.

In addition to English and Spanish, the students used nonlinguistic modes for modeling. For example, when describing their biosphere plan during a gallery walk on Day 11, Luis said:

> I used English, Spanish, and pictures for languages. Then I have a key over here that uses stickers, and that's for the algae .... Then you have the fish, and you have the yellow stickers and then the fish is right here. And then, we just used different languages to describe what they use for energy, what they breathe in.

With this description, Luis identified multiple modes, including languages (English and Spanish), pictures and stickers. Each of these modes offered students a new perspective of the biosphere that was generative for their design; for instance, drawing the plant in the jar raised questions about the size of the plant and the space in the jar. These questions led the group to consider the amount of space a guppy would need. When presenting their plan, Carlos explained that space could impact guppies' survival:

> When we searched it up it said that [guppies] could live two to three years, and then if we would have put in two guppies they would both probably die because it said for one guppy to live calmly, it would take one liter, and this isn't enough.

This example shows that nonlinguistic modes (in this case, drawing) can enable students to participated in STEM activities in new ways, and they can also help students take on new perspectives that support conceptual learning (in this case, considering how space can impact animals' survival).

Despite these positive outcomes, we also identified challenges related to our designed learning activities in this group's interactions. Sean seemed at times to feel excluded when Luis and Carlos used Spanish:

Sean: Why did you say algae?
Luis: 'cause.
Sean: You're pointing to a snail.
Carlos: Yeah.
Luis: The snail eats the algae, right? See that's what I put. ((pointing to 'El caracol usa el algae y respira oxygeno' – The snail uses algae and breathes oxygen)).
Sean: Well, I can't read Spanish!

In this interaction, Sean struggled to understand Luis' multilingual text. In response, he attempted to police the language in his group several times; for example, saying 'Luis, just do it in English, we don't have to do Spanish.' Sean's actions may have been well-intentioned – he was likely trying to understand and engage with Luis and Carlos. Still, these actions reflect and reproduce larger societal discourses, including monoglossic ideologies that privilege English.

This interaction presented an opportunity for a co-shift in instruction; Ms S and I could have responded explicitly to language policing within this small group, or we could have facilitated a whole class discussion that critically examined language ideologies and their impact (in this classroom and in other contexts). However, during class, we did not notice these language-policing interactions. Although we were both focused on trying to see, hear and support students' translanguaging, our positionalities and experiences may have made it more difficult for us to recognize and respond to these linguistic microaggressions in the moment.

This group's participation in translanguaging and modeling reveals successes and challenges of our design. On one hand, translanguaging and modeling created new opportunities for students to participate in STEM learning by leveraging multilingual and multimodal resources. Furthermore, shifting between modes offered students generative perspectives of ecosystems phenomena, supporting conceptual learning. On the other hand, monoglossic ideologies threatened students' use of multilingual resources, even in the context of a design intended to value and encourage translanguaging. Further research is needed to understand how to effectively surface and address these ideologies in English-dominant classrooms to create more inclusive STEM learning environments.

Group 2: Translation to existing and invented terms

Group 2 also included two bilingual students (Jennifer and Jesús) and one monolingual student (Becca). However, their approach to translanguaging in and modeling was different from the flexible strategy employed by the students in Group 1; their approach is instead more consistent with *translation* (García *et al.*, 2020), likely influenced by the emphasis on 'untranslatable' words in the introduction to translanguaging described above. Again, this group's participation in translanguaging and modeling illustrates successes and challenges of our design.

When Group 2 began working on their biosphere plan, they chose to assign each student to a language (Becca chose English, Jennifer chose Spanish, Jesús chose computer code – see Figure 12.3). First, they drew components of their biosphere, and they labeled each drawing three times – each student added a label in their language. Although this activity could be seen as rote translation, Jennifer still saw labeling drawings in Spanish as an opportunity to enrich and add nuance to her understanding of science content, because thinking about Spanish translations helped her see phenomena from new perspectives:

> In English, it's like 'food chain' and you know, like, it has to be connected to something because of the word 'chain,' and in Spanish you have to think of, like, multiple words to describe the food chain because, like, in Spanish there's not really a word to describe food chain, so you have to, like – a sentence will describe a food chain, not just like saying two words.

Although Jennifer was not familiar with a Spanish term for 'food chain,' thinking about how to described this idea in Spanish offered Jennifer a new perspective of 'food chain' – not only as a term, but also as a concept. She explained that 'chain' connotes connection between organisms, which she noticed as she thought about 'multiple words to describe the food chain' in Spanish.

While Jennifer worked on English–Spanish translations, Becca and Jesús invented terms that mimicked computer code. Becca and Jesús

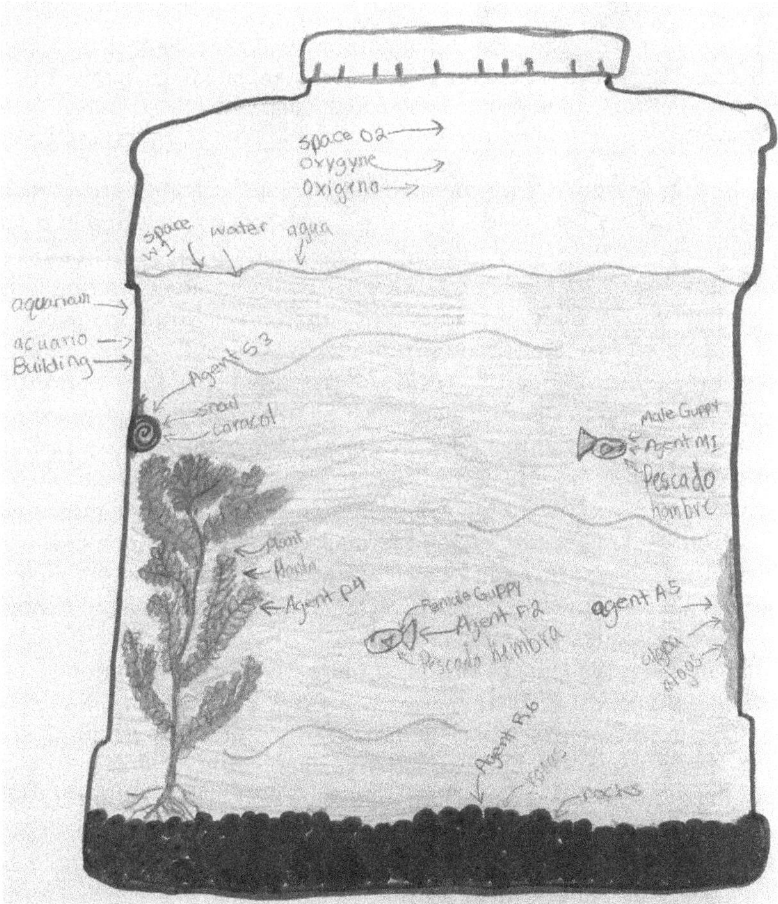

Figure 12.3 Group 2 (Jennifer, Jesús, Becca) – biosphere plan

began systematically naming biosphere components in their invented code-language by classify objects into categories and numbering item within a category. They used 'agent' to describe visible discrete objects within biosphere, like guppies and water. The word 'Agent' was followed by a letter that described a salient attribute of the agent – either the type of object ('S' for snail) or a more specific attribute ('F' for female guppy and 'M' for male guppy):

Becca: This would be AgentF ((points to the female guppy)), AgentS ((points to the snail)).
Jesús: AgentS, water is AgentW.
Becca: Yeah!

A few components were not considered agents – the jar ('building') and the types of space within the jar ('spaceO2'):

Jesús: I don't know what this aquarium would be called.
Becca: Is there like a building? Are there, like, buildings in there?
Jesús: Watch… I'm just going to call it aquarium.
Becca: No, call it building. You tell me and I'll write it down, ok?

Modeling the biosphere with code-language created categories that would not otherwise have been evident. Jennifer, who was not involved in creating the code-language, noted this affordance both in her presentation of the biosphere plan and in her interview two months later, describing the code-language as 'specifying things more' than English and Spanish.

In addition, broadly framing computer code as a language allowed Becca, a monolingual English speaker, to participate in a form of translation. Whereas Becca's engagement with Spanish was limited to asking Jennifer and Jesús about the terms they chose (and in several cases, asking them to help her pronounce new words), creating a 'code-language' offered Becca a new perspective of English terms and the ideas they represented, similar to how Jennifer understood terms like 'food chain' in a new way as described above. In addition, creating code-language destabilizing English-only practices by offering Becca and Jesús a new way to express ideas beyond 'academic' English.

In summary, students in this group interpreted the invitation to use multiple 'languages' in their model as a translation activity, and they translated terms across named languages (Spanish and English) and invented languages (computer code-language). While we did not intend for students to participate in translanguaging and modeling in this way (we imagined students taking up the flexible and fluid approach described in Group 1), we recognized that this approach could also support new forms of learning. Specifically, translating to existing and invented terms offered students new perspectives of terms that helped them deepen their understanding of the underlying concepts and ideas that these terms represented. Even so, we do not believe that pedagogies that focus exclusively on translation could fully realize the potential of syncretic translanguaging and modeling. Translating to *named* languages could inadvertently emphasize 'correct' translations, decreasing bilingual students' confidence in their linguistic resources, and translating to *invented* languages may not disrupt participant structures in which monolingual students take on leadership roles. Further research is needed to understand how to integrate opportunities for translation into STEM classrooms in a way that supports equitable learning opportunities for bilingual and monolingual students.

Reflecting on Successes, Challenges and Implications

The findings above show that valuing and legitimizing translanguaging in an English-dominant STEM classroom can create new learning opportunities for bilingual students and their monolingual peers. These learning opportunities were made possible by the process of teacher–researcher collaboration (Tian & Shepard-Cary, 2020). By building a *co-stance* that prioritized translanguaging, Ms S and I were able to center multimodal translanguaging in our lesson plans and our instruction. Through the process of *co-design*, we were able to build upon research about inviting and supporting multilingual and multimodal practices (e.g. Rowe, 2018; Smith *et al*., 2020) while adapting these approaches based on Ms S's knowledge of her students and her context. Openness to *co-shifts* enabled us to respond in the moment to the ways that students were participating in our unit, for example, by allowing students to use digital tools to mediate heritage language use. In addition, this study contributes to the field of science education by illustrating one approach to supporting multilingual learners through connecting translanguaging practices with the scientific practice of modeling.

As a result of this collaborative process, Ms S and I designed learning activities that invited and supported translanguaging in her English-dominant STEM classroom. Ms S worked intentionally to help students identify disciplinary reasons for translanguaging (Canagarajah, 2013; García & Kleyn, 2016) during modeling activities, and she demonstrated that she valued students' multilingual and multimodal resources (García & Kleifgen, 2019; Rowe, 2018) by inviting multilingual contributions and by positioning herself as a language learner. As a result, when offered opportunities to engage in translanguaging and modeling, students leveraged a wider range of semiotic resources than in previous iterations of our design, integrating English, Spanish, invented terms, and a variety of multimodal representations in service of sensemaking. These findings indicate that translanguaging must be explicitly encouraged to be supported in English-dominant classrooms, and they suggest that future studies should explore ways to invite and support translanguaging.

In addition, analyzing students' participation in our unit surfaced challenges that should be addressed in future research. Specifically, our design did not explicitly address monoglossic ideologies with students (Flores & Rosa, 2015); as a result, students at times drew on these ideologies as resources to interpret classroom interactions (Philip *et al.*, 2018). For example, in Group 1, Sean challenged Luis and Carlos's use of Spanish, and in Group 2, a focus on 'correct' translations and invented terms may have initially undermined bilingual students' confidence in their own linguistic resources. Although examples like these were rare in my data, such interactions could discourage bilingual students from leveraging their full linguistic repertoires in English-dominant spaces. Further research is needed to explore how such resistance to translanguaging could be prevented or addressed in English-dominant classrooms.

Moreover, through my analysis, I became aware of microaggressions (like those described above) that went unnoticed during class. These data speak to the broader challenge of addressing pervasive monoglossic ideologies (Flores & Rosa, 2015; Gutiérrez *et al.*, 1995), not only with students, but also with educators – another important area for future research. They emphasize the importance of work that helps educators recognize and respond to systems of oppression in their classrooms, as well as the need to recruit, prepare and support a population of teachers that reflects the diversity of the US student population.

These findings reinforce that there is still much to learn about designing to support translanguaging in English-dominant STEM classrooms. Still, they also illustrate the promise of teacher–researcher collaboration for adapting and developing translanguaging pedagogies. This critical and reflective approach to design is needed to realize the potential of translanguaging pedagogies across contexts, including in English-dominant classrooms.

Notes

(1) From the perspective of translanguaging theory, 'bilingual' and 'monolingual' are socially constructed concepts; there is no threshold of linguistic knowledge that distinguishes between monolingual, bilingual, and multilingual students. Still, these categories are important in discussions of social identity and sociolinguistic behavior (Otheguy *et al.*, 2015). In this study, I use 'bilingual' to describe students who identified as bilingual and used more than one language (in or out of school), including students who were classified as English learners. I use bilingual rather than multilingual because I did not observe any students drawing upon more than two languages in the data. I use 'monolingual' for students who did not identify as bilingual and used English almost exclusively for speaking and writing. I recognize that 'monolingual' students can leverage other multimodal resources, like gesture and drawing, and sometimes use resources from languages other than English.

(2) In this study, we used an agent-based modeling environment, StarLogo Nova (SLN), to help students explore phenomena related to ecosystems. Students created programs that represented the micro-level actions and interactions of system components (the

'agents' – e.g. guppies, algae). Then, they instantiated large numbers of these agents, using the model to simulate macro-level aggregate behaviors (e.g. population dynamics). SLN combines a block-based programming environment with an agent-based simulation engine and a 3D renderer that depicts agent–agent interactions in a virtual world optimized for modeling complex systems. SLN also includes the ability to use tables and graphs to visualize data.

(3) In these data, I preserve students' spelling and grammar in written text, both in English and in Spanish.

References

Barajas-López, F. and Bang, M. (2018) Indigenous making and sharing: Claywork in an Indigenous STEAM program. *Equity & Excellence in Education* 51 (1), 7–20.

Bezemer, J. and Kress, G. (2008) Writing in multimodal texts: A social semiotic account of designs for learning. *Written Communication* 25 (2), 166–195.

Blackledge, A. and Creese, A. (2017) Translanguaging and the body. *International Journal of Multilingualism* 1–19.

Canagarajah, A.S. (2013) *Literacy as Translingual Practice: Between Communities and Classrooms*. New York, NY: Routledge.

Charalambous, P., Charalambous, C. and Zembylas, M. (2016) Troubling translanguaging: language ideologies, superdiversity and interethnic conflict. *Applied Linguistics Review* 7 (3), 327–352.

Charmaz, K. (2006) *Constructing Grounded Theory: A Practical Guide Through Qualitative Analysis*. Thousand Oaks, CA: Sage.

Cole, M.W., David, S.S. and Jiménez, R.T. (2016) Collaborative translation: Negotiating student investment in culturally responsive pedagogy. *Language Arts* 93 (6), 430.

Daniel, S.M., Jiménez, R.T., Pray, L. and Pacheco, M.B. (2019) Scaffolding to make translanguaging a classroom norm. *TESOL Journal* 10 (1), e00361. https://doi.org/10.1002/tesj.361

Erickson, F. and Schultz, J. (1997) When is a context? Some issues and methods in the analysis of social competence. In M. Cole, Y. Engeström and O. Vasquez (eds) *Mind, Culture, and Activity: Seminal Papers from the Laboratory of Comparative Human Cognition* (pp. 22–31). Cambridge: Cambridge University Press.

Flores, N. and Rosa, J. (2015) Undoing appropriateness: Raciolinguistic ideologies and language diversity in education. *Harvard Educational Review* 85 (2), 149–171.

García, O. (2009) Emergent Bilinguals and TESOL: What's in a name? *TESOL Quarterly* 43 (2), 322–326.

García, O., Aponte, G.Y. and Le, K. (2020) Primary bilingual classrooms: Translations and translanguaging. In S. Laviosa and M. González Davies (eds) *The Routledge Handbook of Translation and Education* (pp. 81–94). New York: Routledge.

García, O., Johnson, S. and Seltzer, K. (2017) *The Translanguaging Classroom: Leveraging Student Bilingualism for Learning*. Philadelphia: Caslon.

García, O. and Kleifgen, J.A. (2019) Translanguaging and literacies. *Reading Research Quarterly* (55) 4, 553–571.

García O. and Kleyn, T. (2016) Chapter 1: Translanguaging theory in education. In O. García and T. Kleyn (eds) *Translanguaging with Multilingual Students: Learning from Classroom Moments* (pp. 9–33). New York, NY: Routledge.

Gee, J.P. (2014) *An Introduction to Discourse Analysis: Theory and Method* (4th edn). New York, NY: Routledge.

Goodwin, C. (2018) *Co-Operative Action (Learning in Doing: Social, Cognitive, and Computational Perspectives)*. Cambridge: Cambridge University Press.

Gutiérrez, K.D. (2008) Developing a sociocritical literacy in the third space. *Reading Research Quarterly* 43 (2), 148–164.

Gutiérrez, K.D. and Jurow, A.S. (2016) Social design experiments: Toward equity by design. *Journal of the Learning Sciences* 25 (4), 565–598.

Gutiérrez, K., Rymes, B. and Larson, J. (1995) Script, counterscript, and underlife in the classroom: James Brown versus Brown v. Board of Education. *Harvard Educational Review* 65 (3), 445–472.

Hall, R. (1996) Representation as shared activity: Situated cognition and Dewey's cartography of experience. *The Journal of the Learning Sciences* 5 (3), 209–238.

Hua, Z., Li, W. and Jankowicz-Pytel, D. (2019) Translanguaging and embodied teaching and learning: Lessons from a multilingual karate club in London. *International Journal of Bilingual Education and Bilingualism* 23 (1), 65–80.

Latour, B. (1999) *Pandora's Hope: Essays on the Reality of Science Studies*. Cambridge, MA: Harvard University Press.

Lehrer, R. and Schauble, L. (2015) The development of scientific thinking. In R.M. Lerner (ed.) *Handbook of Child Psychology and Developmental Science* (pp. 1–44). Hoboken, NJ: Wiley.

Lemke, J.L. (2000) Across the scales of time: Artifacts, activities, and meanings in ecosocial systems. *Mind, Culture, and Activity* 7 (4), 273–290.

Li, W. (2018) Translanguaging as a practical theory of language. *Applied Linguistics* 39 (1), 9–30.

Machado, E. and Hartman, P. (2019) Translingual writing in a linguistically diverse primary classroom. *Journal of Literacy Research* 51 (4), 480–503.

Makoni, S. and Pennycook, A. (eds) (2007) *Disinventing and Reconstituting Languages*. Clevedon: Multilingual Matters.

National Research Council (2012) A framework for K-12 science education. *A Framework for K-12 Science Education: Practices, Crosscutting Concepts, Core Ideas*. Washington, DC: National Academies Press.

Nersessian, N.J. (2008) *Creating Scientific Concepts*. Cambridge, MA: MIT Press.

Norris, S. and Jones, R. (2005) *Discourse in Action: Introducing Mediated Discourse Analysis*. New York: Routledge.

Otheguy, R., García, O. and Reid, W. (2015) Clarifying translanguaging and deconstructing named languages: A perspective from linguistics. *Applied Linguistics Review* 6 (3), 281–307.

Pacheco, M.B. and Smith, B.E. (2015) Across languages, modes, and identities: Bilingual adolescents' multimodal codemeshing in the literacy classroom. *Bilingual Research Journal* 38 (3), 292–312.

Philip, T.M., Souto-Manning, M., Anderson, L., Horn, I., Carter Andrews, D.J., Stillman, J. and Varghese, M. (2018) Making justice peripheral by constructing practice as 'core': How the increasing prominence of core practices challenges teacher education. *Journal of Teacher Education* 70 (3), 251–264.

Pierson, A.E. and Brady, C.E. (2020) Expanding opportunities for systems thinking, conceptual learning, and participation through embodied and computational modeling. *Systems* 8 (4), 48.

Pierson, A.E., Brady, C.E. and Clark, D.B. (2020) Balancing the environment: Computational models as interactive participants in a STEM classroom. *Journal of Science Education and Technology* 29 (1), 101–119.

Pierson, A.E., Clark, D.B. and Brady, C.E. (2021) Scientific modeling and translanguaging: A multilingual and multimodal approach to support science learning and engagement. *Science Education* 105 (4), 776–813.

Pierson, A.E. and Grapin, S. (2021) A disciplinary perspective on translanguaging. *Bilingual Research Journal* 1–17.

Radke, S., Vogel, S., Hoadley, C. and Ma, J. (2020) Representing percents and personas: Designing syncretic curricula for modeling and statistical reasoning. *Proceedings of the International Conference of the Learning Sciences* (Vol. 3, pp. 1365–1372). Nashville, TN: International Society of the Learning Sciences.

Ranker, J. (2009) Student appropriation of writing lessons through hybrid composing practices: Direct, diffuse, and indirect use of teacher-offered writing tools in an ESL classroom. *Journal of Literacy Research* 41, 393–431.
Rowe, D.W. and Miller, M.E. (2016) Designing for diverse classrooms: Using iPads and digital cameras to compose eBooks with emergent bilingual/biliterate four-year-olds. *Journal of Early Childhood Literacy* 16 (4), 425–472.
Rowe, L.W. (2018) Say it in your language: Supporting translanguaging in multilingual classes. *The Reading Teacher* 72 (1), 31–38.
Rowe, L.W. (2020) Hey Siri: exploring the potential for digital tools to support heritage-language use in English-dominant classrooms. *Language Arts* 97 (6), 363–375.
Sherris, A. and Adami, E. (eds) (2019) *Making Signs, Translanguaging Ethnographies: Exploring Urban, Rural and Educational Spaces*. Bristol: Multilingual Matters.
Shin, S. (2017) *Bilingualism in Schools and Society: Language, Identity, and Policy* (2nd edn). New York: Routledge.
Smith, B.E., Pacheco, M.B. and de Almeida, C.R. (2017) Multimodal codemeshing: Bilingual adolescents' processes composing across modes and languages. *Journal of Second Language Writing* 36, 6–22.
Smith, B.E., Pacheco, M.B. and Khorosheva, M. (2020) Emergent bilingual students and digital multimodal composition: A systematic review of research in secondary classrooms. *Reading Research Quarterly* 56 (1), 33–52.
Strauss, A. and Corbin, J. (1990) *Basics of Qualitative Research*. London: Sage Publications.
Suárez, E., Tzou, C., Bang, M., Meixi, Roque, R., Pinkard, N. ... Martin, C.K. (2018) Designing for axiological innovation within family-centered learning environments. In J. Kay and R. Luckin (eds) *Rethinking Learning in the Digital Age: Making the Learning Sciences Count* (Vol. II, pp. 1187–1194). London: ISLS.
Tian, Z. and Shepard-Carey, L. (2020) (Re) imagining the future of translanguaging pedagogies in TESOL through teacher–researcher collaboration. *TESOL Quarterly* 54 (4), 1131–1143.
Vogel, S., Ascenzi-Moreno, L. and García, O. (2018) An expanded view of translanguaging: Leveraging the dynamic interactions between a young multilingual writer and machine translation software. In J. Choi and S. Ollerhead (eds) *Plurilingualism in Teaching and Learning* (pp. 89–106). Abingdon: Routledge.
Vogel, S., Hoadley, C., Ascenzi-Moreno, L. and Menken, K. (2019) The role of translanguaging in computational literacies: documenting middle school bilinguals' practices in computer science integrated units. In *Proceedings of the 50th ACM Technical Symposium on Computer Science Education* (pp. 1164–1170). New York: Association for Computing Machinery.
Williams, M. (2020) Fifth graders' use of gesture and models when translanguaging during a content and language integrated science class in Hong Kong. *International Journal of Bilingual Education and Bilingualism* 25 (4), 1304–1323.
Yin, R.K. (2014) *Case Study Research: Design and Methods (Applied Social Research Methods)*. Thousand Oaks, CA: Sage Publications.
Zapata, A. and Laman, T.T. (2016) 'I write to show how beautiful my languages are': Translingual writing instruction in English-dominant classrooms. *Language Arts* 93 (5), 366–378.

Afterword

Kate Seltzer

Even though Ofelia García, Susana Ibarra Johnson and I wrote *The Translanguaging Classroom* less than 10 years ago, much has changed since it was published in 2017. The ideas in our book have been deepened and evolved by seismic shifts in the field that have called for a reckoning with racism and coloniality (Flores & Rosa, 2015; García *et al.*, 2021). They have also been extended by the editors of this volume, Leah Shepard-Carey and Zhongfeng Tian, who have taken up our framework of translanguaging stance, design and shifts and applied them to the highly important work of teacher–researcher partnerships. While our translanguaging pedagogical framework has been embraced by many in the field, the authors in this book emphasize the urgency and importance of cultivating its *sustainability* in schools through such partnerships.

Disrupting linguistic business as usual cannot be done by teachers *or* researchers alone; it is through meaningful collaborations between the two that translanguaging pedagogy can be implemented and advanced in ways that not only better support bi/multilingual students but also undo monoglossic, raciolinguistic ideologies. As Shepard-Carey and Tian write in their introduction to the book, by emphasizing the ways that teachers and researchers have partnered to developed co-stances, co-designs and co-shifts, 'we can build upon the potential of translanguaging pedagogies in classrooms and further resist linguistic hierarchies that exist in educational institutions today.'

In each of the chapters in this book, readers are introduced to the intricacies, tensions and complexities that define teacher–researcher partnerships. As Lau, Liaw and Botelho explain in their chapter, navigating these relationships is 'never tidy,' and the chapters here shine light on what can be learned when we do not look away from or try too quickly to clear up that untidiness. Through a variety of studies across contexts, the authors of these chapters showcase their collaborations and grapple with the challenges and discomfort inherent to such close relationships. For example, in Lau *et al.*'s chapter, we see how both teachers and researchers faced a 'circuitous journey' on the road to forging co-stances, co-designs and co-shifts as they navigated power dynamics as well as disparate understandings of translanguaging and classroom-based research. Rajendram and Hamman-Ortiz, too, explore this journey with their collaborating teachers, Ms Kavita (Rajendram) and Maestra Carmen (Hamman-Ortiz). In these partnerships, the authors worked closely with the teachers to implement translanguaging pedagogies in the 'English-centric policy context' of an ESL classroom in Malaysia (Rajendram) and a two-way bilingual immersion program in the US (Hamman-Ortiz). Like the teachers in Lau *et al.*'s chapter, Ms Kavita and Maestra Carmen held reservations about translanguaging, but both Rajendram and Hamman-Ortiz discuss how, rather than assert their own scholarly expertise in translanguaging theory, they engaged with their collaborators' reticence and developed a deeper co-stance that valued and took into account the local context and the teachers' on-the-ground expertise.

Like the three examples discussed above, many chapters in this book highlight the emotional work that goes into teacher–researcher partnerships and connect that work to the development of sustainable translanguaging pedagogies. In Vacca *et al.*'s chapter on developing translanguaging co-designs for computer science education in multilingual spaces, the authors focus on the vulnerability that came up for both teachers and researchers as 'agency was re-negotiated in the classroom.' Rather than ignore that vulnerability or move past it too quickly, the researchers explain how it became a central element of their collaboration with the teachers – an approach they refer to as *acompañamiento*. Translanguaging (and, in Vacca *et al.*'s chapter, technologies that re-negotiate learner agency) necessarily disrupts existing linguistic hierarchies, a challenge to the status quo that can bring up intense feelings for teachers. A key element of sustainable translanguaging pedagogies, then, is attending to and *sharing* the emotional work that comes up through their implementation.

Though many chapters in this volume connect the sustainability of translanguaging pedagogies in schools to the relationships researchers forge with collaborating teachers, they also highlight just how integral larger, structural supports are to sustainability. As one teacher from Fine *et al.*'s chapter, Maren, wondered about her development of translanguaging pedagogies,

> I know it's not enough, but is it enough right now? Like in just one class? And I wonder if [the students] believe that we believe in their bilingualism. If only one teacher believes in it. But then they walk out to the school and everything else is in English and every other teacher...

If, as Rajendram writes in her chapter, teachers (and researchers) engaged in the development of translanguaging pedagogies often wear many hats, from 'advocates and proponents of translanguaging' to 'mediators and peacekeepers who spoke to learners about the importance of intercultural understanding and tolerance,' they need larger institutional supports so that they are not, as Fine *et al.* put it, in a 'lone teacher bubble.' Though the chapters in this book set out specific and helpful suggestions for sustainability, more research is needed to fill in the institutional gaps – what would the development of co-stances, co-designs and co-shifts look like with administrators, district and state leaders? How might partnerships between universities and school districts provide structural support for teachers developing translanguaging pedagogies alongside researchers? How might teachers take advantage of existing structural supports to engage in more transgressive pedagogical work? This book brings such questions to the surface, providing future directions for both translanguaging research and meaningful collaborations.

Thinking about sustainability in the development of translanguaging pedagogies is tricky, as inherent to that development is disruption – of deep-rooted ideologies, of 'common sense' policies and practices, of linguistic, cultural and relational hierarchies, and of structures that are rooted in coloniality (García *et al.*, 2021). The chapters in this book walk this line, lending insight into how teacher–researcher partnerships can build sustainability as they engage in disruption. For example, in Ibarra Johnson *et al.*'s chapter, we see how three dual language bilingual teachers worked with researchers to implement translanguaging pedagogies and reflect on their implementation through 'critical dialogue' with one another. As they highlight the three teachers' co-designs and elements of their co-stances, Ibarra Johnson *et al.* put forth a powerful model of translanguaging pedagogy, one that is shaped by engagement with theory, relationships between the bilingual teachers and researchers, *and* by the lived experiences of the teachers themselves as bilingual women of color. In this way, the collaboration was more than just classroom-based work; it was *heart work,* which is particularly important for bringing in and sustaining bilingual teachers of color. A question that arises, then, is how bilingual researchers and teachers can sustain such powerful stances and practices amidst the forces of gentrification that increasingly shape bilingual programs (Dorner *et al.*, 2021)? How can researchers particularly sustain bilingual teachers of color as they do the intensely personal work of disrupting monoglossic, raciolinguistic ideologies?

Another line of questioning brought up by this book is how to build and sustain a pipeline of critical educators of bi/multilingual students. To build capacity and sustainability of translanguaging pedagogies in schools requires both strong partnerships between researchers and in-service teachers *and* strong stance-building relationships between teacher educators and pre-service teachers (see Cataldo-Schwarzl and Erling, this volume, for more discussion of the potential for working with pre-service teachers). The latter requires that teacher educators, like the researchers in this book, develop co-stances, co-designs and co-shifts with their students in ways that support their future pedagogical choices and sensemaking as well as their ability to actively disrupt the maintenance of harmful ideologies through policies and practices that do not serve bi/multilingual students. In addition to designing coursework that engages pre-service teachers in the development of the personal, political and pedagogical elements of their stance (Seltzer, 2022), teacher educators might draw on the work of in-service teachers like those featured in this volume to model what the enactment of translanguaging pedagogies can look like. Broadening teacher education classrooms to include in-service teachers who not only have an understanding of translanguaging theory but can communicate the 'untidiness' of implementing it and standing for it on the ground in schools could be yet another way to develop and sustain critical educators of bi/multilingual students as they learn to disrupt.

Lastly, many chapters in this book prompt a question that has grown in importance as translanguaging has become more widespread – how do we sustain criticality itself within translanguaging research and, particularly, in its translation to pedagogy? A central metaphor in our book, *The Translanguaging Classroom*, is that of the translanguaging corriente, which we define as the 'flow of students' bilingual practices' or the 'fluid, ever present current that they tap into to make meaning' (García *et al.*, 2017: 17). We contend – and the authors in this volume show – that when teachers design pedagogy that brings this current closer to the surface of the classroom, they can better leverage it for student learning. But perhaps there is another element of this corriente that runs through the classroom, flowing below the surface and shaping its terrain: a corriente of power and ideology that informs how language is used, perceived, judged and valued (or not) by teachers and students.

This element of the corriente flows and makes itself visible in several chapters of this volume. For example, in Dobinson *et al.*'s chapter, they describe how researchers and teachers in Australia worked together to 'foster a sustainable stance which sees diverse language practices as valuable resources to be built upon and leveraged in the primary classroom'. The authors describe how one teacher, Gary, implemented translanguaging pedagogies in his classroom and discuss the complexities that emerged as he tried out this new approach. One such complexity was engaging 'monolingual' English-speaking students in translanguaging designs. In a telling moment, one monolingual student told Gary and Toni, first author of the chapter, that he could not participate in the activity because he did not speak another language – 'he just spoke "normal."' In her chapter, Pierson similarly recounts how, during a collaborative STEM activity that grouped two Spanish-speaking bilingual students with a monolingual English-speaking student, the monolingual student, Sean, seemed to feel excluded by his group members' use of Spanish. In response, Sean attempted to police the language in his group several times; for example, saying 'Luis, just do it in English, we don't have to do Spanish.'

These brief classroom moments, as Pierson puts it present 'an opportunity for a co-shift in instruction' whereby she and her collaborating teacher, Ms S., 'could have responded explicitly to language policing within this small group' or facilitated a larger conversation about language ideologies. However, she writes of herself and her co-teacher, both white, monolingual English speakers, 'our positionalities and experiences may have made it more difficult for us to recognize and respond to these linguistic microaggressions in the moment.' This honest assessment of the moment reveals what so many teachers come to know: that they are not necessarily equipped to navigate the shifts of this element of the corriente – the in-the-moment instances where power-laden language ideologies come to the surface. My own work has detailed instances such as these (Seltzer & de los Ríos, 2018), when teachers, and especially white, monolingual teachers, are pushed to evolve what we call their raciolinguistic literacies, or their awareness of and ability to navigate and disrupt ideologies that negatively shape their perceptions of racialized bi/multilingual students' language practices. These raciolinguistic literacies are necessary if educators are to shift with and teach into these highly important classroom moments.

Whether and/or how teacher–researcher partnerships can support and sustain the co-development of raciolinguistic literacies is a question worthy of future research. As teachers and researchers work together to leverage the corriente of students' bilingualism, can they simultaneously develop a co-stance that enables them to shift with and respond to the corriente of power that surfaces when linguistic hierarchy and separation are called into question? The development of such a co-stance and a shared commitment to the internal work needed to recognize how teachers' and researchers' own subjectivities not only shape their own relationship but their relationships with students is integral to the sustainability of translanguaging pedagogies and their transformative potential in the classroom.

References

Dorner, L.M., Cervantes-Soon, C.G., Heiman, D. and Palmer, D. (2021) 'Now it's all upper-class parents who are checking out schools': Gentrification as coloniality in the enactment of two-way bilingual education policies. *Language Policy* 20 (3), 1–27. https://doi.org/10.1007/s10993-021-09580-6

Flores, N. and Rosa, J. (2015) Undoing appropriateness: Raciolinguistic ideologies and language diversity in education. *Harvard Educational Review* 85 (2), 149–171. https://doi.org/10.17763/0017-8055.85.2.149

García, O., Flores, N., Seltzer, K., Li, W., Otheguy, R. and Rosa, J. (2021) Rejecting abyssal thinking in the language and education of racialized bilinguals: A manifesto. *Critical Inquiry in Language Studies* 18 (3), 203–228. https://doi.org/10.1080/15427587.2021.1935957

García, O., Johnson, S. and Seltzer, K. (2017) *The Translanguaging Classroom: Leveraging Student Bilingualism for Learning*. Philadelphia: Caslon.

Seltzer, K. (2022) Enacting a critical translingual approach in teacher preparation: Disrupting oppressive language ideologies and fostering the personal, political, and pedagogical stances of preservice teachers of English. *TESOL Journal* 13 (2). https://doi.org/10.1002/tesj.649

Seltzer, K. and de los Ríos, C.V. (2018) Translating theory to practice: Exploring teachers' raciolinguistic literacies in secondary English classrooms. *English Education* 51 (1), 49–79.

Index

Milton Keynes UK
Ingram Content Group UK Ltd.
UKHW021827270923
429508UK00005B/55

9 781800 413160